The Sword and the Scepter

The Sword and the Scepter

THE PROBLEM OF MILITARISM IN GERMANY

Volume II:
**THE EUROPEAN POWERS AND THE
WILHELMINIAN EMPIRE, 1890-1914**

By GERHARD RITTER

Translated from the German by HEINZ NORDEN

 University of Miami Press
Coral Gables, Florida

Translated from the second, revised edition, 1965 version, published originally under the title *Staatskunst und Kriegshandwerk: Das Problem des Militarismus in Deutschland. Zweiter Band: Die Hauptmächte Europas und das wilhelminische Reich (1890-1914)* by Verlag R. Oldenbourg, Munich, Copyright © 1965 by R. Oldenbourg Verlag, Munich.

Copyright © 1970 by University of Miami Press

ISBN 0-87024-128-1

Library of Congress Catalog Card No. 68-31041

Designed by Bernard Lipsky

Manufactured in the United States of America

Second printing 1972

Contents

From the Preface to the First Edition *1*

Preface to the Second Edition *3*

One: Review of the Military and Political Systems of the Major Powers of Europe Other than Germany

1. The Army and Politics in France, from the Restoration to the End of the First World War *7*

2. Army, Society, and Government in Britain in the Age of Bourgeois Liberalism *33*

3. The Anglo-French Staff Talks and the Entente Policy, 1905-1914 *61*

4. The Role of Militarism in Czarist Russia *77*

Two: The Military and Political Situation in Wilhelminian Germany, 1890-1914

5. The Militarization of the German Middle Class *93*

6. War and Politics in the Military Literature of the Last Decades before the First World War *105*

7. Military and Civilian Authority Under the German Empire *119*

8. Naval Armaments—Tirpitz and the Battle Fleet

   Part 1:   German Naval Policy up to 1914 *137*

   Part 2:   The Arms Race after 1905 and the First Naval Talks with England *158*

   Part 3:   The Further Naval Talks of 1910-1912 and Their Failure *167*

9. Planning for Warfare on Land—Schlieffen and
His Great Campaign Plan

Part 1: Schlieffen's "Purely Military" War Plan *193*

Part 2: Schlieffen and German Arms Policy *206*

Part 3: Strategy and Arms Policy After Schlieffen *216*

10. The General Staffs and the Outbreak of War

Part 1: The Austrian General Staff and the
Notion of Preventive War *227*

Part 2: Understandings Between the Austrian and
German General Staffs *239*

Part 3: Conrad's and Moltke's Share in Manning
the Loom of Destiny *247*

Part 4: The Inexorable Sequence of War Declarations *263*

Notes *277*

Supplement to the Notes to Chapter 10 *315*

Index *319*

The Sword and the Scepter

From the Preface to the
First Edition (1960)

THIS SECOND VOLUME of my work deals with my over-all theme during the era of what is commonly called "imperialism," the time when German militarism, so much deplored, was incubated, so to speak. The questions that emerged were of great diversity, and their full and balanced discussion required so much space that I found myself compelled to call another halt with the landmark year of 1914. A third volume will deal with the political history of the First World War, largely on the basis of unpublished sources. This will form a major portion of the whole work, for it was during the war that the military, full of cocksureness even before, achieved its full potential, soon throwing in its lot with the rising tide of impassioned wartime nationalism, which ultimately led to the complete triumph of the "craft of war" over the "art of statesmanship."

Against this main portion, the history of the Weimar Republic forms no more than a kind of epilogue. The problems posed by militarism did not cease then, but they are better understood as after effects of the preceding era rather than as springing from the new situation. They were, of course, utterly changed by the Hitler movement and its political victory. The spirit of pure militancy, blind to all political considerations, communicated itself from the heads of the army and navy to the political leadership. In the end there arose a totally unique situation, unprecedented in history. It was the soldiers who had to oppose the blind militarism of the civilian political leadership. This shift in our over-all subject in the recent past may make it necessary to move from detailed narrative to a more concise type of presentation.

It will be noted that, in the final chapter of this volume, I find myself enmeshed in the investigation of the war guilt question, a vast ocean of published sources, polemical writings, and voluminous historical treatises by authors of many nationalities. While I have taken note of everything of real importance, I have refused to be drawn into individual polemics, lest I become mired in the morass. Unavoidably, I have at times had to become involved, in my notes, with the latest comprehensive work on the subject as a whole—the three volumes by Luigi Albertini, which thoroughly exploit almost the entire international literature, indeed, add some things that are new; but instead of warming up the endlessly repeated pros and cons of the guilt question, I have here as in the other parts of my work endeavored to limit myself to the original sources rather than include all the monographs and polemical writings. I have sought to find my own answers to my own questions, and to give life and immediacy to the events of history from their concrete reality, without getting lost in subsidiary matters.

In concluding this preface, I hope I may be permitted to confess that I have written this book with many qualms. The prewar Germany I describe is the Germany of my own youth. For most of my life, as I looked back on it, it seemed to me to be bathed in a kind of radiance that did not begin to darken until the outbreak of war in 1914. Now, at the twilight of my life, my probing eye finds shadows far deeper than my generation perceived—let alone my academic teachers.

Preface to the Second Edition

THIS NEW EDITION incorporates many corrections of details over and above typographical errors. I found no occasion to alter my presentation as a whole.

Walter Hubatsch, in a brief review of the book (*Hist. pol.*, Book IX [1961], p. 50), expresses regret that I deal at such length in Chapter 2 with the British army, which was of such little importance in the nineteenth century, and recommends that in a second edition I "discuss the position of the British admiralty in the public life of Great Britain." If this suggestion means that I should contrast German militarism with what has been called British "naval-ism," I can only refer to my remarks on pp. 107ff. and to Note 7, p. 288. For the rest, I need scarcely justify the inclusion of England in a review of the military systems of the major powers of Europe, precisely because the English system is so totally different from the continental ones. The role played by military activists in the establishment of the Entente and in the origins of the First World War, as well as in the war itself, illustrates the difficulties and the significance that attended a balance between military and political thinking in Great Britain too.

As I expected, my discussion of the war guilt question in the final chapter has been vigorously criticized by Fritz Fischer ("Weltpolitik, Weltmachtstreben und deutsche Kriegsziele," *Historische Zeitschrift,* Vol. 199 [October, 1964]) and his disciple Imanuel Geiss (*Julikrise und Kriegsausbruch 1914. Eine Dokumentensammlung,* Vol. 1 [1963]). The latter pointed out two errors in dates (pp. 247 and 272), which I have corrected.[1] His over-all view, however, differs from mine, as does Fischer's, and I am unable to accept either. In essence, both accept the arguments of Luigi Albertini, with which I dealt in the first edition. Fischer has more recently suggested that one of the influences that attuned

Bethmann to war were supposed economic concerns in the Balkans and in Turkey. I have stated my position on this matter in an essay, "Zur Fischer-Kontroverse," in *Historische Zeitschrift,* Vol. 200 (1965). As early as 1963, in another essay, "Eine neue Kriegsschuldthese? " I discussed his older treatment of the July crisis in the first edition of his book *Griff nach der Weltmacht* (1961), Chapter 2 (*Historische Zeitschrift,* Vol. 194, pp. 646-668). For my part, I now consider this debate concluded. One reason there is no occasion to continue it in this new edition of my work is because the real issue here is not the attitude of the Reich government in July, 1914, but the attitudes of the generals—those of the Austrian as well as the German General Staff (cf. my essay, "Der Anteil der Militärs an der Kriegskatastrophe von 1914," *Historische Zeitschrift,* Vol. 193 [1961]). I do agree that a whole series of aspects and insights have come to light that throw new light on the political decisions of the Reich leadership, and I am surprised that these have found so little notice in the most recent flare-up on the war guilt question in Germany.

This discussion has very recently taken a turn I cannot completely ignore even in the framework of this book; consequently, I have appended to the notes to the final chapter a supplement that deals briefly with this question.

Freiburg
March, 1965   GERHARD RITTER

ONE

Review of the Military and Political Systems of the Major Powers of Europe Other than Germany

1

Army and Politics in France, from the Restoration to the End of the First World War

OUR DISCUSSION so far has endeavored to reconstruct the Prussian tradition that dominated the relation of state and army in Germany until the end of the era of Bismarck. It was the tradition of a military state under the leadership of a *roi connétable*. Outwardly this form was retained until the end of the monarchy in 1918. Yet the life that pervaded this state, the actual relation of military and civilian authority, underwent incisive changes after Bismarck's departure. The development that reached full maturity in the First World War had long been incubating—the emancipation of military power from the political leadership—a development that ultimately resulted in a complete reversal of their natural order.

Before we turn to this new phase of our general subject, however, it becomes necessary to devote some attention to the other major powers of Europe, notably France, England, and Russia. How did the position of the army in state and society develop in those countries during the course of the nineteenth century? Did they experience serious problems relating to militarism? And if so, how did they seek to master them?

The political situation in which the restored French monarchy found itself in 1815 was crucial to the development of the French army system. More specifically, the truly militarist policies Napoleon the conqueror had imposed on the Franch nation left a heritage of shock which it took almost a century to overcome.

It has often been said that the French, though a very warlike people—or at least a people with a fierce pride in military glory—are in truth not really a military people.[1] It is all the more curious that no other European nation spent so much effort to cultivate the *esprit militaire* in the nineteenth century. Almost to the end of that century the French army was by composition a national army (the Royal Swiss Guard, restored in 1815, having been swept away in the July Revolution). Yet it was essentially a garrison force, leading its own separate and isolated life. Even more than the Prussian Guards units, with their loyalty to King William I and his reactionary militarist cronies, the French army was intended to be the government's domestic instrument for the suppression of revolution. Oddly enough, the Prussian military system after 1815 came much closer than did France itself to the original spirit of the French *levée en masse,* a fact which the French historian Cavaignac has rightly described as a "crucial element in the history of the nineteenth century."

We know that the idea of a nation in arms was first hatched and practiced in France in the Great Revolution. It sprang naturally from the ideal of a single, united political community that inspired the great Federate Festival of July 14, 1790, and its famous marching song, the Marseillaise. It is true that there was always a big gap between ideal and reality. The revolutionary armies with which the powers of the Convention ultimately proved able to master a seemingly hopeless military situation were not composed of volunteers, but were raised under the lash of coercion. No more than sixty thousand volunteers answered the call of the National Assembly on July 11, 1792, and of these only half were fit for active service. The enforced levies of the following year, when the country was in direst peril, met with the most stubborn resistance. Yet, conceivably, universal military service might have become acceptable and indeed taken for granted, as it was later on in Prussia, had only two conditions prevailed: a just and consistent system of conscription that was economically supportable; and limitation of compulsory service to defense of the native soil, as had been originally proclaimed.

Both of these conditions, however, soon disappeared. Carnot's clear-cut principle of the limitation of military service to all young men from 18 to 25 without exception, without possibility of substitution, and without partisan discrimination was quickly abandoned. Enforcement of conscription was tightened and relaxed in keeping with the military and domestic political situation. The annual levies were called up, discharged, or retained in service as needed. Those who were prosperous, infirm, or essential to civilian life were now permitted, now forbidden to hire substitutes, largely at the whim of subaltern authorities and the police. The fairer system of calling up recruits by lottery was used only infrequently after 1803. The overstretching of conscription in the final years of Napoleonic rule created even greater resentment than these abuses. By 1813, recruits who were mere boys were being dispatched to the battlefields. Almost from the beginning the national character of the French army was watered down by the acceptance of large numbers of foreign defectors and Swiss mercenaries, and it vanished more and more in the course of the campaigns waged by Napoleon, who raised entire armies in the countries he conquered or compelled to allegiance. These he mingled with his French regiments, or at least he had them march together. Above all, the war itself increasingly lost its national defense character, becoming instead the means of carrying out a limitless policy of power and conquest. Finally, after more than two decades of almost ceaseless campaigning, the war seemed to have become an end in itself.

The French people followed the demoniac forces unleashed in this war with mixed and changing feelings. There was constant difficulty with recruitment. Young Clausewitz, taken prisoner in 1807, at the summit of Napoleon's victorious sweep, was amazed to watch day after day "as two or three gendarmes escorted thirty to forty conscripts to the prefecture, tied up two by two to a single long rope."[2] There were large-scale raids, in which woods and hills were sealed off to round up deserters and conscripts in hiding. By 1811 their number had risen to sixty thousand, and only half of them were ever apprehended. Laws were passed authorizing the taking of hostages; flying squads were dispatched; whole families, communities, even cantons were held liable for the escapers. The disaffected were watched over by a growing army of informers, and by 1811 political prisoners numbered 2,500. Even among the generals and marshals there was strong political resistance to the Corsican's tyranny. A few of them, like Pichegru and Moreau, became victims or martyrs to their political and libertarian convictions. Plots on the life of Napoleon never altogether ceased, and in 1812, while he was away in Russia, they even led to a bizarre military *Putsch* in Paris.

Yet there can be no real doubt that for the majority of the French people—especially the most active political segments—Napoleon Bonaparte, during the period of his meteoric rise to mastery of the continent, was the true representative of the popular will, and that his military and diplomatic triumphs were celebrated with general enthusiasm. Here, as everywhere, political success abroad proved to be the government's strongest propaganda weapon, stronger than any libertarian ideals. As for the French army, it idolized Napoleon more and more, right down to his fall and even afterward. After the banishment of Moreau, Napoleon's marshals, on whom he lavished princely gifts, decorations, and titles of nobility, followed him without a murmur in all of his campaigns, all the way to Russia. His guards units, constantly enlarged and almost drowned in rewards and distinctions, formed a sworn fellowship that maintained its undying loyalty into the final weeks of his collapsing regime.

"The guard dies, it does not surrender"—this turned out to be something less than the literal truth. Napoleon was still able to carry out the winter campaign of 1813-1814, but many of his generals were by then resentful and even rebellious. Nevertheless, he was able to continue the last bloody struggles up to the very gates of Paris, even when the situation seemed militarily hopeless. Only at the last moment did the defection of the marshals become a fact, involving on the one hand those who placed France's salvation above the dictator's will, and on the other those who were primarily concerned with salvaging their position and wealth. These groups joined in forcing their lord and master to abdicate; but the old guard did not share their attitude—the majority of the old troopers and noncoms remained loyal to the emperor to the last. Even the disaster of 1814 did not destroy the image of the great warlord among his soldiers. Within the year they again rallied to his standard—his mere appearance on French soil made them forget all that he had done to France and the world. A purely military revolt, issuing from the subaltern ranks, put him back on the throne and hurled the country once again into the horrors of a hopeless war against all Europe. The true meaning of militarism was never more clearly manifested than in the politically senseless campaign of 1815.

But this was precisely the reason why Napoleon's army henceforth stood completely aloof from the life of the nation. Distrust of successful generals and of a conscription system that placed unlimited manpower reserves at their disposal had become almost insurmountable. France now strove passionately to become a truly civilian nation, opposed to the military and all its works and dedicated to peace. A popular storm broke out against the traitors of 1815. A number of Napoleon's generals fell victim to lynch justice; others were arrested, prosecuted, imprisoned, banished, or shot. On demand of the occupation powers and in the interest of European peace, Napoleon's army was disbanded. The officers' corps suffered the penalty of an exacting purge process that lasted for years. Those caught up in it were classified in fourteen categories of political culpability. The country was soon flooded with unemployed officers who felt that they had been unfairly treated and were regarded as a dangerous element of political unrest. Yet the newly created volunteer army—a kind of strengthened police force based on a royal guard and a core of Swiss mercenaries—was unable to win popularity of any kind. Its new officers with their gold braid sought to make up for their lack of military distinction and ability by zealous monarchist sentiments. Many of them owed their advancement solely to connections at court.

So long as the occupation continued, this poorly equipped surrogate army was sufficient. France was glad to be rid of universal military service under the charter of 1814; indeed, its abolition was by far the most popular measure of the Bourbon rulers, the only one that gained them any sizable groups of adherents. Yet the revulsion against war had become so thoroughgoing that after 1815 not even the modest quotas required by the small police army could be met by enlistment. On the average, no more than 3,000 to 3,500 men a year could be persuaded to rally to the colors;[3] and the questionable elements attracted by the generous bonus which was offered usually made wretched soldiers, many of them concerned only with making off as soon as they pocketed the money.

Once the foreign occupation troops had departed, France faced the alternative of permanently doing without a large army, thereby forfeiting its position as a sovereign European power ranking with the others, or of reimposing the burden of military service. For in the post-Napoleonic age a mercenary army in the style of the eighteeneth-century, brought together from antisocial elements by means of all the evil devices of enticement, impressment, and propaganda, was neither feasible nor sufficient, if only for the reason that the Germans had meanwhile taken over from France the system of popular mass armies. Yet how could a great national army be established without raising anew the specter of militarism?

Marshal Gouvion-St. Cyr's great army law of 1818 endeavored to give an answer to this crucial and hotly discussed issue. It became the fundamental law for two full generations. Some changes were made by the July monarchy in 1832 and by Napoleon III in 1855, but the basic outlines were retained. The law accorded as closely as possible with the political needs of the day, with the views of a bourgeois-liberal society. Yet from the point of view of military needs as well as of social justice and political morality, it was a highly dubious compromise.

The revolutionary principle of universal military service was maintained, but its application was in effect limited to only a small fraction of the country's youth, not only in view of the general aversion to military service, but also from fear of a new wave of militarism with a consequent renewal of power politics. Under the law of 1818, the French army was never to exceed a strength of 240,000. When voluntary enlistment proved inadequate, the so-called system of *appel* was to be resorted to in place of the former conscription; but this was no more than a new liberal-sounding word for a draft. In accord with democratic principles, this draft was to hit all twenty-year-olds, with no class distinction. In fact no more than 40,000 were selected by lottery from the year's crop of about 300,000. This was as many as were taken in Prussia—but Prussia at the time had a population of eleven million, not thirty million, like France. Unless a man drew a "bad" number, he was exempt from all military service, in peace and in war. He was not assigned to a militia unit like the Prussian Landwehr or Landsturm.

Even among those actually drafted, a large number were immediately "exempted" or "given dispensation," the former, without reservation, for physical unfitness or family considerations, the latter as theological or other selected students or as winners of prizes for scientific or creative achievement. All these exemptions were liberally interpreted, and contingents were called up only as needed when enlistments fell short. The largest number of conscripts that reached the garrisons in any one year was 34,000. In some years the draft did not exceed 10,000 (not counting naval recruits). In the 1860's the yearly average was 23,000. Even this limited scope of coercion was not absolute. Whoever could pay a substitute could evade military service.

The first and most important consequence of this limited draft was a long term of service, for the desired minimum strength of the army could be attained only by accumulating many annual classes. Initially the term was six years, later it was raised to eight, and finally, in 1832, it was reduced to seven. During the entire term, the soldiers had to live on army posts and remain unmarried. To the liberal bourgeois of the time this was not an intolerable burden, for they could buy their way out of it and send some poverty-stricken wretch instead. Indeed, similar systems then prevailed throughout Europe, even in Austria and Germany, with the exception of Prussia.[4]

In France, both before 1848 and after, it was virtually an article of faith among all the ruling parties that soldiers must be alienated from civilian life by a long term of service. The royalists and reactionaries of 1818 looked back longingly to the mercenary armies of the *ancien régime*. Count de Sabron declared in the Chamber of Peers that this system kept society free of antisocial and inferior elements, bringing them under strict discipline. He seems to have overlooked the pathetic failure of these armies in the kingdom's greatest hour of need despite their segregation from the life of the nation, a failure attributed to inadequate discipline. Hence everything was now staked on a long term of garrison service, during which the *esprit militaire* and a purely passive, blind, and nonpolitical obedience could be artificially cultivated.

These views were shared by the liberal property-owning bourgeoisie, which feared nothing more than a repetition of revolutionary terror. The army was to provide above all police protection for property, and any mingling of the civilian and military ways of life in the style of the Prussian Landwehr seemed suspicious. It was the same distrust of a people's army we know from Prince (later King) William of Prussia, except that he thought he could manage with a third year of service for troops of the line in order to train obedient and absolutely reliable soldiers, while in France at least twice that period was thought to be necessary. It is true, of course, that the French looked back on bitter experience. They were well aware of the Gallic temperament; it was hard to discipline, tended to rebelliousness and anarchism, was resentful of order and punctuality, and was easily exhausted.

Yet this distrust was sharply at odds with the idea of popular sovereignty, on which universal military service and indeed the whole life of the French state had subsisted ever since the Great Revolution. Although French liberals in the nineteenth century made a great show of democratic ideals, they never really accepted them with the confidence and optimism that distinguished the Anglo-Saxon cultural and economic pioneers of America and the British Empire, nor did they share the German liberals' idealistic loyalty to the state, their dedication to the historical image of the monarchy. Having passed through the revolutionary terror and through the Caesarism of Napoleon, French liberalism lived in perpetual fear that its security would be threatened by the street mob on the one hand or on the other by a victorious general who would create a new military dictatorship. Unlike Prussia, which looked back on a great victory, France had to come to terms with a great defeat. Nationalist enthusiasm had been squandered to no effect, indeed had served only to deepen the disaster, and disillusion was rife.

In Prussia and Germany the national army was eagerly embraced as a symbol of the nation's power and will, a "school of national discipline"; but in France it was seen more or less as a necessary evil, at least in peacetime, a burden preferably devolving on the shoulders of the socially weak, with the added hope that it would serve to discipline at least a part of the hated mob. Occasionally the army was even described as the "cloaca of society." These ideas lived on in the French bourgeoisie with surprising tenacity, despite the many disappointments the morale of the French army provided in 1830 and in February, 1848, despite its semitorpor and readiness to place itself at the disposal of revolutionary governments. As late as the 1870's, in the debates over the total failure of the "garrison army" in the Franco-Prussian War, Adolphe Thiers, the principal leader of the traditional liberal bourgeoisie, fervently defended the eight-year term and opposed the creation of a *nation armée.*

An important element in these considerations was the vague and lopsided notion, nourished by the memory of Napoleon's veterans, that French military superiority could be insured only by seasoned soldiers serving long terms. This, it was thought, would guarantee an "army of quality," far superior to the Prussian troops, and trained over a far shorter period of time. What was overlooked was that with a high general level of education modern armies no longer needed long periods of training, if there were a firm training cadre of professional soldiers and a well-disciplined officers' corps. An even more important factor which was ignored was the irksome one that large and well-organized reserves were more essential than long training. It had been shown that modern warfare displayed a voracious appetite for manpower from the first day and could not be sustained without powerful reserves. The real secret of Prussian military superiority in the nineteenth century was the possession of virtually inexhaustible reserves, trained for three years or less, firmly brought into the army system, assigned to fixed units, and clearly integrated with the standing army. In the three Wars of Unification from 1864 to 1871 this superiority was demonstrated to all the world with such clarity that it challenged emulation. Thus began an arms race among the great powers that preoccupied the entire period from 1871 to 1914, especially the last two decades, and that immeasurably deepened the tensions in European grand policy.

Even in the time of the Restoration there was no lack in France of shrewd military men who recognized the virtues of the Prussian system, just as they did the weaknesses of their own, which involved only an extremely limited portion of the nation's manpower, because of the long service term, and which provided no trained reserves at all. For the original provision in the law of 1818, under which servicemen, after completing their six years, were required to serve another six years in the reserves, was revoked as early as 1824, after almost one-fourth of the reservists called up for the Spanish campaign never reported.

Instead, the annual draft contingent was increased, though a part of it was never inducted. Those who were not inducted remained in civilian life and had to play at being reserves for their full term of eight (later seven) years, being forbidden to move or marry, so that in theory they were always "available." In fact they received no military training whatever, nor were they organized in any way, let alone assigned to an existing unit of the standing army. In the event of a call-up, they had neither arms nor equipment—they were purely a paper force; and their enforced celibacy merely served to wreak moral havoc in the countryside. This total lack of reserve units, not really remedied even by 1870, was bound to lead to disaster in any European war; but France at the time did not feel under threat, and the garrison army was quite sufficient for its colonial wars. With an almost incredible lack of realism, public opinion clung to the legend of 1792—that an improvised *levée en masse* would prove capable of destroying any invading enemy. Despite the disaster of 1814 and in curious contrast to the general conviction that the *esprit militaire* could be cultivated only by long service, the French still felt themselves to be Europe's finest "natural soldiers."

As early as the 1820's there were scattered proposals in the French chamber to emulate the Prussian system or to adopt some similar system of national military training; but to the reactionary "ultras" this seemed to pose far too great a hazard to the crown, for they still profoundly distrusted the people's revolutionary aspirations. The liberals on their side kept reiterating in various ways that the Prussian army system was a barbaric institution which transformed the whole country into a great drill ground, as Guizot put it in 1832. This might do for the rural latifundia of East Elbia with its submissive serfs, but not for a highly civilized nation like France, whose bourgeois youth would never tolerate being ordered about by drill sergeants.

We recall similar sentiments from the Germany of the Biedermeier era, and not merely from the lips of the Freiburg liberal Welcker. They were heard over and over in South Germany up until 1870. After 1866 they even found public expression in the protests of Swabian particularists against Prussian military drill, which "violated human nature, and the culture of the age." We also recall the aversion of Prussian reformers, Boyen, the war minister, in the vanguard, to the "barracks spirit" of the standing army; and Boyen's efforts to organize the Landwehr into an autonomous, semicivilian armed force, in which the educated classes would supply an officers' corps of their own. The uncompromising integration of this force into the "garrison army" under the army reforms of 1860, subsequently extended to the whole of Germany, undoubtedly contributed to the militarization of German society, the less edifying aspects of which will still be our concern. The principle of universal military service held dangers brought to full light only in the twentieth century. By militarizing virtually every walk of life, it gave rise to totalitarian war. Our present concern is with the means used in France to avoid these consequences.

The French army system in the nineteenth century in effect amounted to proletarianizing the army in favor of the ruling bourgeoisie, which was able to exempt its sons by paying idle *remplaçants* to serve in their stead. French publicists managed to gloss over this ignoble money privilege by upholding the liberal principle of *liberté* as against the democratic principle of *égalité*. How could there be liberty if state coercion were allowed to ride roughshod over all distinctions of class, profession, and endowment, lumping the whole of society into a uniform mass and destroying all individuality?

These sentiments echoed those of the "ultras" like Boisgelin and Chateaubriand, even though the extremists were cautious in their utterances. French and indeed western European liberalism proclaimed the principle of private and individual liberty with far greater emphasis and consistency than did its German counterpart, which still fed on the principles of idealist Kantian ethics. In the view of the Prussian reformers of 1808-1815, the army was to recognize in theory but a single privilege—the privilege of education and culture.

Yet in Prussia this never led to complete exemption for the educated classes as in France, under the army law of 1818, for those who attended certain institutions of higher education. What happened in Prussia was that the service term was shortened, under the "one-year volunteer" scheme, and that access to commissions in the reserves and the Landwehr was granted or at least facilitated. There was no way of buying one's way out of military service, and such service was therefore never considered dishonorable for the upper classes. On the contrary, it was regarded as a patriotic privilege, as a field in which even the little man could realize his ambitions and by military ability rise to the coveted and respected rank of an officer in the reserves or Landwehr, a kind of military ruling caste in which the aristocracy still set the tone and mode of conduct.

By way of contrast, the bulk of the French army came from the lowest rungs of the social ladder. Initially the officers' corps, especially in the royal guard, was still regarded as a closed corporation for aristocratic youth, continuing or reviving in some measure the traditions of the eighteenth century; but after the second fall of the monarchy in 1830 and the third in 1848, the practical scope for cultivating such a caste spirit grew more and more limited. Even during the Restoration there was bitter conflict between the old royalist aristocracy, returning from exile, and the new Napoleonic aristocracy of the sword. There were countless duels and libel actions, efforts to limit the king's command power, to bring under statutes his authority to make promotions, to replace political caprice with seniority. At later stages the leftist parties conceived an ingrained distrust of the officers' monarchist and clerical prejudices.

At the end of the century, with egalitarian democracy in the ascendancy, this distrust turned into outright hatred, as exemplified in the Dreyfus trial, and the officers' corps came under the severest form of political thought control.[5] Moreover, the profession of officer had never been very attractive from the outset, for from 1815 onward pay lagged far behind even the meager scale of the Prussian military budget. Commissions were uncertain, dependent on political influence and the whims of superior officers, and readily revoked. As early as the 1820's, graduates of the military academies (the so-called St. Cyriens) had to be liberally supplemented from the ranks of veteran noncoms in order to fill the many vacant officers' posts.[6] From then on, these *sortis du rang* formed a powerful element within the officers' corps, impairing its inner cohesion and social prestige; the lower grades, according to French testimony, were about on a level with that of German foresters or gendarmes.

Yet the situation of the officers was enviable compared to that of the noncoms and enlisted men, who were in much the same position as the mercenaries of the *ancien régime.* The young worker, artisan, or countryman, consigned to barracks life for six to eight years, found himself in disreputable company. The *remplaçants* accounted for about one-fourth of total army strength, and they enjoyed the worst kind of reputation. After all, what kind of man would sell himself to a well-to-do member of the bourgeoisie for one or two thousand francs, with the certainty of being excluded from productive civilian life for many years? He must have had no alternative.

It is true that there were a certain number of veterans eager to re-enlist at a much higher premium than the modest bonus offered by the army itself. The truly professionally-minded preferred to volunteer or re-enlist directly, since only in this way could they qualify for promotion to higher rank. Indeed, the whole replacement system could not have functioned without a kind of organized manhunt, no longer in the style of the eighteenth-century press-gangs, but by commercial companies which also provided the premiums under a form of military insurance. Their turnover ran into many millions, and they operated with the same methods of enticement and deceit as the old press-gangs.

No wonder that the men they recruited contributed a large quota of deserters and military delinquents, nor that the army forfeited much of its social prestige in this way. To a greater or lesser degree this was true in all the countries that had replacement systems, even in Germany, but with the exception of Prussia.[7] Military service was the prerogative of the poor and antisocial, who were herded together in crowded and gloomy barracks, two to a single bedstead, eight eating from one bowl; who were scantily clothed and equipped (at least while the government still groaned under the burden of military pensions from the

Napoleonic era); and lastly who were at the mercy of all the moral hazards of an all male society subjected to unnatural celibacy and day after day to trivial and monotonous work without a trace of dignity. Naturally enough, no army post was complete without a brothel.

Did all this, indeed, engender the kind of *esprit militaire* that would have justified such great sacrifices? Was the liberal bourgeoisie right in praising the advantages to civilization of a system that spared its own youth for higher cultural purposes while burdening the poor with the defense of the country? Doubts in this direction were never stilled; and they were confirmed by the fact that the long-serving soldiers, instead of finding pleasure in their profession, with fewer and fewer exceptions only counted the days until their longed-for discharge. Of course, we must not give too much weight to the surprisingly high numbers of deserters and *réfractaires* who sought to evade induction, not infrequently by self-mutilation. Ultimately the French nation grew inured to the system. Yet the new moneybag aristocracy did sharply increase social tension and deepen the resentment of the little man. In order to solve the problems of militarism and avoid militarizing the entire nation, the country's politically most defenseless group was segregated from everyday life and shut away in barracks, to serve as a substitute for the old mercenary armies. A true *esprit militaire* never came into being, and the rest of the nation stood in danger of losing its warlike spirit as well.[8]

In its early stages, liberalism did not consider this a serious danger to the nation at all. Fired by British ideals, the French liberals, like the idealists of 1789, dreamed of an age of universal peace and reconciliation, inevitably impending in the wake of the great upswing of modern capitalist economies throughout the world and supplanting the era of war and power politics on the continent. At such a stage, standing armies would no longer be required at all, for such armies were indeed no more than the instruments of power-hungry adventurers, for purposes of conquest abroad and oppression at home. In the age of the new world economy they had become meaningless. It was Jean-Baptiste Say who most eloquently voiced such sentiments in the 1840's.[9] The pacifism and antimilitarism based on these sentiments could, of course, play a significant role only so long as France still suffered from the repercussions of the disaster of 1814-1815 and had not yet developed any new ambitions in the field of foreign policy. In the military sphere this pacifism found expression in numerous plans and movements which would have replaced the standing army with a mere national militia, possibly organized around a small core of profes-sional troops to secure the border. These trends emerged repeatedly during the period under review and found their most important spokesman early in the twentieth century in Jean Jaurès.

The historical model for all such plans was the National Guard of 1789, a res-toration and expansion of which was repeatedly sought under the Restoration and the July monarchy. Yet such a civilian guard always proved unsuitable, for it was not really a national militia, but simply a makeshift force for the protection of bourgeois property that could be rallied only in exceptional circumstances and was extremely limited in social scope. The last occasion on which a civilian national guard had played any significant part was in the street fighting of June, 1848, when the guard fought shoulder to shoulder with formations of the standing army. Napoleon III began his political ascent almost immediately afterward. The experiment of a modern popular democratic imperialism, beginning with a military *Putsch,* swiftly put an end to all the pacifist dreams; for such a system could not be instituted unless it catered to national aspirations for successes in the field of foreign policy.

The new Bonaparte was neither a soldier nor a military reformer, but he was shrewd enough to sense the weaknesses of the French military system and to endeavor to win the support of the army in every possible way. The first thing he did was to improve its material situation and public prestige by generously lavishing honors, pensions, and pay increases on it. Next he sought to improve the replacement system. In 1855 it was supplanted by a system under which anyone who did not wish to serve could buy his way out before he became subject to the draft by paying 2,000 to 2,500 francs into a state fund.

This large fund enabled the army to induce veterans to re-enlist, which put an end to the wretched traffic in men, although only as long as it proved possible to find such veterans, since otherwise the army itself had to look for *remplaçants.* The new system strengthened the professional character of the army, while the bourgeoisie, to its profound satisfaction, could dispense with its efforts to find substitutes. The whole thing amounted to a kind of "military insurance scheme" for the sons of the bourgeoisie. The army of old *troupiers*[10] thus created was quite suitable for waging cabinet wars in Europe or campaigns of conquest in Africa and even Mexico. It followed the principle Napoleon III had proclaimed at the time of his coup d'état: "The highest duty of the army from general down to common soldiers is passive obedience to the commands of the head of state." The military achievements of this "army of sergeants" in the Crimean War at times left a deep impression in Prussia (e.g., on Roon), perhaps deeper than they deserved.

Nevertheless, this army, as before, was ill suited to a national struggle on the grand scale, to a war against a European enemy of equal stature. Napoleon III became aware of this as early as the Italian campaign of 1859 when, following the bloody Battle of Solferino, he found himself without reserves and without a chance to protect the Rhine border against Prussian intervention, and thus compelled to conclude a negotiated peace at once. From 1861 onward, therefore, he had part of each year's draft contingent of recruits called up for a few months and trained as reservists.

This too, however, proved to be only a half measure, as was shown in 1866, when the Emperor was unable to restore the balance in favor of Austria by effective military intervention in the German war. Prussia's overwhelming victory at Königgrätz and the swift Austrian collapse left an indelible impression; and in 1867 Napoleon III had Marshal Niel prepare sweeping military reforms which all in all would have meant a first approximation to the Prussian-German army system, had they not been cut to pieces by the resistance of the French chamber. The defense act of 1867 was no more than a poor compromise. It did result in a certain strengthening of the army by virtue of increased draft quotas, achieved by legislative approval of a five-year term, which was already informally in effect. But the strengthened reserves Niel had planned were bypassed. In their place came a *garde mobile* to embrace all who did not serve in the army, without the privilege of substitution. Unfortunately this force received no serious military training in peacetime, and its organization was wholly inadequate. It was a militia only on paper, and in a time of war it could at best have been used as an occupation force.

Moreover, the liberal bourgeoisie, opposed equally to Caesarism and to militarism, succeeded in having the old substitute system reinstated and in abolishing the system of exemptions to be paid by all, which had been instituted in 1855. Thus the traditional garrison army with all its weaknesses lingered, and these weaknesses were made far worse by fantastic technical deficiencies, especially in the mobilization and commissary structure, as well as by thoroughly obsolete organization at the higher command level. Embittered patriots were later to charge that the defeat of 1870 was due to the frivolous incompetence of military leaders, undisciplined Gallic temperament, widespread corruption, deficient officer training, and the ossification of a General Staff consisting only of chair-warmers *(ronds de cuir)* out of touch with front-line realities. These complaints were certainly not groundless, but they did not hit the heart of the matter. The crucial failure was national, expressed even by France's parliamentarians at the hour of need. The French simply refused to accept the degree of military effort shouldered by their feared and at the same time despised neighbors under Prussian leadership. The failure of Napoleon's army reforms in 1867 merely confirmed that the policy of power and prestige he inaugurated was quite out of character with the unwarlike and profoundly antimilitary spirit of the French bourgeoisie. It did elicit new ambitions and grandiose foreign claims, but no new military resources that could have been organized to realize them; and in history nothing is more dangerous than chauvinist ambitions based on deluded ideas of one's own strength.

In a military sense, the campaign of 1870 was from the outset a hopeless undertaking for France, and these grand illusions were cruelly destroyed in the course of a single month. Even the old French dream of an improvised *levée en masse*, which Gambetta sought to recreate once again with his people's army, dribbled away forever in the course of the winter. Thus the war became a great historic turning point, and henceforth French defense policy took a totally new course.

When the Constituent Assembly deliberated a new defense bill in 1872, the republican general Trochu, who had been governor of Paris and its environs in 1870-1871, described the German army as "the only modern war instrument in Europe." Like him, other reformers now were eager to emulate the German example, but they succeeded only in part. The defense act of 1872 substantially expanded universal military service, increasing liability from nine to a total of twenty years (including furlough status) and finally abolishing the substitute system. In its place the German one-year volunteer system was introduced for a limited number of men from the educated classes, who had to provide their own equipment as officer candidates.

Undoubtedly the position of the French army in French society was profoundly affected by the fact that educated youths now had to do garrison service side by side with the sons of the proletariat. For something like two decades there was actually military enthusiasm among the bourgeoisie, coupled with hopes for an inner resurgence.[11] Yet the horrors of the Paris Commune also reawakened much distrust of the idea of the *nation armée* among the owing classes. Because of his brilliant oratory and great personal prestige, Adolphe Thiers, their spokesman, succeeded once again in salvaging the garrison army with its long term of service. Only in this way, he and his friends insisted, could absolute discipline and "purely passive" obedience on the part of the soldiers be insured.[12]

Thus the five-year term was retained after all, and this again made it necessary to exempt large sections of the population of arms-bearing age, lest the army budget be excessively swelled. In practice only 110,000 of the annual call-up of 300,000 men were actually inducted for the five-year term, while a "second helping," determined by lot, were recruited for only six months, thus creating a deep gulf between five-year and half-year men. It was this grossly unequal burden, flying in the face of the democratic principle of *égalité*, that was the starting point for further developments in the French military system, associated with the slow decline of grand bourgeois liberalism in the 1880's. These developments were accelerated after the fall of the conservative-clerical regime in 1876.

A petty bourgeois radicalism now began to spread. It would not hear of any distinctions in universal service, and its ideal was indeed the *nation armée* in place of the garrison army. There were also zealous advocates of the idea of a militia among the petty bourgeoisie and even more so among the socialists, who were gaining in political importance toward the end of the century. Yet a militia would have meant that France was in effect renouncing any role of importance as a great continental power, the peer of the German Reich, and this was out of the question. On the contrary, when the inner difficulties within Bismarck's system of alliances became apparent in the Bulgarian crisis in 1887, and especially after the chancellor's fall in 1890, new French hopes stirred for influence abroad, and these were greatly encouraged by the Russian military alliance of 1892.

The French people at the turn of the century were no longer the war-weary nation of 1815 or of 1872. They knew that Russia backed them, and soon afterward, in the Morocco affair, they gained the promise of British support in the event of a new conflict with Germany. In Germany the new confidence France gained from this dual entente was all too often characterized as revanchism. In fact the much-cited *nouveau esprit* of the last generation before 1914 was anything but unequivocal. Memories of 1870-1871 had greatly receded, especially among the younger generation. There was widespread dissatisfaction with military matters. Countless novels voiced bitter and vindictive criticism of garrison life and the officer's profession, and educated readers conceived a profound distaste for all things military. Fanatical pacifism was preached, especially among the state schoolteachers. At times the syndicalist workers' organizations conducted an often alarming campaign of agitation within the army posts, challenging the soldiers to go on strike, i.e., to mutiny and use their weapons against their own officers. These were symptoms of a deep internal weakness of the Third Republic.[13] Yet even France was undeniably carried along in part by the great wave of imperialist expansionsism that pervaded the whole world at the beginning of the century, sweeping away the liberal traditions of the bourgeois era and inaugurating a new iron age.

France, furthermore, played an important part in the new literary and philosophical vogue of "vitalism" that then flickered all over Europe, inspiring young people to reject the bourgeois way of life in favor of "danger," and producing literary lions of the day who celebrated war as an aesthetic spectacle, a "creative crisis," and the fountainhead of all virile virtue. More than that, because of the Morocco crisis of 1904-1906, France once again felt threatened by Germany, which resulted in a complete reversal of public opinion and an instant decline in antimilitarist sentiment. French policy tended more and more in the direction of an arms race with Germany.

The goal, however, was not to approximate the German model but to be specifically French—the radical implementation of equality in civic obligations and the equally radical democratization of the army. Since the early days of the Third Republic, the conservative sections of the grand bourgeoisie and the aristocracy, France's "old families," had found in the army a kind of last refuge from general egalitarianism. Other monarchist elements which rejected the "lawyers' regime" of the new state also rallied there, together with many graduates of Jesuit schools who opposed the increasingly secular course the republic was taking.

The natural desire of the officers for intellectual homogeneity and independence from day-to-day politics had stiffened the resistance of many of the higher ranks to the increasingly radical petty bourgeois government, and it had also influenced promotions more or less in the conservative direction. A gulf began to grow between the *esprit militaire* so carefully cultivated in the French garrison army, kept aloof from political life, and the basic trends toward which the republic was drifting. Owing to universal military service, the garrison army of old had after all become a people's army. Small wonder that the radical democratic governments viewed this more or less conservatively and clerically oriented officers' corps with suspicion, sensing it to be a danger to their policies. The secret split became abruptly manifest in the hapless Dreyfus case in the 1890's, which virtually divided the nation down the middle—on the one side a radical democratic anticlerical, antimilitarist, and humanitarian left, and on the other an anti-Semitic right, which had friends among the leading generals.

After many years of bitter struggle the unfortunate Jewish Captain Dreyfus was rehabilitated, his unjust conviction having severely shaken the moral authority of the nationalist right and the General Staff that sympathized with it. This was followed by a vigorous but poorly managed effort on the part of the Waldeck-Rousseau government after 1899 to root out by force the last remnants of aristocratic sentiment among the higher officers and to compel them to adopt radical democratic views. Highly dubious methods were resorted to in this process—informants were placed in freemasonry lodges, certificates of political reliability were issued by the police prefects, political opportunists were systematically preferred when it came to promotions—and a great deal of resentment, mutual distrust, and jealousy was carried into the officers' corps, with the result that government support was impaired rather than advanced. This was exacerbated when troops were used to enforce Briand's church laws, monastery closings, and expropriation measures, which precipitated many officers into grave conflicts of conscience.

This effort at political thought control soon miscarried. But the gradual leveling of the service term for all classes and the complete transformation of the garrison army into a modern mass army was carried out with far better success. This process began with the curtailment of the service term to three years in 1885-1889 and the abolition of the one-year volunteer privilege, which was replaced by the pre-term discharge of a certain highly educated group and a small group of indispensable family supporters. There was very little difference now between long-servers and short-servers.

This was even further reduced in practice and ultimately abolished by law in 1905, when the term of service was reduced to two years, as in Germany. Other similarities to the German model were an increase in the reserves and the extension of the service term in wartime, with which Freycinet, the first civilian head of the War Ministry, made a beginning; the creation of permanent divisional and corps commands (which began as early as 1873); integration of the reserves into the permanent cadre of the standing army; improvements in mobilization procedures; the reconstruction of the General Staff; and many other measures. After 1905 the internal approximation of the French army to the organization of the German made swift strides, not without many groans on the part of educated French youth, who did not readily take to this continuing increase in their military obligations.[14] Once the race was begun, France was able to keep up the pace only at the cost of straining its every resource, for the reservoir of able-bodied young manhood on which it could draw was much smaller than Germany's. France had to use a full 80 percent of her annual classes for active service and was constantly hard put to reach the authorized strength in the face of the sharply falling birth rate.[15] This explains the feeling of panic that followed the large German army increase of 1913, in consequence of which the peacetime service term was extended to three years, while the number of annual classes liable in wartime was increased to twenty-eight. The military effect of these frantic efforts, pushed through only by the most intensive propaganda, came nowhere near matching the dimensions of the sacrifices made. The efforts, moreover, as Premier Barthou plainly hinted, were not motivated by military and technical considerations alone—they were intended to demonstrate before all the world France's heroic resolve to maintain its military stature. In 1870 France had embarked frivolously on a war of prestige, backed by an altogether inadequate military effort. Now it was prepared even to overstrain its resources in order to assert France's standing as a great power in the face of any possible threat.

The Prussian monarchy has time and again been charged with militarism on account of its excessive military efforts put forward on behalf of political power goals. If the charge is valid, then all the powers of the European continent about 1914 would also have to be regarded as militaristic—they must have caught the contagion of the "evil spirit" of Prussia. Actually, under any other policy, Germany would have had to accept the risk (as will yet be shown) of lagging alarmingly behind its neighbors in land armaments. It seems more correct to me—and here indeed lies one of the basic contentions of this book—to speak of militarism only when the supremacy of political leadership and thinking over the military is challenged. Such was certainly not the case in the France of the Third Republic. On the contrary, the specter of a new Napoleon never receded in the minds of French liberals, and the French were always zealously intent on emphasizing and safeguarding the primacy of civilian over military power in every possible way and even in external forms. The whole army system was aimed at preventing the generals from ever again playing an independent political role. It was for this reason that there were no permanent generalships prior to 1873, nor indeed any higher troop commands in peacetime at all. Every regimental commander was directly subordinate to the war minister, a degree of military centralism that made little sense and was to revenge itself bitterly in the war of 1870-1871, when all higher troop commands had to be improvised. Certain reforms were subsequently instituted, but the basic system was never completely abolished.

The upper-level decisions on all arms questions and even on military and naval campaign plans lay with the Conseil Supérieur de la Défense Nationale, which consisted of the foreign, interior, finance, and war ministers, under the chairmanship of the premier. The chiefs of the general and naval staffs and other higher officers and military officials were only advisory members. This central authority, to which there was no counterpart in Germany, met altogether seventeen times between 1871 and 1914, and its practical importance should therefore not be overestimated;[16] but, in any event, it did provide an opportunity to coordinate all defense measures, even on the high seas, and it vigorously affirmed by its very composition the preponderance of political authority in all defense matters.

Supreme command of the army posed a difficult problem. It was supposed to be placed in militarily competent hands, but with a commander who was also fully responsible to Parliament. It was not at all easy to find this combination, and sometimes the problem seemed as insoluble as squaring the circle. In formal terms the head of state, the president of the republic, exercised supreme command. In urgent situations he had the authority to convoke the superior council on his own initiative, a power of which so vigorous a personality as Poincaré repeatedly made effective use. In normal circumstances, however, the president maintained only indirect links with the army, by way of the premier and the war minister, who alone bore political responsibility. In constitutional terms there was never the slightest question but that the war minister not only directed military administration, as in Germany, but also had full command power. Yet how could he exercise this power unless he was himself a military expert? Even if he were so qualified, there still remained the problem of constantly shifting majorities in Parliament and the swiftly changing composition of the cabinet.

In thirty years the Third Republic had more than thirty war ministers, and even those among them who were generals became, unlike their German colleagues, deeply enmeshed in parliamentary jockeying and party politics. Here as in the other ministries, continuity of performance depended on the civil service, which, for that matter, also had a rather rapid turnover. The War Ministry swelled into a huge central bureaucracy that included the General Staff, the Bureau of Personnel, the National Census, and the various service offices. This cumbersome and diffuse agency, with its numberless committees and departments working side by side without clear lines of authority, has often been criticized. Yet the relative impotence of the various department heads did result in strengthening the position of the war minister himself. The most important department was the supreme war council, made up of ten leading generals, the field commanders to be, who met every month under the chairmanship of the war minister (after 1911 under his deputy, the chief of the General Staff). Here too, however, no independent power was allowed to grow, for the members were appointed for terms of only one year, including the staff chief, the most important figure in the ministry. This caution was further emphasized by the provision that no commanding general could head an army corps for longer than three years without cabinet approval.

Everything was done, in other words, to keep the generals in a state of utter dependence on the political authorities, to insure that even at the top they served merely as technical advisers to the war minister. There was not the slightest possibility of the army playing an independent political role, as a "state within the state," as in Germany. Surely this must be accounted an advantage of the system, like the rule that went into effect not long before 1914 under which the most highly qualified peacetime military expert, the chief of the General Staff, was to become supreme commander in wartime, thus placing leadership in war in the hands of the man responsible for the technical preparations for war. The rapid turnover in the office was, of course, a weakness.

Formally, even in wartime the supreme commander was a mere tool; he was simply the military adviser to the political authorities, who wielded supreme command under the constitution—that is to say, the war minister, who functioned as the executive organ of the Conseil Supérieur; the premier, who bore the principal political responsibility; and the president of the republic, who held the supreme command in the legal sense. The supreme command, in other words, was hierarchically graduated in three or even four steps, from the president down to the commander-in-chief of the army, and any effort to delimit these jurisdictions in sharp detail was foredoomed; for the living dynamics of war do not permit a rigid line to be drawn between *gouvernement* and *commandement,* between political and military responsibility, nor, for that matter, between general war directives and campaign plans on the one hand and their technical execution on the other.

In purely organizational terms, a parliamentary republic can never achieve the cohesion in supreme command available to a monarchy, especially a military monarchy on the Prussian-German model. The French appreciated this before 1914 as clearly as did the Germans.[17] In theory there seemed to be but two alternatives open to France, of which the first possessed a higher degree of probability: A victorious generalissimo would win such glory in war as to win also the undivided trust of the nation. Then all the constitutional safeguards for keeping authority in civilian hands would be in vain, for political authority rested in the end only on *volonté générale,* a consensus. Its bearers were no more than "straws in the whirlwind of public favor," as MacDonald put it on a later occasion in describing the democratic system of government at a London conference.[18]

The Paris government necessarily stood all the more in fear of such an eventuality, inasmuch as, unlike the German monarchs, it stayed at home in wartime and thus had no outward, visible share in whatever military successes were attained. In order not to be overshadowed, it had to stake everything—and this was the alternative—on keeping any one general from winning the highest measure of glory in the field. It had to change commanders often, to play off one generalissimo against another, and above all to join with Parliament in exercising the most detailed control over the army. Yet this of itself created a vital danger, that of constant amateurish interference with the conduct of war, which might be further weakened by the constant fluctuations in the parliamentary majorities.

The Germans thought they were safe from this dual danger, in that military and political leadership were combined in the person of the sovereign, who took the field himself as "supreme warlord," personally exercised supreme command, and endeavored to bridge any gulf between military and political interests. It was an article of faith that in this way any military success would directly benefit the authority of the monarchy—as was indeed the case in 1870-1871, when all hearts went out to the aged "hero emperor" as the true victor, while his much-admired paladins Moltke and Roon lagged a good bit behind in glory, and the various army commanders remained even farther in the background.

The most unexpected development of the war of 1914-1918 was that this anticipated political effect completely failed to materialize. The glamour of the imperial house was outshone many times by the victory laurels of the German generals. There was little sign of integration between the political and military leadership—indeed, the conflicts between them ultimately disrupted the Reich government and even destroyed the nation's unity. We shall have much to say further on about the historical reasons for these events. On the other hand, the practical successes of the French system were no less surprising. These years showed as never before of what small moment political forms of organization are in the face of the fateful power of military success or failure, with its strong impress on public opinion, and also in the face of the achievements and shortcomings of the leading personalities. Germany's downfall was no more prevented by its monarchial system than France's ultimate success and military salvation were due to its republican system. We can say, however, that the political and military traditions that had arisen in France since 1815 did a great deal to keep supreme war leadership and authority over the generals in the hands of the civilian government.[19]

They helped in attaining this goal, but they were by no means the sole factor. Perhaps the strongest buttress to political authority in France during the First World War was the fact that its generals never won sweeping victories. Joffre, to be sure, was accounted the "victor" of the Battle of the Marne, and there were times when his authority was so great that no civilian government could cope with him. He used this authority to secure the highest measure of autonomy to his command, even in administrative matters. He built his headquarters into a kind of central war office and paid very little heed to the ministries in Bordeaux and Paris. He gave the ministers as little information as possible and was extremely sensitive to any effort at "civilian interference." Joffre was widely called a dictator, which was something of an exaggeration, and Clémenceau scornfully called him the French Buddha, but Joffre's power remained undisputed until late 1914, when the French chamber reassembled. Led by the forceful Clémenceau, the French parliamentarians then launched an immediate offensive aimed at regaining the lost political preponderance; and Joffre, of course, had actually scored only half a victory. He had not succeeded in throwing the foe out of the country, and the events of the summer of 1915 made it clear to the whole world that the war would drag on for a very long time. Growing uneasiness took hold of the country, and this provided fertile soil for the sharpest kind of criticism. The generalissimo's military genius was called into question. The government was charged with giving him too free a hand in his negotiations with the allied high commands, in filling his own high command positions, and even in his strategic decisions.

Joffre himself has described the desperate struggle he was compelled to wage against parliamentarians obsessed with an urge to meddle with anything and everything.[20] The war minister was driven to distraction by the ceaseless flood of inquiries, most of them pointless, and by the unquenchable curiosity of parliamentary committees and individual deputies. By the end of the first war year it was no longer possible to forestall or sidetrack parliamentary delegations intent on inspecting the front lines in person. Perhaps the greatest danger to army morale was posed by deputies who were themselves called to the colors and then alternated between military and parliamentary service. In the chamber they would pose as military experts, putting forward all manner of grievances, often baseless or at least hard to verify, providing the press with alarmist news, and in the front lines they even gave political speeches. In their capacity as popular representatives, these much-feared *pékins* even claimed a kind of control function over army commanders, often appointed themselves spokesmen for disaffected elements, and circulated the most enormous military indiscretions—a dangerous state of affairs against which the parliamentary government was for the most part powerless.

All this clearly evidenced the defects of the French army system. Political preponderance did keep the army from becoming a "state within the state," but in turn it deeply involved the army in partisan political strife. The old garrison army of the time before 1870 had been relatively immune to this danger, although even then promotion in the higher grades had in some measure involved playing up to the whims of the political powers; in Germany too "good connections" at court and within the military cabinet were of no small importance in speeding up promotion. In the French parliamentary democracy, however, the party bosses as well as the top generals had to be wooed; and once the garrison army had been transformed into a true mass army late in the nineteenth century, politics made deep inroads into it, especially in the wake of the Dreyfus affair. In his memoirs Marshal Foch complains bitterly that as late as 1914 the baleful effect of political influence was notably felt among general officers in securing advancement from brigadier to corps commander; and he is critical of political protection in the army generally—it was always the ambitious busybodies rather than the really capable officers who lent themselves to playing up to the political bigwigs.[21]

Clémenceau, on the other hand, tells us that Foch himself constantly pursued him to use his influence in behalf of Foch's promotion, sometimes by strange methods, even when Clémenceau, the powerful senator and influential publicist, was not a member of the cabinet. We come to see that this was not an isolated case but a deeply entrenched system. Clémenceau, master of scorn and invective, delights in stripping these proud generals of their pretensions, describing how they elbowed each other out of the way in his and Poincaré's antechambers, intriguing one against the other in their efforts to achieve the highest commands.[22] The wily old atheist and anti-Jesuit may be guilty of considerable exaggeration and malice, but we may be certain that a great many French generals were quite at home in the political arena, which they, unlike their German colleagues, never regarded as an alien world; and, conversely, that French politicians, as a matter of course, were given to meddling in military affairs, right down to technical details.[23] Boulanger, the military orator and demagogue, represents only an extreme case of the typical French political general. During the First World War, British General Staff officers never got over their amazement at the political skill and articulateness of their French colleagues.

From the traditional German point of view all this was bound to appear highly dangerous and even corrupt; but, as we shall see, the rigid segregation of the two spheres that prevailed in Germany held its own dangers, chief of which was that in time of crisis purely military thinking could triumph over political reason. Against this danger at least France enjoyed greater protection, for French soldiers were held in lower esteem and were more amenable to the realities of political life, with which they were in much closer contact. Then too, the French army was not granted a major military triumph until the summer of 1918.

The strongest man on the political side in France, Clémenceau himself, did not come to power until November, 1917; but because of the many military failures ever since 1915, even weaker political figures, supported by various military committees of the chamber and a well organized propaganda policy, were able to keep the upper hand over the military. In 1915 Viviani pushed through French participation in the British Dardanelles expedition over the vehement objections of the military commander-in-chief. Its failure, to be sure, contributed to the fall of his government, but this setback to "civilian strategy" did not keep his successor, Briand, from pursuing his own war policy over the head of his commander-in-chief. Against Joffre's wishes, partly for domestic political considerations and essentially without success, he opened up a second theater of war in Salonica, employing a generously proportioned expeditionary force. It was placed under the command of another general given to playing the political game, Sarrail, whom Joffre had relieved of his previous command; and thus a situation was created in which one commander could be played off against another, the favorite of the leftist republicans against the favorite of the rightist parties. This was all the more advantageous to the premier, since he had brought still a third competent general, Gallieni, into the cabinet as war minister. A group within the chamber was eager to charge Gallieni with direct over-all operational responsibility. Joffre was able to prevent this, and he also succeeded in having Sarrail formally placed under his command; but his own authority was soon undermined by new failures, first the German advance at Verdun and then the failure of his great Somme offensive.

The chamber now clamored for direct government intervention in operations and access to all military news. Joffre, under the continual necessity of defending himself against the *pékins,* had to go. His successor, Nivelle, leapfrogged into the top spot over senior rivals by virtue of excellent political connections, but he had to see Sarrail placed directly under the premier and the government now asserting the right to name all army and army-group commanders. In this way Briand, a master of parliamentary intrigue, satisfied the desires of the chamber.[24] Yet even this concession could not keep him in office when, in March, 1917, his third war minister, General Lyautey, came out against the military indiscretions of the deputies. The chamber had now grown so powerful that the new Ribot government tried to secure itself on all sides before it would allow its commander-in-chief to take any decisive military measure. Nivelle was compelled to defend his plan for a great new offensive, to be put into effect with British support, before a council of war presided over by President Poincaré and including not only the cabinet but Nivelle's own skeptical army commanders. When he met with critical reserve there and handed in his resignation, Poincaré insisted that he stay in office.

The great offensive failed with heavy losses, and Nivelle, once the great hope and darling of the chamber, especially of the left, was described as a "blood guzzler," thrown out of office, and court-martialed, while the troops began to mutiny. It was now up to the calm and detached Pétain, unsusceptible to parliamentary influence and passed over for that reason, to restore order. For the time being he did not dare undertake another offensive but merely did his best to train and discipline the army along modern technical lines. Pétain's powers, moreover, were limited by the appointment of Foch as chief of the General Staff and military adviser to the government, a newly created post with ill-defined jurisdiction, superior to the top general at the French front, with whom Foch was nevertheless on the best of terms. It was from Foch's headquarters that the Salonica operations were directed and liaison with the allies was maintained, a semimilitary, semidiplomatic task of which the capable, ambitious, and always optimistic man from Gascony, with his southern eloquence, acquitted himself well.

All this should make clear the considerable damage to the technical direction of the war done by government and parliamentary intervention up until 1917. Yet Painlevé, the war minister of the summer of 1917 and a civilian, nevertheless managed to put the two ablest generals in the right places after the Nivelle disaster and to create an Interallied War Council which at least laid the groundwork for a unified Allied strategy. After his fall in November, 1917, at last the man whose resistless will for victory would overcome even the weakness of the parliamentary regime seized the helm—Clémenceau, "the tiger."

The man who thus appeared on the stage of history was the kind of popular leader who in his person typified the nation's forward thrust and knew how to make it prevail over all the doubters and vacillators, indeed even over the Parliament. He directed the war in person, as his government program had openly proclaimed. He was head of the government and war minister in one; he turned up everywhere at the front in his soldier's kepi, ordering, encouraging, if necessary threatening. Turning the strong arm of the law on the defeatists, he knocked down all opposition. His fiery oratory and inexhaustible energy swept the weary nation on to new efforts.

It was not that the strategic insight of this civilian was superior to that of the professional soldiers. Foch himself had vainly demanded the creation of a great army reserve in the spring of 1918, prior to Ludendorff's major offensive; and this almost led to disaster, for even Foch's appointment as supreme commander—or rather coordinator—of the Allied troops on the threatened front, engineered by Clémenceau with great diplomatic skill in the famous scene at Doullens, remained without much practical effect in the moment of greatest crisis. But the crisis was mastered, nevertheless, and Clémenceau now staked everything on making his generalissimo the *de facto* leader of the Allied troops, who would press and if possible command the Americans to accept active commitment. Clémenceau, moreover, performed wonders in procuring all possible aid for the armies at home and abroad. Perhaps his greatest achievement was that by the pure power of his rhetoric, in the grave crisis of May 27, when the Germans had advanced all the way to Château Thierry, he once again protected General Foch from the fury of the chamber, which was howling for "punishment of the guilty generals." By the sheer power of his will he held France back from the brink of panic long enough for American participation to come into effect and finally bring the crucial turn in the war.

Yet the fact that the war, under Foch's leadership, did after all turn into a triumphant march to victory for the Allies once again threatened to reverse the relation of political and military leadership. The marshal, proudly aware of his success, now asserted as his right a decisive influence on the armistice and peace negotiations. The unrelenting struggle between him and Clémenceau, which arose in consequence is a matter of record. It led to extremely bitter charges between the two that extended even beyond the grave. As late as February, 1918, when the generalissimo had dared to disagree with him before French and British parliamentarians, Clémenceau, in an oft-described scene, dressed him down in no uncertain terms: "Silence! I am the representative of the French government!"

By the winter of 1918-1919 that was no longer possible. President Wilson himself openly acknowledged Foch as the leading spokesman on the question of the armistice. Later, by his stubborn insistence that French security demanded a frontier on the Rhine, Foch did much to stiffen his country's stand, fighting the British policy of moderation in cooperation with such politicians as Tardieu. Yet the soldier was not, after all, to be allowed to have the decisive voice in the peace terms. Even Poincaré's support could not win this for Foch. In a cabinet meeting of April 25, 1919, Clémenceau brought the supremacy of the political power home to the general in almost humiliating form.

None, to be sure, is likely to claim that this civilian triumph over the military was tantamount to a victory of statesmanlike reason over professional military thinking. In an age of mass democracy, with war grown total, there is no longer a distinction between soldiers and civilians in terms of impassioned militancy. To appreciate this, one need only listen to the old Jacobin's own words—for example, his dreadful speech of triumph delivered in the Senate on September 17, 1918, with its savage outbursts of nationalist hate and its unbridled invective against the vanquished foe; or the no less repellent chapter on the armistice in Clémenceau's memoirs, repeating the abuse and leveling the most vindictive charges of alleged French weakness in the postwar years. "When was the time that man did not relish a fight?" he asks, and in these words characterizes himself.

Things did not look much better in Lloyd George's England, nor, certainly, would the attitude of a victorious German military monarchy have been any better. Unlike the time after 1815 or 1866, Europe after the First World War knew no true political wisdom that might have aspired to an enduring peaceful order. Once again the problems of militarism and nationalism were posed in the most urgent form. Indeed, we may say they became the central political problems of our age.

2

Army, Society, and Government in Britain in the Age of Bourgeois Liberalism

PART FROM Russia, England was the only state that passed through the revolutionary era in the early nineteenth century without serious domestic upheavals. For that reason Britain's weight at the Congress of Vienna was largely on the conservative side; and during the ensuing generations the country was slowly reconstructed in the direction of greater democratization and centralization by economic and social changes rather than by political revolution. In the military sphere this essential process of modernization was particularly slow, for beside the island kingdom's navy its army had always played a subsidiary role. As in France—and in fact in close association with French rearmament for a major struggle with Germany—this delay was made up by leaps and bounds only early in the present century; and in England too the example of the German army system played an important part.[1]

The Duke of Wellington was the dominant military personality in England at the time of the French Restoration; and during this period the British land forces continued unchanged in the tradition of the mercenary armies of the seventeenth and eighteenth centuries. Ever since the days of Cromwell and his "Ironsides," the British upper classes had entertained a deep suspicion of any form of standing army. In 1689 a parliamentary orator had described the "redcoats" as the "curse of the nation," and well into the nineteenth century a standing army was regarded as a threat to liberty. It was tolerated rather than welcomed; and not until the era of world war, when none could escape military service, did civilian aversion to it vanish. As late as 1930 a historian of the British army concluded a multivolume work with a bitter indictment of the nation's ingratitude toward its sons under arms. It was to them that it owed the rise of empire, yet after every war they were sent packing with almost indecent haste, in repudiation of their heroism.[2]

This attitude was certainly not based on historical grounds alone, nor did it bespeak a lack of military aptitude, for the British, while they may have been a "nation of shopkeepers," demonstrated their natural fighting spirit a hundred times over on every ocean and continent. Yet until the First World War insular politics never experienced the strong pressure for land forces which was marked in the continental states. The British need was for a powerful fleet, supplemented by a small force of professional soldiers who served for long periods of enlistment and were suitable for colonial warfare. All that was needed at home was a kind of police force which could be expanded into an effective coast guard in case of a threat of invasion. For the rest, insofar as Britain was involved at all in continental cabals, it was content to manage with the payment of subsidies to allies whenever that was at all possible. To a much greater degree than the military monarchies on the mainland, Britain resorted to neutrality and diplomacy. Only in exceptional circumstances would Britain commit sizable mercenary forces, recruited abroad as well as at home, under its own command on continental battlefields.

By virtue of its naval superiority, originally achieved in the wars against Spain and the Netherlands and secured even more firmly in the struggle against Napoleon, Britain was able to wage large-scale economic war even against mainland opponents. It needed to take part in land war only insofar as this seemed to serve its purposes.

There was no sound reason, even in the nineteenth century, for England to abandon this traditional system which had but recently proved its worth in repelling Napoleon—or at least a French invasion; and Wellington, the victor of Waterloo, was the last one to favor a change. The liberal governments of the Victorian age showed little interest in military reform, especially when it held out the prospect of heavy expense. It was they in particular who turned more and more to peaceful agreement in place of military force; and they even tended to de-emphasize traditional colonial policy. Public opinion in the homeland of Manchester liberalism was averse to all things military, and the pacifist ideals of free trade held even greater power over English minds than French. If there was, nevertheless, piecemeal army reform in Britain in the course of the nineteenth century, this was largely a matter of strengthening the influence of Parliament. Technical modernization, the need for which the Crimean War had so dramatically shown, and the question of creating a reserve, which became more and more difficult with progressive industrialization—these were matters of only secondary importance. It was finally the Boer War early in the present century that brought a decisive turn.

To the continental mind it was almost inconceivable—and Bismarck, in his own parliamentary struggles, often cited this as a warning example—that the very existence of the English army should have been dependent on annual votes in the House of Commons ever since 1688. Every year there had to be a renewal of the "Mutiny Act," which embraced the entirety of a separate military penal jurisdiction and, since 1721, the very peacetime strength of the army. The immediate consequence was that there was always a dangerous measure of uncertainty concerning the continuity of the army. Even during the Congress of Vienna, when the new European order had begun to emerge only in outline, Parliament reduced the army by 47,000 men, with the result that, on Napoleon's return from Elba, Wellington was able to command only a shadow of his old army in Belgium.

Up to a certain point the British army was always more or less a matter of improvisation. There was always hesitation to embark on the construction of permanent army posts, and temporary barracks and old prisons were often resorted to. Even the most elementary provisions for the welfare and adequate education of the ranks were neglected. Little was done for technical officer training and nothing at all for the creation of a modern general staff. In a social sense, soldiers were held in even greater contempt than in France, a natural consequence of the fact that the regular army consisted exclusively of volunteers, who, in the face of the tremendous upsurge in British economic life and the rise of the militia—still to be discussed—had to be recruited largely among antisocial elements. In nineteenth-century England the gulf between soldiers and citizens remained as deep as it had been on the continent before the Great Revolution with its mass armies.

The intrusion of soldiers on ordinary social occasions was considered a shocking event. Privates were thought of as rowdies and habitual drunkards to be shunned whenever possible. They were forbidden to enter public parks and gardens, theaters and music halls. When General-to-be Wilson wanted to conduct a training march to Clacton-on-Sea in 1902, the mayor of that resort implored him to spare the holiday-makers such an invasion by notorious bully boys.[3] At the end of the Napoleonic Wars London society objected to the many uniformed men then seen in the streets, and when an officers' club was to be built in 1817, the prime minister himself voiced serious objections. Until late in the nineteenth century there seems to have been scarcely any public sympathy for "Tommy Atkins," the wretched common soldier, who was herded into filthy, insanitary dormitory slums without mess halls, was miserably paid and fed, and lacked any spiritual sustenance. The mortality rate in the peacetime army, principally because of tuberculosis, was much higher than the civilian average.

The lash—up to three hundred strokes—was officially abolished only in 1867. There was widespread public distrust of the redcoats, who appeared in the role of police, protecting the capitalist class, whenever a working-class rebellion had to be put down. The aristocracy and upper middle class on their part felt themselves to be vastly superior to the private soldier, who was viewed as a mere paid bully rather than as a fellow citizen called upon to defend the country.

Even more than in France, the garrison army was a thing apart from the life of the people. To nineteenth-century England the notion of a nation in arms was utterly unfamiliar, except possibly in connection with the militia units as opposed to the regular army. The idea could not become popular until the government was thoroughly democratized, and that was still a distant goal. Like the French liberal bourgeoisie, the British ruling classes in the nineteenth century—the nobility and the upper middle class—regarded antimilitarism as a basic ingredient of libertarianism.

The image of the professional officer fitted into this concept. It was a career considered suitable and convenient to the younger sons of the gentry rather than as one of honorable service to the country. The educational qualifications were modest and the duties and obligations incumbent on an officer were slight, normally pre-empting at most the time between breakfast and lunch. Troops enlisted for life—or a contractual minimum of twenty-one years—and little training was required for mere guard and police duties. There was no question of realistic war exercises, partly for reasons of economy, and partly because there simply were no large troop units in peacetime. The officers drawn from the nobility had very little contact with their men and often did not even know them by name. Many of them were preoccupied with purely administrative work, and the ratio of officers to men was higher than anywhere else in Europe.

All this was in the interest of the ruling nobility. At the height of its political and social power, in the eighteenth century, there was virtually no limit to the patronage of political cliques, especially since high army rank was quite compatible with a seat in Parliament. Members would secure army sinecures, and the royal court would endeavor to keep such officers out of the opposition in the House of Commons by invoking their military loyalty to the king. Parliamentary influence with the secretary at war could secure immunity from military punishment, even in cases of desertion. Only after the revolutionary wars was this patronage system restricted. In 1793 the office of the commander-in-chief was instituted as a purely military agency whose incumbent could not be a member of Parliament and who was to represent the military prerogatives of the king. The Duke of York, who held this office from 1795 on, vigorously resisted backstairs parliamentary influence, introduced stricter discipline into the officers' corps, and created his own personnel office, staffed with specialists, and an officers' training school. In 1866 soldiers and noncoms were at last by royal ordinance expressly forbidden any participation in political and party demonstrations, a ruling that applied in practice to officers on active duty as well.

All this put an end to many abuses, but it did not alter the preferential position of the nobility, which continued to enjoy excellent connections with the army leadership by way of both the court and Parliament, where it dominated the field to the end of the century. Commissions were for sale, as before, and the higher positions could be obtained only for enormous sums.[4]

This system interfered with both promotion on merit and discharge for incompetence and entirely excluded the candidacy of the unmonied. Not until 1871 was this age-old feudal heritage abolished by law and were examination and pensions for officers introduced.

The sale of commissions was part and parcel of the older form of army organization, taken over intact from the age of mercenary armies in England and elsewhere, and in force in England until well into the nineteenth century. It was based entirely on the regiment as a recruiting organization, and indeed regiments had greater importance in this capacity than as tactical units.

Every regiment of the standing army was in a sense accounted the personal property of the colonel whose distinguished name it carried, who recruited its ranks and paid them from a blanket allowance granted by the government, and who pocketed whatever he managed not to spend. Any financial burden could be eased by the sale of commissions—sometimes to young children of the nobility—and in case of need by the sale of whole companies to other regiments. Fiscal army control did not become possible until Burke's great financial reform of 1782, which was implemented only slowly and even then but incompletely. Procurement of uniforms remained the responsibility of regimental commanders until the Crimean War, and permanent higher tactical units were created only after 1902. Before then the largest tactical unit for the infantry was the battalion, for the cavalry the regiment, and for the artillery the battery.

No clear and uniform plan underlay top army leadership, which was a patchwork of many casual jurisdictions distributed over many authorities, scattered even as to location, and cooperating only poorly. Maintaining an intricately scrambled system of top military authority was, in the eyes of Parliament, the best insurance against the assumption of an independent political role by the army.

In formal terms the army's sole leader was the king, who, since the Napoleonic Wars, did indeed have a commander-in-chief as his deputy, to implement his authority in practice. The crown clung tenaciously to this institution until late in the century, for it meant close contact with the army. Queen Victoria in particular endeavored to maintain and even expand her royal prerogatives in military matters in this fashion. She was concerned, not without reason, that the British system of running the army gave too little scope to expert soldiers as against civilian political dilettantes. At one time there was even a plan to make Prince Albert, Victoria's consort, commander-in-chief. In 1856 the Queen's cousin, the Duke of Cambridge, was appointed to this post, which he retained until 1895. However, by his rigid conservatism, especially in technical matters, he managed to undermine rather than strengthen his authority, although it was severely limited to begin with, extending primarily to appointments and promotions, pardons and decorations, etc., and only in formal terms to the maintenance of discipline and the exercise of command as well.

The position combined the functions of the Prussian military cabinet with those of a commander-in-chief and a chief of staff—except that there was no General Staff in England and the royal command power was extremely ill defined. Without specific constitutional authority, purely by virtue of tradition and the power of the purse, Parliament year after year intervened in the technical details of army administration, down to the use of cavalry lances and the minutiae of recruitment. Early in the nineteenth century no less than thirteen agencies competed with the office of the commander-in-chief. The master-general of the ordnance was charged with all matters of arms, artillery, and pioneers; and the home secretary oversaw the use of the militia, volunteers, and yeomanry and of the army for police purposes as well as all domestic troop transfers. Disciplinary matters and courts-martial were under a judge advocate-general, and all colonial troops were under the colonial secretary. The so-called commissariat, a division of the treasury, was responsible for feeding the troops. There were special agencies for fiscal control, two paymasters-general, a board of general officers, an army medical board, an army hospital board, and still other bodies for construction and recruitment. The commander-in-chief was in practice very dependent on the secretary at war without being his formal subordinate. Indeed, the secretary had long since developed from a mere administrative assistant to the field commander and then into the most important army leader, since under Burke's fiscal reforms he was responsible to Parliament for most of the army budget. Yet he was not a member of the cabinet and thus not a war minister in the true sense. His war office, nevertheless, was accounted the core of civilian army administration, and it steadily gained in importance. Located in Pall Mall, the war office was the major rival of and limitation upon the plenipotentiary power of the commander-in-chief, whose seat of office was the Horse Guards in Whitehall. The inevitable conflicts between the military and civilian (or rather political) views in the army took place chiefly between these two centers.

In an effort to bridge this gulf, Pitt had created a third government agency in 1794, the office of the secretary *for* war, later expanded into the ministry for war and colonies. It was to direct over-all military policy in peace and war. It also represented the war office in the cabinet. Until 1914 no professional soldier ever headed this agency. In practice the secretary for war and colonies was overburdened with colonial concerns. This fact, together with the ill-defined demarcation of jurisdiction, in respect of both the secretary at war and the commander-in-chief, prevented any effective coordination among the many military agencies; and this unresolved dualism of civilian and military authority characterized British army organization until almost the end of the century.

The preponderance of civilian and political authority in practice was, nevertheless, an indubitable fact. It was far greater and less equivocal than in France, where military experts always carried much weight as advisers to the government and where time and again—indeed, until 1888 always—generals were in charge of the war ministry. In a political sense, the British form of organization may have had its advantages, but it seriously paralyzed the army's striking power. Despite his proud title, the commander-in-chief was not in fact the top military commander, let alone the "supreme warlord." He was essentially an administrative official with poorly defined but limited powers. The Duke of Wellington once complained before a commission in 1837 that without the consent of civilian authority he could not even order a corporal with a squad of men to go from London to Windsor or return. Marching orders for troops in the field were drafted at the war office, not at the Horse Guards; and in the Crimean War the secretary for war asserted supreme direction without consulting the commander-in-chief. The latter afterward reported that his advice had never been sought during the campaign and that the only dispatches he saw were those published in the newspapers.

It was the Crimean War that demonstrated the consequences of this chaotic state of affairs to all the world. Inadequate army administration in that conflict cost the British nation immense sacrifices in blood and money, more even than during the Napoleonic era. This provided the first real impetus for administrative reform, by the usual route of a sensational report from a commission of the House of Commons. Even during the Crimean War most of the agencies concerned with army administration were reorganized into a war ministry (the office of the secretary for war) now definitely split away from the colonial office, thus ending or at least greatly reducing the former diffuseness. In 1863 the office of the former secretary at war was also swallowed up by the new war ministry. Since the war minister, as a member of the parliamentary cabinet, could not be a professional soldier, this reform actually strengthened the hands of the civilian elements. Queen Victoria, however, saw to it that the commander-in-chief retained his importance. His authority was actually expanded, in that he was now given military command and disciplinary supervision over artillery, pioneers, and colonial troops, as well as military control of fortifications.

What remained in dispute was the degree of autonomy with which he was permitted to exercise this command power at the immediate direction of the crown, a direction about which the queen was in dead earnest. She was particularly concerned with keeping the appointment and promotion of officers free of parliamentary influence, and here public opinion was on her side. All the same, the reform commissions clung to the view that the war minister was ultimately responsible for all military questions and that he must therefore exercise political control over the commander-in-chief as well. Even the Duke of Cambridge acknowledged in 1860 that in the event of a difference of opinion between him and the minister the latter carried the deciding voice. No other conclusion was possible under a parliamentary system.

The impression may have arisen that this reorganization solved the precarious problem of the relation of political and military authority in clear-cut fashion. Concrete experience shows, however, that there simply is no ideal organizational solution as such which would eliminate the natural conflict between civilian and military thinking once and for all. In practice there can only be a compromise, and its scope depends much less on the particular organizational forms in question than on how deep the conflict itself is at the given time. Nineteenth-century British cabinets were even less warlike in orientation than was the bourgeois French government of the same period. On both sides of the Channel change came only after 1900, in the so-called Age of Imperialism, and the consequences in transforming the whole army system were similar in both countries. In the 1860's, following the reforms of 1855-1863, it was inevitable, even at the height of liberal pacifism, that friction between the Horse Guards and the war office should continue and even intensify. The soldiers complained of civilian parsimony, while the civilians held that the generals asked for far too much; but officer training and promotion, the employment of troops at home and in the colonies, the use of the militia and other ancillary forces—all these could become bones of contention, with Parliament sticking its nose in at every point. Concrete decisions were all the more difficult for the war minister, since the war office had grown into a huge agency embracing many administrative departments, whose details the minister could not possibly keep in his head, particularly since he lacked specialist qualifications. Hence, he inevitably slipped into a kind of dependence on the views of his military advisers, especially his military secretary, whose office grew into a permanent secretariat and who, as a professional soldier within a civilian agency, represented something new and strange to England. Whenever the minister overrode this adviser, he was in danger of being belittled by him as an amateur. In these circumstances, and with the frequent cabinet changes, it was difficult to maintain a clear and consistent military policy.

For that reason there was constant tinkering with war office organization at all levels. The ablest war minister prior to Haldane, Edward Cardwell, succeeded in having the commander-in-chief move his office from the Horse Guards to Pall Mall in 1870 as his subordinate, with the status of a department head in the war office, although the special relationship of the commander-in-chief with the crown continued. The cumbersome war office organization was to be simplified by regrouping the many departments into three major divisions—one, under the commander-in-chief, for matters of command and discipline, another for fiscal matters, and a third with jurisdiction over arsenals and fortifications—although this last one was soon to be reorganized and subdivided again. The two administrative chiefs had access to the House of Commons, while the commander-in-chief, when a peer, sat in the House of Lords, where he sometimes voiced his own personal views, which led to new difficulties.

Indeed, friction between military and civilian officials continued even with the new system. It became necessary to institute one reform commission after another; and in 1888 an effort was made to achieve a formal separation of the two spheres. There was to be a civilian "side" under the fiscal head and a military one under the commander-in-chief, with sole jurisdiction over the military sections. Unfortunately this enhanced the position of the commander-in-chief as military adviser to the war minister to a greater degree than could be tolerated, the more so since the Duke of Cambridge's stubborn conservatism paralyzed all attempts at technical military reform and created deep resentment, particularly among his ablest and most progressive military subordinates.

The minister, on his part, chafed at the Duke's constant invocation of his special relation to the crown whenever disagreements arose. The crown's military prerogative thus appeared as the chief obstacle to organizational and technical reform, while progress became identified with complete integration of the army into the parliamentary system. In 1870 a reform commission under Lord Hartington had proposed the abolition of the office of commander-in-chief, or at least his removal from the war office as a kind of inspector general of home troops. A modern chief of staff on the French and German model was to take his place; and he and the other military and civilian department heads were to meet regularly under the chairmanship of the war minister to provide him with expert advice on all matters. This would have meant reorganizing the war office along the collective lines of the admiralty; the plan also bore a distant resemblance to the supreme war council of the French war ministry.

The plan failed to carry, however, because of the stubborn opposition of the queen and her conservative entourage; and even when the seventy-six year-old Duke of Cambridge was at last persuaded to retire in 1895, the office he had held so long was continued. All that happened was that in the same year the heads of four newly created military subdivisions were made independent advisers to the war minister along with the commander-in-chief, although they were his subordinates. They were the adjutant general, who was in charge of training and discipline; the quartermaster general, who was in charge of supply; the master-general of the ordnance, who was in charge of equipment; and the inspector general, who was in charge of fortifications.

Manifestly this was only a half-measure. It was intended to weaken the powers of the commander-in-chief without eliminating the office altogether, and it merely served to complicate the system even further. The commander-in-chief was now a complete hybrid. He was not a responsible minister himself, nor the minister's sole military adviser, nor chief of a General Staff with clearly marked jurisdiction, nor the top commanding general. In the main he was once again an administrative official, burdened with countless different concerns. It would have been impossible to say who now bore the ultimate responsibility for the state of the army and for war plans. The war minister certainly did not, for he was not a professional soldier. Besides, he had his hands full with parliamentary and political affairs. Nor was it the General Staff, for there was none.

The four division heads did not come into it either, for the jurisdiction of each was narrowly circumscribed and they could not act with full autonomy. Lastly, the commander-in-chief was out of the running, for he lacked plenipotentiary powers and had no contact whatever with the troops and current field experience.

The British army organization had still other flaws, equally serious. The war office was notorious in the army as the "circumlocution office" because of its fragmentation into a host of individual bureaus with diffuse and overlapping tasks; these bureaus worked side by side and all too often against one another. An added difficulty was excessive administrative centralization, with the result that the top officers were burdened with the most absurd detail work. One reason was the peacetime absence of higher troop units that would have carried out administrative services of their own. The administrative districts that were supposed to serve as intermediate links remained mere shadow organization in the absence of such units. For the same reasons peacetime training, mobilization plans, and tactical staff training were utterly inadequate. In emergencies higher staffs had to be painfully assembled. The whole machinery was aimed only at coastal protection and minor colonial warfare, where there was always enough time for improvisation, and not at warfare in the continental style.

Equipped with this incredibly cumbersome system, Great Britain entered the Age of Imperialism, an age marked by constant and severe tensions on the continent. If things had still been in such a state by 1914, the possible over-all consequences for the world situation stagger the imagination. Britain would have been unable to provide France with any really effective support against the German army, and this would have influenced the whole policy of the Entente long before. But things in fact turned out quite differently; in 1899 the Boer War confronted Britain with the clear-cut alternative of either foregoing an imperialist power policy on the grand scale or reorganizing its army system from top to bottom.

Never was a campaign of conquest more poorly prepared for in technical and organizational terms. So disastrous were the consequences, so plain for all the world to see, that the political prestige of the British Empire was momentarily shaken. But the extent of the initial failures was more than matched by the efforts to undo them and to stake everything on military victory. With an even more astonishing and abrupt leap than France, Britain sought to reorganize its entire army system directly after the war, to bring it up to a new level, to match its superior navy with truly modern armed forces, suitable for continental battlefields. This again was possible only by deliberate emulation of the German example. It meant not only recasting military administration but completely reorganizing the army as such, modernizing its training and equipment, and, most importantly, opening up large manpower reserves.

The crucial step was taken by a three-man commission under Lord Esher instituted by the conservative Balfour government in 1903-1904. In essence it reverted to the proposals of the Hartington commission of 1890, but it greatly expanded them. Everyone was by now convinced that thoroughgoing modernization and strengthening of the army were urgent matters. The reforms of the Esher commission were put into effect by order-in-council without much to-do and without the participation of Parliament; and these reforms did indeed once for all end the period of experimentation and of perpetual strife between military and civilian authority within the ministry. Abolition of the office of commander-in-chief clearly established that the war minister was to have single-handed leadership with parliamentary responsibility, and he was now himself considered the executor of the prerogatives of the crown. More and more, his office took on the collective character of the admiralty. All important questions were responsibly decided by a seven-man board under the chairmanship of the minister, on which the military held a majority—chief of the General Staff (in place of the former commander-in-chief), adjutant general, quartermaster general, and master-general of the ordnance (who was also inspector of fortifications). The civilian members were the parliamentary undersecretary, the permanent undersecretary, and the financial undersecretary.

Hence civilian and military department heads no longer worked exclusively in separate compartments, but collaborated on a board in which they shared responsibility. Friction was thus reduced and practical solutions facilitated. This collegiate arrangement had long since served well in the admiralty, which was taken as a model. All the discretionary powers of the war minister, the commander-in-chief, and the adjutant general were transferred to the "army council" thus created. The ministerial responsibilities were regrouped and at last clearly delimited, and the six divisional heads were relieved of petty detail work by administrative officials assigned to them. The administrative duties of the former commander-in-chief were now, on the German model, transferred to inspectors general of the army and to seven different, newly created general commands, each of which received its own administrative staff; thus the former excessive centralization was loosened. The whole cumbersome agency was at last made really efficient.[5]

It is true that such a collegiate administrative system is commonly regarded as cumbersome itself compared with a "bureaucratic" system, in which the ultimate power of decision lies with one man. The latter system, however, usually functions well only when it is headed by an expert possessed of considerable personal stature and skill. Otherwise there is too much scope for intrigue by subordinates, and too much is left to chance. Given the type of civilian minister under the prevailing British parliamentary system, the reorganization of 1904 was undoubtedly the best that could be attained.

The greatest advance made was the creation of a modern General Staff in place of the obsolete office of the commander-in-chief. In retrospect, it is surprising that such a staff had not come into being long before. This step had been urgently recommended even by the Hartington commission, but in 1890 there was as yet little concern over large-scale war plans, and an extremely modest intelligence and mobilization section was accepted as sufficient. The Liberals, moreover, remained deeply suspicious of military planning agencies on the continental model. All that general staffs did, remarked Campbell-Bannerman, was dream up every conceivable kind of war plan. This was, to be sure, a naive prejudice; but we know how tenaciously the Anglo-Saxon world clung to it, right down to the Nuremberg Trials. And, as we shall yet see, Campbell-Bannermann's concern was to be justified precisely in England in the most curious fashion.

Another useful innovation was the establishment of a Committee of Imperial Defense, an improvement and expansion of the older Committee of National Defense, created in 1895 and comprising several cabinet members, which had never carried much weight. The prime minister now had complete discretion to assemble cabinet members, preferably, of course, the war minister and the first lord of the admiralty, together with a staff of officers drawn from all the armed services, including India and the colonies, as needs might dictate. They were heard only as expert advisers, however, and did not function as voting members. The prime minister was thus placed in a position which enabled him to secure any information he desired directly from the most highly qualified experts, and to make his decisions on the basis of the insight he thus gained, which the cabinet merely needed to confirm. Of course it was not an easy matter to bring about truly fruitful cooperation among such divergent interests as those of the British dominions. Practical implementation of decisions was rendered extremely difficult on account of the disorderly structure of empire administration, with its many diverse central agencies with overlapping jurisdictions—the colonial office, the foreign office, the India office, the government of India, the war office, the admiralty, etc. In the end almost everything depended on whether there was a powerful personality at the head of things, a man who knew how to wield the complex machinery in the first place, in addition to having the will to prevail. At the outbreak of war in 1914, the Committee of Imperial Defense simply vanished into limbo, to be replaced by other "war boards." The committee was evidently accounted an institution that could function effectively only in peacetime.[6]

The principle that the prime minister could, in military matters, consult with a cabinet committee advised by military experts was retained; but he was in no way bound in every detail to so large a body as the entire cabinet.

We see that the British, traditionally among the most conservative nations, wrenched themselves free of their obsolete military traditions after the Boer War and created a truly modern and rational army organization for themselves. And precisely because this reorganization took place at so late a stage, at a time when the system of parliamentary democracy had been perfected, it was possible to make the new British army system in some respects more efficient than its older continental counterparts.

With the help of the new British war office, a greatly rejuvenated and much more effective army was now built up in a matter of a few years.[7] Reorganization actually began even before the Boer War was over; for the war pushed capable young officers into crucial posts, compelled numerous technical improvements in training and leadership, and above all aroused the nation to the mortal danger to the whole empire of a defeat that would undermine its international power. It was really only the Boer War that made the imperial cause, previously the concern largely of colonial theoreticians and activists, a truly popular issue. This was especially true in the dominions, which quickly sent more military support on a voluntary basis than England had dared hope for. At home, too, the flow of volunteers was surprisingly heavy, at least in the beginning, under the impress of the early defeats. And all these volunteer units, like the militia, submitted meekly to being shipped overseas to the theater of war in South Africa, though they were originally obligated to serve only at home in the narrowest sense.

The more the army and the war became popular causes, the less it was possible to continue holding the "Tommies" in contempt. Even in outward respects the situation of the soldier was greatly improved. Pay was sharply increased, a necessary step to attract enough volunteers; housing, mess, and training standards were raised; and veteran benefits were bettered. With the expeditionary force swelled to a quarter-million, the lack of properly trained officers became a particular problem, and much money and effort were lavished in this sphere. The age of sinecures for members of the nobility was ended for good and all.

Here, too, the most important and difficult problem was the procurement of adequate reserves for large-scale warfare. This had been brought home to the British for the first time by the overwhelming successes of the Prussian army in 1866 and 1870-1871. Cardwell's reforms had then shortened the term of the British mercenary from twenty-one to twelve years; after 1881 only seven years were spent in active service and the remaining five in the reserves, so that it became possible to increase the cadre battalions. This in turn made it possible to concentrate larger forces at home, whence in case of need they could be dispatched with relative speed to any overseas theater by the modern steam-powered fleet. Every regiment now consisted of two battalions, one of which was always garrisoned at home, serving to train replacements, while the other was stationed in the colonies. Until the Boer War, this system had proved entirely adequate. Short-term universal military service, adopted by France in 1885, was impractical for the British Empire, if only for the reason that raw recruits were useless for colonial warfare, while shipping trained men to India or Afghanistan for only a year or two would have entailed unacceptable transportation costs. Thus the militia were used merely as a reservoir for recruitment, whenever direct recruitment for the regular army failed to provide sufficient reserves.

The British militia system dated back to Tudor times and had not undergone its first thoroughgoing reform until the Seven-Years' War in 1757. The Prussian system of cantonal imposts had then been adapted to English ways. Every county was obliged to provide and maintain a certain quota of men. The lord lieutenant chose these men by lot from a list of all inhabitants liable to military service. He also appointed the officers—only in 1871 did that privilege devolve upon the crown. Anyone called up could procure a substitute—the very poorest even enjoyed a government subsidy to this end. Regulations were repeatedly updated in the course of the nineteenth century. Compulsory levies by lot were raised only occasionally and were actually abolished by law in 1852. The militia was mobilized only when the country was divested of troops by foreign wars, such as the Crimean War, the Indian Mutiny, and the Egyptian campaign, and it was supposed to serve solely for home defense. Its training was extremely limited, up to six months' basic training by regular army personnel, and after that annual exercises of three or four weeks. Since 1882 the total term had been six years. These forces were organized on a purely local basis, and their equipment was poor. In the main they were considered a source for regular army recruitment. Membership in the commissioned ranks in particular was regarded as a means of qualifying for regular army commissions under less onerous conditions. After 1867 there was also a militia reserve, a kind of voluntary force like the Prussian Landsturm, entailing regular army service in the event of war. These forces were further supplemented by various volunteer groups, some of them with very ancient traditions, among which the mounted yeomanry enjoyed particular prestige. They financed themselves largely from their own private means, in return for which they enjoyed certain privileges, especially a shortened training period, essentially limited to evenings and weekends.

In a military sense all these units were of slight value. Yet for large parts of the population they did serve as a preliminary training school and thus provided a basis for improvement. They fell far short, however, of providing an adequate manpower pool for large-scale modern warfare. It is indeed doubtful whether any voluntary system, unsupported by the firm hand of the law, can achieve this goal, and the Boer War made this quite clear. Yet at the end of that war the Liberals once again tended to regard it as an exceptional case, possibly the last of the great colonial campaigns. True, doubts had been created as to the efficacy of Cardwell's reserve system, but there was no unanimity as to what should take its place. In 1903 a reform commission proposed that universal military service should be introduced, with one year of active service and three years in the reserves, but this met with bitter and indignant opposition throughout the land. What purposes were these onerous military burdens to serve? There were indeed no immediately plausible arguments. In the age of the Russo-Japanese War and the first Russian Revolution, a large colonial war with Russia, say over Afghanistan, seemed highly unlikely. In the view of military experts, such a war would have been limited to small expeditionary forces on the Russian side, because of transport difficulties in Inner Asia.[8] There was, of course, talk of a possible French invasion, but in 1905 the Balfour government conducted landing exercises on the basis of which it concluded that such a venture would have little chance of success.

Thus the prospects at the end of the Boer War were that army reorganization would after all solve the knotty problem of reserves. The fact that this did not happen is of considerable historical significance. It was entirely due to a basic shift in British foreign policy under the Liberal Campbell-Bannermann-Grey cabinet. Actually, among the British statesmen of the time, none exceeded the new prime minister in the vigor of his opposition to the militarization of England. None more vociferously proclaimed a policy of peaceful agreement instead of military power. Yet under his leadership a defense policy prevailed that not only enabled Great Britain to intervene decisively in the crucial first weeks of the great continental struggle to come, but served to weave more and more tightly that network of moral obligations that inescapably caught the country up in an anti-German war coalition.

The man to whom England is primarily indebted for its new army was R. B. Haldane, the most talented and vigorous British war minister since Cardwell. From his own testimony we cannot doubt that his whole defense policy was from the very beginning oriented toward taking part in a war against Germany by France's side. Yet he was certainly no warmonger—indeed he called Germany, with whose cultural history he was intimately familiar, his "spiritual home"; and none labored harder nor more sincerely to achieve a military and political *modus vivendi.*

Yet ever since the Morocco crisis of 1905-1906, Campbell-Bannerman, like his friend and colleague Grey, felt that France was seriously threatened by Germany; and the forced pace of German naval growth, together with the plans of the German General Staff for a possible invasion of Belgium, seemed to him to pose a threat to Britain as well. In his memoirs he explains over and over how the naval policies of William II and his adviser Tirpitz shifted the balance of power and virtually forced England into a close entente with France.[9] The age of "splendid isolation," he says, was over the moment England had to stand in fear that its naval superiority might be lost and that Germany might succeed in becoming allied with another major naval power. Everything had to be done to keep France out of any anti-British continental alliance; and France also had to be protected against the possibility of a German victory, for such a victory would have placed the Channel coast in German hands and thus put England into a state of complete dependence on her most powerful rival. Thus

Campbell-Bannerman, as early as 1906, assented to military discussions with French General Staff officers; and from then until 1914 British foreign policy never seriously diverged from the course set by these discussions. On the contrary, military integration with the French deployment plans grew closer and closer. Here lay the major political impetus for the British army reforms under Haldane.

The main goal was the creation of a fully equipped expeditionary striking force that could be mobilized and dispatched to the continent in a matter of days—the very thing that had still eluded the British during the Morocco crisis of 1906. The expeditionary force—i.e., the regular army—was set at one cavalry and six infantry divisions, units modeled on the example of the continental army corps in their equipment and arms mix. The main emphasis was on technical modernization, which followed the continental pattern more and more closely down to 1914. Haldane had studied German mobilization techniques and General Staff organization with particular attention and success. The obvious question as to the political purposes of the expeditionary force, repeatedly put by suspicious Liberal critics, was always evaded in Parliament, though the army itself was quite clear on what was intended.

The need to create adequate reserves against the event of war grew more and more urgent, and the defense act of 1907 sought to meet it. It did so not by introducing universal military service, but by thoroughly reorganizing the militia and the old volunteer units—in other words, by economical expedients. The militia was transformed into a kind of voluntary force like the Prussian Landwehr, intended mainly to provide replacement battalions for the regular army which were no longer locally organized. The old volunteer units were organized by law into a single Territorial Army, intended in the first place for home defense in case of war. In this organization county units were recreated, on the traditional principles of home rule and self-government, and these units soon developed a life of their own. Supported by the government and awarded royal distinctions of every kind, both middle-class and working-class elements joined with patriotic zeal and proved themselves as a military training ground to such a degree that the opposition Labour party soon grew suspicious and began to talk about a "Germanization" and "militarization" of the British nation. Actually, the authorized strength of 300,000 men in the Territorial Army was never reached, but by 1909 intensive propaganda had managed to rally some 270,000.

So long as the voluntary system remained intact, war propaganda remained an essential element in the whole picture; and as conducted by Haldane and the numerous propaganda organs of the Territorial Army, this was something decidedly new in English life. The goal long since attained in Prussia-Germany by the coercion of universal military service—to awaken zeal for the profession of arms in a nation of civilians—was now pursued in England, in somewhat attenuated measure, through the means of modern propaganda. The minister himself did his own recruiting mainly among the educated classes, from which he sought officers and military surgeons. Special one-year officer training courses were instituted and in the secondary schools and universities cadet corps were created for officer candidates. Military fitness was cultivated in every possible way, not least by involving the schools, sports organizations, and Boy Scouts in military and paramilitary exercises and camps. All this found a ready response among the educated youth. Cruder methods had to be resorted to in order to win over the urban masses for Territorial service. The danger of possible invasion was luridly highlighted by speeches, billboards, stage plays, and articles in the press. The growth of the Territorial Army was thus closely associated with arousing nationalist passions and with the anti-German propaganda of the last prewar years.

A particularly heavy share in this campaign was defrayed by the National Service League under the former commander-in-chief, Lord Roberts. Established in the time of the Boer War, its aim was to fight for the introduction of universal military service. Its agitation did succeed in deepening fear, hatred, and bitterness with respect to the "German threat," but compulsory service had not yet come in by 1914, though the General Staff had seriously considered it two years before. In 1913, at the height of the European arms race, a bill was actually introduced into the House of Commons that would have brought limited liability to service in the Territorial Army to all British subjects. It failed to gain government support and was rejected by a large majority. England did not yet feel that the threat was great enough to warrant the creation of a huge army in peacetime. The General Staff itself was apprehensive of changing the traditional system at a time of great international tension. Such a change would have taken years, during which a dangerous transitional stage would have prevailed, and this might have served as the strongest possible provocation to the Germans to fight a pre-emptive war. In 1910 General Hamilton had proposed that universal military service should at least be anchored in law in the event of a national emergency, with prompt registration of all men, but even this plan did not prevail.

Thus the military effectiveness of Haldane's reforms and the striking power of the new expeditionary force were still severely limited. Later critics have indeed scored all these reforms as pathetic half-measures. The generals who had to lead the expeditionary force in North France and Flanders in 1914-1915 complained bitterly at having been sent with utterly inadequate forces, equipment, ordnance, and munitions into a modern mass war—a war for which Britain was still in no way prepared.[10] They were undoubtedly right, yet Haldane's reforms were indeed ultimately aimed at making British participation in such a struggle possible in the first place. And considering the limitations of the parliamentary system, just about everything that could be done by way of military and political preparation in the circumstances was done. Without these reforms, Kitchener could not possibly have expanded the Territorial Army into a great mass army later on—still keeping the voluntary system intact, however. Haldane himself never doubted—and he said so openly on the floor of the House—that following large-scale mobilization the Territorial Army would accept its patriotic duty and be willing to fight for the interest of the nation and the defense of the empire even beyond the coasts of the British Isles.

The great dominions associated with the empire were, of course, to provide aid again, as they had done in the Boer War. The outstanding success of Haldane's defense policy was that he succeeded in methodically organizing the military resources of the former colonies for the purposes of British war policy, without having to apply force of any kind, basing himself solely on the principle of voluntary service. His typically Anglo-Saxon-Liberal faith in the wisdom and patriotism of his fellow citizens proved to be well founded. At the imperial conferences of 1907, 1909, and 1911 he convinced the dominion representatives that successful cooperation of their armed forces in the defense of the empire was possible only if they took advantage of the new technical achievements of the British army. The appropriate way to achieve this end was to allow the General Staff at home to train all the dominion cadres, to collect and transmit all experiences and intelligence from and to all parts of the empire, to work out common plans of operation, and to advise the overseas governments in the training and organization of their troops.

This road was indeed followed, and not without success. The British staff chief received the title and rank of Chief of the Imperial General Staff. The dominions established new troops or greatly increased their strength. The training, organization, arms, and equipment were everywhere assimilated to the British model. The dominions thus achieved the ability to defend themselves, and England could withdraw or greatly reduce its overseas garrisons from Canada and South Africa, while concentrating its military power more strongly at home than before.[11]

The basis was also laid for the successful use of colonial forces within the British army, even on the battlefields of Europe, an expansion that proved of particular importance to England in the First World War. From the very beginning the specter of German world dominion haunted these military consultations, giving them their strongest political impulse. In the critical year of 1911, Grey himself set forth the main outlines of his foreign policy to the dominion representatives. Its purpose was to protect the weaker continental powers against the preponderance of a single major power, that is to say the Germans. Subsequently dominion representatives regularly took part in the deliberations of the Committee of Imperial Defence under Asquith, with the result that their political identity, as distinct from the mother country, was newly strengthened. Thus rearmament was closely integrated with the foreign policy of the British Empire. It was indeed meaningful only in the context of the new anti-German course pursued in Europe, and it intensified that course in turn. The precise details will concern us later.

Before we move to such a consideration, let us briefly examine how the new British army system acquitted itself in wartime, and especially how political and military authority were interrelated during the war years. What did the British parliamentary system accomplish by way of solving the problems of integrated war leadership?

The British government had an easier time of it than the French in one point, the attitude of Parliament. Even in England, however, parliamentary interference with the conduct of the war was not totally absent. Indeed, a measure of political meddling even emanated from the military side. Yet, on the whole, the British war cabinets were in a much stronger position vis-à-vis Parliament and the army. The House of Commons was less inclined to intervene directly in military matters, was more uniformly patriotic in orientation, and was far less volatile. This was in part owing to the fact that despite the German submarines, the threat of war was not felt as strongly and immediately in the island kingdom as it was in Paris, and because the members were less given to shuttling back and forth between the House and the front.

As the war became more and more totalitarian, moreover, pre-empting all the resources of the nation to an unprecedented degree, the advantages of the parliamentary system asserted themselves. The government was in close touch with public opinion, which was skillfully manipulated with the aid of a huge propaganda machine that spanned the globe, with the help of the empire. The role of the prime minister had long since come much closer than in France to that of a true popular leader. The kind of demagogue with almost dictatorial authority, whom France found in Clémenceau only in November, 1917, had appeared on the British political stage as early as 1916.

The supremacy of political over military authority was never seriously challenged in England, if only because no English general or admiral had the opportunity to rise to great public stature by the kind of military triumphs Wellington won. For several years the First World War was limited in the main to the precarious maintenance of a front in Flanders, in support of the French and Belgians, without any freedom of strategic initiative. Such scope existed only in the subsidiary colonial theaters of war and in the Arab-Turkish area. The most immediate and urgent task was to hold the Franco-Belgian front until England had established a modern mass army equipped with appropriate weapons. This called for stubborn and sustained energy rather than strategic genius, and Kitchener, Robertson, French, and Haig were not lacking in energy.

Still, it took a long time, until May, 1916, before Parliament came around to introducing conscription, and months more before the British army was in a position to launch its own major offensive against the Germans on the Somme.

It was conducted with great dash, with new artillery tactics and even new weapons—the first tanks—and it inflicted great damage on the Germans, though in the end it gained less than a complete success. Up until 1918 the weakness of the English generals was that they were not able to report any brilliant victories. This made it all the easier for their civilian critics to charge them with incompetence, especially in view of the German successes. Lloyd George in particular always held a contemptuous opinion of his own commanders and bluntly let them know his feelings on more than one occasion. As early as 1917 he was prepared to place them under French supreme command.

The problem of the proper relation of politics and war thus appeared in England in a new form, almost the precise reverse of the situation in Germany, where, as will yet be shown, the preponderance of public authority shifted lopsidedly to the military. In England the soldiers had an extremely hard time getting any hearing for their military advice and demands. It is truly astonishing how little impact Haldane's reforms had made on a parliamentary system which Salisbury, as long ago as 1900, had described as utterly unsuited to the purposes of war. Asquith did not dream of exploiting the opportunity offered him through the Committee of Imperial Defence to take personal charge of the war by outmaneuvering the cabinet.

Yet there was scarcely a body less suited to run a world war than the thirty-man British cabinet, consisting of civilian ministers, most of whom had no official responsibility for the day-to-day business of the war at all. Matters were made worse by their large administrative staffs, which made the maintenance of security all but impossible. In the early months of the war Asquith, nevertheless, allowed nearly all military decisions, right down to technical details, to be deliberated by this cumbersome body, giving his colleagues the opportunity to meddle in every aspect of the war. Winston Churchill and Loyd George, in particular, the most mettlesome personalities, formulated and in part pushed through their own strategic concepts over the warnings of the military experts. Not a single step could be taken on this slippery pavement without endless discussion and intrigues of many kinds. As a result the war machine was slow to spring into life, and creaked and faltered heavily. Blunders were made, there was much vacillation, and decisions were often unconscionably delayed.

By way of extenuation it should be remarked that none could have foreseen the immense sacrifice and effort this war would entail, a war during which, Grey had once believed, "business as usual" could prevail. Nor was it foreseen that the task of inuring the British people to the new situation, of winning their whole-hearted cooperation in so dangerous an undertaking, would require the participation of all available parliamentary resources. It has become clear from the testimony of those involved that most of these British civilian ministers had not a glimmer of the technical requirements of large-scale modern warfare. Their debates displayed little respect for the judgment of military experts, and here again they ran true to the traditions of the old ruling nobility. Asquith had summoned as war minister Lord Kitchener, a veteran colonial soldier, wearing laurels from the Egyptian campaign. Yet the chief of staff had not even been consulted when war plans were first debated on August 5, 1914. Instead, eight high officers in various posts were summoned, even though they had no access to the intelligence material of the General Staff. For some time to come, until late in 1915, the chief of staff scarcely entered the picture.

According to the elder Moltke and all the lessons of history, there is no more pernicious method of running a war than by a deliberative body, in which opinions tend to be at variance and the ultimate responsibility for decisions becomes obscured. Yet this was precisely the system under which Britain was now waging war, through continuous meetings in London of a war council composed of politicians rather than soldiers. Asquith, the chairman, evidently felt far too uncertain and out of his element in military questions—unlike the self-assured Churchill and Loyd George—to arrive independently at clear-cut decisions. Then too, in order to avoid becoming dependent on a single expert adviser, he preferred to listen to several. This may have been sound political policy, but it did not serve military ends well.

Kitchener was not the kind of man to put an end to this system. As a professional soldier, he was accustomed to submit to political direction. He had no European military experience and lacked assurance in strategic questions. Thus he was ill equipped to serve as a counterpoise to the claims of civilian strategists and politicians. Above all, he was much too preoccupied with building up the great new army to emancipate himself from the politicians, whom he needed for that purpose, and devote himself single-mindedly to strategic tasks. If we can give credence to Robertson, Kitchener's ultimate goals departed widely from the traditional line of British policy—at the end of the war Britain was to have the strongest army in Europe and with its help dictate the peace.[12]

Within a matter of months war leadership by the cabinet as a whole proved so intolerable that Asquith, late in 1914, established a cabinet committee of six ministers, later expanded to twelve members, to take charge of the war. This war council did not greatly improve matters, for intervention on the part of the most diverse political authorities did not cease even now; and the military experts were the very people who did not prevail with this council, which initiated the controversial and ill-starred Dardanelles expedition. In the autumn of 1915 the war council was reorganized as the cabinet war committee, and its membership was cut in half; but all the major decisions still had to be submitted to the whole cabinet, and the General Staff remained out of the picture. The turn came only in December, 1915, when General Robertson, who had been appointed chief of staff, succeeded in being invited to all the meetings of the cabinet and its war committee, and in securing authority to issue all operational orders as the cabinet's sole official adviser in questions of land warfare. Until then the chief of staff had functioned only as one of eight divisional heads in the war office. Now he moved up to become the official operational commander, a position not unlike that of the chief of the General Staff within the German supreme army command.

There was, however, one important difference. Robertson remained formally under the war minister, who alone was responsible to Parliament for the conduct of the army in wartime. Robertson's initial desire to see the war minister limited to purely administrative matters remained unfulfilled, if only because of the objections of Kitchener, who invoked the British constitutional tradition, for very good reasons. The danger was thus avoided that the powers of the chief of staff could assume a political coloration and compete with the political leadership, as had been the case in Germany. Actually, Robertson did not want this. His memoranda on these questions, classical examples of the wartime thinking of the British generals, show no traces of military truculence.[13] They acknowledge the supremacy of the civilian war council in the conduct of the war, not only as a fact but as objectively necessary; and they merely press for swift and clear-cut decisions from the war council through a strengthening of its powers. (Robertson would have preferred to see all such powers in the hand of one man, the prime minister.)

The more powerful position of the chief of staff was to serve the same end. The civilian war leadership was to avoid consulting all and sundry military authorities and listen to only one responsible adviser, the chief of staff, whom it could readily replace if he did not live up to expectations. The military, on their part, must appreciate that the day was gone forever when the civilian power could simply leave all directive tasks to them on the outbreak of war and disappear from the stage until the time came for peace negotiations. For modern war with its multifarious ramifications involves the nation's whole life, and the many questions that arise can be mastered only by experts in the various political departments. There is no longer any hard and fast division between the military and the political and economic sphere.[14] Whoever holds the military threads in his hands must—without becoming a "political general"—develop an understanding of political problems and the political viewpoints of civilian ministers. The latter, on their part, stand in constant danger of being influenced by the powerful currents of public opinion in the direction of plans and by demands that run directly counter to military needs and requirements. They must be ready to be convinced by objective counterarguments put forward by responsible operational leaders and guard against making inappropriate and even impossible demands.

All this sounds far more intelligent than the militarism of a Ludendorff, far more modern than the views of even the elder Moltke. Robertson was indeed worried by the great difficulties that were bound to arise from this modern method of running a war through the cooperation of political and military authority. He thought it unavoidable that modern war could no longer be directed from field headquarters, but only—as was true in England under his own leadership—from the capital city. The chief of staff had to maintain continuous discussion with the ministers of the war council and cabinet, setting forth, defending, and pushing through his plans; reporting on the progress of the war; and standing up to all criticism. Robertson tells us just how he did this for years on end in almost daily, unending sessions—a method probably feasible only during a war of position. From his description it becomes disconcertingly clear that the establishment and maintenance of harmony between politics and strategy in England was not only a difficult task but an extremely time-consuming one.

This was all the more true since the British ministers were apparently less tractable than the soldiers. They did not dream of respecting the lines of military jurisdiction. Time and again the chief of staff was tempted to allow himself to be pushed into blind alleys or dubious compromises in order not to fall out with the political powers. In the end, after all, political dickering must always result in compromise; but on the field of battle compromise is often fatal. Robertson needed all his strength of character and strategic clarity to avoid the easy road of compromise.

He did not always succeed. There were fateful blunders. The great Dardanelles project of 1915, for example, was launched as a typical compromise between political desires and military needs. It was indeed a central issue. Should the British army rest content with defending the soil of France shoulder to shoulder with the French and Belgians, or should it try to bring about a swifter decision on another front, say by striking a blow in the enemy's back? Most of the generals, especially those fighting in Flanders, thought that diversions in the east, in the Baltic or the Balkans, would be a useless frittering away of resources, and from their own viewpoint they were undoubtedly right. But there was also the danger of a deadlock on the Franco-Belgian front, with the endless slaughter of ever more hundreds of thousands leading to no tangible result, the danger that without technical arms superiority the offensive would be stalled forever. Politicians like Churchill and Lloyd George, who felt that any eastern offensive—in the Baltic, Turkey, Arabia, or the Balkans—was essential, saw this danger very clearly. Churchill has discussed this particularly impressively in his magnificent introduction to the second volume of his war history.

When Lloyd George called the generals who opposed him stupid, he was undoubtedly doing them an injustice. Yet the conclusion is unavoidable that intensive participation in a continental struggle such as was taking place on the western front flew in the face of all the political and military traditions of England. Even in the struggle against Napoleon, England had essentially limited itself to operations based on naval strategy, supported by military diversions on subsidiary continental fronts. The new war policy, introduced in 1905, could be implemented only at enormous cost, bleeding the nation white, destroying its wealth, severely endangering its political and economic influence throughout the world, and finally transforming its social structure almost completely.

What Churchill wanted in 1915 was a major offensive in the Mediterranean area that would take Turkey out of its alliance with Germany, win over Italy and the Balkans to the cause of the Entente, and open up the Russian Black Sea ports to arms and munitions shipments; but this could be achieved only if England shifted its main energy away from the western front to the southeast, which would have meant extrication from the long-standing close tie with French policy. The difficulties of such a solution in mid-war are as plain as the advantages of freedom of political action it would have brought in the peace negotiations to come.[15] Because it failed—indeed, for political as well as military reasons, it was not even seriously attempted—the Dardanelles campaign remained a half-measure without hope of military success; and in a political sense it represented a serious blow to its originator. At the request of the Conservative opposition Churchill had to resign, and the cabinet had to reorganize itself into a coalition government. Public opinion grew suspicious of the British leaders and called more and more vociferously for a "strong man." Late in 1916, after the failure of the breakthrough attempts on the Somme, such a strong man came to the helm—Lloyd George.

As minister of war and munitions in the Asquith cabinet, Lloyd George had played an important part in intensifying the British war effort, which now, under his leadership, reached its climax. So great had it grown that in the spring and summer of 1918 the British army not only drew abreast of the French, but appeared in a superior light, especially in respect of its equipment and dashing leadership. Yet in fact no greater measure of unity was achieved under Lloyd George in the way the British ran their war. On the contrary, conflict at the topmost level was increased.

The Welshman was a resourceful but capricious man. His astonishing versatility kept him from thinking through strategic problems thoroughly, and his limitless self-confidence made him look down contemptuously on professional soldiers, whose advice and proposals he was fond of ignoring. He liked to bring home to the generals their subsidiary role, was given to improvisation and surprise effects, took sudden turns without consultation, set little store by confidential relationships, and even had a streak of malice. His own strategic plans for diversions in the east were amateurish and even unrealistic, and in the end none of them was put into effect, partly because he himself felt the risks to be too high, partly because the generals managed to mobilize public opinion against them, and partly because events in France outstripped them. In February, 1918, Lloyd George maneuvered the competent Robertson, a man of character and clear insight, out of the post of chief of staff and replaced him with his own favorite, the pliable Wilson, the epitome of the political general.

The inevitable tensions between civilian and military war leadership were thus needlessly enhanced rather than reduced. In other respects, however, Lloyd George did much to increase the British war effort. He was more adept than his predecessor in getting his way in the political arena, and he knew how to raise popular war passions to the boiling point. He embodied the new type of the modern popular leader, whose character we have already examined in Clémenceau. It is a type that has become characteristic of the twentieth century—the trusted leader of a direct mass democracy who pushes aside (and later, under the Fascist system, destroys outright) the liberal parliamentary system of elected pluralistic popular representation. In the wartime western democracies this was the type who became the true representative and executor of the popular will, of the *volonté générale*, visibly embodied to all eyes in his person. Supported by the roars of the crowd and a huge propaganda machine, he is able to formulate his policies without timid obeisance to the official representative organs and sometimes is able to compel them to follow his lead.

Lloyd George appointed a spokesman minister to represent him in the House of Commons and created his own closely knit war cabinet of five to seven civilian ministers who were freed of all other government business in order to help him run the war. To this small, secretive, and truly efficient circle the generals and admirals had to submit all their plans for approval. They were its servants, as advisers and executors. The prime minister surrounded himself with a huge staff of private secretaries and personal auxiliaries which enabled him to exercise centralized war leadership and, perhaps even more importantly, to control the war economy and public opinion. Only a thoroughly seasoned parliamentarian, steeped in the techniques of party life, could have governed in this way—though it was certainly not a form of government that can be called parliamentary in the traditional sense. It approaches the forms of dictatorship.

It went no further than to approach them, however. It could not attain the dimensions of real one-man rule. The parliamentary traditions of England were too strong to permit such a development. Public opinion could be mobilized even against Lloyd George; we have already seen that this was successfully done at certain critical moments. The top British generals, moreover, were anything but servile. Thus, while Lloyd George was able to delay necessary actions, he could not, by and large, alter the main course of the war. In the end the big German offensive in the spring and summer of 1918 constrained the Allies to common operations, in which the pet strategic plans of the British prime minister lost their importance. The weight of decision now fell naturally into the laps of the army leaders.

All in all one must marvel at how well the British system of government, so ill suited to the centralized running of a great war, stood the test of the First World War, while the German military monarchy failed, for reasons yet to be discussed. A factor not to be overlooked is that England's island position and the sustained immobility of trench warfare facilitated the build-up of a new army while it slowed down the pace of war to such a degree that the dangers of unending debate and the difficulty in arriving at consistent decisions were reduced. There were distinct advantages to the British system, moreover, which greatly contributed to the ultimate success. The traditions of the British cabinet were loose and adaptable. To a talented and determined politician they offered scope for expanding even further the already strong position of the prime minister.

On the other hand, the continuing, close, and direct contact between the parliamentary government and the masses was an important asset in a struggle in which the whole life of the people was involved. Here the British system bears favorable comparison with the German bureaucracy, which was estranged from the people. Again, the British masses had already been progressively politicalized in the twentieth century, and no such deep gulf existed as in Germany to separate the proletariat from the crown, the government, the nobility, and the upper middle class. The bourgeois parties in England held no monopoly on patriotism, and the loyalty of the socialist-led working-class masses was not in question. The Liberal prime minister Lloyd George was able to become a working-class hero as well, and he was able to unify the nation in wartime in higher measure than was true in Germany, as will yet be shown. Lastly, in no other country did the war become so much a popular cause as in the unwarlike island kingdom.

But the flaws in this development must not be overlooked. Lloyd George whipped up a new social and political awareness among the British working class to win them not only to the war but to his party. Yet once the war was over he had to watch as the workers, just like the capitalists, left his party in droves. The newly risen radical lower-middle-class and proletarian democracy he had sponsored had swallowed up so many old British traditions that little scope was left for even a liberal bourgeois party. More than that, when it came to establishing enduring peace in Europe after the war, he himself was no longer able to banish the demons of hate and nationalist passion he had conjured up.

The question arises whether Britain, under Lloyd George, exercised political wisdom in carrying the war to the point of totally destroying the German enemy, rejecting all thought of a negotiated peace. Did militarist thinking play a part in setting this course—a militant zeal that would not rest short of savoring victory to the dregs? In view of the fact that the German militarists were also sabotaging a negotiated peace, would there not have been a chance of foiling or impeding them by pursuing a more conciliatory policy? These questions cannot be answered here. We do know that British policy was in part determined by consideration for France, whose soil was to be rid of the German invader and augmented by the annexation of Alsace-Lorraine. But this does not necessarily mean that political wisdom and self-interest required Great Britain to insure a complete French triumph over Germany.

And here we come back once again to the beginnings of the Anglo-French Entente policy. It is worth inquiring more closely whether and in what degree British policy slipped into its dependence on French policy on account of purely military considerations rather than by reasons of pure political wisdom. We may note that the problem of militarism is a European problem.

3

The Anglo-French Staff Talks and the Entente Policy, 1905-1914

THE ORIGINS of the Anglo-French Entente and its hardening into a war alliance in the summer of 1914 constitute a complex process in which, on the British side, political and purely military and technical considerations were intimately interlinked. Our present interest lies in tracing the military share in the London policy decisions.

The first element which draws attention is that a conviction of the inevitability of a great war with Germany crystallized among the leading British military authorities long before the policy of isolationism was officially ended and the naval arms race proper began. James M. Grierson, later to become a general, went to Berlin in 1896 as military attaché, strongly prejudiced in favor of Germany and its army, as his biographer testifies, only to be deeply disillusioned by the Kruger telegram, the highly personal diplomacy of William II, and many other happenings. By late 1897 he was writing a friend: "We must proceed against the Germans, very soon, or they will proceed against us. A pretext for war should not be hard to find, and I do not belive that even Russia would hold back." Later on this same Grierson, by then head of the operations division of the British General Staff, formulated the doctrine based on the lessons of the Russo-Japanese War, that even an island power could no longer do without a large land army, a doctrine that won the approval of other generals.[1] Late in 1905 he initiated the first military discussions with the French General Staff.

William Robertson, then head of the war office's foreign intelligence section, but soon to become field marshal, was asked for his opinion in 1902 as to whether an alliance with Germany was desirable from a military viewpoint. His answer was a memorandum in which he used essentially political arguments to characterize a German alliance as impracticable and described Germany as England's most dangerous rival.[2] Waters, Grierson's successor in Berlin, has testified that around 1902, i.e., toward the end of the Boer War, the opinion prevailed in the war office that an Anglo-German war was bound to come, "perhaps better sooner than later." The main burden would necessarily devolve upon the British navy, but the British army must cooperate in colonial warfare.[3]

This unequivocal anti-German stand was naturally and swiftly hardened after the great turn in 1904, the Anglo-French colonial pact that marks the beginning of the Entente policy. Even before the Morocco crisis broke out in 1905 the British General Staff had thoroughly discussed the problem of a Franco-German war. A staff conference in Camberley in January, 1905, worked out a war exercise, actually conducted during March and April, in which a German invasion of Belgium was taken for granted, solely on the basis of the total strategic situation and without any supporting intelligence from Germany.[4] Robertson was in command of the "German" side in these maneuvers and advanced strong forces north of the Meuse and Sambre to envelop the French army. It was concluded that France alone would be unable to halt such an advance, and this purely technical conclusion apparently determined the further stand of the British General Staff, which at once envisaged the dispatch of a British expeditionary corps to Belgium and did not rest until such an operation had been prepared for in full technical detail.

It is a remarkable fact that the British General Staff evidently perceived much earlier and much more clearly than the French that the Germans, in the event of a western offensive, would be compelled to outflank the French defenses on the border of Lorraine by a sweeping advance through Belgium.[5] The British generals looked at this possibility quite dispassionately, purely from the military point of view. This violation of Belgian neutrality seemed to them inescapable. Of course, moral arguments also came into play occasionally, to the effect that the Germans would not hesitate to break international law. French professional soldiers looked on the question of Belgian neutrality in the same hard-headed "militaristic" way. We know that under Napoleon III the idea of clearing away the Belgian barrier had played an important role. For a long time after his fall a French offensive was quite out of the question; but as early as the 1890's, when the military alliance with Russia was established, French military writers had begun to deprecate Belgian neutrality, insisting that it must not be allowed to form a serious obstacle to the great Franco-German duel.[6] Shortly before the First World War, with the intensification of French rearmament and the growing intimacy of the Entente with England, notions of a swift push through Belgium to the German border turn up in the deployment plans of the French General Staff. As we shall see, they came to nothing because of British political objections and the negative attitude of Belgium.

The basically liberal orientation of Britain kept government policies from being dominated by military thinking. In 1914 Lord Grey was able to draw cabinet and nation into the war only by proclaiming it a kind of crusade to save

Belgium from German invasion. Actually, in a military sense, it was the security of France rather than Belgium that was the object of Anglo-French operations; and the political Entente between the two western powers was established in 1904-1905 from concern for the fate of France, not Belgium. Belgian neutrality had long since lost its original purpose of protecting Europe against the unquenchable power hunger of revolutionary France. On the contrary, since the Morocco crisis of 1905 it had been considered a French shield against German preponderance. The joint guarantee of the great powers had become a mere legal fiction since the guarantor powers had begun quarreling among themselves. Yet it was still in England's interest to combine its partisanship on behalf of France with its traditional role as the guardian of international law in Europe. Hence the British government never assented to a Belgian surrender to French offensive plans prior to a German invasion. On the other hand, Britain had an immediate and urgent interest in keeping the Belgian coast out of German or, for that matter, French hands. This could be prevented only by the intervention of British land forces in any Franco-German duel.

The question is whether the grave decision taken in 1905-1906 to protect France not merely with naval power but also with a large expeditionary force in the main theater of war was dictated by such political considerations or by the military thinking of the General Staff, already known to us. From the source material that has become available so far, the question cannot be answered unequivocally. Presumably both factors played a part. It is certain that even the admiralty was convinced that British naval operations alone would not be able to give the French enough help. Lansdowne's original promise of aid to Delcassé, formulated in writing on May 17, 1905 during the first Morocco crisis, and the opening gun in what was to become a war alliance, contained no concrete military commitments. The document speaks only of cooperation between the two governments on a basis of mutual trust, primarily in the event of an "unprovoked attack" by a third power, and beyond that in any other menacing involvements during the time to come.

One senses quite plainly the eagerness of the British ministers to win the confidence of the French government. They were worried that French isolation—the Russian ally was then utterly paralyzed by revolution and serious defeat in the Far East—might drive the country into a political understanding with Germany; and they wished to preserve existing French policy by means of generous offers of aid. The colonial pact of 1904 was to be developed into a general political entente, enduring beyond the moment. Ambassador Cambon quite correctly interpreted all this to bespeak a willingness for discussions that might lead to military commitments. Delcassé went even further—he read into it a promise to land 100,000 men on the coast of Schleswig-Holstein in the event of war, as he later told the press. Surely this was not pure imagination!

In some way—King Edward VII has been suspected as the source—Delcassé must have learned that the British admiralty was indeed just then considering contingency plans for landing British troops in Schleswig-Holstein, possibly with Danish assistance, in order to create a diversion for the Germans in the event they invaded France. Possibly the Kiel Canal and naval base might also be occupied and destroyed.[7] But how could such fanciful assurances offer any serious aid, and what practical measures at all could be expected of the British army at the time before its reorganization, if war were to break out in a matter of weeks? Premier Rouvier thought little of it and dropped Delcassé, in hopes that the fall of this minister might lead to a tolerable settlement with the Germans over the Morocco question. Had Bülow now entered into a bilateral colonial pact with France, it is unlikely that the Anglo-French Entente offered by Lansdowne would have hardened into concrete military agreement. As Eyre Crowe later remarked, it might have failed altogether. Even Cambon, the French Ambassador in London, seems to have entertained doubts about such a turn.[8]

But Holstein's and Bülow's hapless diplomacy missed this favorable moment and pushed on. This compelled the calling of a European conference, in the expectation that the worthlessness of British support for France would there stand exposed and the western Entente would be strangled in the cradle. Germany persisted in its menacing stance. This would have been quite incomprehensible if it were not that Berlin was quite familiar with the actual military weakness of Britain. What was insufficiently or not at all taken into account on the German side was British readiness to reorganize the entire army system in order to create an expeditionary force suitable to be dispatched to the mainland—and this under a Liberal government, which Germany, like the rest of the world, expected would de-emphasize military preparedness! [9]

Bitterly disappointed in his hopes for an understanding with Berlin, Rouvier, only a few weeks after Delcassé's fall, wooed the Entente with Britain he had but recently disdained. We hear of deliberations in the British Committee of Imperial Defense in August and September, dealing with the question of whether the Germans would actually invade Belgium in the event of war and what could be done about it. The General Staff regarded such an invasion as a certainty, though not necessarily at the very outset of war, but some ministers were reluctant to accept this view, and no decision was taken concerning the landing of British troops in Belgium.[10] The opposing side put forward a number of substantial arguments and received support from the navy, a stronghold of the British tradition which advocated keeping out of continental quarrels and avoiding large-scale operations on land in favor of blockade and naval warfare, and possibly amphibious operations, in which the enemy would be attacked and weakened on secondary fronts.

To the admirals, especially Sir John Fisher, the army seemed more an auxiliary to the navy than the other way around. Fisher vigorously upheld this position time and again right down to the First World War, and he equally condemned Haldane's reform plans and participation in large-scale mainland warfare. He was fond of playing the role of the rough-hewn and rough-spoken tar. He and Lord of the Admiralty Lee remarked cynically that the German navy should be "suppressed" or "Copenhagened" before it could grow any larger. German naval propaganda gave wide currency to these sentiments, which had a devastating political effect in Germany. They expressed the instinctive militarism of the one service in which the British knew themselves to be superior. We may be certain that Admiral Fisher would gladly have seized any opportunity to use this superiority to destroy the German fleet "better sooner than later"; but in England such militarists were taken seriously only in their expert technical capacity, and they never succeeded with their concept of naval action only—even though the so-called naval school included important figures like Lord Esher, chairman of the military reform commission, and Sir George Clarke, permanent secretary to the Committee of Imperial Defense. In the end the army General Staff officers retained the upper hand, simply because they were able to show that their war plan was more effective and alone met France's concrete military needs.

These needs clamored for attention late in 1905 in two ways—in the form of certain inquiries made by the French military attaché Huguet, and again in representations made by the ambassador, Paul Cambon. What was behind this was the French government's fear that in the event of the failure of the Algeciras Conference France would be open to German attack, which it would have to meet in virtual isolation. In mid-December Huguet carefully sounded out the head of the operations section of the British General Staff on the strength and mobilization time of the British army. To his surprise, Grierson told him that the British General Staff had long since been preoccupied with strategic exercises looking to operations on the mainland. This most welcome news was soon confirmed by further encouraging information from the war and foreign offices, which Huguet was able to obtain through an official middleman, Colonel Repington.

This at once set the machinery of diplomacy in motion. Cambon secured permission from Rouvier to make an official inquiry of Lord Grey, foreign minister in the new Liberal cabinet, as to the degree to which British support might become available in the event of war. It turned out that Grey wished to continue the Francophile policies of his predecessor Lansdowne, indeed to intensify them in some respects. The Frenchman did not succeed, however, in securing a firm commitment for an alliance in wartime. In the face of the antiwar sentiments entertained by most of his colleagues—and indeed most of his fellow countrymen—Grey would have been quite unable to promise such an undertaking. He did make it clear, however, that England would not abandon its Entente partner in the event of an attack in violation of the Anglo-French Morocco pact. Such an act would at once inflame public opinion in Britain.

There was no mention of any violation of Belgian neutrality in these talks. It was France that was at risk, not Belgium. Yet Grey unquestionably knew of the danger threatening Belgium, and perhaps that is why he felt certain of being able to find the tinder to arouse the people in case of need. Lansdowne had always spoken officially of only diplomatic support, merely hinting at his readiness to enter into military commitments on the day of need; but the new minister, after consulting Haldane, expressly agreed to immediate technical talks, in order to make swift military aid possible in an emergency. (He was aware that the naval staffs had already established contact, without the intervention of the diplomatic authorities.)[11]

The way was now open for gradually turning the colonial Entente of 1904 into a military alliance directed against Germany. We know, of course, that this was never expressed in formal terms, that there was no written treaty tying British policy to French—Grey scrupulously avoided such a thing until August, 1914. Yet even British historians today unreservedly acknowledge that the technical understandings between the military and naval staffs in time gave rise to moral obligations that took on binding character in a political sense. Is this an instance in which purely technical military considerations influenced diplomacy, a kind of adulteration of political wisdom by militaristic factors?

Such a conclusion would assume that a proper British *raison d'état* would necessarily and in all circumstances require that the country keep out of the great power quarrels of the continental powers, adopting a continuing policy of voluntary isolation, as in the days of Gladstone and Salisbury, or a policy of the "free hand" à la Bismarck, i.e., of changing alliances, weighted now in this direction, now in that. Since the Boer War and the great increase in German naval strength, however, statesmen in both the major British parties had become convinced that this method could not continue, because England ran the risk of sitting down between all the chairs.

With astonishing unanimity, men like Haldane, Grey, and Nicolson have set down in their memoirs and other writings what the country's leading politicians envisaged as a rational British policy. The motivating force has been identified particularly impressively by the younger Nicolson in his biography of his father—impressively because it is stated with complete detachment and freedom from anti-German sentiments. It was fear of German preponderance. This preponderance was brought home to the British with full clarity for the first time during the Morocco crisis of 1905. As we have already seen, the British General Staff had concluded unequivocally that despite its border fortifications France would be lost without foreign aid against a German attack advancing through Belgium. Since this was well known in Paris, the French would have no choice but to submit to the German will if France remained isolated.

Many memoirs testify that Delcassé's fall, resulting from these considerations, caused great alarm in England as possibly heralding a German hegemony on the continent. The year 1905, moreover, saw the signing of the Björkö

Convention by the German Emperor and the Russian Czar. From the London viewpoint, there were clear indications on the horizon that the imperial government was trying to organize a combination of the three great continental powers, directed against Britain. Should Germany succeed in winning over even one, there would be no further guarantee of British naval superiority, in view of the rapidly growing German fleet. Yet international faith in British world power was based on the prestige of dominion of the seas—not until after 1919 was a substitute for this prestige sought in Britain's role as the main guarantor of world peace within the League of Nations; and whenever British world prestige was endangered—by the naval race prior to 1914, by the weakening of the League of Nations after 1935—a raw nerve was touched in the British Empire. Hence the fear of German naval construction and the eagerness since 1904 for colonial agreements, the most important of which was now threatened by German policy in Morocco. This seemed to challenge Britain's whole world position. The deeper meaning of the British Entente policy of 1905-1906 was precisely to prevent this shift in power by binding France to the British side at all costs.

This policy, however, was also part and parcel of England's peculiar brand of power politics. Absolute rule of the sea by Great Britain had already become more fiction than fact. Even with the greatest fleet in the world, the island power would no longer have been capable of defending its worldwide overseas possessions by force of arms in the event of military conflict with other major colonial powers. London knew very well that no naval threat could prevent Russian infiltration in Persia, for example; and the Boer War had painfully exposed the military weaknesses of pure sea power.

A possible charge against the British policy of 1905-1906 is that it tended to overestimate the threat posed by the German rival, that it wrongly interpreted a German desire for security as a striving for hegemony. Grey was out of his element in military matters, and it can be shown that he failed to realize that the staff talks he sponsored would lead to inevitable political consequences. More than that, Grey and his friends, and Haldane, the war minister, had no idea of the scope and difficulty of the venture in which they were becoming embroiled through these talks by envisaging British participation in major military operations on the mainland—against the opposition of the admiralty, by the way.[12] A final criticism is that most of the members of the Liberal cabinet—whose opposition was anticipated—were left in the dark until 1911 about the grave decision taken in 1906.

Yet there is no conclusive evidence that the decision was dictated by considerations other than British *raison d'état*, i.e., to assert British political power as such; and it must be acknowledged that in January, 1906, Grey faced a clear-cut decision. Either he had to encourage French policy by concrete assurances, or the whole Entente, on which so much depended for the British world position, went out the window. The only real militarists in Britain were the admirals like Fisher, who toyed with the idea of a pre-emptive strike and of totally destroying the German navy. What the war office General Staff succeeded in accomplishing in 1906, the technical preparation for a campaign that would afford France better protection in the event of war, was entirely within the framework of legitimate British political interests, certainly at a time when the British generals were convinced that without such help their Entente partner would be virtually lost.

The results of the military talks of 1906, conducted on the British side under Grierson's leadership, were in close accord with the diplomatic situation. The stronger role during the discussions fell to the British. The French were happy to be able to count on British aid at all and submitted in all essential points to the demands of their Entente partner. Initially they asked that the British expeditionary force be placed under French supreme command, closely integrated with the French army, but this demand they had to drop almost at once. The details of these military talks have been repeatedly discussed by scholars and need not detain us here. The most important element is that Grierson from the outset envisaged the defense of France on Belgian rather than French soil, thus insuring that the British army would be largely independent of French leadership. All France was to do was to provide port and rail facilities and depots for a British expeditionary force, which would reinforce the Belgian army as soon as the Germans invaded Belgium. The goal would be to block a German advance to Antwerp and across the Ardennes. Even if the latter occurred, the road to Antwerp was to be kept open for the British, who reserved the right to move their base of operations entirely to that city once control of the Channel had been secured. In the event of a German Ardennes offensive, the British deployment plan apparently envisaged extending or reinforcing the French left flank.

Such a plan, of course, required close cooperation with the Belgian as well as the French General Staff, and at the very beginning of the talks Grierson secured political authority to approach the Belgian chief of staff, Ducarne, through the British military attaché in Brussels, Barnardiston. Ducarne was as surprised by the British initiative as had been the French, but once he had secured the permission of his war minister, he did not hesitate to reveal to the British all the details they desired about the strength of the Belgian army and its operational plans in the event of war. The result of the ensuing talks, which lasted for several months, was a deployment plan for the British expeditionary force which went into the most minute technical details such as timetables, railway carriages, uniforms, questions of supply and requisitioning, interpreters, etc.[13]

By any narrow interpretation of Belgium's duty to maintain strict neutrality this was undoubtedly an infraction of international law, and Ducarne himself had upheld this strict interpretation in a report only six years earlier. A neutral power, he said, must not grant the smallest advantage to either of the potential belligerents; and unquestionably this one-sided communication to Britain of Belgian war plans represented a very considerable advantage. Brussels was probably well aware of this, as shown by its great precautions to limit knowledge of what was going on to the smallest number of persons. But did this indeed mean, as German war propaganda tried to contend over and over after 1915, that Belgium had formally moved into the western camp? Was this "even without formal ratification a binding military convention, applicable even in the absence of a German attack, if France requested Anglo-Belgian support"? [14]

This would seem plausible only if Belgium, following the military talks of 1906, had felt unequivocally bound to the side of the western powers, through a moral obligation similar to that which grew up between France and England. Quite manifestly this did not happen. On the contrary, the Belgian General Staff was from the outset highly suspicious of the practical effectiveness of British aid; and after the peaceful ending of the Algeciras Conference it practiced extreme reserve. Later on it resisted all further Anglo-French exploratory approaches. Brussels seemed to sense that growing French military strength and the gradual recovery of the Russian ally inspired the French General Staff with increasing confidence, reawakening an inclination to take the offensive. This aroused the suspicion that in an emergency Belgium might have to count on the possibility of a French invasion as well. Ducarne himself retired from active service in 1910, but in the final years before the First World War he headed a vigorous and successful movement favoring increased Belgian military power. The country's borders were to be protected as much as possible by its own resources, to avoid dependence on the policies of foreign powers. To this end the General Staff prepared plans for the defense of the country against either side.

In sum, the 1906 talks did not mark a basic change in Belgian policy comparable to the British shift of 1905-1906. From the Belgian point of view, all that happened was that the military experts sought to formulate concrete deployment plans against a contingency considered to be highly probable, taking advantage of an unexpected offer of outside military aid. Even so, the participants seem to have realized at the outset that the very attempt ran counter to the concept of neutrality, narrowly interpreted under international law. In self-justification they could argue that international guarantees of Belgian neutrality had long since become a legal fiction, and that as soldiers they were obligated to match their actions to military realities. Yet Belgian policy never succumbed to the temptation of drawing political consequences from purely military assurances and of surrendering neutrality in principle, if only for the reason that right down to the First World War the military and political advantages of a link with the western allies were in serious doubt. [15]

Inside the British General Staff the question of neutrality under international law was regarded with considerable detachment. The Schelde Estuary, after all, was under Dutch sovereignty, and Grierson's plan of shifting the British operational basis in time to Antwerp could not have been carried into effect without violating that sovereignty. The British generals, however, did not expect the Dutch to offer anything more than paper protests, and thus they took these difficulties lightly.[16] It is unlikely that they informed the British foreign office of these aspects of their plans.

Just how the British General Staff planned to respond in the event the Germans did not violate Belgium's neutrality is a matter of uncertainty. Evidently there was no fixed plan against such a contingency. At least there is no mention in those years of operational cooperation with the French on French soil. It has recently been contended that the British generals were therefore determined to set foot on Belgian soil in any event and to carry their government along in such a step.[17] It is highly unlikely that such a "militaristic" plan ever existed. A more plausible conclusion is that in such a situation the threat to France would have been considered far less serious. There would have been time to see whether a British expeditionary force was at all necessary, and, if so, where it might best be committed.

In fact British activity sharply declined once the Algeciras crisis had safely passed. Grierson's successor in the General Staff (since October, 1906) was very reserved in his relations with his French colleagues. England had no interest in unnecessarily supporting their war-mindedness. The only development was that the 1906 plans for intervention were further refined and supplemented in many details, and also confirmed by the Committee of Imperial Defense. There was steadfast resistance to renewed French efforts to place the British expeditionary force under French supreme command, assigning to it the role of a French auxiliary. The most important step in preparing for war down to 1910 was the reconstruction of the British army under the Haldane reforms. Only this really put Britain in a position to redeem the pledge given the French in 1906, to dispatch a modern force suited to continental warfare.

Actually, the significance of the great army reform in terms of foreign policy went considerably further. It prepared for the coming war against Germany in a psychological sense as well, by using the army to stiffen the anti-German turn in British foreign policy. One can see quite plainly how a whole generation of young officers, trained for a mainland war against Germany at the staff college at Camberley, grew inured to looking on such a war as inevitable and impending. The crises in foreign affairs were followed at the various staff headquarters with nervous tension. The army came to take it for granted that the coming war would be fought on Franco-Belgian battlefields, by the side of French comrades-in-arms. Under no circumstances was it to be met with the lack of preparedness that marked the Boer War.

For this reason the field and study trips by members of the General Staff and the war academy no longer had the battlefields near Metz as their only goal, but often led to the Franco-Belgian border regions, the presumable scene of the next war. General Wilson, head of the operations section since August, 1910, paid no fewer than seventeen visits to this area and went to Paris on countless occasions to engage in confidential discussions with the French General Staff. He became a close personal friend of General Foch, whom he introduced to his colleagues as the future commander-in-chief of the allied armies when Foch first visited England in 1910 at his invitation. Numerous visits by important French generals in England, reciprocated by the British, created an atmosphere of mutual familiarity and camaraderie, before which the former French contempt for the British mercenary army swiftly vanished. In sum, long before Britain entered into a formal diplomatic tie with France, the generals considered themselves to be allies. The reservations entertained in official policy had long since disappeared from the friendly banquets with French officers, and on occasion London had to issue political warnings against anti-German demonstrations by the officers' corps.[18]

Thus the British officers' corps did have a considerable share in engendering the warlike spirit that overheated the atmosphere throughout Europe in the decade before the First World War. It need scarcely be said that all this represented a great encouragement to French policy; but the French had an even better piece of good fortune. From 1910 on the operations division of the British General Staff was headed by a man who may without reservation be described as wholly in thrall to French aims and ideas, General Henry Wilson, a typical "political general," who was not content to confine himself to his technical sphere but insisted on pursuing political goals of his own. His main goal was quite clear—subjugation of Germany in a common campaign with the western powers, in whose swift victory he believed with astonishing optimism.

In pursuit of this goal, Wilson did not eschew political intrigue. We read in his diaries with amazement how he intrigued with leaders of the political opposition against his own government—in 1913 against the war minister, his superior, to force him to retract certain statements against universal military service which he had made in the House of Commons; in July and August of 1914 to hasten the declaration of war against Germany in the hesitant cabinet and to help settle Grey's fight with the pacifist ministers against the latter.[19] In a military sense, Wilson was entirely under the spell of Foch, who had been translating France's rising self-confidence into strategic plans of attack ever since 1906. Totally at variance with British tradition, moreover, he shared the French General Staff's contempt for the fleet as a weapon in a large-scale war. He more than anyone was responsible for the British army's being drawn into the First World War without the kind of operational autonomy to which Grierson had clung as recently as 1906.

The crucial turn came with the second Morocco crisis in 1911, which France survived in much better shape than it had the first one in 1905-1906. Even then, however, not too much could be expected of the Russian ally, whose armaments still fell far short of the desired level, as will be shown later. Yet Russia had staged a reasonable recovery from the disaster of 1905-1906. France's own armaments had made important progress, and the country's inferiority to Germany was no longer as unequivocal as it had seemed to the British General Staff in 1905. Above all, the French now found in Wilson a henchman prepared to do them every possible favor.

As they had in 1905, the French again pressed for a formal military alliance. General Foch voiced this desire to the British military attaché as early as April, 1911, even before the beginning of the new Morocco endeavor that was to violate the Algeciras treaties. The gloomy and biased picture he drew of the German drive for hegemony that allegedly threatened all Europe found ready agreement in the British foreign office; and in the same month of April, long before there was any real German threat, the British General Staff gave its blessings to the working out of plans for the dispatch of all six divisions of the British expeditionary force. It is not entirely clear to what extent this was done in liaison with Paris and may have encouraged French policy in Morocco.[20] The crucial turn came only when a German warship put in an appearance before Agadir and Lloyd George's well-known threatening speech brought the crisis to a head. Wilson left for Paris and with surprising swiftness—indeed, in almost a matter of hours—concluded a written agreement between the two general staffs which virtually put the British army at the disposal of the French as a kind of auxiliary (July 20-21). Its principal clauses, which remained in force until the early days of the First World War, provided for simultaneous mobilization of both armies, transfer of British troops after debarkation by French rail to the concentration area of Busigny-Hirson-Maubeuge, and operational subordination to the general directives of the French high command.

Thus the British expeditionary force was entirely integrated with French operational plans—plans not even known to Wilson at the time he signed this agreement but only the following September. The fact that the French army had to reserve rolling stock for the British divisions placed a new moral obligation on the British. They would not be able to delay mobilization, since otherwise their allies would be in a serious plight. Foch's desires were now fully met. The agreement did elicit vehement opposition from the admiralty in the Committee of Imperial Defense, but on August 23, in an impressive speech of several hours, Wilson managed to convince the ministers and have it accepted—not as a formal military convention but as a written protocol against the event of a military alliance. The opposing naval leaders were compelled to yield, and it was for that reason that Churchill was then appointed first lord of the admiralty.

There was no more talk of protecting Belgium, only of French security. The British plan of deployment was shifted much farther to the west than in 1906, onto French soil, where it was better protected against German surprise. The

British front was thus turned into a mere extension of the French flank and was implicated in the fortunes of the Allied army for better or worse. The route of retreat to Antwerp was forfeited, and no consideration was given to the British interest in securing the Belgian Channel coast from the German grasp. Contact with the Belgian General Staff went by the board altogether and was never restored; for, as has already been mentioned, the Belgians distrusted the intentions of the French high command and remained quite obstinate when the British, in 1912, tried, with a mixture of threats and enticements to draw them into firm commitments on the side of the western powers in the event of war.

In these circumstances Belgian neutrality, instead of helping the western powers, brought an alarming degree of uncertainty to their strategic deployment plans. This was felt most strongly in Paris. As early as February, 1911, General Michel had proposed a major French offensive straight through Belgium, without regard to whether or not the Germans had already staged an invasion. The suggestion actually came from General Wilson of the British General Staff, which had grasped German offensive plans more accurately than the French under Joffre. In July, 1911, Michel's operational plans and organizational reform proposals were rejected as technically unfeasible. Yet at about this time a new offensive spirit began to prevail among the higher French generals, who wanted to overcome the timid defensive spirit that had existed for so many years. If the Germans were indeed to advance through Belgian territory, as was expected, they were going to be anticipated by a counteroffensive, if at all possible.

General Joffre, chief of the French General Staff since late July, 1911, first thought of an offensive in the direction of Alsace-Lorraine but soon shifted to the idea of an attack through South Belgium.[21] The success of such an operation would depend almost entirely on its being launched in time to strike the incipient German deployment. Hence Joffre repeatedly pleaded for authority for an offensive into Belgium without waiting for a German invasion. Poincaré agreed in principle, but declared that on account of world opinion and especially for England's sake the French entry into Belgium had to wait until threatening steps on the part of Germany fully justified it.[22] We see that in France the military expert was kept within narrow limits by the politician, in sharp contrast to Germany, where the problem of Belgian neutrality never became the subject of formal consultations between soldiers and politicians prior to 1914. Yet the Poincaré government did try hard to influence British policy along the lines its chief of staff desired.

Occasion for this was afforded by Haldane's trip to Berlin in February, 1912, which was intended to relieve the tensions between Germany and Britain, where the danger of war in 1911 had shocked public opinion. Had German diplomacy succeeded in gaining neutrality assurances of any kind in return for concessions in the matter of naval armaments—and from the vantage point of Paris it seemed at times as though this might happen—all the French offensive plans would have been seriously jeopardized. The French army would then on no account have been able to become the first to cross the Belgian border. Germany might well interpret such a move as an unprovoked attack, invoke British assurance of neutrality for the case, and win over British public opinion to this view.

Hence, in March, 1912, a veritable barrage of supplications was launched in London to the end of keeping the Entente from being "betrayed" to the Germans. There were repeated broad hints that France might be compelled to shoulder the onus of appearing in the role of an aggressor because of the strategic necessity of anticipating a German invasion of Belgium.[23] We note with some surprise that the British ambassador, Lord Bertie, did not shrink from inciting Poincare to such representations, warning him that the attitude of his own chief might not be altogether reliable. We are not nearly so surprised to hear that the French diplomats, in putting forward their own aggressive designs, were able to cite the agreement of the British General Staff, i.e., of Wilson.[24]

We can scarcely doubt that these agitated warnings stifled the already slight inclination of the British foreign secretary to conclude a neutrality agreement with Germany. Yet it would probably be an exaggeration to say that technical military considerations exerted a crucial influence on the British policy of alliance. The Haldane mission was doomed to failure long before the French ambassador made his impassioned representations in London, because the cabinet had already rejected the Berlin neutrality formula.[25] England had chosen sides and stood firm. Nor can we say that the British foreign office encouraged French aggressive plans in any way. It is true that Grey and especially his secretary of state Nicolson were extremely courteous to the French ambassador. They never with a single word rejected the notion of a preventive invasion of Belgium; but just how they thought about it is made quite clear. They had previously approved a report by their assistant, Sir Eyre Crowe, which declared it to be an essential aim of British policy to appear merely in the role of protecting Belgian neutrality, as provided by treaty, without forcing the country on the side of the western powers.[26]

Belgium's attitude merely confirmed the British government in this policy. All the soundings and contacts made in Brussels by the naval and military attachés as well as by the ambassador showed that the Belgian government was determined to resist any entry of foreign troops, whether from the west or east, unless it had been expressly requested. Even Wilson now seems to have realized that a hasty invasion would be dangerous, since it might drive the Belgian army, which was still of substantial size, into the arms of the enemy. He even considered that the Belgians might make common cause with the Germans and consulted with the French how this might be countered.

In any event, in October, Lord Grey decided that Britain would on no account violate Belgian neutrality unless the first violation occurred on the German side. On November 27, 1912, General Wilson himself was dispatched to Paris with the mission of transmitting this decision to the French General Staff. He further requested that the French army should under no circumstances move into Belgium ahead of the Germans, since otherwise a very difficult situation would be created for the British government.[27] Joffre's plan was now rejected for good. A decision of great importance had been taken. It followed the famous exchange of letters between Grey and Cambon, in which diplomatic confirmation was given to the military talks, including the new naval agreement. While this may have been a bitter pill for the French militarists to swallow, it clearly shows that in Britain political wisdom prevailed over purely military considerations.

Is this indeed the upshot of our examination of this phase—that in Britain political wisdom proved stronger than the zeal of the militarists, stronger than the claims put forward by the General Staff? It is a serious question whether it was politically wise of Grey in 1912 to confirm the Entente with France by military talks, among other things, more forcefully than had been done in 1905-1906. Was it really necessary even now to encourage French self-assertion, to support the French policy of colonial expansion, to begrudge German successes in Africa? Would not Bethmann Hollweg's peace policy have had a better chance of prevailing over militarists of Tirpitz's stripe if London had offered more tangible prospects of political agreement? Another pertinent observation is that the British army helped intensify anti-German sentiment in the country while encouraging the French chauvinists. Yet there is no evidence that Britain's official foreign policy prior to 1914 was dominated by any other than political considerations. It was never the creature of the military.

Actually, an even greater danger loomed from precisely the reverse situation. It was the eclipse of technical military considerations by political prejudices and predilections that posed a threat to Britain rather than the blind zeal of its militaristic admirals and generals. General Wilson not only sacrificed the operational autonomy of the British army to his Francophile propensities, but was also lured into agreeing to a misguided operational plan. He was taken in by French offensive plans which later proved to have been based on miscalculations. French notions of the capacity of their own forces and of German attack plans were wrongheaded and indeed utterly unrealistic. In his facile optimism, Wilson counted on swift victory, never dreaming of the enormous dangers and sacrifices to which he would commit the British army, despite the warnings of farsighted and sober-minded generals like Haig and Kitchener.[28] England, whose military might had always come into play only slowly, was thus dragged into a war plan based entirely on swift and final decision, with the British navy and the resources of the empire scarcely playing a role in the initial phases, something that ran directly counter to British political doctrine. In the end, this effort was all in vain and produced a mere carbon copy of a foreign model. What ultimately brought British victory was not great triumphs on the battlefield but sheer tenacity and endurance. The enemy was slowly choked to death with the help of the navy and the power of industrial war production.

4

The Role of Militarism in Czarist Russia

OUR REVIEW of the political role of the military in the major powers of Europe about 1900 would be incomplete without at least a brief glance at czarist Russia. Beyond this we cannot go—nor indeed is it necessary; for, so far as I know, historical studies devoted to East Europe have scarcely touched on the questions with which we are preoccupied here. Furthermore, under the regime of the last czar the army does not seem to have played a political role of any importance.

Outwardly the czarist court made a martial impression equal to that of the German court under William II. As supreme warlord, the last czar always appeared in public in uniform, and like the German emperor he was surrounded by a grossly swollen staff of adjutants and other military dignitaries. Yet unlike William, Nicholas actually showed little interest in military matters, of which he had no expert knowledge at all.[1] Above all, the Russian army in its modern form was, unlike its Prussian counterpart, of far too recent vintage to have developed a cohesive officers' corps of fixed professional tradition and strong political views. Then too, the social and political prestige of the Russian officer was incomparably lower, not least because the Russian army, again unlike the Prussian, had gathered few laurels since the end of the Napoleonic campaigns; on the contrary, it had repeatedly suffered serious defeats.

Only since 1874 had Russia known a modern mass army based on consistently applied universal military service on the Prussian-German model. The situation was similar to that in France and England; the swift German victories over France had had a revolutionary effect in Russia. Until then military service had essentially been defrayed by conscripts from the lower classes. These men, sons of peasants and proletarians, served for long terms under officers drawn from the aristocracy who lacked specialized training. The crude conscription laws ordained by Peter the Great in 1705, providing lifetime service for an arbitrarily chosen number of subjects, had been improved in 1825 but were not abolished until after the serious reverses of the Crimean War. Beginning in 1864, reforms had first shortened the term of service to fifteen years and extended it in principle to all classes; but, as in France and the German states other than Prussia, there had been a system of paid substitutes for the scions of wealthly families, together with furloughs after eight to ten years which were geared to performance and education. Mass illiteracy and the low educational level among officers were the most serious obstacles to full introduction of the Prussian system. As late as 1909 an illiteracy rate of 38 percent was taken for granted in the army.[2] Milyutin, Russia's great army reformer, and war minister from 1861 to 1881, found it necessary in his basic army law of 1874 to retain a six-year term of active service for the mass of muzhik sons.[3] This was shortened at the outset only for the educated and could be reduced to as little as one year (originally even to six months), according to the level of education. Further relief was provided by a self-financed voluntary service system on the Prussian model. To improve officer training, Milyutin began to build up modern military schools at higher and lower levels, to promote General Staff modernization, and to introduce many administrative reforms. Corporal punishment was finally abolished, and efforts were made to educate the common man in honorable patriotic duties—efforts in which liberal ideas played their part.[4]

These reforms were in large measure successful, as was shown as early as the Russo-Turkish War of 1877-1878. In time, with Russia's vast manpower resources, an almost inexhaustible reserve of trained soldiers was created. The Russian army became a "steamroller," far surpassing in numbers any other armed force on the continent by the turn of the century. All the same, up until the First World War it never attained the striking power of the Prussian-German army.

Geographic factors were only partly responsible—Russia's limitless, sparsely settled spaces, with thin lines of communication, created extraordinary difficulties in the way of swift mobilization and army deployment. The danger of such delays was always a matter of deep concern to the Russian high command. Actually, with French urging and financial assistance, this was greatly lessened by 1914 through technical and organizational measures; but all these reforms suffered from the well-known Russian administrative weaknesses—corruption, confused jurisdictions, intrigue at the czarist court, lack of discipline among high officials and commanders, and intervention and favoritism practiced by the grand dukes, the czar's closest relatives, whose clumsy and arrogant meddling assumed particularly grave proportions under the weak Czar Nicholas II. Contemporary memoirs are full of complaints on this subject,[5] and diplomatic reports are surfeited with them. Two other essential factors were even more important as handicaps to Russia's ability to engage in modern mass warfare.

The country lacked an efficient large-scale armaments industry; and the people were politically passive and dumbly obedient to the government, without a true sense of patriotism. Despite all the efforts of the war minister, Russian army equipment and weapons always remained inadequate. The Russian masses had not the slightest idea why their last czar exacted such horrendous sacrifices in blood and hardship in the Japanese War and the First World War.

To this extent it was correct to describe the vast Russian Empire as a colossus on clay feet. The army, instrument of the czar's power, never enjoyed the popularity it gained in Germany—and even in the Third French Republic. Conscription had to proceed with much greater caution than in the other countries.[6] Since the nobility had lost its hold on the officers' corps through Milyutin's reforms, a commission was no longer considered an attractive career. Only in the great urban centers like St. Petersburg, Moscow, Kiev, and even Warsaw was officer's rank an open door to the brilliant society of the court and the aristocracy, and even to the czar himself. There colorful uniforms, glittering medals, and superb horsemanship were likely to impress the spoiled ladies; and from the mounted guards units members of the right families could move into diplomatic and other high government posts even without administrative training and law examinations. On the other hand, service in the many remote and poverty-stricken garrison towns was monotonous and poorly paid; and there was constant complaint about the lack of new blood, especially from the small educated class. This situation seems to have improved only shortly before the First World War.[7]

There certainly was no *esprit de corps* among Russian officers, as there was in Prussia and Germany. Milyutin's reforms were decried as "democratic," and that is precisely what they were, in that they were deliberately directed against the traditional claims of the nobility to a monopoly of the leading posts. The new officers being trained in the military high schools, Junker seminaries, and war academies were supposed to value expert knowledge and concrete performance more than the glamour of ancient families and the condescendingly aristocratic airs of the grandseigneurs who had hitherto set the tone.[8] This conflict was felt particularly deeply among the younger General Staff officers who took their military studies seriously and all too often encountered in the higher ranks titled amateurs drawn from the circle of the grand dukes who sought to make up for their deficient expertise by brute energy.[9]

The young men did not have an easy time of it. The General Staff was a privileged and unpopular body in the army, composed of military bureaucrats unfamiliar with combat. Both its active members and its alumni enjoyed preferment in promotion, far and wide, and this aroused much envy. Originally entrusted with every possible administrative task, the Russian General Staff did not take on modern form until very late.[10] Zukhomlinov, who rose to its head only in 1908, felt that still another ten years would be needed to bring it up to par.[11] But even he failed to assign it an autonomous role, always considering it as no more than a department of the war ministry and treating it as such when he became minister. This state of dependence was aggravated by the fact that the position of chief of staff was frequently rotated, while the war minister usually held office for a long time. Thus the Russian General Staff never attained the prestige and independence that fell to the German General Staff.

The question is whether the attitude of the Russian officers' corps discernibly affected the course of Russian foreign policy, especially the deepening differences with Germany. In the view of Alfred Vagt, the officer class should be considered the true protagonist of Russian imperialism.[12] It is true that after Milyutin's reforms the Russian officers' corps was indoctrinated with a decidedly nationalist spirit, in which loyalty to the czar, national pride, and military ambition were naturally blended. Insofar as this nationalism was inspired by Pan-Slavic ideals, these did find entry into the army, but, as shown in many memoirs, they underwent the same kind of transformation that marked Russian society as a whole. Sobering experiences with the Poles, Czechs, and Yugoslavs exerted a push in the direction of a more purely Russian nationalism, which indeed prevailed entirely after the reign of Alexander III (1881-1894), perhaps because it was more compatible with a strictly monarchial system than mid-century Pan-Slavism with its revolutionary or at least markedly liberal features.[13] In general this also meant a shift in the point of view on the Balkan question, from romantic sympathy to cold considerations of power and prestige. Pan-Slavism, moreover, was basically a literary movement, which put a limit to its spread inside the army.

Still, there were individual generals who as writers and speakers helped give currency to Pan-Slav and anti-German sentiments, especially Fadeyev, who from the 1860's on advanced some rather curious notions about expanding the Russian sphere of influence to the Adriatic. He coined the slogan: "The road to Constantinople goes by way of Vienna." Fadeyev was soon relieved of active service as a political trouble-maker. Nevertheless, the German ambassador, General von Schweinitz, certainly one of the most knowledgeable experts on the Russian army, remarked in one of his more brilliant reports in 1892 that Fadeyev was "the true progenitor or at least codifier of Russian General Staff chauvinism." Schweinitz also mentioned some fanciful notions of conquest from the lips of a high Russian General Staff officer, Dragomirov;[14] but he promptly added that Fadeyev was long since forgotten and then showed in detail that "General Staff chauvinism" was far more defensive than aggressive in character even in its Asiatic, let alone its German, aims.

We may say, all in all, that political generals were as much of an exception in the Russian army as in the German army. Here as there the great majority of the officers were nationalist and monarchist in outlook, perhaps even chauvinistic, but by and large they were professional soldiers without political instincts. The best-known exception was General Skobelev, a vainglorious swashbuckler who felt a great sense of mission as a result of his achievements in the Asiatic colonial wars. In the spring of 1882 he delivered fiery speeches in Paris and Warsaw, in which he openly called for a Franco-Russian war alliance against the central powers, creating distinct disquiet among diplomats throughout Europe. A kind of counterpart to Boulanger, Skobelev failed as quickly as the Frenchman[15] and was never able to marshal a war party among the Russian generals. No such grouping came into being even after his death, according to the reports of German ambassadors, for very good reasons.

During the eighties Russia was well aware of its hopeless military inferiority to the German Reich, let alone the allied central powers. Army modernization, begun only in 1874, was still in its infancy, and the campaigns against Turkey in 1877-1878 had ended in dreadful political frustration at the Congress of Berlin, directed, it is true, mainly against the German ally, who—so the Russians felt—had betrayed them at this congress. From 1879 on relations between the two imperial courts cooled more and more, as Schweinitz's reports and memoirs impressively document. The sources of anti-German sentiment, however, lay not only in the campaign of incitement waged by such Russian nationalists as Katkov and Aksakov, whose journalistic effusions in this direction grew all the more intemperate as they were muzzled because of domestic affairs, but also in a very real concern of the military with the excessive preponderance of Germany's material might.

This worry seems to have stirred individual generals like Dragomirov as early as the time of Prussia's overwhelming victory at Königgrätz. The traditional view had been that the Prussian monarchy was a kind of Russian protégé, and that now it had suddenly grown into the continent's leading military power, stubbornly refusing in 1876 to assist its Russian neighbor in plans of conquest in the Balkans and instead allying itself closely with Austria-Hungary. This was bound to give rise to growing uneasiness in Russia. In terms of alliances, Russia felt isolated on account of its continuing quarrels with England in the Orient and with Austria-Hungary in the Balkans. Indeed, it felt dependent on Germany's good will, for, in the eyes of the Russian General Staff, Russia was virtually defenseless in the event of a combined attack by Germany and Austria.

Throughout the 1880's German intelligence reports spoke of Russian troop movements, mainly of large cavalry units, to the western regions of Poland, sometimes close to the German border, as well as of strategic railway construction in these same areas. The German General Staff was inclined to view these regroupings as military threats and caused repeated representation to be made to the Russian government through the German ambassador.[16] The sterotyped reply was that these measures merely served Russian security and improved mobilization methods, which aroused German distrust with the same regularity. As has been discussed earlier (Vol. I, pp. 233 ff.), this distrust led to suggestions of a pre-emptive strike in the German and Austrian general staffs in 1887.

Beyond question the Russian arms measures helped a great deal to deepen political tensions between the two empires as well, yet as described by Russian military writers they were only the outgrowth of fear and caution. The Russians were well aware that the western staging area for their armies, the projecting salient of the Polish plains, could be cut off by a pincers movement from East Prussia and Galicia, as Moltke's plans indeed provided, and they were afraid that this contingency might arise very suddenly; for what had impressed the Russian General Staff most deeply during the events of 1866 and 1870-1871 was the rapidity of Prussian-German mobilization and deployment. Russia saw no chance of rivaling the Germans in this sphere. Hence troop strength was increased in the west, especially cavalry, which was to ride out instantly in an emergency to cut the rail lines and delay enemy deployment as long as possible.[17] The rail network was extended in Polish Lithuania as well. Such technical measures are, of course, everywhere considered necessary military jobs even in peacetime. They have nothing to do with "General Staff chauvinism."

So long as Bismarck was at the helm, political tension between Germany and Russia was always eased again, the last time by the highly artificial means of the Reinsurance Treaty; and it was only the abrogation of that treaty by Bismarck's successor that ultimately drove Russia into the arms of France. The history and development of the Franco-Russian military pact of 1892 are today known in fullest detail.[18] The Russian chauvinist writers, especially Katkov, had long demanded such an alliance; and this propaganda campaign was joined by a general of whom we have already heard, Skobelev.

Yet it would be wrong to say that the initiative for the Franco-Russian military pact came from the Russian army.[19] It is true that Obruchev, the chief of staff who signed the military pact of August 17, 1892, together with the Frenchman Boisdeffre, played a zealous part in its final formulation—he was accounted the main exponent of Russian patriotism in the style of Milyutin. But the original impetus clearly came from the French side, especially from Ribot, the foreign minister and revanchist politican who actually prepared the first draft. Freycinet, the French premier, also played a leading role. The French General Staff served merely as an instrument—it did not provide the impetus, as General Wilson was to do later on in the Anglo-French negotiations. By 1892 the French ministers needed a great diplomatic success to stay in office, and they pressed forward with almost indecent haste while the Russians held back for a rather long time.

This hesitation stemmed from the fact that from the outset the goals of the Russian General Staff were at odds with those of the French. For Russia the Hapsburg monarchy was the real enemy, the conquest of Galicia and the "liberation" of the Balkan Slavs the real goals. Germany was a possible enemy only because it formed a protective shield for its ally. Hence it lay in the interest of the Russian high command to preserve freedom of strategic action and to mass its forces in the event of war where the greater chance of victory beckoned, remaining as long as possible on the defensive against Germany. The French would then bear the main burden of the struggle with Germany; and even in the absence of a treaty it could be foreseen with certainty that France would not remain neutral. As early as the 1870's the German General Staff and Bismarck counted firmly on that eventuality. The Russian foreign minister, Baron Giers, moreover, by a diplomatic exchange in August, 1891, had formally secured French armed aid in the event of war. He had been virtually forced into this Entente. Had he not at last grasped the French hand, which had been extended ever since 1887, Russia would have been consigned to complete diplomatic isolation; for German policy, inspired by Holstein, denied Giers even the most casual assurance of friendship, for fear of trouble with the Austrian ally.

Giers, however, did not intend to let his country be exploited in the service of French revanchist politicians, and he was careful in 1891 to pledge no more than consultations between the two governments on "measures to be taken immediately and simultaneously" in the event that peace in Europe was threatened from any side, not merely by Germany or Austria. That would still leave time and scope for political bargaining. Giers waged a long and stubborn fight against Freycinet's offer to turn the general assurances of 1891 into a formal military convention, an offer which Russia's Francophile ambassador in Paris, Baron Mohrenheim, had at once accepted, without authority. For the French the elastic assurances of 1891 were not good enough. Like the Russians, they feared the speed of German mobilization and the great impact of an initial German attack. The Russian ally was to throw his main force against Germany rather than against Austria-Hungary, instantly, before the German forces were able to penetrate deep into France. Hence Russian mobilization had to be expedited by every conceivable means. Article 2 of the secret military convention of August 17, 1892, provided that at the very first news that any one of the three central powers was mobilizing, France and Russia would, "without need for any special prior exchange, at once and in common mobilize their entire armed forces and quickly move them as close as possible to the border." And Article 3 stated: "These armed forces (France: 1,300,000; Russia: 700,000-800,000) will advance with such speed and vigor that Germany will be compelled to fight at once in the east as well as the west."

This represented an extremely strong and close tie of Russian policy to French. It may indeed be confidently called a crucial turn in the genesis of the First World War, a genuine triumph of the military technicians over the politicians. It prefigured the diabolical circle of inexorable military necessity that robbed the statesmen in both Berlin and St. Petersburg of breathing space, so to speak, leaving them only extremely limited scope for freedom of decision. It was a masterpiece of French diplomacy that General Boisdeffre managed to win over the Russian chief of staff Obruchev to this secret convention, and through Obruchev the hesitant war minister Vannovsky, who at first had opposed the convention, and ultimately even the czar. We need not here discuss in detail the political motivations that persuaded Giers, the foreign minister, in the end to give his approval a year and a half later. The fear with which we are already familiar probably tipped the balance on the side of the Russian generals —the fear of an overwhelmingly swift advance by the central powers into the territory of Poland and straight into the Russian forces, still in the process of deployment.

In spite of this, there was no dearth of criticism and reservation on the Russian side, in relation to the close tie with France. Subsequent negotiations between the two general staffs, resumed every year until 1913, show this clearly. The French generals time and again pressed for a swift advance of the largest possible Russian armed force in the direction of Berlin. In principle the Russian generals had no good counterarguments, particularly since they were dependent on French loans to extend their strategic rail network; but they kept arguing the difficulties posed by their vast spaces and especially the need for having large armed forces ready against possible Austrian attacks. The invariable answer they got was that once Germany, the most dangerous enemy, was downed, Austria-Hungary and Italy would no longer amount to much in a military sense. The French tried to protect themselves by pinning the Russians down to specific deployment plans, timetables, routes, and even rail lines, but after 1912 the Russians seem to have dodged them by nominally yielding to the French desires while not actually changing their plans at all. They reserved substantial forces for a counterblow against an Austro-Hungarian offensive in Galicia, the plans of which had been betrayed to them in detail; nor did they cancel their earlier shifts of garrisons and staging areas from West Poland to the east.[20] After the war there was much criticism of the military pact on both sides, each charging the other with unnecessarily having drawn the other into irrelevant political conflicts of interest.

All this was hindsight. It can be plainly seen that at the time, during the 1890's, the new alliance sharply enhanced both French and Russian self-confidence. The domestic conflicts between czarism and republicanism never vanished, but public opinion in both countries enthusiastically welcomed the new Entente, outwardly manifested by the exchange of visits of fleets and rulers. On both sides exaggerated hopes were pinned to the alliance, and reports from German diplomats in St. Petersburg show that especially among high Russian generals totally unrealistic notions of Russia's future power began to spread.[21] The general imperialist trend that prevailed at the turn of the century laid hold of Russian society as well and, in keeping with the Russian character, often took on wishful and fanciful form, applied to Russia's supposed world mission.

Such ideas played a fateful part in turning the head of the last czar, who was weak and easily influenced. Indeed, the relation of the last Russian czars with public opinion in their country is one of the great puzzles in the mysterious history of Russia. As absolute rulers, they seemed quite independent of the popular will, which until 1905 did not even have constitutional representation. The small segment of the population that called itself Russian "society" was fickle and split along many lines, and it was difficult to determine what it stood for.[22] The moral foundations of the Russian government had been hollowed out by anarchistic forces, leaving it with a haunting sense of insecurity, even with regard to the army's officers' corps, which the secret police watched with the same care it gave to other parts of the population.[23] Quite evidently this insecurity affected czarist foreign policy, which had always resorted to the expedient of papering over domestic tension by some brilliant coup—*exercitus facit imperatorem.* Against the background of Russia with its vast spaces, such a policy led to more than the normal quota of military adventures. Under Nicholas II the first of these great adventures was the Russo-Japanese War, the second the First World War.

It would be wrong to hold military circles primarily responsible for the Russo-Japanese War, if only for the reason that it is probably impossible to determine who was to blame—apart from the czar himself, who was driven into this criminally frivolous venture by a blind underestimate of Japan's military capacity as relayed by military observers, by his own stubbornness and wishful nationalism, by the insinuations of irresponsible adventurers, and by the brutal egotism of his grand-ducal relatives. The man who bore official responsibility as war minister, Kuropatkin, was an outspoken opponent of this war, which he nevertheless had to conduct as commander-in-chief. Kuropatkin himself was by no means a chauvinist. Two years after the grave Balkan crisis of 1908 he published a book entitled *Russia for the Russians,* in which he characterized Pan-Slavism as dangerous and nonsensical. Furthermore, at the time, he offered the German military plenipotentiary von Hintze a peaceful agreement with Germany and Austria concerning the future of the Balkans and Turkey, expressly declaring that Russia would need a long period of peace for purposes of reconstruction.

To be sure, this was in the wake of the hapless Russo-Japanese War and the almost complete disintegration of the Russian army in the years of revolution. The domestic authority of the czar had crumbled to such an extent that military ventures were out of the question for the foreseeable future. At the climax of the Balkan crisis of 1909 War Minister Roediger had to confess to the crown council that the army was no longer capable even of defending the empire. It had been established before this that the army would not be able to risk war with Turkey, and the same thing was true of the Black Sea fleet.[24] A "council of national defense," instituted in 1905 under Grand Duke Nicholas Nicolayevich, had failed utterly. A change came only with the summoning of Zukhomlinov to the war ministry in 1909. A favorite of the czar who also enjoyed the general support of the newly created parliament, the Duma, Zukhomlinov with ruthless energy procured large sums of money for army reconstruction. He was aided by the surprising expansion of the Russian economy in the final prewar years.

We need not here discuss the details of his reorganizational efforts.[25] Their main results were an increase in military efficiency and a marked speeding-up of mobilization procedures, which were zealously tested. By 1913 the Russian army had been infected, even in terms of numbers, with the hectic rearmament fever that marked the last years before the war throughout the continent. French urgings and promises of major new loans helped, of course. The term of service was increased by half a year, and an immense improvement in numerical strength was contemplated and authorized by the Duma in July, 1914. Peacetime strength was to be raised by almost forty percent within a few years, i.e., by far in excess of 300,000.

This great program could not, of course, have been implemented before 1916. Zukhomlinov himself described the state that had been reached in 1913 in these words:

> The machinery was ready to set in motion an army of any desired size, but the finished army was still lacking, both in numbers of trained men and in terms of equipment, arms, and supply, for the means to those ends did not become available until 1913. . . . The great framework had been built, into which an army commensurate with Russia's size could grow within a decade, and within which such an army could be run. If efforts were successful in time to improve the level of new blood among the officers and administrators . . . and to sweep aside the rudiments of former years by abolishing the privileged position of the grand dukes, the czar and his diplomats could count on having a political instrument at their disposal within a few years that would rival the world's finest armies.[26]

The statement has a cautious ring. Unfortunately, Zukhomlinov did not always speak so carefully at critical moments. In January, 1914, a ministerial conference discussed the risks of using military power against Turkey in an effort to compel it to dismiss the German general Liman von Sanders, whose activities as corps commander in Istanbul and head of a German military mission were agitating Russian nationalists. Zukhomlinov was asked whether the Russian army was ready for war, if it came to that. Together with his chief of staff Shilinsky, he gave assurances that the Russian army was well prepared to fight Germany as well as Austria-Hungary; but they added that such a contingency was unlikely.[27]

The crucial cabinet session of July 25, 1914, dealing with the Serbian crisis, approved partial mobilization against Austria-Hungary in principle, if that country were to institute war action against Serbia. Zukhomlinov volunteered no warnings on that occasion, by his own testimony.[28] By way of exonerating himself, he insisted that the intervention of a soldier in political matters was inappropriate and also mentioned what happened to his predecessor, General Roediger, who openly admitted the military weakness of the army in 1909 only to be dismissed from office soon afterward. Unlike the situation in 1909, he added, however, Russia in 1914 "seemed justified in looking the possibility of war in the eye with confidence. The country had never been better prepared for war." This testimony from his own lips seems to me to possess high evidential value. It provides a reliable clue in answering the question of the extent of responsibility of Russian army leaders for the outbreak of war in 1914. All the reports by German diplomats and military plenipotentiaries from St. Petersburg in the years after 1909 give essentially the same picture.[29]

Russian chauvinism was deeply disillusioned by the disappointing end to the Bosnian-Serbian crisis of 1908-1909, which also stimulated resentment of Germany, whose diplomatic intervention had compelled Isvolsky to retreat. The army in particular regarded it as intolerably humiliating that its own weakness had made such a retreat unavoidable and chafed to make up for this defeat. Hence its redoubled zeal to reorganize and work out an aggressive war plan in close collaboration with the French General Staff. As Zukhomlinov had put it, in a few years the czar was to have a political instrument at his disposal that would rival the world's finest armies.

This was purely a professional military reaction and had little to do with political considerations and concrete power goals. The army was no more committed to Pan-Slav or "Neo-Slav" ideals than the rightist parties in the Duma which were closest to it and did most to foster its growth. Indeed, the extreme monarchist right regarded Russia's traditional Balkans policy as misguided, as we have already heard from General Kuropatkin. The Octobrists under Guchkov did support an active Russian interest in the Balkans, but they also favored an understanding with Germany; and the remaining conservative groupings at least avoided joining in the anti-German propaganda, since they regarded the German Reich as a bastion of the status quo.[30] For the rest, the inflated hopes of Russian imperialism constantly fluctuated between Asiatic and European power goals; and perhaps nowhere was there any clear picture of what the future should hold in store for the Balkans.

There was certainly no widespread and undivided sympathy for the Serbs, who had once again disappointed their Russian protectors after the Balkan War of 1912. Yet in the end it was not concrete power goals that determined the course of Russian foreign policy, but simply greed for power as such. These ambitions clashed with those of the German-supported rival, Austria. Many Russians could not stomach the diplomatic defeat of 1908-1909. Ever since, savage hatred of Austria-Hungary had dominated virtually all the parties. This hatred ultimately stemmed from jealousy mixed with contempt and a slowly rising conviction of military superiority.

Such sentiments could not but find a particularly strong echo in the army, but that did not necessarily mean that the military were warmongers. Naturally there were hotheads among the generals, as is true in any army. Yet those who really knew the Russian army knew its weaknesses. All the reports agree on the point that the responsibile army leaders were well aware of the danger of war up until 1914, and that they were far too familiar with the secret weaknesses of the instrument in their hands to agitate for war. Count Pourtalès repeatedly stated that there was no single personality who might have emerged as the leader of a military "war party," in the way Skobelev had once tried. Like their German colleagues, the Russian generals were first and last professional soldiers, and the separation between military and political jurisdiction was no less watertight than in Berlin.[31] It was only that Czar Nicholas, who supposedly combined both powers in his person, was even less capable of exercising those powers than William II. He was certainly far less of a militarist than the Kaiser, less given to having his mind made up for him by his military advisers. His uncle Nicholas Nicolayevich seems to have exerted a strong influence over him at times,[32] but because of his grand-ducal position he was not the spokesman of the army. The mobilization order was wrested from the czar not by his military advisers, but in the end, after all, by the civilians, Foreign Minister Sazonov in the lead.

The war guilt literature has always strongly emphasized that it was because of the chief of the General Staff, Yanushkevich, supported by Sazonov, that the partial mobilization order against Austria, agreed on in principle on July 25, was changed to complete mobilization on July 30; and certainly this ended the last hope that the race among the general staffs to unleash the horrendous war machine, a race measured in days and hours, could still be halted. Yet there can be no serious doubt that even Yanushkevich was already acting in a preordained pattern. In a technical sense, partial mobilization was impossible, for it would have thrown the whole Russian deployment plan into confusion and exposed the Polish theater of operations to the gravest danger, so long as there was no certainty—and how could there be? —that Germany would stand by idly while a Russo-Austrian duel developed. Mobilization plans, moreover, happened to be in the midst of still another process of reformulation, and there were, in fact, no complete plans whatever for partial mobilization. Last but not least, partial mobilization flew in the face of the Franco-Russian military agreement of 1892 as well as of the plans worked out between the two general staffs.[33]

In view of these circumstances, General Yanushkevich's intervention can scarcely be said to involve the Russian General Staff in the responsibility for the decisions that led to war. It is different in the case of War Minister Zukhomlinov's attitude at the crown council session of July 25, already mentioned. He failed to give warning on this occasion because he felt that his role was purely that of a soldier; and as a soldier he felt obliged to display the kind of personal courage that would be required in war, when there would be no full certainty of victory and obstacles would have to be surmounted with the help of confidence and will power. Quite evidently Zukhomlinov was badly deceived about the capabilities of the army he had reorganized.[34] But did that make him a warmonger? It must not be overlooked that the basic decision to effect partial mobilization in a specific eventuality was by no means tantamount to a final decision to make war. The immediate aim was merely to use a strong military threat to support diplomatic measures on behalf of Serbia. Even after the general mobilization of July 31, Sazonov still clung to the hope that the door to diplomatic negotiation might remain open. Zukhomlinov's attitude seems to have been similar. As late as July 27 he had assured the German military attaché that he urgently wished to preserve peace, and the attaché felt that these assurances were sincere and insisted that the minister seemed very nervous and worried. Those who would dispose of these assurances as no more than tactical maneuvering should bear in mind the immense political pressure to which the general was subjected. Even in Russia the time was long since past when those who governed could adapt their policies to the calm dictates of political wisdom—the ideal of monarchial government, as envisaged by Bismarck and seriously attempted by Foreign Minister Giers. The last Russian exponent of calculating cabinet diplomacy, the premier and finance minister Kokovzov, had been eased out of office in the spring of 1914 by chauvinists and generals, including perhaps Zukhomlinov, who felt that he was not effective enough. Foreign Minister Sazonov was unquestionably afraid of war, and Nicholas II was even more so. Both were convinced, however, that the Russian throne would be in peril if the Serbs were now abandoned to their fate. They simply did not dare to confront Russian public opinion with another retreat before threats from the Austrian rival, in the manner of 1909. In view of the hostilities which the Austrians had already opened against the Serbs, this second defeat would be even worse. What finally tipped the balance among the czar's counselors, however, was not warlike ambitions but political motives of prestige and self-assertion considered appropriate to great-power status, as nearly always in the history of states.

TWO

The Military and Political Situation in Wilhelminian Germany, 1890-1914

5

The Militarization of the German Middle Class

S TATED CONCISELY, the difference between the military situations of the great powers of West Europe and Prussia-Germany in the nineteenth century is that among the former the military were considered a kind of necessary evil while in the latter they were the nation's pride. This was true around mid-century, at least, during the high tide of liberalism. We have already seen that soon after 1870 a change took place which tended to soften the contrast. With the onset, late in the century, of the great colonial expansion and the conflicts among the powers which it brought with it, military might began to enjoy added esteem even among the western powers with parliamentary systems of government. Soon after 1900 this led to the formation and consolidation of the great power blocs that explosively discharged their potential in the First World War.

As we have shown, imitation of the Prussian-German army system played an important part in this process, primarily among the major continental powers, east and west. The miracle of the abrupt German rise to power under Bismarck, first manifested in the incredibly swift and decisive victories on the battlefield in 1864, 1866, and 1870-1871, upset professional soldiers all over Europe. Within only a few decades this led to a militarization of political life none would have thought possible as recently as 1860. An arms race ensued, in which Germany soon lost its numerical advantage over France. Indeed, by 1890 Germany was already lagging far behind the military strength of its later enemies, who nevertheless, long before 1914, still regarded the new German Reich as a real threat. Later they were to charge the Germans with having indulged a reckless ambition for European if not world supremacy, in pursuit of which they wantonly destroyed the peace.

The question of how such a thing was possible and what we are to make of these charges will form a central theme of this second volume of our study. Even within the framework of the general problem of German militarism the Wilhelminian Reich, to which we now turn our attention, constitutes an altogether new epoch. The world has always seen it in that light. During the entire life of Bismarck's government, it was never charged with posing a threat to European peace. On the contrary, nothing could be more impressive than to see, in the reports of foreign diplomats during the 1870's and 1880's, how initial fears that Bismarck might misuse the massed power of the new Reich for forcible expansion quickly evaporated, how distrust slowly gave way to confidence. Despite its vigorous assertion of power, the country at Europe's heart appeared as a guardian rather than as a disturber of the peace. It is true that the notion that Bismarck's *Realpolitik* presaged a purely military brand of nationalism, putting might before right and staking its case entirely on "blood and iron" rather than on peaceful negotiation, had its roots in the domestic political struggles of the 1860's. But only after Bismarck's fall did this become a political catchword in the anti-German propaganda campaign. So long as he was personally at the helm, none could seriously doubt that German policy would be set by political reason rather than by nationalist passion and military zeal.

What were the factors that shook confidence under Bismarck's successors, bringing Wilhelminian Germany into disrepute and giving it the odor of being dominated by a spirit of violent militarism? To find the answer, we must first of all consider the position of the army within the whole of German political life.

In the first volume of this work we tried to define the vague and much-abused term "militarism" by describing it as an "exaggeration and overestimation of the military estate, unbalancing the natural relation of statesmanship and war." The charge of such exaggeration and overestimation, leveled even against the eighteenth-century Prussian soldier kings, is one of the staples of anti-Prussian propaganda. The standard of comparison was seen in those eighteenth-century courts which preferred to invest their funds in princely pomp—predominantly during the first half of the century—and in economic welfare—during the age of "enlightened absolutism"—rather than in the establishment of large mercenary armies. Later critics proceeded, whether consciously or not, from the ideals of modern welfare policy and maximum civil liberty. Our own analysis has emphasized that while economic welfare, rule of law, and cultural development played an important part in the policies of Frederic the Great, he like his father saw the rise of independent Prussian power as the foremost task of his government. While this task could not be accomplished without the creation of a large army—some say too large an army—Frederic was nevertheless, as we sought to show in our first chapter, quite free of any one-sided overestimation of the military estate; for battle and conquest were never to him ends in themselves, the highest goals of his life, and even in war his actions were guided by political rather than by narrowly military considerations. Whoever studies Frederic's foreign policy and style of warfare in depth will almost have to reject any characterization of him as a "militarist."

This is not to deny in the least the obvious fact that, in the old Prussian military state after Frederic William I, public life was dominated by the existence of a grossly swollen army to a degree quite unprecedented in Europe. When Frederic the Great ascended the throne, more than two-thirds of his country's revenues—five of 6.9 million thalers—went to maintain an army (including many foreign hirelings) that numbered no less than 3.8 percent of the population.[1] Compulsory army service by the nobility and its peasant serfs, the use of army veterans in numberless government posts, introduction of the principle of military subordination into the entire official hierarchy all the way up to the ministerial level—all these things, we know, incisively altered the Prussian way of life. This may well be described as a "militarization" of the Prussian people, in town as in country, but at the same time it should be realized that it was a kind of compulsory militarization that fell far short of kindling a military spirit among the mass of the citizenry like the "militarism" which is thought of when that term is applied to the German character on the eve of the First World War. The origins of the neo-German militarism cannot be traced directly to the military system of the old Prussian soldier kings, which tended to beget blind obedience. The militarist strain in the new German bourgeoisie, on the other hand, was a kind of perversion of patriotic pride, of the sense of power that pervaded free citizens who were, indeed, rather inclined to oppose official government policy.

The inversion of the natural relation of statesmanship and war shown in the wars of our era, i.e., the displacement of political wisdom by impassioned militancy and self-perpetuating military exigencies, requires that the whole nation be pervaded with patriotic and warlike ambition, as was demonstrated in the third chapter of Volume I of this work. This was scarcely the case with the subjects of the Prussian soldier kings. The radical innovations of Frederic William I, creator of the Potsdam military state, were thrust upon them as a kind of revolution and appeared at first as a dreadful misfortune.[2] Until the wars of Frederic the Great the army was anything but popular. The middle class was as hostile toward the arrogance of the high-born officers as it was toward the coarse rabble in the ranks, plucked from the dregs of many lands and held in check only by the cruelest discipline. There was much cursing and muttering at the many burdens and abuses—mercenaries with their women and children billeted in town homes; villages saddled with cavalry units; levies for service, forage, and transport; the muster of whole townships to recapture deserters; the long arm of brutal military justice; the rude manners of officialdom; ruthless military intervention in home rule; competition by craftsmen-soldiers fattening up their meager pay; and not least the heavy military tax load weighing on the peasantry.[3] Officers habitually addressed civilians with terms of abuse, and citizens in turn looked down on common soldiers as rowdies and ne'er-do-wells.[4] Public drill-ground whippings were not calculated to raise the esteem in which the army was held. In the garrison towns there had always been frequent clashes and riots between soldiers and civilians.

The social prestige of the soldier's estate was not greatly changed even by the victorious campaigns of Frederic the Great, which brought him so much admiration and aroused so much patriotic pride. We have already heard of the bitter criticism of the Prussian military system which flowed from the political pamphleteers of the late eighteenth century with their humanitarian ideals (Volume I, Chapter 2). Prussian military reformers prior to 1806 and especially after fully shared this hostility. The great groundswell of militant patriotism came, at least among the upper classes, only with the Wars of Liberation from Napoleonic rule with their mass levies, which supplemented (though they did not immediately supplant) the old professional army.

Yet our earlier scrutiny has shown that this great resurgence swiftly faded, while the restored Prussian monarchy tried to restrain the "Jacobin" patriotism of the war years and to indoctrinate the army with the spirit of a royal guard to protect monarchial institutions, despite the defense acts of 1815. The resultant garrison army, painstakingly drilled mainly for parades, offered little inspiration to civilian patriots.

In the rest of Germany, until 1866, the relation of the liberal citizenry to the army was much the same as in France. The wealthy could buy their way out, depriving the army of all representation from the educated classes, which became completely alienated from military life. The army fell to the despised status of a force of poorly equipped watchmen, unfit even by its small size[5] for anything better than police duty.

To the credit of the South German states it should be said that among their officers the caste spirit was far less marked than in Prussia. There officers did not shun social intercourse with civilians, and they displayed a far greater interest in cultural matters. Yet prior to 1870 the military were perhaps even less popular in South Germany than in Prussia, even though in South Germany army service was the prerogative of the lower classes, restricted in practice, despite long terms in principle, to a few brief training periods and pre-empting only a limited share of local resources. Nevertheless, especially in Württemberg, the army was the butt of constant attack in the chamber. The liberal bourgeoisie, far from taking pride in the army, viewed it as an unnecessary burden, a foreign body if not a canker in the body politic, a "breeding-place for venal servility," an "instrument of despotism," quite in the style of Karl von Rotteck, with whose laments we are already familiar (Volume I, Chapter 5).

In Prussia prior to the Revolution of 1848 there was no opportunity for such antimilitary mutterings, since there was no corporate representation; and perhaps there was not even an inclination, for neither the prowess of Prussian arms in the great liberation struggle nor the glories of the army of Frederic the Great had faded from the people's memory. Yet the course of the revolution in Berlin abruptly revealed that here too soldiers and civilians were at loggerheads. This tension was more responsible for the revolution than any other factor. Berlin's upper middle class actually loathed the aristocratic officer caste, especially in the guards regiments, and beyond that the whole system of the military state, which was essentially inimical to civil liberty.[6]

What the rebellious Berliners really wanted was a nonmilitary bourgeois monarchy in the style of Louis Philippe, based entirely on a citizen militia—in other words, a complete break with Prussian tradition. The course of the revolution throughout Germany later that year showed that the country could not be united under Prussian leadership in this way, and this was sealed by the failure of Prussian plans for such a union at Olmütz (Olomouc). The controversy over military reform that erupted in 1860 merely warmed up the conflict of 1848 in weaker form (see Volume I, Chapter 6), though it remained bitter enough at times to pose a serious threat to the Prussian monarchy. In any event, no one would have dreamed of calling the majority of the Prussian and German people "militaristic" by nature.[7]

All this must be borne in mind if one wishes to assess properly the almost incredibly strong effect of Bismarck's "Wars of Unification" on German political sentiment. This is perhaps most vividly shown by a comparison of press and public opinion in Württemberg before and after the war of 1870-1871.[8] As late as 1867 Moritz Mohl had ringingly implored his fellow countrymen to protect South Germany against the extremity of barbarization by Prussian military take-over: "I am convinced, gentlemen, you will rue it on your deathbed!"

The Stuttgart *Beobachter* wrote that it would be preposterous to expect the talented sons of Swabia to go through the unnatural contortions of Prussian drill, "useful as these might be for the children of the North German plains, who lag behind in so many respects." Of what possible benefit to the South Germans were exercises needed "up there to attain at least a tolerable general level"?

All these objections were swept away at a single stroke by the war against France. The Württemberg field division had occasion to distinguish itself on the Upper Rhine, at Wörth, Sedan, and Paris, and received high praise for its impressive record from King William himself. The tempestuous events in the course of the great patriotic war were enough to blow away the stubborn old Swabian particularism like a wisp of vapor. The Württembergers grew proud of being numbered among the national army's crack troops, and they maintained this reputation in both world wars.

The notorious military docility of the German bourgeoisie thus turns out to be of comparatively recent vintage. Considering the crucial role of the Wars of Liberation of 1813-1815 and the Wars of Unification of 1864-1871 in the origins and success of German union, we can scarcely be surprised that after the founding of the Reich the Germans, flushed with power and unity at last achieved, looked on their army as a priceless national treasure. Long-nurtured resentment of Prussian militarism and drill-ground spit and polish paled and vanished, inside Prussia and out—at least among those segments of the populace that felt a strong awareness of historical, national, and political traditions, i.e., the larger part of the German bourgeoisie, led by the academic circles which had played such an important part in the national uprising of 1848.

As bourgeois liberalism succumbed more and more to Bismarck's blandishments, allowing its ancient libertarian ideals to become submerged in the single-minded power drive of the new age, now served up as *Realpolitik,* its military docility grew apace. Complaints against certain abuses in the Prussian army never ceased—mistreatment of soldiers, brutal noncoms, arrogant and class-conscious officers, miscarriages of military justice, etc.—but they became more or less the prerogative of the left liberal opposition. [9] As shown by the party programs of these groups, even they, however, did not reject outright the Prussian defense system with its strictly applied universal military service, nor the royal army based on it. [10] That would have cost the Progressive People's Party all election chances. All the bourgeois parties were convinced of the general excellence of this military system—though they had fault to find with certain details. Only the young Social Democratic Party, which was against tradition and without one of its own, kept out of step and demanded a militia system in place of a standing army.

Nor was the German parliament as such basically disinclined to authorize the necessary financial means for defense, even when larger and larger programs were called for. The notorious conflicts that broke out with Bismarck on this issue in 1886 might have been avoided altogether had not the chancellor aroused the Reichstag's ire by his efforts to fix the army budget over a longer period of time, thus limiting the deputies' power of the purse. There were more difficulties over Caprivi's army bill in 1892-1893, perhaps because of the Reichstag's desire to exploit the greater financial freedom of action it had acquired after Bismarck's fall rather than from any lack of patriotic fervor, which was, it is true, a bit dampened by the unfavorable situation of Germany in the world. As in 1887, all it took to foil this opposition was to prorogue the parliament and go to the country with an appeal to patriotism.

In subsequent government bills—in 1899 and 1905—the Reichstag did obtain certain military economies. This was of small importance at the time, since the war ministry, as will be discussed later, did not then regard a substantial army increase as necessary, German arms emphasis having by 1898 clearly shifted to the navy. And public opinion was such that the political parties shunned no sacrifice on behalf of the navy. When, after the second Morocco crisis of 1911, it became clear to every German that the country's political isolation had put the Reich in grave jeopardy, the Reichstag was the first to criticize the government's budget requests as too modest and press for swifter rearmament, again supported by a groundswell of public opinion.

Of course German militancy was further deepened because the so-called "Little German" historical view propagated by Sybel, Droysen, and Treitschke—i.e., German unity under Prussian rather than Austrian hegemony, as achieved through the great triumphs of Bismarck's policies—was now taught in all the schools. The royal army to which Prussia owed an incomparable succession of brilliant victories from Frederic the Great to William I as well as its rapid rise to power, and to which Germany owed the removal of particularist obstacles to national union, shone with a dazzling and unprecedented glory. Not long ago the liberal bourgeoisie had looked on the army as a bastion of reaction, but now it was seen as the embodiment and guarantor of true political progress. History itself was turned upside down, and the traditions of bourgeois liberalism were allowed to gloss over the true Prussian-German past. This new historical perspective found its most extreme expression in Heinrich von Treitschke's lectures on political science at the University of Berlin during the 1890's, which drew enthusiastic audiences not only from among students but from army officers as well. Treitschke dramatically underlined the "divine majesty of war," praised universal military service as the foundation of political liberty and training in blind discipline as the finest school of character, and described the Prussian generals as an elite of open-minded men of character. "A true general," he declared, "is always a statesman as well." He lauded Moltke's political insight and called the old swashbuckler Blücher "a political genius."

Small wonder that celebrations of national holidays bore a marked military character. Throughout the world, after all, war heroes are the preferred subjects of monuments, and great victories are what stand out in the mind of the masses. In the new German Reich there were countless unveilings of monuments in memory of generals and victorious battles, and these were always combined with military parades. At such events the local leaders and generals and other celebrities played the main roles, while the common people were permitted participation only through their veterans' organizations and glee clubs. After 1871, the anniversary of the French surrender at Sedan supplanted the memory of the Battle of the Nations of 1813; and, as I recall it, this annual celebration did bear the character of a true popular holiday, at least in the countryside. Only after the turn of the century did it begin to fade away.[11] It is significant that this date became the first new patriotic festival rather than January 18, the date on which the Reich was established—which may have been, however, in part because September was a more suitable season.

As for Emperor William II's birthday, January 27, its celebration was always a preponderantly military affair.[12] The greatest impression on these occasions was always made by the ceremonial parades with their crashing military bands. All this was often the subject of criticism in the democratic press and the

Reichstag, but the spectacle remained as popular as it is today throughout the world, even in countries like England, which prides itself on being antimilitarist. "Prussian ladies never tire of watching the soldiers," said a Turkish diplomat to the empress' ladies-in-waiting on the occasion of a long parade in 1889. "That was spoken straight from our hearts and made us not a little proud," commented Countess Keller—nor was she speaking purely for the court circles.[13]

Over-all the new German patriotism was at first strongly nostalgic. Its inspirations were the "great deeds of the fathers" and the happily achieved national union. On January 27, 1871, Heinrich von Sybel, chronicler of the Reich's birth, wrote to his friend Baumgarten: "Now at last has come the fulfillment with such infinite magnificence of what for twenty long years was the great goal of all our yearnings and aspirations! At my stage of life, how can there be any new meaning for my remaining years?"[14] It was a natural sentiment in the circumstances, and it was fully reflected in the political attitude of the Reich's founding father, Bismarck, who insisted time and again that Germany was now sated in the field of foreign affairs and would henceforth seek to augment only the resources of peace rather than outward power.

But patriotism, to stay in character, cannot forever subsist on nostalgia. Then too, almost from the first day German domestic policy took a most unfortunate course, for which Bismarck bears greater blame than the political parties; and the nation's pride in the deeds of the fathers was in danger of lapsing into a deepening awareness of German power, especially among the younger generation, and of reaching out for new foreign goals. Scarcely was Bismarck dismissed when he grew into a legend, the "giant from the Saxon woods" who supposedly owed his political successes largely to the mailed fist, the ruthless use of military power. Bismarck himself was partly responsible for nourishing this legend, by his public opposition to the policies of his successors. His authority alone could have kept German public opinion within the narrow confines to which history and geography inexorably consigned Germany, despite its inherent vitality, which was fully unleashed only with the establishment of the Reich. The younger generation impatiently pushed against these barriers. Those who, like the author, have a living recollection of the Wilhelminian era know from personal experience that the new catchwords about world power and sea power had a tonic effect on the younger generation, as a welcome change from the everlasting nostalgia of traditional patriotism.

Gratitude and admiration for the great achievements of the army in three victorious wars naturally enhanced the prestige of the officer class even more. The old Prussian soldier kings had long ago given it top ranking, which was now acknowledged without reservation by the entire middle-class society. Complaints about the arrogance and supercilious bearing of the younger officers continued, but on the whole widespread respect of the uniform prevailed, especially in Prussia, somewhat less so in South Germany with its differing tradition, and least of all in Alsace. How far this servility, which infected the upper as well as the lower middle class, could go was shown in 1906, by the successful escapade of the grotesque "Captain of Köpenick," who was actually a cobbler named Voigt dressed up in a uniform.

The officer class owed much of its social prestige to the fact that it alone pre-empted the firm Prussian heritage of a disciplined way of life, with a strict code of honor and a strong *esprit de corps*. This made it stand out from the inchoate, traditionless mass of modern democratic industrial society, lending it the appearance of a true elite. As the army grew into the millions, officers drawn from the nobility naturally declined in proportion. Still, aristocrats continued to play an important part, especially in the top echelons, the guards units, and certain crack regiments.[15] German military literature has always insisted on the importance, indeed the indispensability, of this self-sufficient *esprit de corps*, with its highly developed sense of honor, in providing effective army leadership. Following the First World War, however, there was also much self-criticism of the dangers and weaknesses that stemmed from the caste system—the wholly unnatural segregation of the officers' corps from the life of the people; the artificiality of its increasingly formalized code of honor with the grotesque institution of the duel that limited "fitness to respond to a challenge" to an exclusive class within the nation; the curious aversion of the higher officers, adhering to the aristocratic pattern, to everything that smacked of the technical, which led to dangerous lags in arms technology;[16] the overbearing manners, intended to make up for the lack of intellectual sophistication; the frequent preferment of well-connected noblemen, when it came to promotion; etc., etc. One danger to the officers' corps, peculiar to the Wilhelminian era, arose from the intrusion of numerous elements from the world of industry and high finance. These young men brought to their regiments, especially in the cavalry, a style of living that was neither aristocratic nor traditionally Prussian but simply luxurious, putting the "gentility" of the officers' corps in a rather unedifying light.

This intrusion of "plutocratic" elements was a direct consequence of the social prestige enjoyed by the officer class. Many were tempted to follow this road to status, possibly even to direct access to the imperial court.[17] Even here we touch on a point at which the militarization of German life began to gain direct political influence, within the meaning of our broad theme. Military patterns of thinking came to invade the ideology of the middle class.

This happened primarily by way of the reserve officer, a military figure who began to play a major role in the German army only after the founding of the Reich. In the War of 1870-1871 reserve officers were still numerically insignificant.[18] Until Roon's army reforms, one-year volunteers, once they were commissioned as "officers on furlough status," usually transferred to the Landwehr. This changed only with the close amalgamation of Landwehr and line, in which the character of the Landwehr as an autonomous field force beside the regular army was destroyed. One of the major changes was that Landwehr and reserve officers came into much closer contact with regular officers, as a result of which the regular officers' corps grew much more selective. Military efficiency was no longer the sole criterion. The district commander, whose officers picked the candidates to be recommended for commissions to the military cabinet, was enjoined to consider civilian position and conduct outside the service, a discretion which opened the doors wide to political considerations and social prejudices. Men with leftist leanings or Jewish antecedents had virtually no chance to secure reserve commissions.[19] Candidates from the peasant and artisan, let alone the working classes, were only seldom eligible. This was also true of shopkeepers and sometimes even of men with wives of lower middle-class origin.[20]

The reserve officers' corps regarded itself as a social elite, and it became the ambition of every young German citizen to have his status as a member of "society" confirmed by a reserve commission. The degree to which class differences in Germany were thus hardened is almost unimaginable. In certain professions, such as the law, and in the higher echelons of the civil service, it was a matter of honor to hold not merely a simple reserve commission, but preferably one in a regiment in which most of the officers belonged to the nobility, best of all in the cavalry. Thus a military pecking order arose even in civilian life, reminiscent of certain aspects of the traditional Russian system. Deserving statesmen received military rank as a mark of distinction. Bülow became a colonel in the hussars; Michaelis was promoted from captain to lieutenant colonel in the reserve; Finance Minister von Scholz advanced from sergeant to lieutenant, Landwehr (retired). It was the accepted fashion even for higher officials to wear uniform on every suitable occasion. On his first appearance as chancellor before the Reichstag, Bethmann Hollweg wore the uniform of a major, a practice for which Bismarck, who perpetually dressed up as a cuirassier general, was certainly to some extent responsible. To be accounted a man's man, it was essential to wear the silver epaulettes, better yet to be a cavalry captain in the reserve or the Landwehr. Aristocratic conventions and condescending tones were adopted in civilian circles to an almost ludicrous degree, perhaps most of all in the student societies, where callow youths sought to find and confirm their manhood by stiff and labored mannerisms. An aggressive demeanor and instant readiness to fight a duel were widely copied attitudes in academic circles.

But mere imitation of outward manners was not all. Regular officers were ineradicably indoctrinated with royalist sentiments, which were indeed considered natural and appropriate in a monarchial state. This orientation was even more deeply entrenched by virtue of the fact that so many of the officers and most of the generals came from the Prussian military nobility. As in France, only more so, the German army was basically unpolitical, though its sympathies inclined unequivocally to the right. There are many startling incidents illustrating how this operated within the reserve officers' corps.

General Liebert tells of a case dating from the 1890's in which several reserve officers from Hanover were summoned before a court of honor and cashiered because bar gossip had revealed that they had voted for the Guelph (Hanoverian) party in a Reichstag election. As chief of staff of the tenth army corps, Liebert thoroughly approved of this action, but had recommended that it be effected without publicity.[21]

Prince Henry of Schönaich-Carolath, a chief county magistrate, highly respected nobleman, and supernumerary cavalry captain, was severely reprimanded by the military cabinet in 1884 because he had dared, as a deputy of the Free Conservatives, to speak before the Reichstag in favor of equality of family pensions for subaltern officers and civil servants—even though he had immediately afterward voted for the contrary government bill. The following year, after he had supported a motion by the left liberal deputy Eugen Richter, which would have kept the army from arbitrarily exceeding its budget, the prince's military status was terminated.

According to Waldersee, Bismarck originally approved; but the case threatened to blow up into a political scandal, and the prince's aristocratic colleagues in particular grew highly agitated. After protracted negotiations, in which high officers and officials threatened to resign, a pardon was held out, on condition that the prince, who avowed his loyalty throughout, would not again fall from grace; and nine months later the dismissal was withdrawn. Yet the prince continued to be under suspicion in high places, and as late as 1912 he had serious difficulties with the military cabinet when it became known that in the wake of the great electoral victory of the Social Democrats he had cast his secret vote for the election of the socialist August Bebel as a member of the Reichstag presidium. As the *Deutsche Zeitung* wrote indignantly, no worker who voted for a Social Democrat even for town councilor would have been tolerated in any veterans' organization. What was one to make of such a prince, then? As an aggravating factor, the military cabinet charged him with having, while in uniform, patronized an innkeeper suspected of socialism.[22]

As a politician, Prince Schönaich became known to a wider public at home and abroad only in 1890, when he delivered a famous speech in which he warned against harsh unilateral measures against the Social Democrats and challenged the educated middle class to come to grips with the ideology of socialism. His own contribution to that debate is not particularly important, but his speech touched one of the sorest spots of Bismarck's domestic policies, the fateful split of the nation into two camps—the militarily docile middle-class right and the basically antimilitarist left. This division was greatly deepened by the fact that the liberal traditions of mid-century had, by the 1880's, faded among the upper middle class and officialdom. Under the aging Bismarck and his secretary of the interior Puttkamer, anyone who wished to get ahead in the Prussian civil service had to be absolutely "reliable," in the Conservative party sense. The political influence wielded by the officers' corps served only to strengthen this trend.[23]

Once Bismarck had gone, this proved to have a dangerous effect on the way the German middle class as well thought about foreign affairs. More and more, the terms *stramm* (smart) and *schlapp* (slack), borrowed from drill-ground and casino jargon, came to dominate talk about foreign affairs in nationalist-oriented middle-class clubs and in the hangouts of the patrioteers.

Soldiers live with the idea that mere will power can overcome all obstacles; but such a primitive notion will not hold in the sphere of politics, and especially not in diplomacy with its many subtleties. Statesmanship calls for the ability to attain one's goal indirectly, sometimes even by compromise and surrender, if need be. It was a great misfortune that within the rapidly rising German nation the idea spread so widely that civilians were "pen-pushers" and "slackers" by nature. This served only to encourage postures of muscle-flexing and saber-rattling. We have already mentioned the Bismarck legend that began to proliferate soon after the great chancellor's fall. This legend caused much trouble for his successors, and there can be no question that the militarization of the nation had a major share in these developments. It helped to create a disposition and a pressure in nationalist circles which the feeble Reich governments of the Wilhelminian era were often able to resist only with considerable difficulty.

6

War and Politics in the Military Literature of the Last Decades before the First World War

I N THEORY the German officers' corps was supposed to be above party politics, beholden solely to its "supreme warlord." This, however, did not keep military writers from developing a literature that often went beyond military matters narrowly into the sphere of politics. These writers were for the most part retired or unassigned officers, for it was not an easy matter for officers on active duty to engage in literary work. They could do so only with the permission of their superiors and thus had to observe many professional limitations. For an officer publicly to criticize military institutions and official views of the nation's history, especially the "glorious deeds" of the Wars of Unification, was considered a breach of professional etiquette, running counter to the *esprit de corps* and the principle of military subordination. It could indeed endanger the author's career.

As a matter of fact, the military cabinet also sought to stifle hostile journalistic efforts by retired and often disgruntled officers, and William II, in occasional outbursts, was prone to threaten them with courts-martial and honor courts. The General Staff maintained a formal censorship system for writings on subjects which it had previously dealt with in its own studies.[1] The literary activities of reserve officers, of course, could in the long run be neither controlled nor restricted. Still, even reserve officers faced the risk of being summoned before a military court of honor for their public statements.[2]

The public utterances of German officers are of interest to us only insofar as they tell us something about the political orientation of the higher ranks, especially the General Staff. Naturally, the views of an individual writer cannot be automatically regarded as those of the officers' corps as a whole. Yet there are certain common features that come through everywhere.

One striking characteristic is a keen—indeed, often an exaggerated—sense of

Germany's precarious world position, at least since the fall of Bismarck. Germany was seen to be surrounded by enemies on all sides. All were convinced that none of its neighbors was to be trusted. As early as 1887, Count Waldersee, speaking as a General Staff officer, concluded "that it was better to seize the initiative than to leave it to one's opponent."[3] What he was recommending was, of course, a pre-emptive strike against Russia; and we already know that the elder Moltke, too, constantly toyed with the idea that Germany should act swiftly to anticipate any dangers that threatened it, a thought on which he repeatedly clashed with Bismarck. Are we justified in concluding that the idea of preventive war handed down within the General Staff as a firm tradition?

This cannot be proved for Waldersee's immediate successors, Count Schlieffen and the younger Moltke, at least not in transparently recognizable form. In contrast to Waldersee, Schlieffen was a completely nonpolitical officer, a pure technician of strategy. During his term as chief of staff, as will be shown, he never meddled in politics, and in particular he never officially urged preventive war. The singularly military character of his political ideas is shown by his extensive writings on history and politics, on which he embarked after his retirement. Bismarck is there shown entirely in terms of the traditional German legend—"the statesman of blood and iron, who cut the knot of politics with the sword on the battlefield. This herald of conflict, this mighty champion whose powerful voice inspired Germany's sons to fight the enemies of the fatherland's freedom and grandeur was a soldier, even though he owed only formal allegiance to the army." Acting swiftly, he began the War of 1870 before a hostile coalition could come into being.[4]

In an essay of 1909 entitled "War in the Present," which quickly became famous, Schlieffen projected the view that Germany's then complete military and political encirclement had begun almost at the moment the Reich was founded; and he saw all of Europe pervaded with irreconcilable and uneradicable hatred of Germany. France's thirst for vengeance "had summoned all Europe to arms"; England loathed "the once-despised German rival"; Russia was dominated by "the traditional antipathy of Slav for German," Italy by Irredentism and hatred of Austria. Only the towering might of German arms had so far prevented Germany's enemies from engulfing the country. They were merely waiting for the opportune moment to fall upon it from all sides. "Danger looms large," he wrote, but if and when war would come remained uncertain. What was essential in such a situation strong armaments, a firm political stand, and sure military leadership.

Yet there is no word about a timely strike, about preventive war. Nor does any such hint appear in a confidential memorandum of 1912 which contains Schlieffen's last great operational plan. Here he expressed keen regret that German policy, during the Morocco crisis of 1911, had failed to display a firm will to use the army if necessary. This, however, is not because Schlieffen desired preventive war, but merely because he was firmly convinced that the enemy would again have recoiled from a serious threat of war, as in his view had been the case in 1905 and 1909, from fear of the German army.[5]

This was a rather primitive and oversimplified view of political reality. To Schlieffen's mind Europe lived in a perpetual state of crisis, so to speak, and strong armaments and vigilant preparedness were the only means for keeping this crisis under control. In a way, Schlieffen the soldier was using historical arguments to confirm the central importance of his profession. Yet he did stick closely to his lines of authority, leaving the decisions on war and peace to the statesmen; and it is also noteworthy that Schlieffen seems to have lacked the inflexible fatalism so often encountered in the military literature of the time— the idea of the absolute inevitability of impending war.

This fatalism emerges with particular clarity at those points at which the Darwinist doctrine of the "struggle for survival" invaded political thinking. The kind of philosophy this could engender in the minds of soldiers is so strikingly illustrated in the memoirs of Conrad von Hötzendorf that I must mention him here, even though he was not a German general but rather the chief of the Austrian General Staff.

Looking back on the First World War, Conrad concluded that the Austrian and German emperors delayed far too long, ignoring the fact that struggle had been a basic law of nature from time immemorial, long before the appearance of man. All living creatures were perpetually engaged in a struggle for survival. Predators killed, and man indiscriminately killed animals for his own ends. "Rather than standing above nature, he too is subject to its laws and powerless in the face of its inexorable workings," which include struggle. Religion and ethics might at times help soften the crasser forms of conflict, "but they will never succeed in abolishing it as one of the driving forces in the world."

For Conrad, the First World War had the same inevitability as "a thunder-cloud inexorably moving toward the moment of discharge." It would have come even without Austria's ultimatum to Serbia. To him "imperialism" was no more than the natural drive of unfolding mass forces, inevitably leading to violent conflict when they encountered resistance, a spectacle that had been repeated in history for millennia.[6] True, all this was hindsight; but similar thoughts un-doubtedly dominated the mind of their author even before the war. In the final decade before 1914 no one advocated preventive war with such impassioned truculence as did Baron Conrad. We shall return to his role later.

Thus there were marked differences in political attitude between the chiefs of the German and Austrian general staffs. This was certainly connected with the fact that Vienna was far less exposed than Berlin to the fearful pressures and responsibilities entailed in a two-front war with its doubtful chance of success. Austria, moreover, was always inclined to overestimate the capacities of its German ally. There was, furthermore, fear of the rapidly progressing internal disintegration of the Hapsburg Empire. War might be the most effective means for reconsolidating a shaky government authority. For the rest, Conrad was by no means alone with his Darwinist theories of war. On the contrary, he was swimming with the tide. This must be borne in mind in any fair assessment of the militarist excesses to be noted in Austrian and German military literature.

This is not the place for a thoroughgoing account of the political ideologies of the time around 1900, the era of imperialism, for which I refer the reader to another of my books.[7] I note here only that Germany was not the only country where people believed in the moral justice of war, in war as destiny, a notion which we have traced in the literature of German idealism and its successors (Volume I, Chapter 8, Part 3). This sentiment was widespread throughout the western world, including America, though it did not set the tone of public opinion elsewhere to the degree that it did in Germany. In the era of the new, overheated, and intensely aggressive colonialism that went by the name of imperialism, political thought took on a highly militant character throughout the world. Political Darwinism was not the only contributory factor. There was the so-called "unmasking" of bourgeois idealism by the Marxist movement with its gospel of the class struggle. The *Lebensraum* theories of militant geopoliticians and economists also played a major role, with their insistence on the need for secure markets and raw-material sources.[8] New schools of philosophy, represented in Germany especially by Nietzsche, glorified the idea of the superman and put their reliance on unerring instinct in place of "cowardly" and vacillating intelligence; and these in turn influenced the political sphere and helped to crowd out humanitarian and pacifist trends.

Reading the political literature of the turn of the century, one sometimes gets the impression that the cultured elements of Europe were tired of the overlong peace and almost yearned for the great and challenging adventure of a new war that was to serve as a "bath of steel" and destroy the comfortable complacency of middle-class life. There were militarists in England and France too, and during the last decades before the First World War, as the international political atmosphere grew more and more inflamed, they gained a wide hearing. The English variant of this movement has lately come to be called "navalism," since its exponents were mainly found among the bumptious admirals, the Navy League enthusiasts, and the followers of Captain Mahan and his doctrine of the role of seapower in history.

Indeed, there is no German militarist catchword that cannot be found widely represented as early as the 1890's in British navalist writings, sometimes in modified, often in very blatant, form. The simile of war's "moral bath of steel" recurs there, as does the Darwinist doctrine of the everlasting struggle among nations and races and the inevitability of impending war. Even the absolute necessity of preventive war to preserve British dominion of the seas by swift and complete destruction of the German fleet without prior warning had its advocates—this threat was heard more or less openly on more than one occasion in public speeches by British sea lords. In the lower reaches of journalism, what is customarily called warmongering was widespread almost everywhere during the last decades of the peace.

On the German side the *Alldeutscher Verband* (Pan-German League) clearly had a major part in sweeping the German people into the imperialist wave of the times. The aims of its foreign policy propaganda remained vague and shifted repeatedly, but the central theme was that Germany was to rise from the status of a mere continental power to that of a "world power." If necessary, the country was to be prepared to fight for this goal. In pursuit of their aims, the Pan-Germans wanted a hard German foreign policy. Non-German elements in the Reich and the Danubian realm were to be "Germanized," and German elements throughout the world were to be supported. A "Greater Germany" was to be created, reaching from Berlin to Baghdad, etc., etc. Many of these projects were half-baked and are scarcely worth discussion, and they found little support among the German middle class. Yet the idea of German ascent to world power did in some measure embody a common dream of the German people, or at least of those Germans who considered themselves nationalist oriented.[9] As to what world power meant, ideas were vague. Moderates like Paul Rohrbach and the historian and publicist Hans Delbrück did not view it so much in terms of acquiring more colonies as in terms of implying a voice in great-power decisions and of economic and cultural influence throughout the world—though certainly not in terms of continental expansion. But imperialism, in whatever guise, always called for a great navy that would, by its mere existence, inspire British respect and protect German overseas trade.

As we shall discuss later, the German navy under the leadership of Tirpitz fanned these imperialist sentiments in Germany and exploited them for purposes of building up a powerful battle fleet. Did the army too foster these imperialist trends?

There were many retired officers in the *Alldeutscher Verband* besides high officials, business leaders, and professors. One prominent member was General Liebert, who had caught the colonial contagion during a term in Africa and drifted into the nationalist movement following his early retirement. In addition to being one of the Pan-Germans, he was active in colonial and naval groups as well as in a Reich League Against Social Democracy, founded in 1904; he was also a Reichstag deputy. He represented an officer type hitherto unknown in traditional Prussian army circles—the general as popular orator and political functionary, who was wooed by political groups because of his high social prestige, and who impressed mass meetings with frowning remarks about civilian failure in the foreign office even more than by hollow patriotic pathos. At bottom he knew nothing about politics.[10]

General Keim could boast of better political training. He had written for the press as a young man, and Caprivi had for a time used him as a propagandist for the army reforms in 1892. He too had left the service early and afterward became the bustling president of the German Navy League. Even Tirpitz's big navy bills did not satisfy him, and there was soon trouble with the Reich navy office, as well as within the league and with the Centrists. Keim ultimately had to resign. He immediately threw himself into other fields. First he founded a youth organization which sought to supplant religious sentiment and humanistic culture with a nationalist outlook. He then became active in the *Alldeutscher Verband* and in a patriotic propaganda group that distributed large printings of pamphlets peddling the views he favored. In 1912 he organized the German Defense Union, which vigorously agitated for army expansion.[11]

Figures of Liebert's and Keim's extreme nationalist and Pan-German stripe certainly had many sympathizers among German officers, even though political busybodies were quite foreign to the traditions of the Prussian army, which loathed the noisy new nationalism with its turbulent mass meetings and imperialist goals. While the German Navy League, despite some quarrels with the naval office, became its semiofficial propaganda agency, General Keim's *Wehrverein* met with resistance and distaste in the Prussian War Ministry, where it was considered a nuisance.[12]

When Major Liebert, recently returned from East Africa, submitted an enthusiastic report on that colony, the new Reich chancellor Caprivi coldly retorted: "But how will you defend East Africa against England?" thoroughly disconcerting the officer.[13] To his press adjutant Major Keim, with whom he had many arguments on the subject, Caprivi repeatedly said: "The less Africa, the better for us!" This shrewd and clear-headed soldier and statesman never allowed himself to be carried away by political fads. Although he had commanded the navy for many years as chief of the admiralty, he was convinced that it could play only a subsidiary role in an emergency and should never be allowed to stand in the way of a *rapprochement* with England. Thoroughly impressed with the risks of a two-front war, he insistently warned against neglecting army expansion in favor of the navy.[14]

On this point Caprivi was in complete agreement with his political opponent Count Waldersee, who in 1889 had his subsequent successor as chief of staff, Count Schlieffen, compile a report, in which the protection of German ports and sealanes was projected as a task for an alliance with British navy and the possibility of accomplishing this mission with German resources alone was not even mentioned.[15] Waldersee opposed colonial expansionism as well. In a confidential letter of 1889, he said that he hoped Germany would soon get rid of Samoa by some reasonable method, and if possible of all of East Africa as well. He entertained profound doubts about the Kaiser's great naval plans—they would only draw British enmity without holding out any real hope that Germany could ever seriously compete with British sea power.[16]

Schlieffen thought along similar lines. He is reported to have looked on a great war fleet as an unproductive luxury.[17] During the Russo-Japanese War he remarked to his quartermaster general, Freiherr von Freytag-Loringhoven, that Kiao-chow could indeed cause one to have sleepless nights. Freytag himself said he never could understand how the Germans could hope to defend their overseas territories in wartime by means of their battle fleet. Freytag also rejected Tirpitz's contention that the German navy should be large enough to pose a serious risk to the British, who would then be deterred from war.[18]

Of course the German General Staff was deeply concerned as it watched the immense cost of naval armament—no less than 59.3 percent of the army budget in 1911—encroach on army expenditures. At a meeting of top government and army men called by the chancellor in 1909, Moltke declared that the German fleet would never be strong enough to wage a naval war against England with any chance of success. Hence, war with England must be avoided at all costs. After the Battle of the Marne, Moltke's World War I successor, General von Falken-hayn, argued bitterly with Tirpitz that but for the navy the Germans would have had two additional army corps at their disposal, the very two which, in the event, had to be shifted from the western front to East Prussia, with disastrous consequences.[19]

That there should have been rivalry between the two services was quite natural. It appears in the armed forces of almost all nations. If the German staff chiefs failed to share the popular naval and colonial enthusiasm, however, it was not so much from jealousy as from their awareness of the heavy responsibilities that a two-front war would bring to them. An added factor was that the conservative old Prussian gentry, with its close connections with the officers' corps, followed the new trend of the times only hesitantly, harboring a certain distrust of the new influx of middle-class naval officers.

In summary, let us fix in our minds that the General Staff and the war ministry, the army agencies with the greatest responsibility, had no discernible share in the imperialist wave, the colonial ardor, and the naval enthusiasm of the pre-war decades. Of course this does not gainsay the fact that certain generals and General Staff officers were indeed swayed by these trends.

There was Colmar Freiherr von der Goltz, for example, an enormously talented soldier and writer whom William II disliked so intensely that his gifts were never fully exploited in Germany. Entrusted with the job of reorganizing the Turkish army, von der Goltz seems to have drifted into a pseudoromantic imperialism. As early as 1899 his correspondence contains remarks about England that are entirely in the style of the German Navy League, together with fanciful ideas about an occupation of Egypt by Turkish troops under German leadership and an advance on India to break British world dominion. There is even talk of German troops landing in the British Isles, in league with Holland.

These were dreams rather than serious plans, yet they do illuminate the writer's basic political orientation; and in a comprehensive exposé of 1899 he hinted that he was not unsympathetic to the idea of a strong navy capable of taking the offensive.[20] Nor does von der Goltz seem to have been a stranger to the idea of preventive war. As early as 1886, in a letter to Waldersee, he spoke of the "overlong peace" and of the "need" for a prompt war. The editors of his memoirs say that during the Morocco crisis of 1905 and the Balkan crisis of 1908-1909 he desired a military rather than a diplomatic solution. In a confidential letter of 1908 he expressed the hope that the German people would at last become convinced that even in a war with England they would, because of their superior manpower resources, "ultimately emerge victorious, if the war were waged long enough."[21]

In a brilliantly written essay published in the spring of 1900 and intended to give support to Tirpitz's second great navy bill, von der Goltz tried to make this view plausible to a wider audience. Even a German landing in England, he declared, was not altogether impossible. Essentially, he advanced the same historical, economic, and political arguments habitually put forward by the German Navy League to justify the need for a German naval presence beside England's.[22] On occasion, Treitschke's philosophy of war is echoed in his letters. In one instance, in 1908, he wrote: "I have two principal recommendations for restoring a state of health to the German nation. First of all, it should engage in a bitter and protracted struggle for survival. This would then necessarily bring about a return to the simple circumstances of our fathers."[23]

Taken out of context, this sounds alarming today, but it must be understood primarily as an expression of a Spartan approach to life rather than warmongering. Indeed, von der Goltz made his more extreme utterances only before a circle of intimate friends. In its later editions, his most popular book, *Das Volk in Waffen (Nation in Arms),* intended as an exhortation to militant thought, steers quite clear of glorifying war and wandering off into politics. Nor did von der Goltz share the illusion of many of his contemporaries who thought the coming war would be as brief as Bismarck's Wars of Unification. On the contrary, he projected it as a war of annihilation, waged over many years by armies running into the millions, with terrible destructive power.

Much more dubious in a political sense was the work of another literary general who also filled a major post in the General Staff for a time—Friedrich von Bernhardi. His writings have played such an uncommonly prominent role in the war guilt debate that we must here deal with them at length.

Bernhardi was certainly not mediocre—indeed, he can be described as a rare exception among German generals. He was the son of the most important military writer of the Bismarck era, Theodor von Bernhardi, whose several volumes of fascinating diaries he edited. He had soon developed his own literary ambitions and, also like his father, a vigorous interest in politics. He widened his horizons by world travel, and his writings show a more than ordinary measure of historical knowledge and literary sophistication as well as much military expertise. During his career as a soldier he was full of reformist ideas which were usually considered "off beat" and in any event brought no practical results. As head of the General Staff's historical section from 1898 on, he was extraordinarily enterprising, hard working, and productive, but he soon ran afoul of Schlieffen, who found him too radical in his endeavors to substitute ruthlessly critical studies for the traditional style of war history that cast a harmonious and patriotic patina over everything.

The result was that Bernhardi was prematurely transferred to a line command, with no effort made to preserve the amenities. He never returned to the General Staff. A proud and stubborn man, he subsequently repaid his former chief by subjecting his tactical and strategic principles to outspoken criticism, heedless of the Schlieffen myth of infallibility among the top generals. His critique, objective and not to be ignored,[24] took the form of a two-volume work, *Vom Heutigen Krieg (Present-Day Warfare),* that aspired to replace Clausewitz's theory of war never carried to completion and to adapt it to modern conditions.

Bernhardi finished it in 1911, two years after retiring from the army. Well informed and even brilliant, though discursive, it was based on studies he had begun while still a member of the General Staff. It is essentially a technical work, and Bernhardi clearly consulted many specialists. His chapter entitled "The Influence of Politics on Warfare" echoes the views of the Moltke school, with which we are already familiar, but it does so in greatly moderated form, clearly in an effort to do justice to the statesman's claims to influencing the conduct of war.[25]

Originally the technical portions of the work were embedded in a political and historical study. At the request of the military publishing house of Mittler, the latter was lifted out and published in 1912 by another publisher, Cotta, as a separate book called *Germany and the Next War.* This book became a best seller and a political disaster. It went into seven editions in a few years and was translated into virtually all the major languages, including Japanese: no other book ever did so much harm to the reputation of the German General Staff. The fact that it was written in a purely private capacity by an outsider not in the General Staff's good graces was completely ignored. It was cited on countless occasions as proof that the German General Staff was systematically fostering war, with the aim of making Germany the principal power in the world.

Actually Bernhardi had given much earlier evidence of his political immaturity. In 1890, while still a captain in the uhlans, he had published an anonymous pamphlet, *Videant Consules, ne quid Respublica Detrimenti Capiat! (Let the Consuls See to It That No Harm Befall the State*–a traditional instruction by the Roman Senate). This tract challenged the new chancellor, Caprivi, to relinquish Bismarck's ingrained distaste for preventive war and do nothing less than attack the formative Franco-Russian coalition before the two countries could further advance their armaments. In the long run, it contended, such a war was unavoidable; and a peace policy as such must be regarded as the root of all evil.[26]

Bernhardi was doing no more than voicing the views of Count Waldersee, who was then chief of staff and with whom he was on the closest of terms. In Bernhardi's view, Waldersee was Bismarck's logical successor, destined to become Germany's savior; and Bernhardi shared Waldersee's opposition to Caprivi's reasoned and moderate policies at home and abroad, an opposition common to other General Staff officers.

His 1912 book did not pose so open and direct a challenge, though it was written at a time when the author had been driven into vehement opposition to the government's "shameful peace policy."[27] In typically journalistic fashion, Bernhardi stuck for the most part to vague generalities. His aim seems to have been on the one hand to defend the justice and necessity of war against the pacifist trends of the day, and on the other hand to exhort the German nation to put forward every possible military effort, at the time of the second Morocco crisis and the open threats of Lloyd George.[28]

The right to wage a preventive war was argued purely theoretically. Such a war should be embarked upon only when the chances would seem particularly favorable or when war threatened directly; but Bernhardi's examination of the world situation as of 1911 concluded that the external circumstances were highly unfavorable, and he gave a particularly gloomy view of the prospects of a naval war with England. He foresaw quite correctly that England would put a broad blockade into effect, against which Germany would be virtually powerless. This, however, was not to preclude an aggressive naval policy and the building of a huge war fleet.

Bernhardi's main postulate was an aggressive foreign policy that would secure for German supremacy in Europe—abolishing the obsolete "balance of power"—as well as an entirely new "world stature," if necessary at the risk of war. Just how this was to be done and what Germany's precise stature was to be Bernhardi never made clear. He speaks in turn of German moral leadership in the world, to be safeguarded by political means; of a new Middle Europe under German dominion; of "decisive political influence" on Germany's markets; of new *Lebensraum* needed for Germany's rapidly growing population. Yet Bernhardi almost immediately adds that there is no more free *Lebensraum* in Europe, nor for that matter in the eastern regions, and that expansion of Germany's African colonies would not help the population pressure.

There is extremely blunt talk about the need for crushing French power once and for all, something that actually should have been done long before, in order to protect Germany's rear for the pursuit of world aims; yet in the context of such plans it is England that turns out to be the archenemy. On the question of

Belgian neutrality Bernhardi expresses himself contemptuously—it had long become a mere shadow and no longer had any semblance of authority since Belgium's acquisition of the Congo. Besides, permanent neutrality really flew in the face of the inherent nature of the state and must, in a sense, be regarded as immoral. In the face of German war contingencies it should not constitute any more of a barrier than the similarly mistaken principle of nonintervention in the domestic affairs of another country. Law was not a superhuman reality but an arbitrary device of man's intellect. It had a different aspect for every nation, and treaties were valid only insofar as they coincided with national self-interest.

In sum, war must be neither shunned nor delayed when it became necessary. The most important need of the moment was the highest possible level of armaments, on land as on sea. Germany must put forward a supreme effort to be ready to strike at any moment, not, at bottom, because there was a direct external threat of war—which was acknowledged, but is not at the heart of Bernhardi's reflections—but for the sake of an extremely ill-defined goal of enhanced German power. "World power or decline" was the catchword; and once the hour of war had come, a situation unequivocally favorable to the deployment of the German armies had to be created immediately. This meant that the western powers must on their part be compelled to attack, by means of some form of political action in Europe or even in Africa, thus allowing Germany to take the immediate offensive without inviting the odium of aggression. How to achieve this was a matter for diplomacy to consider.

These thoughts cannot be disposed of simply as the notions of an extreme outsider. Too many of them recur in the military writings of the First World War, especially from Ludendorff's circle; and that is the reason why they had to be set forth here. The political mentality that speaks from this book has symptomatic value, rather than its details. It is the first comprehensive expression of the militarist orientation, i.e., of a spirit of militancy that begins to reach out from the purely military sphere—where it enjoys a certain legitimacy—into the political arena, in deliberate and direct pursuit of political aims. Bernhardi expressly demanded that the entire German educational system be reorganized along the lines of his program. He regarded the Germans as far too peaceable and legalistic, and these traits were to be methodically expunged, so that the nation would at last stand ready to discern its historic mission in the world and achieve it in a life-and-death struggle.

To the world at large the terrifying thing about this book was the way it leaped over the restraints of international law in its dynamic assertion of political power. Every possible idea and argument in favor of militant patriotism which had been voiced in Germany over the past century was here rounded up, from Schiller's reflections on German grandeur and the freedom fighters around Arndt and Stein to the political philosophy of the German idealists and their successors, already discussed in the first volume of this work (Chapter 8, Part 3).

One of the central authorities cited by Bernhardi was Heinrich von Treitschke, especially his lectures on politics with their paeans in praise of war as the nations' moral taskmaster. These sentiments were inflated to the point that peace appeared almost as a state of depravity and a statesman's stature was measured by his willingness and courage to strike in time, even without the certainty of success, indeed sometimes merely for the sake of honor! The lofty idealism of German political liberalism, which saw man fully realized only in voluntary dedication to the whole of society, was naively coupled with Nietzsche's philosophy of power and the Darwinist doctrines of the struggle for existence and the survival of the fittest. War was no longer the school of true morality but a "biological necessity," a salutary purge of inferior elements. The biologists were not the only authorities cited. Goethe was occasionally summoned as a star witness; and together with materialist arguments even Christian doctrine was invoked.

All in all, a whole compendium of German war philosophy was here assembled for the reader, declaimed not with the crass and naive brutality of the Pan-German pamphleteers, but with undeniable literary skill and the inflections of a man of culture. Small wonder that this book did so much to confirm the impression abroad that the German mind was giving way more and more to innate instincts of pugnacity, that under Prussian influence the nation which had given birth to a Goethe had ardently embraced the cult of militarism, a notion which is far from extinct even today. Bernhardi's books may be regarded as the classic example of a brand of German dogmatism that swallowed a theoretical principle whole without paying the slightest attention to its dangers when it is driven to excess. Later on Bernhardi himself in all seriousness put forward the excuse that he could not have dreamed of the effect his book would have abroad.[29]

I have no idea how the top generals in Germany reacted to the book, but I do know that after its publication Bernhardi received an order-in-council which "could not have been more sharply worded."[30] Undoubtedly the attitude of Bernhardi's former colleagues was influenced by the confidence with which they themselves viewed the chances of victory in a coming war. The younger Moltke, then chief of staff, had little such confidence, and he called Bernhardi a "perfect dreamer." When Freiherr von Freytag-Loringhoven, a member of Moltke's staff, tried to dispel his chief's doubts of the prospects of victory in a three-front war with encouraging words, Moltke replied: "You may believe me, *viele Hunde sind des Hasen Tod*" (many dogs are the hare's death). To Freytag-Loringhoven's mind such inner uncertainty smacked of a pacifism unseemly in a soldier. Yet his own memoirs show quite clearly that he himself was deeply worried.[31] To have simply ignored these doubts might have been "soldierly," but in a man who understood Germany's true situation as well as the uncertainties inherent in all the supposedly foolproof recipes for victory, it would have been unconscionable rather than valorous. Optimism alone, no matter how firmly held, is a poor foundation for aggressive designs. The over-all attitude of the General Staff on the problem of war is perhaps best characterized in these words from a General Staff study of 1902: "We are not out for conquest, but seek merely to defend what is ours. We shall probably never be the aggressors, always the attacked. The swift successes we shall need, however, can be achieved with certainty only when we take the offensive."[32]

7

Military and Civilian Authority Under the German Empire

THE HISTORY of the second German empire is a classic example of how little constitutional forms as such mean as against the powerful drives and ideological trends that set the pattern of political reality within the state. Bismarck's empire had arisen on the basis of a military monarchy with a soldier pure and simple as its ruler. That ruler's first minister had been summoned for the express mission of guarding the sovereign's unlimited power over the army against the encroachments of the people's representatives. To the end of his tenure the confidence he enjoyed rested on his jealous and unrelenting defense of the crown's privileged command power, and we shall soon see that for the sake of that prerogative he relinquished not only formal authority over the central military agencies but their firm integration as well. Considered purely in organizational terms, the German army was even in Bismarck's time a state within the state. Yet so long as he was at the helm, civilian preponderance over the military was never seriously in question. It was he alone who set the political course of the ship of state, even in arms matters and military understandings with Germany's allies. So long as William I was alive, at least, no willful military leader was able to challenge the chancellor's authority, not even the restless and ambitious chief of staff Waldersee, who attained passing political influence only after William II ascended the throne.[1]

There were no major changes in army organization and the constitutional position of the chancellor under Bismarck's successors, but the political climate did at once change, with an abrupt emergence of the weaknesses inherent in an unsystematic constitution tailored preponderantly to Bismarck's personal power needs and the political docility of his "old man." The fateful flaw that came to full light in the course of the First World War had actually been foreshadowed long before: the constitution did not confer on the political authority a preponderance over the military sufficient to keep the army in a state of dependence and to make possible an autonomous course, free of militarist influence.

This changed under the Weimar Republic, in which the armed forces were formally placed under civilian jurisdiction, in the persons of the war minister and the Reich president. The army seemed totally shut off, after the disaster of 1918, from regaining any influence on the course of German policy—its only possible role was to serve as a shield to the republican government. Yet this strict constitutional integration did not enlist the allegiance of the army to the republic. Indeed, in the great crisis of 1932-1933, the army had become virtually useless to the government as an instrument to be employed in the event of civil war.

Subsequently Hitler, the dictator, did make the army abjectly dependent on civilian authority, in both the constitutional and the political sense rigidly centralizing military control in his own hands to a degree Germany had never seen before. But since Hitler, nominally a civilian, was actually the arch-militarist incarnate, the life of Germany was militarized through and through in the utmost measure, and German policy took on a radically aggressive character beyond the dreams of even the Prussian soldier kings.

These observations should teach us not to overestimate the importance of constitutional and organizational forms in the life of the state. On the other hand, neither must they be underestimated. Few will doubt, in particular, that the peculiar army system Bismarck left to his successors even further limited their already narrow scope for political maneuver, while they dangerously fostered William II's autocratic propensities. Already possessed of a military command power no minister could touch, the Kaiser felt himself qualified and entitled to exercise a similar power in political questions. This delayed unduly the process of codifying personal rulership, inevitable in a modern state with its growing complexities. In a military sense too much mischief was done by the fiction of the soldier king, the *roi connétable,* with which we are already familiar and which persisted into the twentieth century.

Even in Manteuffel's and Roon's day, resistance to any interposition of a minister responsible to Parliament between the king as supreme warlord and his army had prevented integration of the Prussian war ministry into a central military authority combining every aspect of command and administration, as had happened everywhere else (see Volume I, Chapters 7 and 8). Military cabinet and General Staff had developed into independent organs of the royal command power, limiting the war ministry more and more to purely administrative tasks, a process which continued into the second empire—indeed, with Bismarck's support. In 1883, when War Minister von Kameke showed himself willing to make certain concessions to the Reichstag in the matter of local tax exemption for officers in return for a military pension law, Bismarck proceeded against him with unexampled vigor. The war minister was averse to countering parliamentary demands with blustering threats and invocations of the sovereign's unlimited command power. Bismarck, in a direct report to the king-emperor, accused von Kameke of pusillanimity and compromise. Since von Kameke was himself a general on active duty, Bismarck said, he did not have the right of an English civilian minister to "bargain for parliamentary favors," certainly not without the chancellor's prior knowledge. "A parliamentary general on active duty always cuts an un-Prussian figure, and a dangerous one when he is war minister. This forebodes a future in which the monarchial traditions of our army will be slowly but surely eroded."[2]

This sounds like a return to the fighting mood of the great army controversy. Taken literally, it meant depriving the war minister of all political autonomy, turning him into a mere watchdog of the imperial command power, and almost reversing his accountability to the Reichstag. This was something von Kameke could not possibly have accepted, and he at once submitted his resignation, which was accepted. His fall had, indeed, been carefully planned by Waldersee, then Moltke's deputy in the General Staff, and by Albedyll, since 1871 chief of the military cabinet and a faithful disciple of Manteuffel. In this way they secured an even greater detachment of their agencies from the war ministry and recognition of them as formal coordinates with direct access to the sovereign, a situation which von Kameke's successor, Paul Bronsart von Schellendorf, was required to acknowledge even before he was appointed.[3] Albedyll, unlike his predecessor von Tresckow, had tried for years to expand the powers of his office and to limit the war ministry's claim to the right of countersigning imperial rescripts. Bismarck vigorously supported this endeavor, too, and in 1885 he obtained a ruling that only orders affecting the army budget required a ministerial countersignature.[4]

It would be wrong to conclude that in military matters Bismarck was simply lapsing back into an absolutist approach. Directly after von Kameke's dismissal he advised Albedyll on one occasion that "the war minister is no longer a general subordinate to His Majesty, as was true before the constitution came into force," but an official accountable to Parliament.[5] Thus this parliamentary accountability of the war minister was not simply swept aside; and even after von Kameke's fall, incumbents steadfastly declined to invoke the principle of military obedience and ignore their parliamentary responsibilities.[6] Yet Bismarck was quite willing to use the war minister as an instrument and means for limiting the priviliges of the Reichstag as sharply as possible, with the help of the military command power.[7] When von Kameke resisted playing this role, as did Stosch, chief of the admiralty, Bismarck dropped both of them in 1883. He did not stop to consider that no constitutional minister, no man of character, could have fallen in with his designs. Bismarck was not greatly concerned over the everlasting jurisdictional disputes between the War Ministry and the military cabinet. Nor was he particularly worried that the military cabinet might become too powerful through the elimination of ministerial countersignature which he had engineered. Edwin von Manteuffel, after all, had already been sidetracked.

Bismarck, in other words, was willing to leave the broad and ill-defined area of royal command power to the emperor—which meant, in effect, to the military cabinet and the General Staff. On the other hand, he was all the more intent on bringing the war ministry under his control as an administrative agency, even though it carried little political weight. Within the framework of the Prussian constitution, the war minister occupied a privileged position among his colleagues, as we have already seen (Volume I, pp. 177ff.). He had direct access to the king without going through the minister president, which compelled the latter to tread carefully and removed the army from his political control. Bismarck tried to remedy this state of affairs in the Reich constitution. Military affairs had become a Reich concern, yet there was no Reich war minister, since the Reich army consisted of troop contingents from the constituent federal states, some of which had their own war ministers. As Prussian war minister, Roon had to look after Reich military administration, but he tried in vain to achieve the title of Reich war minister. Bismarck would not hear of it and continued to be firmly attached to the principle of remaining the sole Reich minister accountable to the Reichstag. Roon became Prussia's plenipotentiary in the federal council and chairman of its military affairs committee; and it was in this capacity that he appeared before the Reichstag, where he had to stand up to questioning and sometimes criticism, without really being accountable to the Reichstag. That political responsibility was borne by the chancellor alone, and Bismarck used this as the basis for sweeping powers. He regarded himself as chief of the Reich administration for the land forces, and even more so of the navy, which was a Reich institution in the first place, rather than Prussian.

However, he was not able to get the Prussian war minister under his thumb in the way that the chief of naval administration, as a minister, was his subordinate and deputy. What Bismarck did do was to keep his position of pre-eminence alive in the minds of successive Prussian war ministers by occasional but deliberate intervention in administrative details, down to the improvement of infantry and artillery weapons, the fixing of allowances for mounted officers, and questions of appointment and promotion.[8] Since the army budget was a Reich matter, Bismarck, in his capacity as Reich minister of finance, was able to keep the military administrative authorities in a state of dependence.

Despite all this, it must be said that in Bismarck's Reich there was no strong and clear-cut political leadership, superimposed on the military; nor was there a truly unified military high command, nor a combined central agency in which military and civilian authority collaborated in methodical war preparations. It is true, however, that the initial friction between the military cabinet and the war ministry gradually ceased, when the ministry, following a rapid succession of several incumbents under William II, became reconciled to being merely an administrative agency in the narrower sense.

Who, then, had responsibility for over-all military planning, beyond the handling of current business? It was not the war minister, who had become a mere auxiliary of the chancellor, who was left out of the secret plans of the General Staff and was able to gain the emperor's ear far less frequently than the chief of the military cabinet. In the matter of actual field service, too, the war minister had little influence, for the commanding generals and inspectors general of the various branches were not subordinate to him but were directly under the sovereign. As for the navy, the war minister had nothing whatever to do with it.

The General Staff, for its part, did not function as a central agency either. In peacetime its authority was strictly limited to strategic plans and exercises, the training of General Staff officers, the collection and evaluation of military intelligence from abroad, and, lastly, historical studies. Until almost the eve of the First World War, such war ministers as von Einem and von Herringen were jealously intent on gaining priority over the chief of staff in arms matters.[9] As for the head of the military cabinet, he was even less suited to bear a heavy political as well as military responsibility—he was a courtier general whose technical jurisdiction was essentially limited to matters of personnel in the broader sense.

Yet by Prussian military tradition, the head of the military cabinet was much closer to the throne than any of the others. He functioned as a means of liaison with all the highest echelons of the army. He was able to exert considerable influence on major military and political decisions when the sovereign, as happened repeatedly, proved incapable of filling the role assigned to him under the constitution—the rule of supreme warlord, living focus of every branch of the armed services and source of the crucial initiatives. William II was certainly not able to play this part. Restless and constantly on the go or absorbed in festivities, he had no time for serious and sustained work. He remained, furthermore, an amateur in military matters, or at best a semiprofessional.

In other words, the independent command power, with its immunity from ministerial intervention, which Bismarck did so much to preserve, contributed little or nothing to the unification of military leadership. On the contrary, it led to a mere juxtaposition of numerous agencies with direct access to the sovereign and without any clear hierarchical order. The unresolved differences between command and administrative affairs continued to beget friction and confusion. In 1873, Bismarck fleetingly considered creating a federal war office or national General Staff, but regrettably nothing came of these plans.[10] It might indeed have become the central agency—provided, of course, the Kaiser had left to it the practical exercise of his command power.

General Verdy du Vermois developed a similar plan in 1889. He would have limited the military cabinet to pure personnel matters, while expanding the General Staff into a "staff of the high command," to which would have fallen "all command matters relating to army training and operational preparations." The war ministry would have been limited to administrative, government, and parliamentary affairs; in other words, it was to secure the necessary appropriations, with the help of the Reichstag.[11] Although Verdy became war minister himself soon afterward, this plan was never seriously discussed.

It was only for the navy that a high command had been created as early as 1859, understandably enough, since in this area the king's personal leadership could not be maintained even as a fiction. The fleet, moreover, was quite small at the time. Yet there was soon friction between this naval high command and the war ministry, which had administrative charge of the navy. Hence, in 1870 Bismarck combined naval administration and command in a newly created navy ministry, styled "Imperial Admiralty" beginning in 1872, and administratively under the chancellor.

One of William II's first acts was to destroy this unity. In 1889 command was again severed from administration and placed directly under the Kaiser. The administrative portion, now called the "State Secretariat of the Navy," was even more narrowly circumscribed than the former navy ministry, although in the naval sphere command and administration are particularly hard to separate. In justifying the change to the Reichstag, Bismarck once again sharply emphasized the need for a command power high above all parliamentary influence. "I regard any intervention by the Reich chancellor in the command of army and navy as something to be scrupulously avoided, since the chancellor is always in a certain state of dependence on the Reichstag, and any Reichstag intervention in command matters would pose a grave danger to the state."[12]

This meant virtual abdiction of civilian authority in the most important military matters; and William II promptly expanded the scope of his personal rule by creating a naval cabinet on the model of the military cabinet. Count Philipp Eulenburg, William II's favorite, describes Admiral von Senden-Bibran, summoned to head the naval cabinet, as a man of rather limited outlook, though a staunch supporter of naval armament. He too proved unable to steer a clear and consistent course in matters of naval policy.

In Tirpitz's judgment the ensuing years, until he took charge of the naval secretariat in 1897, were a period of utter aimlessness, with the naval agencies constantly bickering among themselves. To end this and strengthen his own office, Tirpitz supported the endeavors of the Kaiser—whom he knew to be very dependent on him—to expand his personal rule even further, eliminating all intermediate stages between himself and the naval line commands, as with the army. "Your Majesty is now in a position to be his own admiral," he remarked to William II in 1899.

The naval high command was dissolved, and nothing was left of it but an "admiralty staff" with very limited powers. The Kaiser declared himself commander-in-chief and granted direct access to a whole series of command authorities—the chiefs of the two naval stations in the North Sea and the Baltic, the inspector of training, the commanders of the first and the cruiser squadrons, and the newly appointed inspector general of the navy. The result in the technical chain of command was chaos, as experienced and bitterly lamented by Tirpitz himself in the First World War. What happened in practice was that here too the power of the cabinet chief was inordinately enhanced, in fact often almost absolute, since the Kaiser, generally speaking, lacked sufficient experience and technical knowledge in naval matters to make decisions on his own.

In the army sphere the results of personal rule by the emperor were probably not quite so unfavorable. In wartime, at any rate, it was of virtually no importance, since from the first day the Imperial General Staff became the sole source of leadership that mattered, while the military cabinet was restricted to personnel matters and the war ministry turned into a mere auxiliary of the supreme command—the Kaiser becoming virtually isolated from all operational decisions. In all fairness, it must be conceded that there were important advantages in excluding civilian authority, and especially parliamentary influence, from the sphere of imperial command power, as we have already seen from a comparison with other European countries. In Germany the military technicians suffered far less interference with their work from captious civilian demands and intervention; but this gain exacted a price.

The first and foremost failure stemming from the German army's self-imposed isolation has already been mentioned. The point of total planning for war was never reached. Unlike the defense councils in other western countries, Germany's top military and political agencies never got together. Diplomats and generals, economic and military agencies—indeed, even the army and navy themselves—had no opportunity to adjust and harmonize their plans. In the second chapter following, we shall consider the devastating effects to which this led, in strategic planning as well as in armaments and preparations for economic warfare.

The second baneful factor was the profound alienation of the German officer class from the nation's political life. We know, of course, that professional soldiers are prone to inveigh against party politics and parliamentary chatter in other countries as well, to suspect the anti-authoritarian and often antimilitarist and pacifist sentiments of the leftist parties. We have traced this especially in the case of France. Naturally these attitudes are even more intense under a monarchy. Still, it was a great misfortune that the basic differences dating back to the crisis period of 1862-1866 were never reconciled, that, indeed, they were intensified under William II, with increasing industrialization and the sweeping rise in the numbers of social democratic voters.

The Kaiser himself, disappointed over the failure of his initial welfare policies, resorted to shortsighted devices. Of recruits newly sworn in he demanded that, if need be, they must fire on their own parents. He berated the Reichstag deputies as a "rabble without a country"; in his Königsberg proclamation of 1893 he warned of the danger of "rebellion." All this made the army appear to the socialist masses once again in the light of a monarchial bodyguard meant to combat the "internal enemy." Reading the memoirs of War Minister von Einem, for example, one cannot help being startled at the total lack of understanding of the need for parliamentary review of army deficiencies.

The soldiers acknowledged only reluctantly, if at all, that the German parliamentarians and their constituencies actually were prepared to make sacrifices for genuine military needs—if only their power of the purse was respected. In military circles only the militant and nationalist parties of the right, drawn from the upper middle class and the conservative gentry, were considered acceptable. The left was regarded with a hatred which naturally engendered hatred in return. Thus the conflict between militarists and antimilitarists exacerbated the natural hostility between right and left in Germany to a far greater degree than elsewhere. Ultimately this enmity developed into a chasm that was to yawn open until the end of the Weimar Republic, dangerously disrupting the entire life of the nation.

A third parlous element was the overemphasis on the natural differences between soldiers and civilians. As the officer class was increasingly pervaded with the spirit of being under the direct and exclusive command of "His Majesty" and of constituting his personal paladins, it was more and more alienated from civilian life. Officers felt very little allegiance to the citizenry as a whole. Whoever earned the privilege of wearing the king's colorful uniform seemed to belong to another and higher world. The Kaiser himself never got beyond the kind of political ideology that was traditional in the casinos of the Potsdam guards regiments. "I have never read the constitution and don't know anything about it," he is supposed to have said on one occasion.[13] Accordingly, he viewed irksome decisions by his government as a form of insubordination.[14] When Reich chancellor Hohenlohe advised him in 1896 that the government would probably accept constitutional responsibility for changes in the code of military justice which the Kaiser desired, he added this note at the bottom of the letter: "The government has nothing whatever to do with the army and its internal affairs, which the constitution expressly reserves to the king as his exclusive sphere. Hence the government is in no position to assume any constitutional responsibility for the army I command."[15] Under this concept "civilians" had no voice at all in military matters.

After Bismarck's fall there never again was a Reich chancellor of truly commanding stature, and the almost purely military background against which the Kaiser's daily life unfolded turned into a political menace. One of his first government acts was to combine his entire *maison militaire*, his entourage of adjutants and generals *à la suite* and the chief of the military cabinet, into a peacetime "imperial headquarters" under the command of a general. This was apparently the outgrowth of a desire to present a solid front to the influence of civilian advisers at court. The appointment calendar kept by the new head-quarters commandant beginning in 1889 is heavily weighted on the side of direct reports from the military. The Reich chancellor does not appear on the list at all, perhaps because his audiences took place irregularly and usually on Saturdays. The chief of the civilian cabinet appears only twice, military repre-sentatives eight times.[16] Among the latter, the war minister appears once. The Kaiser, however, usually asked the war minister to submit written reports, to be presented through the chief of the military cabinet.[17]

William II actually prevailed with this "government from the cabinet," in the style of Prussian absolutism before Stein's reforms, even toward his civilian ministers. Apart from the Reich chancellor, he seldom received them more than once a year—on the occasion of the naval review at Kiel—and he had their current submissions processed and presented by the chief of the civilian cabinet. His military entourage surrounded him like a dense cloud. Within this circle he could always find an eager echo to his political tirades, his arrogant and imperious airs. The Kaiser's countless marginalia on official documents clearly reflect the aggressive and vulgar style of political discussion at court and the condescension with which the "spineless civilians" in the diplomatic service were regarded. In contrast to his imperial predecessors, William II never showed the slightest respect for the objective achievements and official dignity of his ministers.

As early as the 1890's there were frequent charges of a military kitchen cabinet, voiced in the press as well as in more intimate circles. There were worried reminders of Frederic William IV's "camarilla." By and large such fears were certainly exaggerated. Most of these officers and adjutants came from the isolation of garrison life, having grown up in the exclusive atmosphere of the officer class. They did not have the deep political interest that had once inspired the Gerlachs to a consistent course of action. They also lacked political experience and knowledge, and their intellectual caliber was not very high— although William II was prone to view every guards officer as the "quintessence of good manners, culture, and intelligence" and to look on his personal adjutants as members of an elite.[18] Still, at certain critical moments, the influence of politically irresponsible soldiers on the Kaiser's decisions does become discernible, especially when army or navy interest were directly touched.

The most dangerous of these personages, in a political sense, was Count Waldersee, until 1888 quartermaster general, then chief of staff. We have already dealt with his effort, in 1887, to whip the aged Moltke into a preventive war against Russia, and with him the whole policy of the Reich (Volume I, pp.

233ff.). A firm military understanding was even to be reached with the Austrian General Staff on such an undertaking, but the entire plan failed because of Bismarck's steadfast calm.

Waldersee's restless ambition then drove him to exploit the position of close personal trust he had meanwhile gained with William II for purposes of toppling the aged chancellor. He was not entirely without hope that he himself might become Bismarck's successor. The intrigues he hatched toward this end with Baron Holstein and other enemies of Bismarck are too well known to be set forth at length here. At the last critical moment, certain consular reports from Russia are known to have played a part. They supplied the Kaiser with a pretext for the almost hysterical charge that Bismarck was withholding from him vital information pointing to an impending Russian attack.

It would scarcely have occurred to the Kaiser to inflate these rather harmless reports to such an extent, had not Waldersee been making similar accusations for many months, on the basis of other Russian intelligence material.[19] This was a political trick Waldersee used repeatedly. He would fill the Kaiser's ears with alarmist reports from abroad, thereby seeking to convince him that his official diplomats were incompetent and that he must strengthen his ties with the General Staff, which was so much better informed and more clear-headed. Like his Austrian colleague Conrad von Hötzendorf later on, Waldersee maintained a lively correspondence with the German military attachés in the principal European capitals—Paris, Rome, Vienna, St. Petersburg. These were hand-picked young General Staff officers whose job it was to support the work of the ambassador in question by gathering appropriate military intelligence. Naturally they were intent on gaining the confidence of the chief of staff. As soldiers they were conditioned to regard any arms measures abroad as a direct threat to Germany, and what they reported was likely to be what the chief of staff wanted to hear.

All German military attachés were required to submit their reports to the head of the diplomatic mission to which they were assigned. The ambassador would annotate them if he saw fit and dispatch them by courier to the foreign ministry in Berlin, whence they might be passed on to the military cabinet, the war ministry, or the General Staff, as the case might be. Waldersee circumvented this irksome diplomatic control by means of private correspondence, in which he actually encouraged the attachés to voice criticisms of their diplomatic superiors. He proposed that the Kaiser place these attachés under his direct control, without the interposition of the aged chancellor, and as a beginning conduct a direct political correspondence with von Deines in Vienna and von Huene in Paris, who were also aides-de-camp to the Kaiser. This would make him independent of the political monopoly the two Bismarcks, father and son, had established. The Kaiser, Waldersee argued, should always listen to several advisers side by side and carefully distinguish between them. Undoubtedly the reports of the military attachés were far better and more reliable than those of the professional diplomats who wrote only what their doddering chief wanted to hear.

Under the elder Moltke there had never been such conflicts between civilian and military reporting. Bismarck had always regarded the reports from the military attachés as valuable additions to those of his diplomats. Occasionally he had even asked them for their political impressions, though they were in principle strictly limited to the military sphere. He set special store by the reports of the "military plenipotentiary" at the czarist court, who traditionally occupied a special position among the diplomats. At critical times he was not content with the general military situation reports of the General Staff, but demanded precise data on the potential enemy's troop strength, garrison locations, railway lines, etc. As the statesman in charge, he had at his disposal the complete machinery of military diplomacy.

All this changed the moment Waldersee officially succeeded Moltke. In the spring of 1889, Bismarck seems to have begun to grow suspicious of the political machinations of the military attachés. In any event, he suddenly tightened foreign office superivision. The military attaché in Berne was to receive new instructions under which even his reports on purely technical military matters would have come under diplomatic control. His military assignments were to be issued by way of the foreign ministry. The war minister objected, and there was a compromise; but the chancellor reserved the right to have the foreign ministry issue a new general directive for all the military attachés. This initiative met with vehement opposition from Waldersee, who now found it intolerable that any Prussian officer should have a civilian superior. The naval high command also voiced serious reservations. It insisted that naval attachés had heretofore been briefed solely by military authorities with whom they were in direct correspondence over many matters.

This was in the autumn of 1889. Even then Bismarck's power was no longer what it had been, and this may have been the reason he never got around to putting the new directive into effect. Soon after his fall, his successor, General Caprivi, returned to the problem of the military attachés, not at all in the spirit of his former professional colleagues, but as a statesman, following in Bismarck's footsteps. A general directive of June 20, 1890, sought to stem the political zeal of the military attachés by requiring them to communicate all their political intelligence orally to the chief of mission, while their military reports were placed under tighter diplomatic control. In December the expanded directive envisaged by Bismarck was issued, in coordination with the war ministry and the General Staff. It definitively subordinated the military attachés to the chiefs of mission and subjected all their reports to diplomatic supervision, in the Bismarckian tradition. This general directive of December 11, 1890, remained in force until the end of the monarchy, except that in 1900

Bülow, the courtier, made the Kaiser in person the direct superior of the attachés in place of their local military authorities, requiring their reports also to be addressed to him.

That William II approved this directive may be viewed as a victory by Caprivi over Waldersee. The impassioned struggle waged against it by the chief of staff may be traced in a series of petitions and memoranda which are among the most impressive testimonials to the militaristic caste spirit then prevalent in the officers' corps.[20]

Waldersee's attitude, however, must be considered an extreme case. When he protested heatedly to the draft of the directive, General von Hahnke, head of the military cabinet, replied dryly that he "must agree with Caprivi on the impermissibility of letting political views he could not control reach the Kaiser through reports by attachés." To Waldersee's intense disappointment War Minister von Kaltenborn declared hearty agreement with the principle of the directive that military attachés abroad should conduct themselves as officers and only officers and keep away from any real political activity. Their instructions, however, were to continue to come from the war ministry.

Waldersee had hoped there would soon be a break between Caprivi and the Kaiser and tried to pave the way in his characteristic manner. But things turned out quite differently. Waldersee himself suddenly fell into disfavor, because he deeply wounded the Kaiser's pride and self-esteem in a maneuver critique. In January, 1891, he was silenced by being transferred to Hamburg as commanding general. His successor, Count Schlieffen, had no political ambitions whatever and offered no objections to Caprivi's wishes. In a directive of his own to the military attachés, he expressly confirmed that their reports were not to be sent directly to him.[21]

It has been pointed out that the 1890 directive as such was not calculated to prevent the military attachés from engaging in unofficial political reporting. They could still write the chief of staff directly in their private capacity, and if they were aides-de-camp to the Kaiser they retained direct access to him as well. Indeed, even after 1890, William II occasionally used Waldersee's favorites as his political advisers[22] —though by 1895 none of them was any longer posted abroad.[23] Besides, since the new chief of staff would not hear of political reports, no attaché could venture to dispatch any such reports on his own without the chief's authority. Even so, there was no longer talk of preventive war within the General Staff under Waldersee's successor; hence political reports from military attachés would have been rather pointless. As far as we know, after 1890 Captain von Hintze, military plenipotentiary at the czarist court from 1908 to 1911, was the only one to provide political intelligence of any importance. His reports, however, agreed in general with the dispatches from the German ambassador in St. Petersburg, to whom they were usually submitted beforehand.

It would seem, therefore, that the danger of backdoor military diplomacy on the part of the army came to an end with Waldersee's fall and Caprivi's shrewd and resolute intervention. It was a rather different matter in the case of the reports of German naval attachés from London. With Tirpitz standing over them as their protector and inciter, these gentlemen engaged openly and often in political activities. All the brakes supposedly applied in official directives were to no avail. The London naval attachés did not even need the evasions of private correspondence or aide-de-camp reports to gain a hearing for their political views in the highest quarters. Tirpitz's protection kept the official reporting channels open to them. We shall deal in the next chapter with the baleful effects of these machinations on the course of Germany's policies with regard to England.

Waldersee's political role, by the way, was not entirely at an end even after his fall. From the vantage-point of Hamburg he soon established ties with Bismarck, now living in retirement at Friedrichsruh (owing not a little to Waldersee's own efforts); and he used his many trips to Berlin for purposes of keeping in touch with his former political cronies. He was particularly eager for news of political tensions that might have developed between William II and his chancellor Caprivi, who was unwilling to accept the overaggressive character of the Kaiser's domestic policies. When Waldersee regained imperial favor in 1895, he cautiously sought to commend himself as a "strong man," against the event of a crisis. Ever since the Kaiser's Königsberg "rebellion speech" of September, 1894, there had been much talk in Berlin about plans for a coup d'état. Court and conservative circles toyed with the idea of precipitating a conflict with the Reichstag over new antisocialist laws and then pushing through changes in the national election laws by force. The Saarbrücken "coal king" Freiherr von Stumm-Halberg was nudging the Kaiser in that direction. Naval people, on the other hand, were more inclined to predict trouble over continuing Reichstag resistance to the Kaiser's big-fleet plans in 1896-1897.

At this juncture Waldersee, who was not at all a big-navy man, edged up to the Kaiser and petitioned him on January 22, 1897, to start a kind of preventive war against the social democrats. In his view the high degree of organization the working masses had already achieved was shown in the great Hamburg ship-builders' strike, in which the strikers preserved exemplary discipline under their leaders, scrupulously avoiding all violence. According to Waldersee, it was in the government interest not to "let these well-organized masses and their leaders, pervaded by class hatred, set the time for the great reckoning, but to advance that time as much as possible." In the long run socialist propaganda in town and country might imperil even army morale.

Waldersee's prescription was the introduction of bills with teeth in them, for the purpose of provoking the socialist leaders. In a conversation with the Kaiser he hinted that he was prepared for ruthless action, should he be summoned as

chancellor—"only the test must not be too long delayed, else I shall be too old."
The Kaiser received Waldersee's memorandum with enthusiasm and read it to
the Prussian cabinet; and he held out to Waldersee the prospect of the long-
sought appointment—not at the moment, but should there be a need for ruthless
action and even "fireworks."

The war minister at once queried the commanding generals on their views. In
his own reply Waldersee recommended setting aside the Reichstag electoral law
if need be. If any of the federated governments failed to agree to this step,
Prussia could, as a last resort, leave the Reich, which would be reconstituted on a
different basis. He was not alone in these ideas (reminiscent of Bismarck's earlier
coup d'état plans), as shown, among other evidence, by a letter from his friend
Verdy, the former war minister, who insisted that a collapse of constitutional
parliamentary institutions was a prerequisite to strengthening the authority of
the state. For a while the Conservatives now considered Waldersee the "coming
man," in whom they staked all their hopes, and Waldersee himself zealously
made contact with rightist Reichstag deputies. In the end, however, William II
decided against the perilous venture of summoning this military activist to the
highest office in the land.[24]

Since the days of Edwin von Manteuffel, the Prussian army had not seen a
political general as busy and ambitious as Waldersee; nor was there to be anyone
like him down to 1914. As for the collective machinations of "imperial
headquarters" as a whole, with its adjutants and aides-de-camp, not a single
figure emerges with any degree of clarity. Even so, however, the harmful
political influence this circle exerted on William II is well documented, especially for the 1890's, when his personal rule was still in full flower and there was
virtual chaos among his advisers, for lack of a commanding leader. The Kaiser's
autocratic leanings were undoubtedly reinforced by his military environment.
As Admiral von Senden put it, what these people considered the ideal was a
strong government that could do without a Reichstag.[25]

Caprivi never tried nor desired to govern without the Reichstag, or in
defiance of it, but deliberately abandoned Bismarck's everlasting fighting
stance. For that reason alone he was considered *schlapp* and unreliable at
imperial headquarters. Astonishingly enough, this man of character, cast altogether in the soldierly mold, met only criticism and opposition, rather than
support, among his former professional colleagues. At court his great army
reforms, not superseded until 1913, were fought because they introduced the
long overdue reduction of the service term to two years, so that the army could
be enlarged. The inevitable compromise with the Reichstag in 1893 (involving
the introduction of half-battalions) was condemned as a feeble concession.

The agrarians and reactionaries hated Caprivi because of his liberal tariff
policies and his opposition to the sedition bill the Kaiser wanted, and this brand
of opposition was also strongly echoed at imperial headquarters. General von

Plessen, commandant of that institution after 1892 and an old friend of the chancellor, dared to speak up for Caprivi only diffidently, according to Eulenburg.[26] And indeed, the chancellor soon fell before the intrigues of his arch-conservative adversaries.

His successor, Prince Hohenlohe, also soon got into trouble with the Kaiser and his military entourage. There was a most unedifying quarrel over reforms in the military code of justice, in the course of which the highly competent war minister Paul Bronsart von Schellendorf was ousted, while Hohenlohe's own position was at times in danger. The whole train of events illustrates how William II's rigidly conservative attitude was stiffened by his military environment.

What the Kaiser chiefly opposed was that courts-martial should be thrown open to the public, though this had long been the custom in Bavaria and had carried in the Prussian cabinet with but one dissenting vote. To his friend Philipp Eulenburg he confessed what his main motive was: "What kind of figure would I cut in the eyes of the army, which would be bound to conclude that all the protective walls were being torn down?" This was indeed the view of General von Hahnke, head of the military cabinet: "The army must always remain a separate body, closed to critical eyes," he declared to Reich chancellor Hohenlohe.[27]

The "shadow government" was bitterly attacked on this question in the press and the Reichstag, as was the Kaiser's personal rule. These attacks struck a sensitive nerve. When the *Kölnische Zeitung* criticized Adjutant General von Hahnke, the Kaiser's answer was an instruction to the Reich chancellor that all state officials were to be enjoined from having anything to do with this (hitherto semiofficial) newspaper, on pain of instant dismissal.[28]

The extent to which Baron Holstein, the "evil spirit" of the foreign ministry, was involved in these press attacks on the "military clique" is not clear, but in the Kaiser's circle the foreign ministry was generally believed to be behind them, and its head, Freiherr von Marschall, was held responsible. Marschall fended off these imputations by the well-known device of inviting publicity himself. He sued his detractors, Inspector Tausch and other agents of the political police, who had acted as informers and talebearers in a subterranean struggle among different ministries. It was a brilliantly conducted trial and the minister won complete vindication, yet the men behind the agents remained in obscurity; and at the imperial court Marschall was now reproached with having publicly compromised Prussian state organs through the scandal he had created—in short, of having engaged in extremely "un-Prussian" conduct. The Kaiser's dislike of him grew, and complaints about the "South Germans" Marschall and Hohenlohe, men with whom Prussia could scarcely be expected to govern, met a ready echo from his military circle. The end result was that Marschall was ousted in the summer of 1897.[29]

His successor, Bernhard von Bülow, gained a position of such confidence with the Kaiser as foreign minister that he became more and more the leading figure on the political scene. We know today—not least from Bülow's own memoirs—that he was little more than a sinuous courtier and lacked the stature of a true statesman. Yet he did bring one undeniable virtue to the affairs of government, a far higher degree of integration. Irresponsible machinations—including those emanating from the military—were pushed into the background.

At the same time it would seem that William II, fully preoccupied with his great task of building up the navy, had begun to lose interest in domestic issues. He had become inured to the steady democratization of the German electorate and had begun to accept the progressive leftward shift in the Reichstag as inevitable. At any rate, he sharply rejected any notion of a coup d'état in the years directly preceding the First World War.[30] Despite all his autocratic airs he could not stem the tide of parliamentary government, for the chance of finding pliant majorities by dissolving the Reichstag steadily lessened. Yet nothing really changed in his total lack of understanding for the legal limitations of a constitutional monarchy and the principle of ministerial responsibility, not even when he had his fingers burned in the so-called *Daily Telegraph* affair of 1908. As late as 1911 the Kaiser characterized the attempted resignation of a Reich minister as a "hair-raising instance of insubordination."[31] Even then he still expected his ministers to toe the mark like soldiers.

The more William II felt the power of political decision slipping from his hands, the tighter he clung to his military command power. Year after year his war minister had to defend it against leftist attacks in the Reichstag, directed against its ill-defined scope and the exemption of the military cabinet from all parliamentary control. All the former bickering among the various military agencies became submerged in this common cause. Actually—in the final decade of peace, at least—these attacks missed their target, insofar as they were directed against an alleged military shadow government. Yet the events in Alsace associated with the town of Zabern demonstrated that the army's privileged position within the state under the protection of the imperial command power could turn into a serious political menace. What occurred then was an open power struggle between military and civilian authority, and its issue once again exemplified the defects of the Bismarckian constitution.

The newest treatments of these events[32] rightly emphasize that the sovereign's absolute and uncontrolled command power rested on the unspoken premise of complete internal harmony between him, the people, and the army—the kind of unity forged in Prussia in the Wars of Liberation and confirmed and deepened by the great victories in the era of the founding of the Reich. Such unlimited monarchial command power could be tolerated in a modern nation only when the popularity of the army was beyond all question.

No such harmony prevailed in Alsace. The majority of the settled populace still looked on the army as a kind of occupation force, while the army in turn looked on Alsace as a kind of buffer. This alone led to friction and many clashes between civilians and the military, which only increased with the adoption of a new provincial constitution in 1911, while at the same time the ominous foreign situation once again turned Alsatian eyes toward France.

The most important incident took place in October, 1913, in Zabern. It was by no means the first one of its kind. The military authorities were prone to react to slurs and insults with an exaggerated degree of acerbity which went far beyond legitimate self-defense, let alone the strict observance of the law. To some extent this was the fault of individual officers (like General von Deimling) who either simply lost their nerve or wanted to look "sharp" to their superiors; but another reason for it was the difficult situation of the military in this politically unsettled border region, where French rather than Prussian traditions determined local sentiment and way of life. On the other hand, the civilian administration under Count Wedel, the governor general, watched with horror as ruthless military measures foiled its every effort to win over the Alsatians and allow them to strike roots in German political life through their new home-rule constitution.

The conflict between the two authorities was real and serious. Both were able to marshal good arguments for their attitudes. It should have been the task of the central government to find and enforce an acceptable compromise under which the civil rights of the people would be rigorously protected while the public authority of the army was in no way harmed. Such a solution should not have been too hard to find; but whose business was it to find it? Bismarck had neglected to reserve to the chancellor's office not merely a personal but an institutional influence over the government of this province, which was directly under the Reich. Everything had been left to the emperor's command power, as in occupied territory. The governor general was his direct subordinate, just as were the generals stationed there. Officially, the Reich chancellor had no voice, either in administrative or military matters. All Bethmann Hollweg could do was to come to the governor general's aid by interceding with the Kaiser. All military and civilian authority was combined in his person, and he alone could have saved the mismanaged situation.

But when we study what actually happened, we find our worst fears confirmed. The Kaiser utterly failed in the face of this challenge—indeed, he did not even recognize it as a challenge. Whatever the incident, he was always on the side of the military, sight unseen, praising and rewarding his officers for their *Schneid* (snappiness). At the height of the Zabern crisis he refused even to receive the governor general, and only the most extreme pressure, the threatened resignation of the governor general and his provincial government, persuaded him to take even halfway conciliatory steps. These, however, were always proportioned in such a way that the appearance of a victory by the military over the civilian authority was essentially maintained. Their sole purpose was to give the chancellor and the war minister a sop with which to assuage the ire of the Reichstag majority. The people of Alsace received the impression that the civil authorities were virtually powerless to protect them against military caprice.

Worst of all was the plight of the Reich chancellor. In the face of the vehement opposition in the house, all he could do was to defend the imperial command power as well as he could, deny that the conflict between civilian and military authority was serious, and shield the army as much as possible. The vote of censure passed by a very large majority (293 to 54) in the Reichstag he simply had to accept without the slightest chance of revealing the true state of affairs or his own sentiments—not that they were in any sense antimilitary, since he hewed rather closely to the military line. Any other stand, any show of opposition to the military viewpoint, would have at once ended his tenure. More than ever before, the Zabern affair showed the pitiful situation of the German Reich chancellor, caught between Reichstag and military command power. It was to be the prelude to even crueler experiences during the First World War.

8

Naval Armaments–Tirpitz and the Battle Fleet

Part 1

German Naval Policy up to 1914

THE PREPONDERANCE of military over political considerations in Wilhelminian Germany, as revealed in the Zabern affair, had a particularly fateful effect in the field of armaments, on land and at sea. German naval policy in the era of Tirpitz crucially worsened Germany's international position. Ever since Schlieffen, the strategic planning of the General Staff had been dominated by technical military considerations, ultimately creating a situation, at the moment of the great crisis in July, 1914, in which German diplomacy was completely hamstrung and boxed in.

Germany's greatest patriotic pride and hope in the era of William II were staked on the astonishingly swift creation of a great battle fleet, the second largest in the world. To the German middle class, at least, nothing made the Kaiser seem so progressive and modern—despite his autocratic airs and incurable romanticism—as the leading role he played in building an up-to-date German battle fleet. It was this fleet that seemed to epitomize the international aspirations of the Germans, newly united in the Bismarckian Reich and now reaching out for new goals, for a world role. It was Admiral Tirpitz who really created this fleet, a sustained construction project to which he brought an amazing measure of energy, tenacity, thoroughness, and technical skill. Moreover, it was this same energy that enabled Tirpitz first to arouse and then to fan German ambitions to become a great sea power on the same level as much admired England.

Tirpitz upset all previous notions of how a military government agency should conduct itself by turning his Reich naval office *(Reichmarineamt)* into a political intelligence and propaganda agency, systematically campaigning in support of his navy bills in a fashion never before seen in Germany. He did all this with unofficial financing, chiefly from heavy industry.[1] The propaganda was addressed to every sector of society, the educated classes, from schoolboys to university professors, receiving the lion's share of attention. The whole gamut of modern promotion techniques was brought into play—thousands of popular science lectures; skillfully written books and articles; mass rallies; personal visits by high naval officers to influential politicians, not forgetting even the prince-lings of the federated states; and special days on which the public at large was invited to inspect the warships. The older patriotic clubs were, of course, utilized—the colonial society, the "Pan-Germans"—and in addition a special *Flottenverein* (Navy League) was established. In a matter of a few years it had almost a million members.

An element that paved the way for navy propaganda was that even in 1848 the fleet had played a special role as a symbol of national unity, the expression of a new national self-awareness. Memories of the medieval glory of the old Hanseatic League had played a part in this development. Even a Bavarian could feel tempted to serve in the navy, which was German rather than Prussian to begin with. Besides, many young inland Germans entertained romantic notions of the seaman's carefree, roaming life, the hardships and monotony of which were known in full only to people living along the coasts.

In any event, German naval propaganda swiftly met a powerful response throughout the country. The old Hanseatic cities, to be sure, had been accus-tomed for centuries to conduct their trade under protection of the British fleet, to take full advantage of the British free trade system, to maintain a thousand and one personal contacts overseas. Why was a large German navy needed? they asked suspiciously at first. It could never be the equal of the British and would only arouse resentment in England. But these inhibitions were soon overcome, as was the aversion of the East Elbian agrarians and conservatives to this expensive new toy, so foreign to Prussian tradition.

Naval enthusiasm soon exerted its effect on the Reichstag as well. In 1896 it had still balked at petty naval bills, but two years later, there was virtually no opposition to the introduction of Tirpitz's basic law, which was intended to lay the groundwork for the systematic construction of a powerful battle fleet; and in another two years a new naval act was authorized, under which ships of the line were doubled in number [2] and the Reichstag committed itself to extremely high appropriations for a period of seventeen years. Supplementary bills in 1906, 1908, and 1912 had easy sailing—indeed the one of 1908, politically the most provocative, was in part inspired within the house. If any measure sponsored by the imperial government was ever popular, it was certainly intensive naval armament, even while it was viewed abroad as hasty and blustering.

During the final decade of peace, Tirpitz, creator of the German navy, was widely regarded as the strong man among William II's advisers. Not only was he accounted a particularly able naval man as such, and an uncommonly skillful political maneuverer to boot, but many, especially on the right, thought him a statesman of stature, to whom the whole business of government should of rights be entrusted. During the First World War, even after his battle fleet had let down patriotic expectations, he was still able to play a major political role as leader of the nationalist opposition. And the disaster of 1918 did not really shake his own confidence in his political mission, nor could it quite obscure the luster of his name, at least not among the rightist parties. Even today the debate on whether his naval policies were a will-o'-the-wisp or a statesmanlike achievement continues.[3]

Viewed in the light of his post-1918 writings, he appears as a typical Pan-German militarist. "As long as man has dwelt on earth," we read in the preface to his documentation, "might has gone before right in the life of nations. . . . The German people may have proved themselves ill suited or disinclined to rise to world power, but they certainly had the requisite resources. . . . Their way pointed to the heights, even while they allowed their evil instincts to sweep them into the abyss."[4]

He described his own work in organizing the German navy as "building German world power" and the course of political events (in which he no longer had any part) as "the German world war policy of impotence." This grandiloquent style was the hallmark of the "fatherland party" he and his followers founded in 1917. Yet one would not be doing him justice by describing him as essentially a nationalist agitator or a man with a consuming ambition to have his way. Prior to 1914, at least, Tirpitz never aspired to the chancellorship in the way Waldersee did. On many occasions he held out against the Kaiser's more extreme naval fantasies which, in his view, collided with realities; and even in other areas he did not avoid serious conflict. He was not at all a flatterer and courtier but rather a serious man, who sprang from the old Prussian civil service tradition, was pervaded with a strong sense of duty, and did his best to be swayed only by rational argument. His unswerving objectivity often got on the nerves of the Kaiser, who was given to romantic caprice and pride in his ideas.

Tirpitz, moreover, did not share all the extravagant dreams of conquest of his Pan-German followers; and he opposed the more extreme demands of the Navy League with such firmness that after 1905 he was regarded as a creature of the Centrist party. All contact between the Reich naval office and the league was disrupted. It is true that Tirpitz's total dedication, from youth, to the creation of a great battle fleet as the basis of German world power came close to fanaticism. Yet if he was indeed a fanatic, he was certainly no adventurer. Everything he did and planned was considered with the greatest care; and he was always extremely concerned to avoid any conflict with England, so long as the new navy was not yet in full being. His calculations never included a preventive war, nor indeed any manner of attack on the British navy. On the contrary, Tirpitz explained and avowed time and again that the German navy, far from wanting to provoke war, desired only to prevent a British attack, by its very existence and power. Tirpitz was no daredevil. The passions of war never inflamed his breast.

From the vantage point of the present, however, the only possible verdict is that Tirpitz's lifework as a whole was an utter failure, resting on both military and political miscalculation.

The political argument always cited in support of the need for powerful German naval armaments was the German people's enormous vitality, pushing with elemental force beyond its traditional continental scope and clamoring for a new world stage to satisfy its political and economic requirements. The population of the Reich was growing by three-quarters of a million a year, and outlets had to be provided for this pressure, either in newly acquired overseas colonies (those secured in the era of Bismarck being largely unsuitable for settlement) or by swiftly expanding export industries. Neither alternative was open, however, unless Germany could take its place among the traditional naval powers with a fleet of its own, able to strike at a moment's notice and to command respect.

Such a fleet was to give Germany equality among the great world and sea powers, i.e., participation or at least a voice in the carving up of the globe that was underway just then. The navy was also to protect German overseas trade by safeguarding free access to markets and raw material sources. Opinion was virtually unanimous among the educated classes that this goal was both neces- sary and attainable—nor was this merely the result of pro-navy propaganda. Among the political parties only the extreme left, especially the social demo- crats, were in opposition to these ideas. None did more to gain them currency and authority in public opinion than German scholars, especially economists and historians, including some of the most renowned. The economists never tired of discussing the possibility that worldwide free trade might give way to a system of closed national markets. Their prophecies had not come true by 1914, nor were they able to say just how German battleships might prevent the British Empire from moving toward a protectionist system.

As for the historians, they soon added a political theme. The navy was to secure for Germany—if necessary by armed action—a world position enabling it to break the British hegemony and create a new balance of world power in place of the now obsolete balance of Europe. German power politics was thus given the glittering veneer of a "world mission," and such thoughts continued to work their spell far into the First World War.[5] They were, of course, aired over and over again (and often vulgarized) in Navy League propaganda.

Did these ideas make sense? Did they stem from rational insight, based on scholarship? Or were they, more or less, wishful dreams?

The first thing to be established is that German political writers were extremely vague about what they meant by the term "world power."[6] If it was meant to describe a colonial power with large overseas possessions, then

Germany was clearly much too late with its effort to become a "world power" on a level with Great Britain or France—to say nothing of America and Russia, whose ascent to world power began only in 1900 or was still impending. We are familiar with the extremely modest results of Germany's efforts, under Bülow's chancellorship, to acquire colonies anywhere and everywhere in the world. Ostentatious political naval displays could not change this and only served on occasion—the Manila incidents of 1898, the Venezuela conflict of 1901-1903—to create international tension and disenchantment, without bringing Germany any real advantage.[7]

German diplomats did learn from these experiences, and under Bethmann Hollweg German interest in any and every colonial intrigue throughout the world gave way to concentration on the acquisition of a large and contiguous colonial territory in equatorial Africa (supplementing German economic and technical activities in Turkey). This African goal was pursued with the blessings of the British Empire rather than against its will.[8] It was the only policy that promised any success. Yet, as we shall show, construction of a large battle fleet hindered rather than fostered this.

Germany did, of course, require a navy of respectable size in order to appear in character beside the other major European powers overseas. In the thousand and one pinpricks that are the concomitant of overseas trade with various lands at different levels of civilization, the German flag had to be shown and German claims and economic interest backed with a show of force. This, however, required a fleet composed of long-range cruisers rather than battleships. Such a fleet existed even in Bismarck's time, though it did require expansion as German world trade grew.[9] To use it effectively, and independently of England, overseas bases had to be acquired for coal, food, and supplies, preferably with drydock facilities. Kiao-chow was intended as such a base, to enable the German navy to act on its own in the Far East without, as Tirpitz put it, being abjectly at the mercy of British whims and the Hong Kong docks.

The acquisition of this port was the only colonial action in which the German navy—and Tirpitz personally—played a crucial part. It was administered by the Reich naval office, which turned it into a major commercial port as well—and into an important center of German cultural influence in China. Yet Germany got nowhere in its efforts to supplement this single base with a whole chain of others, which had been the dream of Bülow and Tirpitz in 1898,[10] and which the Reich naval office envisaged as the prize of victory over England in the First World War. At the time this would have cost Germany dearly, politically as well as financially—it would have meant throwing down a direct challenge to the British Empire. Thus Kiao-chow remained an isolated acquisition that led to much diplomatic friction and created an unwanted political conflict with the new major power, Japan. In any event, Kiao-chow could not be held against either Japan or Britain in time of war.

This, indeed, was the fatal weakness of German world policy in its application to colonies and world trade. In the event of war with Britain, there simply was no way of giving armed protection to German colonies and overseas trade—unless British sea power were destroyed, or the island kingdom conquered or starved into submission. And British dominion of the seas could not be successfully challenged with a fleet of cruisers.

Tirpitz saw this clearly, and it became the guiding star of his life's work. From the outset it was his goal to concentrate every resource on the construction of a great battle fleet for a struggle in the North Sea, while giving only second place to an increase in the long-range cruiser fleet.[11] As has been emphasized of late, Tirpitz was only following a general trend of the time, indeed, actually basing himself on older German armament plans.[12] Yet the single-mindedness with which the idea of a battle fleet was pursued in Germany after 1898, to the point of an outright arms race with England, stemmed very largely from Tirpitz personally and leaves him with a special burden of responsibility, in the perspective of history.

The building of the German battle fleet was from the beginning deliberately directed against Britain, not from any innate hostility, which was quite foreign to Tirpitz's nature, but because of the elemental fact that Britain was the chief obstacle to German aspirations to world status.[13] What a German cruiser fleet could never achieve, recognition of Germany as an equal on the world scene, the threat of the big men-of-war was to enforce. This is not to charge Tirpitz with deliberately having tried to steer German policy along an anti-British course. Indeed, he feared nothing more than a serious conflict with Britain until such a time as the German fleet had reached its full strength. Consequently, he was by no means consistent in his advocacy of a pro-Russian policy or of other continental alliances.[14] He did not at all relish the Kaiser's boasting to the English of his navy, nor the fanatical anti-British propaganda of the Pan-Germans and the Navy League. At heart his foreign policy views, down to 1914, were that German diplomats should tread softly, so as not to interfere with the building-up of the navy, and secure success for that navy in case of war by means of some anti-British alliance. Yet this really meant turning the means into an end and inverting the natural relation of scepter and sword. German foreign policy was indeed severely circumscribed in its freedom of action by virtue of the fact that German naval policy was so highly concentrated on a North Sea fleet.

Heretofore the North Sea had been relatively free of large men-of-war, the British navy being originally intended for other fronts and stationed primarily in the Mediterranean. Now the North Sea became the scene of a steadily accelerating naval arms race between the two largest countries on its coasts. Did all this have to be? Was there no alternative to bitter hostility, bent on mutual destruction, between these two ethnically related peoples whose cooperation—or even peaceful coexistence—might have secured peace in Europe for an indefinite time to come? What share did the German naval program have in these developments?

Those in search of answers must learn to distinguish between surface and background motives for the conflict. The deeper motives will come into full view only in the further course of our study.

On the surface was mutual fear of sudden attack or invasion. Most Englishmen completely failed to comprehend William II's naval policy. Why on earth didn't those Germans rest content with being the strongest land power on earth? Why did they put forward such immense effort to become a first-class sea power to boot? —unless it was to attack England one day? They were always talking of the need for protecting their world trade, but the question was: Who in all the world was limiting their freedom? Were they not Britain's keenest competitors in Britain's own colonies and dominions? And was it not plain that their new battle fleet was altogether incapable of protecting any shipping lanes outside the North Sea? Why, then, mount such an effort, unless it was in order to destroy the British home fleet? Was it plausible that the Germans would sacrifice billions, actually prejudicing their land armaments, merely in order to become a sea and world power, i.e., solely for reasons of prestige? Fear of secret German invasion plans, which played such an important part in British public opinion, was more than mere propaganda talk. It was a tradition of insular politics.

Naturally these fears were quite groundless, in view of the continuing and overwhelming superiority of the British battle fleet. Equally unjustified were the fears voiced on the German side of a British surprise attack for the purpose of destroying the German fleet and German overseas trade. They turned up in the German press whenever a new navy bill was up for discussion, and Tirpitz dusted them off repeatedly in his memoirs. It has long been established, however, that there was no real significance to the statements by British militarists and "navalists," by colonialist types and irresponsible journalists, which the propaganda section of the Reich naval office so carefully assembled.[15]

Naturally, some old British salts in high office occasionally vented their anger at the German naval competition in blustering threats, gaining thunderous applause on the hustings or at patriotic rallies, and suggesting that a broad section of the British people were responsive to "navalism." But it says nothing about the attitude of the British government; nor must it be assumed that primitive ideas of getting rid of irksome German export and shipping competition by sinking the German merchant fleet were widely shared in Britain. The leading firms in the City of London, in particular, feared nothing so much as an Anglo-German war.

It is indeed a fallacy—deliberately nurtured by Tirpitz and his naval propagandists, however—to maintain that the Anglo-German tensions that ultimately reached the breaking point in the First World War essentially stemmed from economic causes, i.e., that the war must be viewed as the outgrowth of British "commercial envy." There is no question that English businessmen and industrialists were extremely disturbed over growing German competition and German business methods. At times their panic led to ugly anti-German outbursts in the press; but the age of mercantilism and trade wars was long since over for good. The economies of different countries were so interdependent internationally that when one flourished, the other was also likely to benefit, and the strongest competitor might very well also be the best customer.

The British government certainly never gave any thought to putting down German competition by force. Even severing the empire from the world market, something anticipated at times before 1900, when the notion of "imperialism" was at its height, was not feasible in practice. The most intense period of competition between England and Germany, moreover, was already over by 1905. In both countries there was a sharply rising economic boom. Competing enterprises had adjusted to one another far better than before. Germany was England's principal European customer—indeed, the second largest in the world—while England was the best market for German goods. Above all, German exports were not really oriented toward overseas markets at all, but quite naturally toward European markets, a situation entirely different from England's.[16] As for the volume of trade of the German colonies, it was vanishingly small.[17]

Thus there was really no need for a great German North Sea battle fleet to protect German industry and foreign trade from British commercial envy. In the kind of free world economy that prevailed before 1914, competition could be fought only by economic means. Tirpitz and the German Navy League often described it as unworthy of a great nation to eke out a mere "parasite" existence in the sphere of world trade. But how could construction of a great battle fleet have altered such a situation? If the British government had actually shifted to a system of economic protectionism and imperial self-sufficiency, a German battle fleet would have been the least suitable means to force it to adopt a liberal trade policy.

Were there, then, political issues that divided Germany and England—issues serious enough to warrant construction of a great German battle fleet? This was certainly not true at the time of the first two German navy acts of 1898 and 1900. What is true, however, is that German public opinion was to a large extent anti-British. These sentiments fed on indignation over the Boer War and a number of incidents, such as the seizure of German mail packets along the African coast during the war, which were eagerly exploited by German naval propaganda even though the British government showed itself quite conciliatory and these issues were promptly settled.

The official mood, both in London and Berlin, was anything but quarrelsome. There was, indeed, a predisposition to reach a definitive understanding, perhaps even an alliance, and this was at times even more marked in London than in Berlin. As we know, these efforts ultimately failed in 1901, not merely because the Germans were overcautious and put forward excessive demands, but because in the end Salisbury and his cabinet were disinclined to enter into firm ties with a Germany threatened from two sides. But the German naval program played a part in this failure which was by no means insignificant.

In defense of the first naval act of 1898, it might have been argued that on purely technical grounds Germany needed to expand and improve its coastal defenses by the creation of an oceangoing fleet capable of striking minor offensive blows; but the second act in 1900 brought about a much more marked change in the balance of power. Once Germany's naval program had been carried out, the Anglo-German sea power ratio changed from 2 to 1 to 3 to 2. As was rightly observed, this invested the German naval construction program with a political and aggressive bias,[18] for it posed a serious threat to absolute dominion of the seas by Britain, which, after all, had more to defend than merely its North Sea coasts. In the Reichstag debate on this act, Britain was expressly referred to as Germany's enemy, and it was only a question of time before the British would take note of this great change and draw their own political conclusions from it.

This did take a number of years; and the British government was at first inclined to reassure the public about the German naval program, as long as there was any hope of a general political settlement with the Germans, and as long as the Boer War limited Britain's freedom of action. Despite sharp warning voices in some of the British newspapers, the naval question was not even discussed in the exploratory talks about a possible alliance conducted until 1901. On several occasions the British government publicly stated that it understood quite well the German desire for a large navy, in the light of Germany's growing overseas interests.

Yet the British press and the House of Commons showed increasing concern when it became clear that the German naval programs did not exist merely on paper. From 1902 onward the chorus of warnings swelled, especially in the fateful years 1903-1904, when the great Franco-British rapprochement began to take shape. The German ambassador in London, Count Metternich, and his deputy Count Bernstorff kept warning of rising British resentment.

Worry about Germany does not yet seem to have played a direct part in the Anglo-French colonial pact of 1904, which dealt with North Africa and was later to have such far-reaching consequences; yet only the following year this pact was to give rise to a political entente, namely when the German government tried to take advantage of its momentarily favorable situation abroad to intervene in French colonial policy. Even in this fateful turn, which took Germany by surprise, fear of the great new German fleet may not yet have been the determining factor; but undoubtedly the fact that Germany was now adding naval to the already unwelcome economic rivalry greatly deepened the British conviction that it was not merely an irksome and arrogant neighbor and competitor, but a threat as well. Fear of the German fleet among the British people made it much easier for the government to effect its political reorientation in the direction of France.

Once that turn had been made, there was little further restraint on anti-German outbursts in the British press, which now regularly warned the country of the German fleet and alleged German invasion plans. As early as the winter of 1904-1905, long before the Morocco crisis began, a kind of naval panic broke out in England. The response from the Pan-German press and the German Navy League was a torrent of abuse and even more uninhibited naval demands, while William II and Tirpitz promptly exploited the situation to announce a new navy bill. Thus began an unwholesome naval propaganda race between the two countries, which alienated them more and more from each other.[19]

Before taking a closer look at these unhappy developments, let us pause for a moment to inquire into the ultimate motives that drove England into the arms of France and sealed Germany's fate. They are, I think, most plainly discerned in the comprehensive and much cited memorandum of January 1, 1907, from the pen of Sir Eyre Crowe, the British expert on German affairs, in which the then dominant attitude toward Germany in the British foreign office is set forth and justified with precision, and the recommendations of which clearly exerted major influence on British policy in the final prewar years.

Crowe was not just seeing ghosts. He thought it possible, however, that Germany was planning to achieve dominion of the seas and political world hegemony by force, thus threatening the integrity of her neighbors, especially England. Such plans had, after all, been proclaimed loudly enough in Pan-German propaganda; but Crowe also considered an alternative possibility. German dreams of world dominion might indeed be no more than just that— vague dreams, expressing no more than a desire to play a leading role on a basis of equality among the great powers of the world, to increase German foreign trade methodically, to spread German culture far and wide, and to create by peaceful means new centers of German interest throughout the world. Perhaps the Germans were willing to let the future decide whether some day a change in general world conditions might afford them the opportunity to play a larger part in the control of overseas territories than heretofore. Even such an unwarlike attitude, however, seemed to Crowe to pose a terrible threat to the rest of the world; and he held that Britain must do everything in its power to keep German expansion within firm limits.

Why did he reach this conclusion? The German fleet does not seem to have been his principal worry. It is, of course, true that the combination of the largest fleet in the world with the largest army in the world would have created an intolerable situation. Yet Crowe acknowledged that Germany had every right to build as large a fleet as it liked. He rejected any intervention in German naval policy and was convinced that the Germans would appreciate the hopelessness of their naval arms race once they saw that England would inevitably lay down two keels for every one they did.[20] No note of petty jealousy rings in these thoughts, but on the contrary a spirit of self-assurance. Crowe did not envisage any immediate danger of war. What he feared and what repelled him was "restless, explosive, disconcerting German activity"—in other words, Germany's enormous vitality and the incalculable dynamics of its diplomacy.[21]

Crowe's attitude is reminiscent of the concern felt in a later age in the free West about the concentrated militant power and restless dynamics of Bolshevist Russia. Of course, domestic differences between the insular and the continental approach, between libertarian and authoritarian forms of government, had played their part ever since the beginnings of the Bismarckian empire. On the English side there was a deep-seated distrust of Germany's peaceful intentions, a distrust nourished by Pan-German propaganda and the Kaiser's grandiloquent phrase-mongering—"the trident of the deep befits our fist"; "our future lies on the water"; etc.—and not least by the German naval program itself.

In the end, however, these were not the crucial factors. What really mattered was the simple fact of German preponderance on the continent, compounded by the Russian collapse in the war against Japan and the revolution that followed. It was for the purpose of keeping this preponderance within bounds rather than primarily because of the German navy that England openly sided with France in the Morocco conflict and entered into the system of mutual military pledges with France that has already been discussed in Chapter 3 and that was henceforth to be unshakable.

Never did it become clearer than in those years that the scope within which German power was able to unfold was extremely limited. Scarcely had Germany, owing to its own natural growth in power as well as the Russian collapse, eliminated the danger of simply being crushed in a two-front war, when its first step in exploitation of this new situation, the Morocco policy of Bülow and Holstein, involved it in even greater hazards. In place of a two-front war, there was now the danger of complete encirclement. Could this new danger be banished by the expedient of increasing naval armaments still further?

We are familiar with Tirpitz's theory of a "fleet of risk," already cited in justification of the second German naval act. The German navy need not equal the British in strength, it was argued, since the British would not be able to concentrate their full power against Germany. Hence, even a weaker German navy would constitute a danger to Britain—a danger so great that, even in the event of a British victory at sea, Britain might be sufficiently weakened to be unable to stand up to a coalition of lesser naval powers, i.e., to maintain the so-called two-power standard. Tirpitz added the further argument that possession of a powerful fleet would enhance Germany's prospects of finding allies.[22] Behind all this was the idea widespread in Germany that all second-rate naval powers had a common interest in breaking Britain's seagoing monopoly under German leadership and thus winning "freedom of the seas" in the war to come.

Each single one of these propositions turned out to be a cruel fallacy; and Tirpitz later tried in vain to blame allegedly incompetent German diplomacy for the failure of his policies. Increased naval power did not win Germany a single ally, for no major European power would have dreamed of trying to outstrip British naval armaments, let alone of making common cause with Germany against Britain—neither France nor Russia nor the rising sea powers of Japan and America. The risk to Britain of being weakened in naval battle to the point that the two-power standard could no longer be maintained vanished the moment Britain fell into France's arms and thus gained the opportunity of concentrating its entire battle fleet in the North Sea.[23] This concentration, prepared for ever since 1902, was finalized after the second Morocco crisis, when Britain took over protection of the French north and west coasts against German attack, leaving the defense of the Mediterranean to France.[24] England was thus enabled to maintain absolute superiority over Germany, despite the huge German naval program. And with France at its side, Britain no longer needed the old two-power standard, especially with Germany lacking any powerful naval ally, and even more so since the colonial agreement with Russia in 1907, which brought even this old adversary into the western camp.

The hope that a powerful German fleet would intimidate the English to the point of avoiding battle with it also proved to be a gigantic miscalculation. It is both tragic and ironic in retrospect that in 1909, at a meeting of top army and government officials called by Bülow, Tirpitz declared, in response to a question, that within two years "the danger zone in our relations with England will have been considerably reduced, and in five or six years (i.e., by 1915) we will be safely out of it."[25]

German naval construction, far from intimidating Britáin, simply drove it into the arms of the French. Not that the entente of 1905 stemmed essentially from England's maritime worries—though these ultimately stiffened it beyond possibility of dissolution; for since the naval accord of 1912, which led to the shift of the French battle fleet entirely to the Mediterranean, it would have been morally all but impossible for the British to leave the French undefended against a German naval attack—as none saw more clearly nor with greater concern than the then first lord of the admiralty, Winston Churchill.[26]

Tirpitz's naval program ultimately rested on an overestimate of German resources that was characteristic of the Wilhelminian era. It would seem that from the outset the idea that Britain's capacity to enlarge its navy would soon be exhausted played a fateful role within the Reich naval office.[27] It is undoubtedly true that the need for increasing naval expenditures at an ever-growing rate in order to retain superiority over the German navy at times created financial stringencies for the British, especially since the shift in 1905 to dreadnoughts, which were vainly expected to leave the German competition behind.

This was all the more true since the great social reforms Lloyd George was pushing through at the same time exacted tremendous sacrifices, especially from the upper classes. But the notion held by German navy fanatics that England, the notorious "nation of shopkeepers," would be deterred from maintaining its supremacy at sea and the security of its islands by financial and technical impediments represented a complete misreading of the character of this proud nation. German diplomats never ceased to warn against this delusion; and when Tirpitz, citing the reports of his naval attachés, belittled British arms zeal as nothing but propaganda inspired by shipbuilders and munitions makers, he was merely displaying his limited political outlook. He blandly ignored the fact that German finances were far from inexhaustible and that despite the fiscal reforms of 1909 simultaneous enlargement of army and navy, as planned in 1911, simply transcended German resources and was bound to throw the Reich budget into serious confusion.[28]

The German naval construction program could bully the British into neither neutrality nor political friendship. The belief that this might succeed is a typical element of the militarist ideology. Actually, if Germany sought to escape the danger of a two-front war, a good relationship with England was absolutely essential. The Germans, in truth, had much more to fear from war with England. They would be threatened with the loss of all their colonies, exclusion from overseas trade, and even a hunger blockade. Could a battle fleet have guarded Germany against these perils?

Improved defense against a possible blockade had actually been at the heart of the whole German drive for a stronger navy. Even in Admiral Stosch's day the wretched German record of ineffectual coastal defense in 1864 and 1870-1871 had lent impetus to rearmament. The central idea of Tirpitz's brilliant *Dienstschrift IX* of 1894, which first made a name for him in the navy, was that pure coastal defense was insufficient in the face of a powerful hostile navy, that a blockade could be broken only by offensive forays of mighty high sea squadrons.[29]

Basically, Tirpitz was undoubtedly right, though only if the enemy—as was then generally anticipated—were to place a tight blockade line not too far away from the German coast and facing its ports. But the coal-fired ships of that time, especially the torpedo boats, were limited in range, and the farther away from home waters the battle, the greater the threat to the survivors on the way home from mine fields, torpedo attack, and pursuit. Tirpitz's report says that "advocates of a defensive naval policy proceed on the assumption that an aggressive enemy will accept battle wherever we wish. Actually, this is true to only a very limited extent; for the enemy's harassments need not be close in—they may very well take place at sea, well away from our own defenses, leaving our navy only the alternatives of inaction, i.e., complete loss of morale, or of accepting battle on the high seas"—which, of course, means that it must have the requisite technical capacity.

When Tirpitz wrote this, he was thinking of a clash between the fleets in the Bight of Heligoland, somewhere between that island and the mouth of the Thames, a belief he continued to entertain down to 1914. But what if the British were not to do the Germans the favor of accepting battle where the latter wished it? What if they preferred a broader blockade, bottling up the entire North Sea at the Channel on the one end and from the northern tip of Scotland across to Norway on the other? In that case the German navy would be unable even to attempt breaking the blockade and the situation which Tirpitz feared would be brought about—the German navy would be consigned to inaction and its morale would be destroyed.

This is what actually occurred in the First World War, and the lifework of Grand Admiral Tirpitz thus stood revealed as a failure in the military sense as well, a failure with immense consequences. The German navy was unable to loosen the strangle hold of the blockade, and the longer the war lasted, the more German resistance and vitality were paralyzed at their roots. The German fleet had been built for swift decision at sea, but this simply did not happen, any more than did France's rapid collapse, on which the German General Staff had so confidently counted. It was small comfort that the great German battle fleet did manage to control the Baltic, and indirectly the Bosporus as well, hindering Russian liaison and shipments to the western allies, but it was never able to fulfill its proper and most important task. Tirpitz had often given assurances that the British navy, because of its offensive spirit and highly developed sense of prestige, would be compelled to accept decisive battle near Heligoland or the Dogger Bank.[30] What a great error that turned out to be!

True, this error could have been recognized only at a late date. Until 1911 the British admiralty actually planned a close-in blockade of Heligoland Bight along the lines Tirpitz had envisaged. Light naval forces would be stationed at the mouths of the Elbe and the Weser, backed by stronger fleet units in close support and reserve, the whole force being based on one of the Frisian islands, which the British expected to capture immediately after the outbreak of war and fortify as a depot. As early as 1907, however, doubts about the feasibility of this strategy had been voiced, though they did not then prevail.[31] Not until Churchill's intervention as naval minister in 1911 were British fleet dispositions shifted in such a way that the blocked lines were virtually inaccessible to the Germans, and the entire North Sea turned into a kind of "dead sea." The decisive factors were the technical problems which the older plan posed, which were enhanced by the new fortifications on the North Sea islands.

The British naval high command had by no means renounced battle at sea as such—indeed, during the First World War it repeatedly sought such a confrontation, making bold forays into the North Sea to that end,[32] but to no avail. For, like the British navy, the German was reluctant—and indeed quite unable—to accept a crucial battle far from home waters in unfavorable conditions. After the fact Tirpitz derided the German naval command as lacking in aggressive spirit, in an attempt to shift the blame for the failure of his naval policy; but, of course, it can be argued that the destruction of the German battle fleet at the outbreak of the war would have brought disastrous military and political consequences. And Tirpitz himself, during the decisive weeks in question, demonstrably took great care not to counsel any unconscionable adventure, despite his insistence for some show of force.[33]

The long-range blockade of 1914, by the way, did not take Tirpitz and his naval staff completely by surprise. In 1907 the Reich naval office had submitted to the chancellor a memorandum on the law of prize at sea; and here the question of a long-range blockade was dealt with in a manner that revealed a startling drift in German naval strategy. Tirpitz conjectured that the British would within a few years no longer dare a close-in blockade, on account of the growth of the German battle fleet. They would therefore seek to block Germany's way to the south and north of England; and this type of expanded blockade would have in the main an effect on Germany very similar to a coastal blockade. In the long run Germany would be unable to stand up to it in economic terms. The only defense against this eventuality, in Tirpitz's view, would be a ruthless policy of taking prizes, in the broadest sense, constantly harassing the British coast and its ports with the German battle fleet, in whole or part; for, as the British well knew, the German had no other countermeasure at their disposal. A German blockade of England was out of the question for a long time to come. The prospect of German landing operations was similarly unrealistic. The only chance was to disrupt sea commerce by capturing ships.

The question was whether such disruption by means of attack on the eastern coast of Britain would pose a serious threat to the British Empire. The German ambassador in London, Count Metternich, expressed doubts in a counter-memorandum. The bulk of British sea traffic, he pointed out, proceeded through western ports that would be inaccessible to the Germans. The Reich naval office had confidently asserted that the German navy would conduct ruthless war against England "across the British fleet, beyond the British fleet, and around the British fleet"; but in Metternich's view that was mere phrase-mongering. He anticipated that in the event of war Germany would be completely cut off by sea, unless efforts were successful to limit the traditional law of prize under international law, and especially to insure free sea trade between neutral ports, as against the British doctrine of *voyage continu*. Metternich's proposal that such an effort should be made at the Hague Conference, which was meeting at the time, met bitter resistance from the Reich naval office, which displayed exaggerated confidence in its estimates of the practical prospects of a German strategy of seizure of merchant ships at sea.[34]

Yet continuity of supply by sea could certainly not be guaranteed by cruiser forays and penetration of a close-in blockade, expected of the German battle fleet. Tirpitz himself left the highest Reich authorities under no misapprehension in this respect. In a memorandum in 1906 he set forth the situation quite clearly for the war minister and urged top-level consultations on what might be done to prevent or at least mitigate Germany's economic strangulation by severance of its sea lines in wartime. This report was indeed the starting point for such consultations, though these did not accelerate until 1911-1912, with the Reich naval office constantly warning and pressing forward.[35]

German civil authorities were inclined to put their faith in the London declaration of 1909 on maritime law, in which certain limitations on the law of prize, as proposed by Metternich in 1907, were actually agreed to. The German navy, however, always doubted that England would observe such agreements. The German admiralty at first hoped that at least some of the neutral ports, especially those in Holland and Denmark, would remain open to the Germans for purposes of transit. For that reason, in 1905, Chief of the Admiralty Staff Büchsel protested against Schlieffen's plan, which would have turned Belgium as well as Holland into a theater of war.[36]

Schlieffen's successor, General von Moltke, saw that this objection made sense and rearranged the plan, with considerable difficulty, in such a way that Dutch neutrality, at least, was spared. Holland, he said in a note in 1911, must remain German's "windpipe," so that the country could breathe. And if England were indeed to declare war on Germany over Germany's violation of Belgian neutrality, England could not very well herself commit the same breach of international law against Holland.[37] These and similar hopes and considerations preoccupied the highest German authorities right down to 1914. They were particularly fond of staking their faith in America, which they felt was bound to protect freedom of neutral maritime commerce.[38] The British, on the other hand, were under no illusions that to respect freedom of Dutch transit shipping would mean a highly effective breaking of any total maritime blockade. Long before the war, Britain considered whether the country "could afford to recognize international law which in this case would militate so onesidedly in favor of Germany."[39] That was the reason the British government finally declined to ratify the London declaration on maritime law of 1909.

Thus Tirpitz, who had always predicted this, was proved right. Nevertheless, the question arises whether, in view of his warnings of a total blockade of Germany by sea, his whole naval policy was not proved a hollow sham, since it ostensibly pursued more important goals than the traditional one of coastal defense. What were the Germans to do with their great big battle fleet if the British refused to put in an appearance in Heligoland Bight? This was a question that did indeed give some of the German naval experts sleepless nights. In 1910, Chief of the Admiralty Staff von Fischel openly disputed Tirpitz's pet notion in a memorandum that scored as wishful thinking any assumption that "the enemy, from pure bravado, will precipitately attack us in a position we occupy solely because it promises us a tactical advantage." All the British were interested in was cutting off German overseas commerce. They would think twice before risking loss of substantial tonnage and block the exits from the North Sea instead. The bulk of their fleet would remain together in some Scottish port, and only light forces would advance into Heligoland Bight.[40]

Admiral von Fischel was soon afterward relieved of his post, and the Reich naval office, ignoring the admiralty staff, conducted special strategic studies and exercises concerned with possible operations in Heligoland Bight. Between 1899 and 1914 the admiralty had a succession of seven chiefs, unlike the General Staff, and in consequence it was scarcely in a position to crystallize a fixed strategic tradition. It never reached a clear conclusion as to what Britain would really do in the event of war. Yet it seems that the possibility of a long-range blockade as the sole British measure was perceived as early as 1909. The trouble was that the admiralty staff never quite believed in this possibility and therefore developed no clear-cut plan against such an eventuality.[41] It remained unsure, and in the end even Tirpitz himself seems to have begun to waver. On the occasion of an exercise in May, 1914, he is supposed to have asked Admiral von Ingenohl, chief of the high-sea fleet, what he would do if the British did not show up. Neither Ingenohl nor any member of his staff had any answer. Tirpitz himself, as he stated in a note made at the time, counted on a long-range blockade and spoke of offensive and prize warfare, for which two additional cruiser squadrons would have to be created. He was, in other words, merely reiterating his views of 1907.[42]

Were there no better choices for a war against Britain? In 1907, when Tirpitz was just preparing the transition to the construction of dreadnoughts, Vice Admiral Galster, in a pamphlet that drew much attention, pronounced expert criticism on the Reich naval office's construction policy of great "parade ships" (as Admiral Pohl later called them) and on its limited battle plans. Galster also clearly foresaw that Germany's maritime trade would inevitably cease with the outbreak of war. He did not think it likely that Germany would come out of any great naval battle the winner and advocated emphasis on "naval guerilla warfare." To that end he recommended an increase in torpedo boats and submarines, the greatest possible fleet mobility to disrupt enemy dispositions, and systematic harassment of peaceful maritime commerce by swift and well-armed cruisers that could withdraw to fortified bases in the German colonies.[43]

Tirpitz's subsequent argument that technical development and assembly-line production of U-boats were feasible only after the diesel engine had been invented, and that a great deal was done on the torpedo side, may have been well taken. In any event, it is not immediately plausible how piecemeal warfare could have broken a total blockade. On the other hand, the rigid North Sea fixation of the fleet and the ultimately hopeless race to build more ships of the line inevitably resulted in a certain inadequacy in Germany's light naval and reconnaissance forces at the beginning of the First World War. Yet the dogged consistency with which Tirpitz carried out his construction plans surely had certain virtues compared to the disjointed policies of his predecessors. Unfortunately, in the absence of a similarly steady hand in naval strategy, Tirpitz's policy took on a purely dogmatic character that paralyzed the admiralty staff in its freedom of decision.[44] The strategic concept by which the fleet was built and for which it was alone suited was fixed for all time. What scope was there left for strategic planning? But again, when one looks at the different strategic directives which the admiralty staff issued over the years, it quickly becomes clear that much uncertainty remained on whether and where Tirpitz's great battle fleet could ever be brought to bear.

How could it have been otherwise? Modern naval warfare with armored, steam-driven battleships was something completely new and had been given its preliminary tests only in the Spanish-American and the Russo-Japanese wars. As for the Germans, they were without the slightest experience in modern sea battle or even in the strategic exploitation of their home waters. Britain's naval wars had always concerned protecting or cutting off trade routes or troop landings. If the British managed to blockade the entire North Sea, any naval battle in the lee of Heligoland, as planned and hoped for by Tirpitz, became merely a sterile exercise—huge floating hulks firing on one another in a dead sea.

If the British long-range blockade were to be broken at all, this could be accomplished only from northern waters. Considerations of naval strategy made the opening of the Channel a completely hopeless undertaking. Indeed, the Germans would not even be able to stop British troop transports to France.[45] Thus Denmark or perhaps even Norway would have to be occupied as a base for gaining access to the world's oceans.[46] The admiralty staff did at one point propose an advance into Danish waters, long before any thought was given to a British long-range blockade. This was in the winter of 1904-1905, at the time of the British naval panic, when indignation over the German naval act of 1900 was at its height. The civilian lord of the admiralty, Lee, threatened a possible devastating surprise attack on the German navy, and the German admiralty and General Staff held worried consultations on what would happen if such a threat were implemented.

Tirpitz was unwilling to believe that the British would ever launch such an attack and in any event thought that Germany might win an improvised naval battle in the North Sea; but the German admiralty staff regarded any venture such as a naval battle in Heligoland Bight as completely hopeless. Chief of the Admiralty Staff Büchsel, however, developed an audacious offensive plan under which the German fleet would have ventured from the Kattegatt into the Skagerrak, thence to attack the British offensive fleet in the flank—an operation that would have required firm German control of the Danish sea routes, by the military occupation of Denmark if necessary.

This plan came to grief because of the political objections of Bülow and the German foreign ministry and the military objections of Schlieffen, who insisted that he could not spare the necessary troops from the western front.[47] By that time (probably unknown to Büchsel) the advance through Belgium was already fully decided upon, and it was considered far too risky to seek to correct the quirks of geography by committing still another violation of neutrality, for the sake of a very uncertain naval success.

Thus the North Sea remained the contemplated operational scene. Yet the tug of war long continued as to whether the Baltic should not after all be used as a staging if not an operational theater, and whether an offensive strike should not be based on Skagen. Indeed, German admiralty directives down to 1914 showed a good deal of uncertainty as to where and how a naval attack from Heligoland Bight might promise success. At the height of the German arms fever in 1909, one of these directives stated that a German offensive would have to prevent the German sea routes from being cut off at the very outset of war, even in the event of a long-range blockade, but where and how that was to be done was left completely in the dark.

There was even talk of a "strike into the empty air," in the event that the enemy was not encountered in the North Sea—advances to the enemy coast which were to win at least a "moral victory" by means of mine-laying and damage to enemy shipping. After 1912 even such forays were described as unpromising. A naval battle could be expected only if circumstances were exceptionally favorable. The first step would be vigorous strikes of minor scope against the blockading fleet, to weaken it as much as possible.

An admiralty memorandum of 1913 actually gave an outright warning against a battle at a location so remote that German torpedo boats could not follow; and this warning was emphatically confirmed in naval maneuvers conducted in the winter of 1913-1914. Even then the Germans anticipated that the main British naval force would be stationed at Scapa Flow rather than in the Firth of Forth. A personal report by the chief of the admiralty staff to the Kaiser on May 26, 1914, concluded that the Germans must not commit too large a part of their naval forces, and that any long-range offensive must be waged solely with submarines and mine-layers, the main fleet at first contenting itself with "pushing out" the blockade farther and farther—apparently it was still envisaged as being placed in Heligoland Bight. Not until British preponderance had been cut down by many minor actions could the Germans think of risking their battle fleet as a whole.[48]

Thus, even before the First World War began, the idea of a naval *Blitzkrieg,* which would deprive the British of their supremacy in a single great decisive battle, was abandoned as a hopeless undertaking. Nor was any satisfactory operational plan agreed upon by 1914 under which army and navy would collaborate in wartime—even though the admiralty staff was always punctilious in discussing its basic directives with the General Staff, which it kept currently informed of any major changes.[49] Beginning in 1903, there was even an occasional exchange of admiralty and General Staff officers, for informational terms of service.[50]

By 1899 both staffs had agreed that any landing of German troops in England was impracticable.[51] Until the great political turn came in 1904, Schlieffen had always envisaged a two-front war, in which Britain would not be involved, and he desired active fleet support, whether in the east or the west. In the 1890's there were appropriate naval plans which provided for strikes in the Channel or the Baltic, which were, indeed, based on older plans conceived by Caprivi, who had hoped and planned for at least an impressive initial success against the French fleet—in contrast to 1870.[52]

As late as 1902 Schlieffen desired a battle of annihilation with the French fleet, to which end all available naval forces would be concentrated in the west, in keeping with what were then his operational plans for war on land. But he dropped this demand when exchanges with the admiralty showed that the German fleet would almost certainly be destroyed if it challenged the far superior French fleet to battle and was furthermore quite incapable of maintaining control of the French coast. The alternative plan was to forego any offensive action in the west, limit the German naval forces to North Sea coastal defense, and gain control of the Baltic. To Schlieffen's mind, this strategy promised considerable advantages. Sea lines to Danzig and Königsberg would be kept open. The threat of troop landings might be held over the Russians' heads, thus relieving pressure on any eastern front. This seems a likely plan today, but apparently it was never really implemented, because both army and navy committed themselves more and more to a western strategy.

Nothing could alter the fact that since the second German naval act England had become Germany's chief potential enemy and the breaking of a British blockade the major challenge to the German navy. Even so, Schlieffen undoubtedly underestimated the danger Britain posed for Germany, not only in respect of a total blockade but from a British expeditionary force as well. Only in a supplement to his great operational plan of 1905 did he deal at all with the possibility of British intervention on land. No doubt he was motivated by the highly circumstantial reports of the German military attaché in London on the prospective strength and make-up of that British expeditionary force.[53]

Schlieffen's 1905 plan mentioned the possibility that the British troops might land either in Antwerp or on the coast of Jutland. The latter contingency seems at first to have been taken quite seriously by Schlieffen's successors, because of the danger to the Kiel canal and naval base and to Hamburg and Lübeck.[54] Schlieffen himself did not assess this danger as very great, believing that the British would prefer the security of Antwerp for their expeditionary force, where he on his part thought it might well be encircled. On the other hand, Schlieffen was also confident of his ability to deal with any German landing in Jutland without too much trouble.

In the meantime, the striking power of the German North Sea fleet grew apace, and in its directives after 1905 the German admiralty staff spoke of the possibility of venturing under particularly favorable circumstances on that battle of annihilation on the open sea, even against England, which it had declared to be hopeless against France as recently as 1902. Moltke, the new chief of staff, was a complete convert to Schlieffen's idea of a great offensive in the west. In 1908 he said he considered it probable that the British would undertake large-scale landing operations along the German or Danish coast in the event of war, and he added that he did not think such operations would have any crucial influence on the main theater of war. In any event, the navy was under no circumstances to allow its forces to be frittered away on defensive action against such landings or on other subsidiary missions in support of the land forces. It was to keep its power intact for the decisive engagement at sea. Even control of the Baltic was no substitute for tactical success in a great naval battle and could exert no influence on the war on land.

Thus everything was now staked on the decisive land battle on the western front. The possibility of exploiting German dominion in the Baltic for forays into the Gulf of Finland and against St. Petersburg or for landing operations behind the Russian front was not even considered. The eyes of both service chiefs were riveted on the west. The General Staff chief was thoroughly convinced that a decisive victory on land was indeed possible there, while the chief of the admiralty staff did not wish to weaken the North Sea fleet by ventures in the Baltic.

Moltke actually proclaimed his basic principles to the naval high command more than once, in 1909 and 1911. Both services were to act independently of each other, in accordance with their contingencies. He went so far as to say, in 1910 or 1911, and again after the outbreak of the First World War—or so it is at least reported—that he did not consider interference with British troop transports to France important. Indeed, he could only wish that the British expeditionary force would land, so that the German army "could take care of it."[55]

Moltke must have known that the German navy was in fact powerless to offer any serious resistance to British Channel crossings. His brave words may therefore have been little more than bluster, to conceal the harsh realities. Did he then seriously believe that the Germans could win a great battle at sea? His statements before a council of top government and military authorities on June 3, 1909, were in a rather different vein.

Tirpitz said on that occasion that at the moment the German navy could scarcely contemplate a clash with the British navy with equanimity, though the danger would be over in another five or six years. Moltke retorted dryly and forthrightly: "Since the navy cannot wage war against England with any hope of success, such a war must be avoided. It would be a different matter if we could count on finding allies against Britain, but according to the chancellor such a thing is not to be expected. ... I cannot really foresee how this unfortunate situation will ever change, for our navy will always be substantially weaker than the British.[56] ... Hence I believe it would be desirable to reach an honorable understanding, perhaps on the basis of slowing up the rate of construction."[57]

The chief of staff was clearly displaying no confidence in victory with a view to Tirpitz's navy. If he continued to advise the navy to husband its forces for a great battle, he was probably motivated by a desire to escape any responsibility for the fortunes of naval warfare—which he might have incurred by asking naval aid in support of army missions. It is equally probable that neither he nor, for that matter, the admiralty staff really believed the German navy could win a great naval victory in the early weeks of the impending war. If Tirpitz sustained his own faith in such a victory in undiminished form down to 1914, he was very much alone among highly placed German defense officials at the outbreak of the First World War.

Part 2

The Arms Race after 1905 and the First Naval Talks with England

LOOKING BACK from the turning point of the outbreak of the First World War, the bitter struggle for limitation of the naval arms race to mitigate international tension which was waged between the civilian and military authorities in Germany during the preceding decade appears in an almost spectral light. The naval people were fighting for an illusory goal. Chancellor and foreign office wished to see statesmanship prevail over blind militarism, but on the domestic scene theirs was a lost cause. In the final analysis this was true in terms of foreign policy as well, for Europe was ineluctably falling apart into two hostile blocs. To bridge this gulf by diplomatic means proved no more possible than did a negotiated peace later on, after war had broken out.

Our concern is to pick out from the struggles of the years from 1904 to 1914 those junctures at which the conflict between military and political thinking manifests itself with particular clarity.

We note at once that technical exigencies play a particularly important part in matters of naval policy. This kind of constraint, narrowing the scope for free decision and giving technical considerations preponderance over political, is indeed typical of modern militarism. In the naval field it was shown particularly in the transition to the dreadnought after 1906. After the first naval panic in England in 1904-1905 and the Morocco crisis that followed, the British navy under Lord Fisher tried to shake off its irksome German rival by increasing the size and armaments of its new battleships and battle cruisers at one fell swoop to the point that all the older types immediately became obsolete. Inevitably the German navy sought to follow suit by enlarging its own models—indeed, ever since the Russo-Japanese War navy people all over the world had been clamoring for supermodern ships of tremendous power and speed.

Unfortunately, increasing the size of the individual naval unit brought a tremendous rise in cost, to be compensated for in the long run only by a reduction in the number of units, a trend that ultimately affected all navies. This, of course, made good sense, since the great new battleships carried much greater fire power. In a confidential talk with von Müller, chief of the naval cabinet, Tirpitz himself once voiced doubts "whether we shall be able to maintain the scheduled rate of battleship construction in the long run, since the cost per ship has already grown beyond the government's means and is still growing."[58] But if Tirpitz appreciated the problem, he never did anything about it.

Despite the move to the dreadnought type in 1906, he clung stubbornly to the number of keels provided for in the naval act—indeed, he increased the number with a supplementary bill that reinstated six battle cruisers the Reichstag had refused to authorize in 1900. Purely technical considerations played their part in this policy. Full utilization of naval shipyard capacity meant three ships a year, and the German navy was anxious to maintain this rate.

There was also, however, a political goal in the background. The British were to be pushed to the utmost limits of their own technical and financial capacity. In the long run they were to be stretched beyond any hope of laying down two keels for every one laid down in Germany. Within only two years Germany had accelerated to four ships a year, even though the international situation did not particularly call for such a rate—it was largely a matter of taking advantage of a favorable climate of opinion in the Reichstag, while the so-called "Bülow Bloc" wielded influence. The authorized life of naval vessels was cut from twenty-five to twenty years, and this alone greatly speeded up the rate of modern dreadnought construction.

In an age of rapidly accelerating technology, this shortened life may have been useful and even inevitable, but there can be no question that a rate of four new naval vessels a year also posed certain political dangers. The *Reichsmarine-amt,* however, had long since passed the stage of being a mere technical agency and was setting its own foreign policy goals. Enjoying the Kaiser's personal confidence, the navy minister knew that he was more powerful than the foreign ministry diplomats, whom he despised one and all. Although he was nominally the chancellor's subordinate, he had long since claimed equal rank, threatening to resign at the slightest sign of being balked, in the full knowledge that he would always prevail. So long as the courtly Bülow himself enjoyed the Kaiser's favor, the navy secretary usually managed to stay on good terms with him.[59] This was made all the easier since Bülow, with his lordly airs, seems to have paid little attention to the details of naval policy and was fond of sweeping political problems under the rug, especially when they bade fair to bring him into conflict with the Kaiser's pet notions.

Bülow signed the first big supplementary navy bill of 1905-1906 without objection; he even encouraged the naval head to set his demands as high as possible, though both the German ambassador in London and the foreign minister, at a meeting on December 21, 1904, had urgently cautioned against a big bill of this kind. There are indications that Bülow would have been ready to yield to the clamor of the German Navy League and the armament industry that stood behind it, by putting before the Reichstag a naval bill even bigger than what Tirpitz proposed, making "a big national cause" of it.[60] Tirpitz withstood this temptation, at the cost of quarreling with the Navy League, from fear of immediate war with England and perhaps even more for technical reasons.[61] Bülow later had words of praise for this "act of statesmanship" by Tirpitz. Bülow also approved without objection the naval bill of 1908, which was to have such fateful political consequences. He told his intimate adviser, Baron Holstein, at the time that he was confident Tirpitz would ask for "only what was absolutely necessary." Bülow's letter of approval, however, shows quite clearly that he had not the least idea what the new bill meant in terms of dangerous power politics.[62]

The international repercussions did not take long. Germany's shift to a rate of four ships a year (even though it lasted for only a few years) forced the British into a breathless pace of their own in dreadnought construction—if they were to stick to their two-keels-for-one standard. Coupled with the contemplated social reforms, the burden on the British taxpayer rose steeply, and a great deal of domestic discord resulted. One consequence was the emasculation of the House of Lords, the most important constitutional change in a long time. The British tax burden, by the way, was even then substantially higher than what weighed on the Germans; and, as it rose, so did resentment of Germany. German diplomatic and military observers had been reporting for years that the German navy took pride of place as a cause of anti-German sentiment in England.[63]

In time, however, these reports began to impress even Bülow, the optimist. German foreign policy had little by little got into a predicament that left no more room for optimism. The Anglo-French colonial pact had been followed in 1907 by a similar British agreement with Russia, which had also swiftly grown into a political entente. The Germans had banked firmly on an unbridgeable gap between England and Russia; but for the time being, at least, it had been bridged, and Germany's international isolation had grown even more sinister than before.

This new situation was made plain to all the world by the anti-German bias of

British policy during the protracted Balkan crisis in the winter of 1908-1909, as well as by the now irreconcilable hostility of the Russians. This had been deepened when Germany offered Austria such massive military support that Russia had to pull back grudgingly (see Chapter 4). Europe was now completely split into two enemy camps, and Germany had to give serious consideration to the question whether to provoke the British even further by again stepping up German fleet armaments, or whether perhaps an attempt should be made to soften the conflict by some measure of compromise in the sphere of arms.

We already know what the answer of the Reich naval office was—"keep on building until they have to venture out to challenge us." It was a typically militarist answer, based on the delusion that great political problems can be mastered only by military effort. It completely misread Britain's will to maintain its integrity, which threats only served to stiffen. It also overestimated German strength by far, and in typically militarist fashion failed to see beyond Germany's own vital interests. It further failed to appreciate deep-seated British fears for the security of their sea approaches and the cohesiveness of their empire, both of which depended on British supremacy on the high seas.

There had been differences of opinion within the German camp on the details of naval rearmament, but on the whole it had been effected until this time with the full support of the Reich government, for which the chancellor took full political responsibility before the outside world. But now that the naval arms race began to pose a direct danger to Germany's foreign policy, Bülow himself began to have doubts as to whether the course pursued so far had been correct. This happened at about the same time that William II's authority was so badly shaken by the *Daily Telegraph* affair.

Admiral Galster's strictures on dreadnought construction seem to have left a strong impression on Bülow.[64] Was there a valid alternative—shifting to coastal fortifications and the construction of submarines and thereby eliminating the main reason for tension with England? Late in December, 1908, Bülow suddenly inquired whether Tirpitz was really sure that the great German battle fleet would ever be used, or whether it might not be better to move to the defensive by strengthened coastal fortifications, procurement of sea mines, and enlargement of the U-boat fleet. He suggested, furthermore, that the rate of construction be lowered for the next three years from the four-a-year pace, to assuage the nervous British.

For Grand Admiral Tirpitz this inquiry, after so many years of painstaking organizational work, came as a severe shock. He protested and again threatened to resign, and Bülow, himself no longer quite sure of royal favor, gave way at once. Yet the question of a naval understanding with Britain soon came to the fore again.[65] The initial impetus came from repeated suggestions by British cabinet members, especially from the chancellor of the exchequer, Lloyd George. From the summer of 1908 on they had pleaded that mutual interest called for an Anglo-German agreement to limit or slow down dreadnought construction.

In August, 1908, King Edward VII visited the Kaiser at Kronberg, and on that occasion the idea was mentioned to him personally by the British minister Hardinge. The Kaiser brusquely rebuffed this feeler as an invasion on his sovereign rights, and for the time being the British government was not of a mind to pursue the subject further. The British, however, had good reason to fear that by 1912 they would be lagging behind Germany in dreadnought construction, and the government decided on a dramatic counterblow. In March, 1909, in a mood of near panic, Parliament decided to lay no less than eight dreadnought keels within the year, if necessary.

Tirpitz had already anticipated in the fall of 1908 that the British might sharply step up their rate of construction. For Germany this prospect was particularly unwelcome, since the German naval program was passing through a new "danger zone" of its own. The dreadnoughts made it necessary to widen the Kiel canal, and neither this work nor the fortification of Heligoland could be finished before 1914. According to Tirpitz, he spent hours during the imperial fall hunt at Rominten in September in an effort to convince the Kaiser that too abrupt a rebuff of the British advances was politically unwise, if only because it would invite the charge that Germany was irrevocably committed to a thoroughly militant stance.[66]

Later on, Tirpitz reproached his diplomatic colleagues with having missed an opportunity that would never recur for binding the British to a ratio between the two navies that would be favorable to Germany—say 3 to 4.[67] It is plain, however, that he himself did not even dare put forward any proposal for such negotiations at Rominten. Nor, for that matter, did he breathe a word of such a possibility to the chancellor. On the contrary, as late as January he indignantly rejected as an unnecessary humiliation Bülow's suggestion that the four-a-year rate be reduced to three a year.

Yet Tirpitz soon changed his stand.[68] He seems to have realized only then that the British desire for an understanding in naval matters might be used for limiting their dreadnought program by treaty as well. He now gave it as his opinion that the British should on no account be rebuffed again if they reverted to their earlier proposals. Germany should offer Britain a treaty in which it would agree to build no more than three capital ships a year for the next ten years, while Britain would agree to build no more than four.

Tirpitz held to this idea and seems to have felt confident of winning the Kaiser over to it. It was indeed a tempting opportunity to show a conciliatory attitude toward the British and avoid the odium of appearing truculent in the eyes of the world, while surrendering none of the naval strength contemplated in the naval act of 1900. On the contrary, it was necessary only to delay until after 1912 the laying down of the two dreadnoughts planned for 1910 and

1911, and then regularly to begin three ships a year, rather than the two hitherto contemplated, under a treaty that would cover the years from 1912 to 1917. By 1920 this would give the Germans four ships more than were planned in 1908.[69]

Unfortunately, the Kaiser regarded any and every British proposal for naval arms limitation as insolent and any and every German compromise as humiliating weakness. He was totally unwilling to see anyone lay hands on his hobby, the "legally authorized" fleet strength. His attitude toward the British was a curious blend of envy and arrogance, and he was convinced that sheer military power on the part of Germany would some day cause them to come to him "on bended knees" for help and friendship.[70] Yet to persuade them to forgo the two-power standard by treaty—that was, indeed, an idea that might appeal to him.

The question became acute in the spring of 1909, during the budget debates in both the House of Commons and the Reichstag, when there was much criticism of the latest phases of naval policy and party politicians urgently pleaded for action to reduce the enormous burdens of the arms race by negotiation. The British foreign secretary Grey was sharply questioned on whether he planned or had undertaken any steps to that end, and he now pressed Berlin for a declaration that would enable him to reassure Parliament without bringing the Kaiser's person (and his brusque rebuff in Kronberg) into the debate.

Bülow, quite evidently still intimidated by the Kaiser's aversion to any discussion of naval matters, endeavored to formulate an answer that would show great reserve without slamming the door in Britain's face altogether. Tirpitz gave clear warning against the latter course, recommending an effort to win over both the Kaiser and the Reichstag to a policy of negotiation.[71] In fact, soon afterward he did succeed in convincing William II that negotiations might be possible and even useful. The Kaiser blustered vehemently about the outrageous conduct of the British negotiators at Kronberg and about Metternich, the German ambassador in London, who of rights should have required them to apologize; but on April 3, he charged the chancellor to initiate naval talks, as proposed by Tirpitz, "provided England sincerely requests such negotiations."[72]

Bülow at once sounded out opinion in London, and, when he found that the climate was not altogether unfavorable, he summoned a meeting of high military and civilian government officials, including Count Metternich. The meeting, which was held on June 3, was to agree on guidelines for German proposals, in the event that the British government again expressed a desire for naval talks.

This meeting turned into a duel between Tirpitz and the ambassador, whom the chancellor at the outset felt called upon to defend against highly unfair attacks from the Kaiser, inspired by Tirpitz. Metternich for his part described Tirpitz's proposed 3 to 4 formula not only as inappropriate but as dangerous. If the Germans insisted that the strength of their navy must come as close as that to the British, it was bound to lead to war promptly.

Tirpitz, greatly angered, at once counterattacked. Meanwhile, he himself had grown uncertain whether his proposed 3 to 4 ratio really stood any chance of bringing the British to the negotiating table. Now that the House of Commons had passed the great British naval bill, he declared, the favorable moment for talks had been missed—this was, of course, as usual the fault of the diplomats! Germany would now have to wait and see whether the British were still at all in the mood for talks, and if so what they might have to propose. He, Tirpitz, was certainly not prepared to provide the ambassador with some kind of formula or ratio that might be misrepresented or garbled. He absolutely rejected Metternich's proposal to postpone the 1920 expiration date of the German naval act by five years; but when Bethmann Hollweg, the interior minister, conciliatingly intervened with the proposal that the ambassador be empowered to offer, if appropriate, a slowing down of the German rate of construction, without mentioning any figures for the time being, this was accepted. Tirpitz even conceded to Bethmann that a reduction from four to three ships in 1910 could be effected without difficulty, if the British offered a *quid pro quo*.[73]

All in all, it was an extremely modest upshot; but Bethmann Hollweg, soon afterward himself appointed chancellor, at once used it to continue his efforts to achieve a better relationship with Britain, a goal which he regarded as the most important mission of his foreign policy. To his surprise Tirpitz now was willing to agree to a formula that seemed to go beyond his earlier proposals. The 3 to 4 ratio of dreadnoughts was to be limited to 1910. In each of the years from 1911 to 1914 only two German capital ships were to be laid down for every three British ships; and a supplementary naval bill for 1912 was to be expressly foregone.

Tirpitz had it in mind to spread the three ships not to be built in the next years over the years from 1915 to 1917. Total German naval strength to be achieved by 1920 under the naval act would be undiminished. There would only be a delay for the years up to 1914, i.e., until the German "danger zone" had been passed; but in return there would be the inestimable advantage to Germany that the British naval construction program—which was then under no temporal legal limitations at all—would be sharply restricted for a period of five years, by treaty.

The British government had repeatedly allowed it to leak out in the preceding years that it was prepared to accept a 2 to 3 ratio of new construction, and Metternich had confirmed this on June 3. Tirpitz now calculated that if only the new keels to be laid down in the next five years were added up, the British would indeed have a superiority in this proportion. What he carefully failed to mention was that if all the new ships from the beginning of the dreadnought era to 1914 were added up, the ratio would still be 3 to 4.[74] Bethmann Hollweg at once saw through this trick and had grave doubts that the British would find such an offer acceptable. Like Bülow before him, he warned the naval experts against being responsible for dooming any political understanding with Britain in advance, by virtue of their military demands. Yet he was at the same grateful enough for gaining any scope for his policy of conciliation. Reporting to the Kaiser at Schloss Wilhelmshöhe together with the navy minister, he was able to secure authorization for initiating official negotiations at once, without waiting for any more British overtures.

Bethmann Hollweg agreed with Tirpitz that the naval talks should not at the outset be burdened with political problems, i.e., negotiations on trade, colonies, and neutrality, as Bülow had planned. This might endanger the whole project. But, of course, he did not consider an arms agreement as an end in itself, only as the opening gun in a general rapprochement between the two powers—quite unlike Tirpitz, who was at bottom interested only in limiting the British naval construction program. Tirpitz always rejected the idea of unilateral German concessions regarding the naval program, solely for political ends. He was inclined to regard British political assurances as little more than empty words.[75]

The Chancellor was well aware of this different in outlook and was intent from the beginning on running the talks without military interference. When the grand admiral urged him to relieve Ambassador Metternich and replace him with a more pliable diplomat, Bethmann Hollweg did not even deign to reply, at once drawing upon himself the great man's distrust. What Bethmann did do was quietly move the scene of the talks to Berlin, where he himself conducted them with the British ambassador Goschen.

Actually, the Chancellor at first avoided mentioning any definite figures for a disarmament agreement, presumably in the hope (characteristic of his whole political style) of being able some day to extract better terms from the Kaiser and the Reich naval office, once the concrete prospect of an understanding with Britain beckoned. This was the very tactic recommended by Kiderlen-Wächter, the German ambassador in Bucharest, whose written opinion Bethmann Hollweg closely followed in his negotiations.

Kiderlen-Wächter also suggested that the technical naval discussions be left to the professionals, since they were bound to be extremely complex. The government would do well to escape responsibility for the poor impression which the first concrete German proposals were bound to make on the British.[76]

Was Bethmann Hollweg overplaying his hand? Count Metternich was skeptical from the outset—and he was unquestionably one of the shrewdest German diplomats, a man of incorruptible objectivity in political matters, as well as one who was passionately concerned with improving Anglo-German relations. He was well aware of Britain's close ties with its Entente allies and felt that for the time being little more than general assurances of friendship could be expected of London. Above all, he regarded the formula for a naval pact proposed by Tirpitz as utterly inadequate. He kept emphasizing that the British, unlike the Germans, were only interested in an arms agreement, since they did not really need Germany's friendship. A mere slowing down of the rate of construction was of small value to them, since they wished to effect real economies. Once Tirpitz's 3 to 4 ratio was brought into the discussion, the British would no longer dream of assuming any political obligations; and Germany would be compelled soon enough to turn up its cards.

All these predictions promptly came true. Sir Edward Grey showed himself basically well disposed to an understanding, but kept pressing for concrete arms proposals. In his view, British public opinion made any political rapprochement a hopeless undertaking, unless there were a naval pact. Nor did he leave any doubt on the score that any Anglo-German political understanding must in no way endanger or loosen the Anglo-French and Anglo-Russian Entente. When Bethmann finally got to the point of mentioning a possible naval pact, suggesting with the greatest caution that new keels in both countries might be limited for a fixed number of years, without, however, relinquishing the German naval act, he was at once told that this was not enough, since it would not result in any appreciable lightening of the British naval budget. Within a matter of weeks, the negotiations simply dribbled away; Tirpitz's proposal was not even discussed.

Had it ever been presented to the British, it would have very soon become clear that this was not really a genuine concession on the part of the Germans, entitling them to a *quid pro quo,* but, on the contrary, that it offered more to Germany than to the other side. Bethmann, to be sure, said that Germany would be making "a substantial sacrifice by acknowledging the actually existing British supremacy at sea." Yet this acknowledgment would have had practical value for England only if Germany had actually been in a position to break the British supremacy.[77]

What the British really wanted was quite simply a reduction in the German naval program instituted by the German naval act with its various amendments. Bethmann Hollweg declared that "in view of the current state of German public opinion as expressed in press and Reichstag this was out of the question." Whether he was right in this contention remains doubtful—Kiderlen apparently did not feel it was quite so impossible; but such an agreement almost certainly would have brought a veto from the Kaiser and his naval advisers.[78] Indeed, Bethmann could not even have put forward such an agreement without risking instant dismissal. There was a limit beyond which civilian authority could not go in Wilhelminian Germany—and that limit would have here been transgressed.

There were still other difficulties inherent in the naval situation itself. The Chancellor himself outlined them tellingly:[79] "No country can give absolutely binding assurances that it will under no conceivable circumstances build more than a certain number of ships." Even an agreement limiting the rate of construction over a very long period of time held dangers for both sides, in view of the swiftly developing technology and the possibility that the political constellations might abruptly change. All this, however, predicated that a strong German fleet, approximating the British, was indeed indispensable to the maintenance of a strong German image among the powers—and this was the prevailing conviction among the opinion-forming German classes, which no chancellor could ignore. Subsequently the Germans came to see that the great naval program had been all in vain, an enormous blunder, but this developed only in the actual course of the First World War.

Thus the entanglements that brought the Chancellor's preliminary talks to grief in 1909 are not lacking in an element of tragedy—nor is this element limited to the purely military side. It is a moving experience to read the diplomatic documents of those years, with their sharp analyses of the international problems facing Germany and England—on the German side especially those by Metternich and Kiderlen. How much sincere striving to understand the situation and vital interests of the other side, to find routes of approach, to discover ways in which conflict might be bridged and overcome! —and in the end it was all in vain.

The Chancellor and his advisers were under no illusions that England would ever yield what Germany needed most desperately—firm assurances of neutrality in the event that Germany became involved in a two-front war against its will, by virtue of its alliance with Austria-Hungary. Bethmann saw clearly that "the conflicts which others have with us are ultimately based on their fears that we will outstrip them, and they are therefore likely to be solved but slowly and with difficulty." Yet the Germans were at pains to find some form of political agreement with England that would prevent that country from "showing up in the enemy camp on every occasion."[80] Unfortunately, it was never found. The division of Europe into two hostile camps had already hardened to such a degree that British diplomats declared quite openly that the balance of Europe as embodied in the Triple Alliance and the Triple Entente must not be upset, and that Germany could not receive assurances beyond those given to Britain's Entente partners. The fact was that even in the absence of fixed obligations Britain was joined to its partners in a real comradeship-at-arms.

Part 3
The Further Naval Talks of 1910-1912 and Their Failure

THE NAVAL TALKS in the fall of 1909 faltered in part on account of domestic developments in England, chiefly election campaigns that at times endangered the whole liberal government; but there were other reasons, too, why there were no further talks until August, 1910. England now realized that she could not count on any substantial savings with respect to the naval construction program through any form of agreement with Germany. On the other hand, British apprehension over the German supplementary naval act of 1908 had begun to subside. The extraordinary efforts British naval shipyards had devoted to dreadnought construction after 1909 restored the British sense of naval superiority and security. Time had been gained, and Grey took advantage of this breathing spell, particularly in view of the distrust and even open hostility toward Germany that had accumulated among his foreign office colleagues—to read the record in British diplomatic documents is quite an experience!

Voices of protest were raised, nevertheless, in both countries, demanding an Anglo-German *détente;* and late in July, 1910, the British minister once again extended the hand of friendship across the Channel. Knowing that nothing could be done about authorized German naval strength, he put forward another proposal. The naval authorities on both sides were to keep each other informed of the progress of naval construction and each year's program, in order to reduce mutual distrust and avoid incidents, such as had arisen in England the preceding year, on the basis of false rumors and misunderstandings.[81]

Grey also tried to blaze a new trail in naval negotiations by suggesting a German pledge not to increase naval construction beyond the limits of the naval act. The year before both the Kaiser and Tirpitz had envisaged express renunciation of an expanded program, as provided for in the prospective 1912 naval bill, if this were necessary to secure limitation on the British dreadnought program. William II seems to have taken Grey's new memorandum of July 16 to mean that Grey was offering in return some limitation on British naval construction—even though the text of the document contained no such hint. In any event, the Kaiser immediately and enthusiastically agreed. "Agreement with England most welcome," he wrote in the margin, already dreaming of an alliance that would support the Open Door everywhere in the world, and that might be made attractive to the British by the offer of a German guarantee of British colonial dominion in India.[82]

As for Tirpitz, while he was suspicious of what might lie behind the British memorandum, he did wish to respond with a counterproposal. Germany would agree to reciprocal informative shipyard visits by the respective naval attachés; and, furthermore, Germany would agree to build only two ships annually over a five-year period from 1912 to 1916, if the other side would cut back to three a year. This sounded like a repetition of his proposal of the year before, except that the term of the agreement was put forward two years, beginning in 1912 rather than 1910.

Actually, the plan contained nothing more than a confirmation of the German naval act, 1908 version, which already provided for no more than two keels a year for the years from 1912 to 1917. In other words, there was no longer anything in it about slowing down the rate of construction by postponing certain ships.[83] Tirpitz reported to the Kaiser in person on October 24, 1910, and his presentation shows quite plainly that he was worried that the British might outmaneuver the Germans by an unlimited increase in the rate of their naval construction. This would have destroyed the whole idea of a German "risk navy" and stamped Tirpitz's life work a failure. Tirpitz now realized that a ratio of 3 to 4 was not within reach at that time and pressed with renewed zeal for maintenance of a 2 to 3 ratio as a fulcrum for his entire naval policy.[84]

The German Chancellor's reply to Grey's suggestion had been formulated before Tirpitz's proposals were received, and it did not even get down to military details. Bethmann declared that he was ready in principle to discuss the British proposals and hinted that he was also still prepared to negotiate on slowing down the rate of construction "within the framework of the naval act"; but, he insisted, he must know what counterconcession Britain was prepared to offer. There was a slightly sharper emphasis than in the year before that a naval pact was pointless for Germany unless "secure mutual relations" were achieved through concomitant political agreement—a locution that distantly hinted of a neutrality treaty.[85]

The Chancellor tried to be as concrete as possible and to exemplify the German desire for improved Anglo-German relations with many detailed complaints of British lack of cordiality. On the other hand, he sought to underline his sincere desire for understanding by means of a variety of diplomatic courtesies during the ensuing months. And indeed, by mid-December Metternich was reporting an unexpectedly firm willingness on Grey's part to do something for the improvement of Anglo-German relations. This, however, did not keep the British minister from stubbornly delaying a reply to Bethmann's proposals until late in March, 1911! In addition to this unconscionable delay, the British foreign office did not neglect to inform its Entente partners regularly about the progress of the Berlin negotiations (which were nominally "secret"), emphasizing that they were politically harmless and explaining that Britain had found itself unable simply to reject Bethmann Hollweg's approaches out of hand, even though there was much doubt whether any political agreement could eventuate.[86]

Thus, it is not very easy to believe that Grey was indeed in full earnest with his conciliatory policy. In the House of Commons he did mention the possibility of "a certain delay in German naval expenditures within the framework of their naval act" as well as of the Germans foregoing an enlargement of their naval program—but he gave no hint that the British might offer concessions in return. His official reply to Bethmann was an exercise in generalities. It emphasized the difficulty of making the Germans any political offer that would not cause resentment in Paris and St. Petersburg, proposed that initial discussions deal with Middle East questions, and only incidentally mentioned an "arrangement on fleet expenditures," remarking that political and military aspects should be dealt with at the same time.[87]

At bottom, the whole thing still constituted an evasion of the need for helping the naval talks along by means of practical proposals. The German response of May 9 was in turn couched in rather chilly and aloof terms, showing the influence of the new foreign minister Kiderlen-Wächter. It swept aside the offer of an arrangement on the Baghdad railway and the Persian question as quite unsuitable to provide a basis for a general political understanding. No words were minced now in stating that only an Anglo-German neutrality treaty could guarantee peace in Europe in the long run, and Britain was challenged to put its relations with Germany on the same basis as those with France and Russia. An agreement to slow down the rate of German naval construction, it said brusquely, had now become inopportune, since under the German naval act the rate would sink to two ships per year from 1912 on anyway. Still further limitation would not be acceptable, for budgetary reasons and also from considerations affecting the German shipbuilding industry.

The Anglo-German naval exchanges had thus reached a point of no return.[88] The main reason, though certainly not the only one, was the inflexibility of Tirpitz's construction schedule. It must be said, however, that Britain showed little willingness to make any military or political concessions and put forward no concrete proposals at all. The sticking point was ultimately Britain's massive interest in maintaining its power, together wtih its newly strengthened confidence in its political and military superiority over the irksome German rival.

London now became reconciled with icy resolution to the fact of the German naval program. This comes out in the speeches of British ministers in the House of Commons in the spring of 1911. McKenna, the navy minister, like Sir Edward Grey himself, insisted that Britain had achieved a perfectly satisfactory margin of security—thirty modern capital ships by 1914, as against twenty-one on the German side. The German military attaché Widenmann reported this as a capitulation by the British and a great triumph of the steadfast German naval policy. The proud Britons had at last been reduced to the point of relinquishing the two-power standard and compelled to submit to a 2 to 3 ratio.

The Kaiser was elated and wrote underneath the report: "Had we stopped building four or five years ago, as Bülow and Metternich wanted, we should have had our own 'Copenhagen.' Instead, they respect our firm will and are compelled to bow to the facts. Build on!" What was implied was that more than two capital ships a year might be built even after 1912.[89] The Kaiser never let go of his desire to extricate the British Empire from its ententes and draw it over to the German side.

This he now tried to achieve by blustering threats and tirades against the anti-German stand of British statesmen—although he still talked to Goschen, the British ambassador, about a naval pact, to follow a political understanding.[90]

Such a pact, however, "must neither prevent nor delay the further expansion of our fleet . . . nor offer any guarantees that our naval construction program will not be increased. This latter eventuality will depend entirely on what measures Britain takes." We see from these marginalia to a report from Metternich precisely how William II envisaged a naval pact—England was merely to be tied down to a 2 to 3 ratio, without any limitation on how many ships the Germans might build.

Tirpitz later reproached Bethmann Hollweg for having culpably missed the opportunity that existed in the spring of 1911 for embodying the 2 to 3 ratio in a treaty with England. "The road was clear for a firm agreement that would have done away with all the public squabbling and made another naval panic in England impossible. The German Chancellor needed only to reach out for it." We have already seen that such an assertion was nonsensical, in the light of the British attitude. It is hard to believe, moreover, that Tirpitz made this charge in good faith, when we recall how he felt about a naval pact at the time. He and his henchman, Commander Widenmann, the naval attaché in London, seem indeed to have expected something like a British offer to agree to the 2 to 3 formula. Such a thing, of course, never came about. Nevertheless, the two naval men were constantly importuning the Kaiser with warnings that such an offer would merely represent an attempt to reduce Germany to a two-a-year construction rate, even in the years after 1917, during which, to provide replacements under the naval act, the rate would automatically have to be stepped up to three a year. Any naval pact would now have the effect of destroying the German naval act.

Now that Tirpitz had "victory" in his pocket, however, and felt confident that the British had reached the end of their tether, he was no longer content to maintain the German naval act as it had been. He protested against Bethmann Hollweg even giving the impression, in his note in answer to Grey's of May 9, that Germany was still prepared to discuss British proposals for a naval agreement. In his view the British might conclude from this that Germany was prepared to accept a two-a-year rate of construction for the years 1912-1917 and a three-a-year rate for the ensuing years, when in actual fact a three-a-year rate was the "heart of the German naval act," and it might become necessary to move on to it even in 1912. If Germany built on a two-a-year schedule from 1912 to 1917 (as contemplated in the supplementary naval act), parliamentary difficulties might make it impossible to return to a three-a-year rate in 1918. "That would mean that the whole naval act were knocked into a cocked hat."[91]

It might be argued, however, that such sophistry itself made mincemeat of the law as the fixed pattern. We perceive quite clearly that to this fanatic in naval matters there were no limits to militancy, no hostages that had to be paid to political reason. It was obvious even then that he was merely waiting for a pretext, a political crisis, in order to push his long-cherished new amendment to the naval act through the Reichstag.

Such a political crisis occurred that very summer—the second Morocco crisis. We know that it led Germany to the very brink of war—naval warfare with Britain. The well-known speech of July 21 by Lloyd George, then British chancellor of the exchequer, combined with a trial mobilization of the British fleet, left no doubt that Britain would not hesitate to range its entire might on the side of France should that country become embroiled in an armed conflict with the German Reich over Morocco. Here was the first distant rumbling of thunder over Europe, and whoever (like the author) lived through those days will not soon forget the wave of fear that swept the German people.[92] It was on that day that Germany suddenly grew aware of the fearful possibility that a future war would hit Germany not on two but three fronts. Indeed, down to the First World War, Germany's peace of mind never returned. Concern for the future led to widespread and effective propaganda for army expansion (conducted through General Keim's *Wehrverein*); but for the first time serious doubts were voiced about any large new navy bill, even among circles which had hitherto been staunch supporters and admirers of Tirpitz's big-navy policy. To keep stepping up the pace of the naval arms race had begun to appear like a bootless undertaking—for did it not increase rather than reduce tension with Britain?

Tirpitz shared no such doubts. Almost his first thought after Lloyd George's speech was that it would arouse great indignation in Germany and bring a new navy bill nearer to realization. What should he now demand? Heavier guns, perhaps, larger crews, and, most importantly, three or four heavy cruisers over and above previously authorized strength? He at once began working with his staff.[93] When one follows these discussions in detail, one notes at once that there was scarcely any real technical reason for such increases, merely various desires that were deliberated to and fro. Capelle, Tirpitz's deputy, would have liked to request continuance of the four-a-year rate beyond 1912, but admitted that this would require "strong nerves" and also noted that so far the requisite popular indignation and enthusiasm had not materialized at all. Indeed, he retained general doubts whether a new bill would be opportune at the present time, from the point of view of domestic as well as foreign policy. He never did reach full clarity on these points.[94] In any event, he advised that no new bill should be introduced until 1913.

An interesting memorandum by Capelle, dating back to the fall of 1911 and intended only for internal use within the Reich naval office, has recently turned up among Tirpitz's papers. Capelle here seems to be trying to outshine his chief by contending that the British were even then incapable of implementing in the long run their principle of "two keels to one." Sooner or later they would have to seek a political understanding with Germany. "We hold the trump cards, not England. All we need to do is to wait patiently until our present naval act has been fulfilled." Any understanding to come would be possible only on that basis, hence there should be no further increases in the number of ships. Imperial naval policy was still to find its ultimate culmination in "an alliance with Britain that assures full political and military equality."[95]

Tirpitz can scarcely have shared Capelle's naive political expectation that England would soon be forced to seek an alliance with Germany. The reservations entertained by his closest collaborator seem to have had no effect on his own arms planning. As early as August, during a stay in the Black Forest, he had more and more excluded any thought other than that advantage must be taken as soon as possible of the opportunity to make a new navy bill palatable to the government by representing it as compensation for the setback suffered in the Morocco controversy, as a demonstration that the Germans were unwilling to accept a diplomatic slap in the face without reaction. This, of course, was typically militarist thinking. A war to restore the Algeciras agreement would certainly have been neither popular nor rewarding. "If the British, however, should wish to prevent us from passing a new naval bill, we should have our *casus belli,* understandable to everyone in Germany, and we should not be able to stand in the way of destiny"—even though right then, before the Kiel canal had been widened and Heligoland fortified, was the worst possible moment for a naval war. The four-a-year rate was too much, but Germany should retain the three-a-year rate and in addition opt for large ship types, increased personnel strength, procurement of airships, and a possible stepping-up of submarine construction.

Quite evidently the question was not what was of the greatest technical urgency but only how much could be extracted. By August 30 a report had already been submitted to the Reich Chancellor putting forward concrete demands: formation of a third naval squadron on active service; accelerated replacement of obsolescent armored cruisers; a three-a-year rate for six years instead of a two-a-year rate, i.e., six capital ships more than were provided in the old naval act. These points were presented to Bethmann Hollweg orally the following day. With his usual blend of caution and indecision, he did not at once reject them, but after consulting with Kiderlen and Wermuth, the Reich finance minister, he voiced serious reservations. The new bill might bring on war, and it imposed an intolerable financial burden. Tirpitz was shrewd enough not to press too hard and proposed that any decision be postponed until after the Morocco negotiations with France had been concluded.The Chancellor willingly agreed.

The aid of Widenmann, the naval attaché in London, was now enlisted. He was to make it clear to the Chancellor and especially to the Kaiser that Britain had long been expecting a new German naval bill that would supersede the two-a-year rate and would certainly become reconciled to it, since British public opinion had changed since Lloyd George's speech. There was a certain sense of guilt, of having pushed too close to the brink of war. Political circles were openly reproaching Grey, the foreign secretary, with being too anti-German, and a change of course was being demanded. If this was indeed true—and up to a certain point it was—this report from a military attaché nevertheless represents a classic example of militarist thinking: England's growing willingness to reach an understanding lessened the probability and danger of immediate war—hence the proper German response was to step up armaments!

Shortly before, the Kaiser had already hinted at increased naval strength in a Hamburg speech.[96] Tirpitz arranged for Widenmann to make a personal report to him on the yacht *Hohenzollern* on September 4. The result was quite as expected. On Bethmann Hollweg, however, the effect of listening to a similar report was horrifying—if we can believe Widenmann's own deliberately derisory account of his audience with the Chancellor. It was soon to be shown that the naval attaché, enjoying the imperial favor, had by far the greater leverage. He even served as the instigator of his ultimate chief's policies, and he pushed his immediate chief, the ambassador, into the background with his political reports, subsequently replacing him in office. As his reports show, Widenmann was a hard-working naval officer of unusual talent, equipped with expert knowledge and carefully cultivated contacts in high British naval circles. Unfortunately, he was ineradicably prejudiced against the British, arrogant and presumptuous in his relations with the diplomatic service, and a politically dangerous dilettante. Metternich characterized his work as "hired incitement."

There were, however, some immediate reactions. Not only the Chancellor and the finance minister protested to the Kaiser, but also naval officers at the highest level, Admiral von Holtzendorff, chief of the high seas fleet, in the lead.[97] On the basis of practical experience, the admiral sharply rejected the idea of still more ships, demanding instead that existing navy deficiencies be remedied by increased personnel and improved fleet maintenance. According to a report by Capelle, Holtzendorff was only reflecting the rebellious mood of naval line officers as a whole.

Clearly, the rate of construction had far outstripped the facilities for procuring trained personnel, especially officers. The discussion on this question between Tirpitz and his deputy reveals that Tirpitz was unsure of himself and no longer had a firm grip on the Kaiser—he kept talking of his impending resignation. Then too, the Chancellor clandestinely inspired press protests on a broad front against a new naval bill at this perilous juncture.

But Tirpitz was a seasoned tactician and regained control of the situation with enviable skill. In a cleverly calculated personal report to the Kaiser at Rominten on September 26, he suddenly reverted to the idea of a naval agreement, which he had so vehemently fought in the spring. Only this time there was a completely new twist.[98] Since a naval bill would now encounter so much difficulty, besides providing grist for the social democratic mill during the impending elections, he advised that its introduction be postponed a year. To pave the way for it, however, a public offer should be made to Britain immediately after the elections, perhaps in February, proposing a permanent ratio of 2 to 3 between the two navies—in total numbers, that is, not in new construction.

If the British accepted, the way would be cleared for a new German naval bill, since in point of fact Germany had not yet come near to reaching such a ratio,[99] and the absolute number of naval units would not be fixed under the agreement. If the British refused or, as was likely, used dilatory tactics, the Germans would have a fine propaganda weapon. They would have demonstrated their good will to reach a firm agreement, proved to the Reichstag that the navy was not pursuing "open-end" construction plans, and shown the people that the British were indeed recalcitrant. The catchword about a "risk navy" was worn out in any event, and the 2 to 3 standard would quickly take its place in popular propaganda. A new naval bill could be passed without trouble in the fall of 1912, especially under Tirpitz's new proposal that it be limited for the time being to three rather than six ships of the line beyond the old naval act, distributed over a period of six years. Creation of a third line squadron (using reserve vessels in part) would then become possible, as well as a substantial increase in effectives.

It was indeed a crafty proposal. Under the guise of voluntary self-limitation to a fixed ratio with the British navy, the Germans were to be free to raise the number of their ships. Naturally, the Kaiser was delighted over his admiral's brilliance, and he stated his conviction that their very financial situation would compel the British to accept. In a rescript issued to Bethmann Hollweg he gave the Chancellor directives that followed Tirpitz's proposals exactly. "A decisive turn has come in the history of the fatherland," he said, describing the whole project as a "national deed" that would properly channel German enthusiasm along lines he now proudly professed to have discovered himself.

Tirpitz pressed on, now sure of his sovereign's backing. The very next day he demanded that the Chancellor announce the new bill at once and introduce it next spring rather than in the fall. Only one of the reasons he himself cited for this haste is plausible. The bill was to enjoy the benefit of public support, while the memory of the Morocco crisis had not yet faded, and the hesitant Chancellor was to be publicly committed. Bethmann, however, stubbornly sought to avoid such a commitment. He totally rejected Tirpitz's proposal to offer the British a fixed naval ratio of 2 to 3.[100] His first response to Tirpitz hinted that he had seen through what lay behind such an "offer" and was under no illusion as to how it would be received in England—as an announcement that German armaments would be enormously stepped up, in order (as Tirpitz put it) "to narrow the military gap between the two navies."

A stubborn controversy between the civilian and military authorities now ensued, the details of which we need not follow here. Bethmann declined to pave the way for a new bill by sounding the keynote of a future 2 to 3 ratio, and von Heeringen, chief of the admiralty staff, also voiced reservations. Tirpitz and the Kaiser then dropped the idea of an agreement with singular rapidity. It was cut from the preamble of the bill on November 25, and thus the "decisive turn in the history of the fatherland" was deliberately foregone. The Kaiser and the grand admiral, however, were all the more intent on committing the Chancellor to the new bill as soon as possible. It was to be included in the proposed budget for 1912. "The people," William II insisted, "are clamoring for a new naval bill."[101] Since the Chancellor was unable to prevent it, he tried to delay it as long as possible—at least until after the elections, lest the prospect of large new naval expenditures feed fuel to the social democratic opposition but also in the unspoken hope that he might get out of the whole affair with a new Reichstag in session.

Wermuth, the minister of finance and Bethmann Hollweg's most important ally, was of the opinion that strengthening the German army was much more urgent than building still more new battleships; and he stoutly resisted any effort to rip new holes in the Reich budget, which had but recently been painfully stabilized by financial reforms, for such holes could be plugged only through loans. At the very least, the needs of both army and navy would have to be harmonized and projected over a longer period of time, within the framework of a general fiscal plan.

Wermuth was a clear-headed man of oldfashioned Prussian stripe, austere and uncompromising, and his judgments of Germany's international situation and real needs were astute. More than that, he was a man of character, and when he found himself unable to put over his financial plans he resigned immediately.[102] Bethmann Hollweg himself was not a fighter by nature nor a man to make up his mind quickly. He was also in the difficult predicament of always having to weigh whether he could in good conscience pass over the helm of the ship of state to someone else for the sake of a single issue.

Faced with the opposition of the Kaiser, behind whom he now saw a powerful pro-navy propaganda machine rally, the Chancellor was convinced that he could not prevent a new naval bill.[103] He sought recourse in all manner of compromise proposals to avoid formal expansion of the naval act, while still meeting the demand for a higher degree of naval preparedness, which even Holtzendorff favored.[104] All he succeeded in accomplishing was a reduction of the demand for new construction by one half (three ships of the line, and alternation of two-a-year and three-a-year rates). He could not keep the Kaiser, in his speech from the throne on February 7, from announcing the new defense bill even before the necessary means were assured.

What troubled Bethmann Hollweg most about the navy bill were, of course, its international repercussions. All the reports from London—actually even those from the naval attaché—indicated that after the waning of the second Morocco crisis a kind of self-appraisal had taken place in England, a delayed realization of the menace inherent in the specter of war, appearing so suddenly, a widespread questioning as to why Britain should allow itself to become embroiled in a European war for the sake of French colonial interests. Criticism of government policy culminated late in the year in a kind of uproar in the House of Commons, when Russian ruthlessness in Persia called the value of an entente with that country into serious question and even seemed to threaten the security of India, the British Empire's problem child.[105] The opposition in the House kept pressing more and more strongly for an understanding with Germany. The Asquith-Grey government yielded, at least to the point of engaging in protracted negotiations with German diplomatic representatives on colonial questions, in the course of which the tempting prospect opened up of settling old differences about the Baghdad railway and rounding out Germany's fragmented African possessions into a large and cohesive Central African dominion by the later acquisition of Belgian and Portuguese territories.

Berlin had to ask itself whether this might not be the right moment to make at least an effort to loosen the Entente ring before it was finally too late. Was this not the time to demonstrate to the suspicious British by conciliatory gestures that German policy was indeed peaceful, that the Bismarckian Reich was once again the bastion of peace in Europe, its government the world's "honest broker," who harmonized tensions rather than accentuating them by military bluster? There were many sharp conflicts of interest within the Anglo-Russian Entente throughout the world—in China, in Persia, at the Bosporus—many points, in other words, where German diplomacy might volunteer its services to the British. Indeed, as tensions with Russia were seen to grow more and more acute in London, it became more important than ever for Germany to clear up its policy differences with the British Empire.

Since the crisis of 1908-1909 everyone had known from what quarter the next and most immediate danger of war threatened—from the Balkans and Russia, where German support of Austria-Hungary had drawn bitter resentment. Bülow himself has stated that at the end of his term he urgently counseled the Kaiser on no account ever "to repeat the Bosnian action of 1908."[106] Everything, indeed, now depended on curbing the Balkan ambitions of Germany's Austrian ally, so that war with Russia might be postponed as long as possible or even prevented altogether. The longer that effort succeeded, the better the prospect that the Anglo-Russian Entente might some day begin to dissolve on its own. If the effort failed, everything depended on Germany's ability to make the upcoming war appear unequivocally as a defensive struggle on the part of the Central Powers against Russian aggression, thus leaving a loophole through which British policy might avoid becoming embroiled.

Even in peacetime this would have required war plans unambiguously pointed at the defensive in the west, with every resource marshaled in the east, and a naval policy that would have at least avoided deepening British suspicions beyond the absolute minimum. The last thing the Germans should have done in the circumstances was to bring in a new naval bill that would give the British the feeling that they were at the beginning of a new phase in the arms race with the Germans and bury all their hopes of at last being able to devote their tax money to better purposes. Only in September, 1911, Reginald McKenna, the first lord of the admiralty, had held out precisely such a prospect to the electorate, and two months later Churchill, his successor, reiterated the same hope.[107]

The German ambassador, Metternich, did everything in his power to paint the situation in its true colors to the Kaiser and the German government, in a series of clever and courageous reports and private letters in which he displayed no fear of the Kaiser's disfavor, though he must have known just how much displeasure they would arouse. But the effect of Metternich's reports was largely nullified by the counterreports Tirpitz inspired his naval attaché to provide. These met strong approval on the part of William II, whose marginalia on the ambassador's reports ran to "rubbish" and "incredible nonsense."

Neither the naval attaché nor his boss really understood the political concern of the diplomats. They were satisfied that the new naval bill would not bring on an immediate declaration of war. Metternich, on his part, predicted that a continuation of the arms race was bound to lead Britain to the conviction that a war with Germany was inevitable, a prophecy which the Kaiser merely characterized as "chicken-livered." Kühlmann, who described the possibility of coming to a favorable settlement with Britain on colonial matters, was told in no uncertain terms that the Kaiser wanted ships, not colonies. "We have colonies enough! If I want any more, I shall buy them or take them without England's leave!" In a highly discourteous hand-written decree, the legation councilor was brusquely advised to "stick his nose into naval history," from which he would learn that colonies without strong naval power were worthless. When the German diplomats in London made representations to the effect that one more large battleship, finished only four years hence, was not worth foregoing a colonial understanding, and that even six more ships would not really improve Germany's situation, since Britain would promptly outbuild it, they were not even deemed worthy of a reply.

Bethmann tried to weaken the effect of Widenmann's reports on the Kaiser by having the ambassador add his critical or ironic comments to them, but without avail. The Kaiser always wholeheartedly took the side of the military against the ambassador; and when the Chancellor sought permission to reprimand the young naval officer for his constant encroachments on the political sphere he was roughly told off: "No! He is an officer, and no civilian superior can reprimand him, only his *Oberster Kriegsherr* (supreme warlord)."[108] Small wonder that the attaché, basking in imperial favor, dared to criticize his civilian superior quite openly in his "private" reports to Tirpitz, which, of course, the *Oberster Kriegsherr* promptly saw. Widenmann went even further. Indirectly, he cast suspicion on Metternich as one who was particularly intent on currying favor with Churchill.[109] Widenmann himself took pride in the deliberately brusque tone he used (or professed he used) with British ministers and admirals in representing German interests. William II described all of his reports as "excellent." To take British desires in matters of naval construction into account, he declared, would mean "the interference of a foreign nation which I, as supreme warlord and emperor, cannot countenance and never will! It would be humiliating for our people!"[110]

In these circumstances, it must be considered something of a miracle that there were, nevertheless, further negotiations between the two countries in early February, 1912, and that these were initially greeted with great hopes. This was the mission to Berlin of Lord Haldane, the British war minister. It is an effort that bulks large in the controversy on the war guilt question. Viewed in retrospect, it appears as the last and most important of the "lost opportunities" before the war, meant to bridge the gulf between the two nations, and its failure seems particularly fateful. But, when one looks closely, one finds that it would be wrong to overestimate it, for at bottom it was doomed even before it began.

The very manner in which this meeting came about was based on a kind of misunderstanding. Much as in 1909, it began with well-meant but purely private and somewhat overzealous efforts on the part of two international business tycoons, Albert Ballin, head of the Hamburg-America Line, and his friend Sir Ernest Cassel, a British banker. At Ballin's suggestion, Cassel, a friend of Churchill, the first lord of the admiralty, offered to serve as an intermediary in bringing about a personal discussion with William II on naval matters.

This must have been done in such a way as to bring Churchill to believe that the Kaiser himself was behind the invitation—subsequently diplomats of the two countries argued as to which side of the Channel the initiative did come from. Churchill, in any event, thought that a personal appearance in Berlin on his part would be inopportune, though he was in basic agreement that confidential negotiations on naval matters should take place—a view which was vigorously supported by Lloyd George, who had long been pressing for reductions in fleet expenditures through an agreement with the Germans.

With the approval of Asquith and Grey, the two ministers provided the negotiator with a brief memorandum as a basis for his talks with the Kaiser. The memorandum demanded that Germany acknowledge England's need for supremacy on the seas and agree not to increase its current naval program, indeed, to curtail or slow it down, if possible. In return Britain offered to give favorable consideration to German colonial ambitions and to proposals for a political understanding under which the two powers would be bound not to participate in aggressive designs directed at each other.

As Grey reports in his memoirs, he looked on the whole undertaking with great skepticism and was firmly resolved that nothing would tear him from

France's side. To the Germans, this seemingly new British initiative came as a surprise, even though the proposals did not really offer anything new; but, surprisingly enough, the Kaiser responded with enthusiasm. In a dramatic discussion with Cassel, Ballin, and Bethmann Hollweg, he personally drafted an essentially affirmative note of reply, without first consulting Tirpitz. Very probably the two intermediaries, inspired with hope that their private efforts might result in a great political achievement, painted a highly optimistic picture of the readiness of the British cabinet to reach a peaceful agreement with Germany; and the Kaiser's volatile imagination quickly took fire with the prospect now beckoning that his lifework, the building of a German fleet, might be crowned by an Anglo-German friendship pact.[111] Had he not been always told that the British, at the end of their arms tether, were bound to come some day with offers of an alliance? Now it would seem that they had really come.

In fact, the basic outlines of British policy had not changed at all. According to Churchill's memoirs, what really prompted him and the chancellor of the exchequer was a desire to probe whether the Germans, as had long been feared, were planning another great leap forward in their naval construction, spoiling the economy program of the British liberals, which had been rendered all the more urgent by the recent domestic issues in Britain over the inheritance tax and the House of Lords. If the Germans did plan a new naval bill, they might possibly be dissuaded by the offer of a political agreement. If not, the British government would have made an attempt to reach an understanding, to which it could point before the country.

Such a tactic had become particularly urgent because the chorus of criticism of Grey's Entente policies was rising to its highest pitch in the House of Commons during those months, while the Russian advance on Teheran in Persia had constrained the foreign secretary to lodge a vehement protest. More and more voices were demanding an understanding with Germany. Thus it seemed a promising time to renew earlier attempts at achieving a limitation of German naval construction by treaty, by a more direct approach than in 1909. In any event, the British would gain an unambiguous picture of the German naval program. [112]

The Kaiser, on his part, did not dream of dropping the new naval bill, even though it had not yet been publicly announced by the time Cassel arrived in Berlin. On the contrary, the note of reply he drafted in person for the German negotiators demanded that the German budget estimates already prepared for the year 1912 be included in any naval agreement, i.e., the provisions of the new naval bill. To leave no possible doubt in the matter, the Chancellor gave Sir Ernest Cassel a summary of that bill, "a priceless document," in Churchill's words, over which the British admiralty sat up all night.

The negotiations now took a second surprising turn. They were *not* immediately broken off on the British side, even though Churchill noted at once that the new German bill meant a considerable reinforcement of the German navy, mainly the establishment of a third active squadron of line ships and a sharp rise in effective strength. The British navy would have to spend enormous sums, in fact withdraw the Mediterranean squadron to the North Sea, to maintain the necessary superiority. Yet it might be possible to avert part of this burden by persuading the Germans to spread out implementation of a new naval act, possibly from six to twelve years. A rate that slow, Churchill wrote Grey, "would make it possible to establish friendly relations, and we could reduce our own rate of construction, although I would be reluctant to submit this to negotiation." A change of policy, however—i.e., relinquishing the existing Entente—would certainly not be possible, he added, even if it were desirable.

This was a simple and clear-cut program. It left very little scope for a political understanding—no more than a slight hope of a gradual *détente*. Yet it was the first time, so far as I can see, that there was any mention at all on the British side of a contractual limitation—or at least slowing—of their own naval program. And British eagerness to reach an understanding was emphasized by the dispatch to Berlin of a cabinet member—not Grey, the foreign secretary, whom the Kaiser had invited, but Britain's most knowledgeable expert on Germany, Lord Haldane, the war minister, an ardent admirer of German culture as well as of the German military system. His visit was carefully camouflaged as a purely personal one, for informational purposes only. Yet Haldane was empowered to speak on behalf of the British cabinet and to offer proposals, which represented remarkable progress over the situation that formerly prevailed.

Haldane himself, full of idealism and almost religious zeal, looked on his mission as a great historic opportunity to make a contribution toward international reconciliation.[113] He encountered in the German Chancellor an equally genuine and highminded readiness for understanding. The meeting between these two men turned into a deeply moving human drama. Indeed, Bethmann Hollweg's whole personality had from the outset aroused much sympathy and trust among the British. With all his inner qualms and doubts, he seemed to them almost like another Abraham Lincoln.

Thus the scene seemed set for an understanding, but the long discussion for which the two statesmen met on the afternoon of February 8 revealed the full difficulty of the undertaking. Despite an earnest search, no satisfactory formula for a political entente could be found. With respect to the central problem of a naval agreement, Bethmann dared not simply throw the new naval bill overboard. All he promised was "to think the matter over again."[114] Paradoxically enough, the ultimate decision lay neither with him nor with the Kaiser, but with Tirpitz, the naval expert.

Tirpitz had been deliberately kept out of the picture during the initiation of the meeting, for even the Kaiser was afraid of his obstinacy. It must even be doubted that Tirpitz would have agreed to the agenda William II fixed for the talks on February 4. This agenda provided that the naval bill was not to be an immutable point beyond the initial exchanges. Apparently some compromises might be made if the British gave up the two-power standard, as applying to Germany, and were prepared to conclude a clear-cut alliance or at least a neutrality pact. It was soon to be shown that such expectations were illusory. Indeed, Metternich had never for a moment shared them, while Bethmann clearly had entertained most serious doubts.

These doubts had come out plainly on February 6, when the Chancellor talked with Tirpitz, to whom the Kaiser had communicated his program the day before. Bethmann's own negotiating position was severely circumscribed, for he had assented to the inclusion of announcement of the new naval bill in the speech from the throne, to be delivered the day before Haldane's arrival in Berlin. This can also be said of William II. He had been half-hearted in championing his initial program with Tirpitz on February 5, no longer suggesting that the bill might be negotiable but stating that it should be insisted on with "firmly expressed will." Foreign interference would be impermissible, he added, and the Germans should press strongly for mutuality and reciprocity.

What about Tirpitz himself? In the notes he made for the crucial session with Haldane on February 9, to which William II summoned him, only doubt and rejection are expressed. The British were not even considering a true neutrality pact in the political sense, he wrote, and their colonial offers were practically worthless. In military terms, Germany must insist on a fixed 2 to 3 relation, even though there was no mention of such a relation in the British offers.

Was Tirpitz, then, determined from the very outset to sabotage any agreement? The Kaiser himself was afraid of this and asked Admiral von Müller, chief of the naval cabinet, to urgently exhort Tirpitz not to impede the conclusion of a great Anglo-German entente by petty obstinacy. The fate of Germany and the whole world now hinged on his conduct during the talks with Haldane; and, if they led to success, the Kaiser would see to it "that the world was told it was to Tirpitz that Germany and the world owed peace and a heap of colonial territory to boot." Tirpitz would then "have a position in the world, the like of which no German minister had held since Bismarck, and he would then be able to play catchball with the Reichstag." A list of large colonial acquisitions was appended, allegedly promised by Haldane. The Kaiser seemed greatly taken with this, in curious contrast to his earlier utterances, which we have noted. He appeared to be enthralled with dreams of a political alliance, presumably on the basis of the Chancellor's report on the favorable impression received at the first meeting with Haldane the preceding day.

Tirpitz himself later insisted that he would have been prepared to drop the entire naval bill if the British had given a real *quid pro quo,* in the form of a serviceable neutrality declaration of mutual fleet limitation. Actually, before the meeting with Haldane, a meeting took place at the Reich naval office, to which Tirpitz summoned his deputy Vice Admiral Capelle, Rear Admiral Dähnhardt, Chief of the Central Division Hopman, and other high naval officers. This is what Hopman reports on the exchange that ensued:

> Admiral Capelle spoke to the effect that if Britain were really to make substantial concessions in the colonial sphere and showed an intention to settle the conflicts that were retarding the development of both countries, then it would be the right thing for us to do to drop our naval bill without reservations. It would have become quite illogical; for the establishment of friendly relations would be diametrically opposed to an increase in our naval strength and the creation of a third active squadron. Should an acceptable understanding with Germany come to pass, this would be tantamount to recognition of Germany as a world and sea power, and none could be prouder of that than Admiral von Tirpitz himself.

Capelle proposed that the bill be withdrawn as soon as "concessions held out were assured beyond doubt. This found support from the other gentlemen, as well as the approval of the navy minister."[115]

It must be seriously doubted whether the final sentence of this report, written from memory, accurately represents the situation that existed. True, there is seeming confirmation from a new find among Tirpitz's papers—a slip of paper, in Capelle's hand, on which the results of this talk are again given as above. Yet it remains uncertain whether this reflected Tirpitz's views, for his assent is not specifically mentioned.[116] If he really gave it, it could have been only half-hearted; for, when it came to the climactic discussion, he showed an entirely different face.

In a note, probably written later, on the course of this discussion, Tirpitz himself says that he "held to the principle of the bill from the beginning," since he thoroughly distrusted British willingness for political concessions and had had to yield a good deal in the winter negotiations.[117] In the discussion itself he stubbornly fought for retention of the bill and impressed both the British minister and the Kaiser with his hard, unyielding demeanor.[118]

Haldane showed a great deal of understanding for the German desire for strong naval armaments and even for the basic principle of the bill; but, while he was quite willing to make concessions, he held strictly to the program Churchill had set up and reaffirmed in his famous Glasgow speech about the German "luxury fleet." Haldane proposed that the new German construction program should be extended over at least twelve rather than six years and clung firmly to the policy of laying down two British dreadnought keels for every German one.[119] He said that the 2 to 3 ratio demanded by Tirpitz would be conceivable only as the result of Anglo-German amity extending over a longer period.

In effect, this already marked the failure of the talks, and the question of military concessions which the British might offer in return for more substantial

German concessions was not even mentioned. The only concession Tirpitz was willing to offer—and this only on the Kaiser's intervention, according to the Kaiser's report—was a respite in the tempo of construction. The three new capital ships to be laid down would be slightly delayed—the first by one year, the second by two, the third by about three.

Haldane was desperately eager to avoid an outright failure, and he may have hoped that better terms might yet be forthcoming through Bethmann Hollweg's intervention. In any event, at the end of the discussion he seems to have expressed himself in such optimistic terms that the two German negotiators thought agreement was assured. The Kaiser, especially, already entertained ardent hopes of great new colonial gains. Goschen, the British ambassador, on the other hand, was horrified that Haldane should have even considered such trifling German concessions; and Goschen got the impression that Haldane was deeply depressed over his failure.[120]

Haldane, however, did not yet abandon hope, especially since the Chancellor sent him word to remain firm on the armament question. He, Bethmann, "would not allow an agreement to fail on account of Tirpitz." But Bethmann, of course, could have wrung further concessions from the Kaiser only if he had been able to show far-reaching political concessions from the British side. In their final meeting, the two statesmen therefore promptly got down to an effort to formulate some mutually acceptable neutrality and colonial agreement.

Negotiations along such lines continued between Berlin and London for several weeks after Haldane's departure. Tirpitz had given the British minister a printed copy of his naval bill with its preamble, perhaps in the expectation that the other side might be willing to haggle further over details, a process in which the Germans might jettison certain items in return for political advantages. The bill would thus have become a kind of bargaining counter with which to extort political concessions.[121] If this was indeed Tirpitz's plan, it was a complete miscalculation. When the British admiralty scrutinized the bill, it was found that German combat power, and with it the costs of British countermeasures, would rise even higher than Churchill had feared from the outset and Haldane had assumed in Berlin (before actually seeing the text of the bill). In essence, therefore, London regarded Haldane's mission as a failure. No British minister would have dreamed of having any part in an agreement extorted by military blackmail, even less of offering military counterconcessions.

A question that cannot be unequivocally answered from the available diplomatic documents is whether the hardening British attitude on Haldane's return to London was really based on technical admiralty objections against the German naval bill as such, and especially against the increase in effectives, which now suddenly came to the fore; or whether there may not have been political considerations, especially with respect to the feelings of Britain's Entente partners. Such thoughts played an important part from the beginning.

Even in Berlin, Haldane himself had assured the French ambassador that he regarded continuance of the Triple Entente as absolutely essential as a counterpoise to the Triple Alliance of the Central Powers, for the maintenance of the balance of Europe.[122] If this was indeed his view, he could not even have been thinking of modifying the existing bloc structure by an understanding with Germany. Grey, for his part, was at pains to emphasize the political innocuousness of Haldane's mission in Paris and St. Petersburg; and anti-German diplomats like Nicolson and Lord Bertie made no secret to the French of their disapproval of the whole undertaking—indeed, they rather encouraged the French to protest. There can be no question that concern for his Entente partners made it very difficult, if not impossible, for the British foreign secretary to find a formula for a political understanding that would have really satisfied the Germans.

Yet, as we have already seen in Chapter 3, it was not really Poincaré's protest that led him and his cabinet to reject the German formulation.[123] Nor was it really (or predominantly) Francophilia, let alone Russophilia, that was responsible for this negative decision. To the British it seemed impossible to imperil the Triple Entente, let alone abandon it, for they did not think they could rely on the friendship of a Germany whose policies were not trusted. We have already noted that this distrust was closely associated with fear of German preponderance on the continent. Yet that was not the only reason. The danger of German hegemony was bound to wane year by year, as France and Russia gained in military power. By 1912 it was already disappearing and giving way to mounting concern over Russia's growing strength. What lay at the heart of the distrust in which Germany was held was doubtless its record of unrestrained naval construction.

By the time Haldane went to Berlin, Churchill had already been compelled to bury his hopes for achieving a fixed quota or reduction in that program, in return for political concessions; but he still looked toward slowing its pace substantially, which would have meant much to Britain in financial respects. What Haldane actually brought back was bitterly disappointing—not only because the slight spreading out of the German building program did not greatly lessen the financial burden of British countermeasures, but for another reason that Tirpitz and William II never really understood. The good will of the German powers-that-be to join in a true partnership was once again called into serious question, seemingly confirming British suspicions. The Germans apparently expected the British to embark on this new friendship even while they were being compelled to increase their naval armaments. "The world would scoff at such an agreement," Haldane had told Tirpitz even in Berlin, "and our people would think we had been hoodwinked." This was, indeed, the view that subsequently prevailed in London.

Would dropping the bill altogether, as urgently recommended by Metternich time and again, have led to a satisfactory agreement? The bargain that would have been offered in return was settled, after much backing and filling, at a crucial British cabinet session on March 17. It amounted to a promise by the British government "not to participate in any unprovoked attack on Germany," to refrain from aggressive policies against Germany, and to enter into no aggressive alliances or ententes directed against Germany.[124] As obligations under international law, these pledges would have been of small value. They would have made political sense only if they could have been regarded as the beginning of a continuing *détente,* friendly rapprochement, and reduction of distrust sought by both sides. This was the precise meaning Grey wanted to give them, and he strongly emphasized his government's confidence in Bethmann Hollweg—much too strongly for William II's self-assurance as a sovereign.[125] The misfortune was that the German Chancellor could have prevailed with his policy of conciliation only if he had been able to offer the Kaiser a firm neutrality pact with Britain. It was this vicious circle that so fatefully prevented mutual confidence—the Germans insisted on firm treaty terms first, while the British wanted an end to the naval arms race above everything else.

Under the powerful impress of the Haldane visit, Bethmann Hollweg fought desperately to water down the naval bill even further to make it acceptable to the other side if at all possible—say, by canceling the new keels or postponing them indefinitely.[126] These efforts were supported by the German foreign minister Kiderlen-Wächter, and part of the time by the naval cabinet chief von Müller as well. They failed because of the opposition of Tirpitz, who kept imploring the Kaiser in his memoranda to "stick it out with an iron will" (a catchword that was to recur in the First World War), to tolerate no foreign intervention in German naval policy, and valiantly to withstand the blandishments of the British, as Widenmann put it; for all they were after was a naval agreement under which the German fleet would no longer constitute the slightest danger to Britain. There was no way of breaking out of the vicious circle. Germany could command friendship and respect only by naval power, while the other side thought it could find security against German power only by an entente with France.

These exhortations were strongly supported by the London "reports" from Commander Widenmann, who, as before, did everything within his power to demonstrate to the Kaiser that British policy was devious and insincere—all the British wanted was to trip up the German naval bill. Widenmann at the same time lamented the alleged incompetence of the German diplomats, especially Legation Councilor Kühlmann and Ambassador Metternich. "If only Metternich were to depart from here! He is a national misfortune," Widenmann said in one of his "private letters" to the Reich naval office.

By late February matters had reached the point at which the Kaiser rejected any yielding on naval questions beyond what had been discussed with Haldane and urged that the naval bill be introduced into the Reichstag as soon as possible, so that the Chancellor would be committed to it.[127] When Bethmann hesitated, still unwilling to abandon hope that an agreement with Britain might be achieved even without further concessions, the Kaiser's impatience exploded. Metternich was sharply reprimanded for not simply having refused to pass on to Berlin a response by the British admiralty to the German naval bill which the Kaiser characterized as "outrageously insolent." Under the evident influence of his military entourage at Wilhelmshaven, the Kaiser then attacked the Chancellor and the foreign ministry directly. In sharp military accents the latter was imperiously forbidden to take any steps in "the British matter" without first securing imperial directives. On March 5 the Chancellor was brusquely ordered to publish the bill by the following evening—i.e., even before consultations in the *Bundesrat* were completed, a most unusual procedure. If Bethmann failed to comply, the Kaiser would have the bill made public through the army and navy ministers. "My patience is at an end, and so is that of the German people! "

Count Metternich was advised by wire, over the heads of the Chancellor and the foreign ministry, that what had been discussed with Haldane was final. "If Britain withdraws its ships to England and the North Sea from the Mediterranean [which actually happened immediately afterward!], this will be interpreted here as a threat of war and be answered with a stronger naval bill—providing a three-a-year rate of construction—and possibly with mobilization."

The resignation Bethmann Hollweg thereupon submitted bears impressive testimony to his clear insight and his desire to keep the peace: "If war be forced on us, we shall fight and with God's help not perish. But for us to conjure up a war unless our honor and our vital interests are touched—this I should regard as laying impious hands on Germany's destiny, even if, by human foresight, we could count on complete victory. Such, however, is not the case, leastwise not at sea. Your Majesty's navy will fight heroically, but according to statements repeatedly made to me by the navy minister we cannot count on its victory over the British and French navies."[128]

The effect of Bethmann's offer to resign was that publication of the bill was once again postponed. Initially, William II even said that he was prepared to leave the construction schedule for the three ships open again, but Tirpitz at once forced him to withdraw this concession by offering his own resignation in turn. The controversy with the Chancellor was thereupon renewed, and even the empress intervened. She went to Bethmann and implored him to end her husband's torments of uncertainty. It would seem that all she achieved was a statement from Bethmann that he no longer absolutely insisted on changes in the bill.[129]

As before, however, he did refuse to make it public so long as there was still the slightest ray of hope that the British government might give favorable political assurances. Bethmann tried to blunt the effect of Widenmann's reports by adding his own comments and attempted through Kiderlen, in vain, to have the naval attaché enjoined from submitting any further reports of a purely political character. On March 12, through Kühlmann, he sent newly formulated proposals for a political agreement to London, attempting a compromise between the German and British desires. It came as a bitter blow to him that the British cabinet decisions of March 14 and 17 refused to entertain his new formula as well. For the Kaiser this British reply settled the matter. "Such impudence," he said, "makes any further action unnecessary. . . . The Haldane talks and the agreement discussed in them are dead." The British were now to be offered a defensive and military alliance, to include France, which would, of course, be rejected, thereby "putting Britain flagrantly in the wrong before all the world."

Tirpitz tells that William II was in "an extremely jolly mood" over this negative issue of the affair, and that he thought he had finally got the better of his reluctant Chancellor; but the official documents do not bear out Bethmann's total nervous breakdown which Tirpitz derisively described to his admirals.[130] Apparently Bethmann never paid the slightest attention to the Kaiser's directive to offer both the British and the French an alliance, though the Kaiser himself had made such an offer in a personal letter to King George V. Bethmann sent further directives to England for continuing the negotiations and even desired Kühlmann to enlighten individual British cabinet members on the situation in Berlin through personal discussions—which Metternich protestingly rejected. Bethmann delayed publication of the bill until March 22 and did not finally break off the whole project until April 3, after still a third British cabinet decision late in March had led to another rejection of the German alliance formula.

The Kaiser's triumph was complete:

The consequences of misguided German diplomacy have been the loss of much valuable time and effort and infinite trouble, while the tangible results were zero! I trust the lesson has not been lost on my diplomats and that in future they will listen more attentively than in the past to their master and his orders and wishes, especially when anything is to be accomplished with the British, with whom they do not know how to deal, whereas I understand them well! . . . Thank God no part of the bill has been sacrificed—that could not have been justified before the German people. . . . I saw through Haldane and his fine fellows in time and thoroughly spoiled their game. I have saved the German people their right to sea power and self-determination in arms matters and I have shown the British that they bite into granite when they touch our armaments. Perhaps I have fed their hatred, but I have also won their respect, which may at the proper time persuade them to continue negotiations, let us hope in a more modest tone and with a favorable issue.[131]

It would be hard to imagine a more typical and flagrant outburst of the militarist mind. Tirpitz shared in the Kaiser's triumph, but he affected a mien of conciliation toward the vanquished foe. It was Count Metternich who fell victim to his victory. Long before the naval bill was approved without change and by a large majority in the Reichstag (May 14-21), Metternich was recalled from his London post, with the vigorous cooperation of Tirpitz and Widenmann. Diplomatic procedure required that the naval attaché also be replaced; but Widenmann, after being relieved, was given evidence of the highest imperial favor, a decoration and a promotion to higher rank. The Kaiser, in two long private audiences, asked Widenmann's opinion of the recently ousted ambassador, and the former attaché used the opportunity to vent floods of hateful invective and to urge strongly that Metternich's successor be given better instructions by Tirpitz.[132]

The empress invited Widenmann to a family dinner at Potsdam and expressed her deep appreciation for his excellent London reports, which had been of such value to her husband. Soon afterward Widenmann had the satisfaction of learning that Tirpitz had indeed been charged with instructing the new London ambassador, Freiherr von Marschall; and Widenmann himself was ordered back to London until August, to "introduce" the London ambassador, whom he boasted he had won over completely to his own political views.[133]

If anything, Widenmann's successor, Senior Lieutenant von Müller, outdid him in political narrow-mindedness and eagerness to meddle in purely political matters. From the outset he apparently felt called upon to serve as a kind of naval watchdog over the London embassy. Many of his reports consist of nothing but political rumor-mongering. He never for a moment took seriously the admonitions of the ambassador, Prince Lichnowsky (who succeeded after the early death of Freiherr von Marschall), to stick to his naval sphere. For Müller there were two clear-cut German political camps—the diplomatic service and the navy. One had to be on guard, he wrote, lest the "pen-pusher diplomats," always inclined to compromise, take a stand that "we, the imperial navy, cannot accept." More than that, it would be best if German diplomats scored no successes at all in colonial negotiations.

> . . . Our diplomats hope that any progress in that direction would at last rid German public opinion of anti-British sentiments [incited by the navy and the Pan-Germans] and make it amenable to a policy of conciliation—in other words, that navy influence . . . on the person of the All-Highest and the people and their representatives be broken, so that the foreign-ministry policy of concessions to Britain would gain the upper hand as the more fruitful one. . . . The diplomats would then try to follow up with other successes and undoubtedly solicit any suggestions for a naval agreement.[134]

Understandably enough, this worthy partisan kept on pressing for a stronger

German navy even after 1912, favored radical implementation of the three-a-year construction rate, and zealously opposed Churchill's proposal to lighten the naval burden at least by a "battleship holiday." To his mind the only purpose behind this proposal was to wreck the German naval act, and he allowed the Reich naval office to dictate to him word for word what he reported on the subject.[135] This amounted to an attempt to fob off responsibility for rejecting the year's holiday as far as possible on the diplomats. All these efforts earned Müller high favor with William II, who wrote "excellent and statesmanlike" on a long report from Müller in March, 1914, in which the demand for a three-a-year rate of capital ship construction was again put forward. At the same time, the Kaiser reproached the Reich naval office with alleged deficiencies in its construction policies.

Yet this report made it abundantly clear how hopeless the arms race had become for Germany, ever since British naval policy had come under the influence of Churchill's tremendous energy and organizational talents. It provided what may have been the first instance in which Tirpitz felt constrained to disown the excessive zeal of his own subordinate and tool by adding a critical commentary. Germany's international situation had grown so critical by 1913, the danger of a holocaust from the direction of the Balkans so great and immediate, that one had to be completely blind to miss the most urgent priority of the day. Rather than new armored cruisers and replacements for obsolete ship types, what Germany really needed was to make up in a hurry for the long neglect in increasing its land forces. In his negotiations with the Chancellor and war minister on new defense bills, Tirpitz soon had to realize that there simply was no money for any further increase in shipbuilding, such as he and the Kaiser wished and demanded. Even the long overdue internal consolidation of the fleet, requested by Holtzendorff in 1912, was bound to swallow up immense tax funds and take at least another six to eight years. Tirpitz had always prophesied that England would some day reach the end of its resources. That day had now come for Germany as well.

What, then, was the net result of German naval policy, pursued with such immense resources not only in terms of financial sacrifice, but of untiring energy and political skill, not to say cunning?

In his final report in 1912, Widenmann, the naval attaché, maintained that the British had become reconciled to the fact of a powerful German fleet and had accepted even the new German naval bill without a murmur. Indeed, Germany's firm stand on the naval question had made the British far more amenable to political understanding than they had ever been before. Tirpitz makes the same claim in his memoirs and takes personal credit (rather than giving it to Bethmann Hollweg, with his unswervingly cautious and conciliatory foreign policy) for the fact that the last two years before the First World War went by without Anglo-German friction, while during this period the two powers repeatedly cooperated in the diplomatic sphere, and even colonial agreements were ultimately negotiated. By virtue of its naval policy, he insisted, Germany had matured to the rank of a recognized world power, with which England was no longer eager to pick a quarrel.

This was a wild misjudgment, as 1914 was to show. It is true that from 1912 to 1914 the British showed no desire to take on Germany. On the contrary, directly after the failure of the Haldane mission and the negotiations that followed, Sir Edward Grey declared his readiness to continue discussing colonial questions, in an attempt to reach a political understanding. His motive, however, was not fear of the German navy, but of war itself.

9

Planning for Warfare on Land – Schlieffen and His Great Campaign Plan

Part 1
Schlieffen's "Purely Military" War Plan

THE POLITICAL ATTITUDE of the army command in Wilhelminian Germany presented the sharpest possible contrast to that of the Reich naval office. Neither the war ministry nor the general staff were concerned with political activity, propaganda, publicizing new weapons or inciting nationalist ambitions. The former regarded itself as a purely administrative agency and, as we have already seen, a mere executive organ of the imperial command power. Its heads considered their ambiguous position as army generals and ministers with parliamentary responsibility a heavy burden, which they sought to lighten as much as they could by limiting themselves to purely military concerns. In the General Staff, on the other hand, Moltke had created a tradition of reserve and self-effacement, which was promptly revived in the person of Count Schlieffen after the abrupt fall of Moltke's busybody successor, Waldersee. Schlieffen's ideal was to cut as inconspicuous a public figure as possible, to "be more than one appeared to be." We have seen before the distrust, if not outright rejection, with which the General Staff—with a few exceptions—regarded the Reich naval office's propaganda campaigns on behalf of sea power and international political goals.

Schlieffen endeavored to equal his great preceptor Moltke in every respect, even in his outward bearing—taciturnity and chilly reserve in official intercourse and even in language, with clearly formulated sentences in a concise military manner. A truly Spartan excess of hard work, however, had to serve Schlieffen as a substitute for the easy flow and abundance of creative genius. Even so, he was accounted a master strategist among his staff officers and enjoyed the highest respect throughout the army. Like Tirpitz in the navy, Schlieffen became a much-admired leadership image in the army within a matter of a few years. Yet he never tried to expand his power within the military hierarchy nor to make himself into a central figure, let alone to engage in political intrigue like his predecessor Waldersee.

Limiting himself strictly to his proper jurisdictional domain, Schlieffen did not even secure for himself any dominant influence on armament questions, which he left almost entirely to the war minister. At almost excessive pains to avoid any conflict with the Kaiser, he apparently never thought of intervening in favor of the army in William II's naval policies. He was a military technician pure and simple, with no head for politics, and he was certainly not a fighter by nature. Indeed he was, if anything, inclined to self-criticism rather than arrogance.

One cannot, in Schlieffen's case, speak of a militarist orientation, if that is meant to imply a basic propensity to place military considerations ahead of political ones. When the temptation was greatest for Germany forcibly to disrupt the Franco-Russian military alliance by a pre-emptive strike against France and thus banish the specter of a two-front war for a long time to come—and there was such a time during the Morocco crisis of 1905-1906, when Russia was paralyzed by revolution—Schlieffen did not lift a finger to bring about such a war, though he was, of course, aware that such a favorable moment was unlikely to recur, as he occasionally hinted in discussion with close friends. [1]

Schlieffen always studiously avoided political digressions on his own, at the same time conscientiously maintaining close contact with the foreign ministry. For years on end he paid regular visits to the director of the political section, Privy Councilor Holstein, to secure information at first hand. As I have shown in detail, Schlieffen called the attention of the Chancellor and the foreign ministry to the politically dangerous aspects of Holstein's operational designs, the contemplated march through neutral territory, even when those designs were in the initial stage.

In the political sense, therefore, Schlieffen's conduct was above reproach. Yet no other judgment is possible but that the sum total of his work—his great campaign plan of 1905—was even more baneful to German political life than the excessively swollen German naval program in the Tirpitz era. (We shall yet discuss this at length.) But responsibility for this result accrues only in small measure to the staff chief himself. The full burden rests on the German political leadership, which accepted such a plan without objection, indeed without even thoroughly considering or deliberating its possible political consequences—in other words, it falls on chancellors Hohenlohe, Bülow, and Bethmann Hollweg, and on Baron Holstein, who was the first to learn of it. It was a clear case of statesmanship capitulating before military planning, the scepter falling before the sword, with its inexorable technical exigencies. How did this fateful plan come about? What were its repercussions?

Of itself, there was nothing unheard of in the idea of simply leaping over the irksome barrier of Belgian neutrality, created in 1831, in order thereby to bring about a swifter issue in any Franco-German power struggle. In the military literature and staff studies of England, France, and Belgium it had long been regarded as the most likely form of German offensive strategy—not on the basis of espionage, for the secrets of the German General Staff were strictly preserved until the outbreak of the war, but from purely technical strategic reflection. It was simply that such was the preordained configuration, in view of the powerful fortification barriers along the eastern borders of France—we have already reviewed the details in Chapter 3 of this volume.

In the end, the German march into Belgium in 1914 was nothing more than what the world had expected, except that it exceeded all expectations in the boldness of its conception. And, indeed, when one studies the origins of Schlieffen's great deployment and campaign plan of 1905 in detail, it is found that the German staff chief was motivated exclusively by military considerations that took on their final mature form through decades of war exercises, staff journeys, and consultations.

Schlieffen, of course, fully realized that a German invasion of neutral territory—Luxembourg, Belgium, and, under the 1905 plan, even Holland—would have serious political consequences, at the very least the augmentation of Germany's enemies by the accession of the Belgian and probably also the British army. He smoothed over such qualms with arguments that can only be described as typically military. "If we were to attack along the entire Belfort-Montmédy front with blind faith in the sanctity of neutrality," he wrote in 1905, "we would soon be effectively enveloped on our right flank by a realistic and unscrupulous enemy advancing through southern Belgium and Luxembourg. Belgian countermeasures would either be inadequate or come too late to take effect. Maintenance of Luxumbourgeois and Belgian neutrality . . . is therefore precluded for Germany by the right of self defense. The French are presently as convinced of this as we are."

The right of self-defense was thus invoked in justification of an open breach of international law. Those who lived through the events of 1914 will remember vividly the dominant role this very thought then played in German public opinion. There was, in effect, no other way to military success—thus the Germans generally rationalized their consternation at the fact that they began the war with an attack on a peaceful and politically aloof nation. In his memorandums Schlieffen time and again cited Germany's military predicament in extenuation of the contemplated breach of neutrality, together with his conviction that if Germany hesitated the enemy would be "realistic and unscrupulous enough" to choose exactly the same method—in other words, resort to *Realpolitik*. Not until 1912, long after his retirement, did he add a political argument in one of his notes, possibly under the influence of opinions voiced in the press: "Belgium is accounted a neutral country, but in point of fact it is not. More than thirty years ago it made Liège and Namur into powerful fortresses to ward off a German invasion, while it left its French border open."

We have already mentioned in Chapter 3 of this volume that this charge against the Belgians was unfair, and why this was so. It was also made plain there that Schlieffen's view of "unscrupulous" French plans was distorted or at least greatly oversimplified.[2] On this point he was—perhaps unconsciously—sharply at odds with the views of the elder Moltke, who, in his operational plan of 1887, had expressly described a French advance through Belgium as "extremely unlikely," for military as well as political reasons. In a military sense, the Germans could easily halt such an advance by a flank attack from the south. Besides, it would bring in the Belgian army and greatly disconcert the British and perhaps even challenge them to "take action" against France.

Moltke never even considered an advance of the German offensive forces through Belgium to outflank the French. Had he done so, he would undoubtedly have met opposition on the part of Bismarck, who, in 1887, in response to certain soundings in the British press, had declared in the semiofficial press that Germany would never begin a war with a breach of a European treaty. The possible strategic courses open to the German General Staff were by no means exhausted with the idea of an advance through Belgium. It was a fallacy, moreover, to believe that German policy was dictated by the General Staff.[3]

Schlieffen, in 1905, entertained an even more distorted view of the Dutch attitude. The idea of violating the neutrality of Holland evidently caused him some qualms—he contemplated traversing the southern tip of the province of Limburg, covering the Meuse. "The Netherlands," he ultimately concluded, "see in an England allied with France no less an enemy than does Germany. It should be possible to conclude an agreement with them." This was an illusion, as Schlieffen's successor soon recognized, when any prospect of such an agreement evaporated.[4]

Although violations of neutrality were certainly not unique in the recent history of Europe, there was in fact no practicable way in which political arguments or diplomatic pacts might have avoided the impression on the world of an act of brute force in the event that the Germans launched an offensive through neutral territory. Military necessity was the only justification that could be put forward. But was this really an inescapable necessity? It is not easy for the historian to find an authoritative answer to this question, yet it cannot be evaded.

There can be no doubt that a direct onslaught on the strongly fortified eastern French border along the Meuse and the Moselle offered little realistic chance of success, certainly not over a short period of time. Schlieffen himself briefly contemplated such a course in 1894, but he soon grew convinced that it was hopeless. The elder Moltke, too, did not think it would be possible to repeat the 1870 offensive against and across the greatly strengthened fortified lines along the Moselle and the Meuse. Moltke had given up faith in the possibility of swift decisions in war in the age of modern mass armies, citing German experience in France during the "popular war phase" of the War of 1870-1871. In his last Reichstag speech in May, 1890, he said that it was quite unlikely that a war between major modern European powers, armed to the teeth and provided with inexhaustible reserves, could be settled by total subjugation of one contestant in one or two campaigns. "It could very well become a Seven-Years' or even a Thirty-Years' war," he warned prophetically. Caprivi and the younger Moltke were inclined to similar views.[5]

Schlieffen, on the other hand, thought that a modern industrial country simply could not afford the "luxury" of protracted warfare. It must seek a swift issue, so that the halted wheels of its economy could begin to turn again as soon as possible. German military opinion evidently underwent considerable fluctuation on this whole question prior to 1914. In effect, however, the view predominated after Moltke's retirement, both in the General Staff and in the war ministry, that it was more important to provide resources for a swift rather than a protracted war. It was hoped that France could be subjugated by powerful blows so quickly that the main German forces could be hurled against Russia in a matter of weeks. When such a goal was envisaged, there was, to be sure, no way open other than an advance through Belgium to achieve rapid envelopment of the enemy.

Did such a strategy, indeed, offer the prospect of certain or at least extremely likely success? The fact that the great Moltke never envisaged such a course must give us pause. We have already heard about his strategic reflections and plans after 1871 (see Volume I, pp. 67ff.). As early as April, 1871, barely returned victorious from France, he counted on a two-front war the next time, since the recently vanquished foe would never dare strike again without Russian aid. With astonishing objectivity, he wrote: "Germany cannot hope that a swift and lucky offensive in the west will rid it of one enemy in short order, leaving it free to turn on another. We have only just seen ourselves how hard it is to finish a victorious war even against France alone."

Once only, during the Balkan turmoil in 1877, did Moltke design a strategic plan in which the first strike was directed against the French, to the end of forcing them to accept a great decisive battle in Lorraine. Even here, however, there is no suggestion that such a battle might lead to an advance on Paris. Instead, it was to be left to the diplomats after this victory to see "whether they could restore order in this direction, even if only on the basis of the *status quo.*" Success in the decisive battle, in other words, was seen as nothing more than creating the basis for a negotiated peace, so that the full armed might of Germany could then be hurled against the east. If the issue went against Germany, the only possibility would be to maintain a stubborn defensive in the west, falling back on the Rhine if necessary.

All of Moltke's subsequent deployment plans confined themselves to the defensive in the west, using only tactical offensive sallies, always employing favorable defensive positions in the limited area between Metz and the border between Lorraine and Belgium, the southern flank being protected by the fortress of Strasbourg. The main offensive was always contemplated in the east. In those endless plains that lacked any substantial natural barriers, an effective defense of Germany's 500-mile border was possible only by means of a large-scale offensive. Such a strategy, jointly conducted with the Austrians, held out a good promise of success. The peculiar configuration of Russia's western border virtually invited a great pincers movement by the allied armies, bottling up the czarist armies in the projecting Polish salient. There was, moreover, a clear political imperative not to abandon the Austrian ally to the Russians at the outbreak of war. Bismarck would not permit firm commitments to the General Staff at Vienna—fearing always that the Austrians might then be tempted to adopt irresponsible policies in the Balkans—and Moltke had no choice but to submit (see Volume I, pp. 233ff.); but he clung to the idea of a great eastern offensive to the last, even though war with Russia seemed quite unpalatable as such. Moltke, however, indulged in no dreams of Russian conquest—"they have absolutely nothing worth taking away from them, even after the most complete of victories," he said; nor did he aim at total destruction of the Russian armed forces. He merely wanted to weaken them sufficiently and push them far enough to the east (thereby shortening the front) to eliminate any immediate danger to Germany. He rejected the idea of penetrating deep into the Russian interior. In the event of a two-front war, he had apparently abandoned any thought of total victory, of the kind won in France in 1871.

What distinguished Moltke's strategy basically from that of his successor Schlieffen was this foregoing of the goal of total victory rather than merely a different direction of deployment, as it is usually represented. Moltke's stature is perhaps best demonstrated by his steadfast refusal to allow his great victory in France to delude him about the natural limitations of German power. We have seen (Volume I, p. 225) that at the peace of 1871 Moltke stubbornly insisted on the cession of Lorraine and the great fortress of Metz. His subsequent deployment plans clearly reveal his reasons. He wanted to strengthen the German defense lines in the west substantially, since he foresaw even then that the next war would be a two-front war, and he wished to secure his rear for massive offensive operations against Russia. He always regarded Lorraine as nothing more than a defensive buffer, eminently suitable as the scene of great field battles, and he was always prepared to fall back on the broad and deep river barrier of the Rhine if need be.

Schlieffen, on the other hand, viewed this same territory as the point of departure for a great western offensive—though he was constantly intent on widening this staging area more and more toward the north, ultimately all the way to the Lower Rhine at Wesel. This would have been possible only by concentrating virtually all of Germany's armed might on the western front, in keeping with the time-honored principle of the Clausewitz-Moltke school to keep one's forces together, in order to achieve numerical superiority at the crucial point. Strangely enough, however, this was at odds with the views of the elder Moltke himself, who never felt himself bound to any doctrine and would have preferred a formal division of the German army into two parts, though with a great preponderance on the eastern front.

Count Schlieffen always regarded himself as a faithful disciple of Moltke and, as we have already heard, was eager to emulate his great master. He was certainly no impatient daredevil like Waldersee, nor in any sense an adventurer, but rather a conscientious and calculating planner. Yet his plans partake in some measure of the enhanced confidence characteristic of the younger generation in Wilhelminian Germany—a generation too young to have fought for the achievement of German power in Europe under Bismarck. That power had been handed down to them ready made, and they stood in danger of misjudging its limitations, on land as well as at sea. They were, in a sense, prisoners of a powerful trend of the times, which none could easily escape. In the age of Bismarck it may still have been possible to envisage a strategy that might forego total victory on principle, leaving it to diplomacy, if need be, to bring to an end through understanding at cabinet level a war but half fought. Half a generation later this was out of the question.[6]

Schlieffen's much-discussed offensive plan took on its maturest form—in which it was passed on to his successor—in the year of crisis, 1905, when Russia had become virtually paralyzed in the international sphere on account of its defeat in the Far East and its revolution at home. To plan for a war directed exclusively against France, while ignoring the eastern front, seemed an obvious step. Yet this special and passing phase does not explain the plan's audacity and singlemindedness. The notion of first winning total victory in the west before an eastern offensive could begin occurs in a memorandum as early as 1892. Indeed, the idea of turning the enemy flank by advancing through Belgium was actually hinted at a year earlier, and after 1897 it developed into a clear-cut plan.

As late as 1912, long after his retirement, Schlieffen drafted a final great operational plan in which he recommended that the eastern front be initially left completely bare of troops. The fate of the Austrians, he remarked, would in the end be decided on the River Seine rather than on the River San; and a great German victory in France might deter the Russians from entering a war against Germany. This plan was formulated at a time when the danger of war clearly loomed from the Balkans, not from the west; and we can see that purely military rather than political considerations were behind this fixation on a western offensive. Schlieffen was convinced that the French were the more dangerous enemy and that total victory—swift total victory—could be won only in the narrow spaces of France, clearly delimited by mountain and sea, rather than on the vast plains of Russia. And total victory had to be the goal—not a mere partial victory, but the total destruction of enemy fighting power at a single blow—if the war were to be brought to a swift end. Such a victory was to be brought within the bounds of possibility even in a two-front war. The pride and ambition of the soldier is always to achieve the seemingly impossible by concentrated force and will power.

Count Schlieffen thought he knew a method by which such total victory could be swiftly won with certainty. So reliable did he consider this formula for victory that he was willing to stake everything on this one card. The plan involved the strategic envelopment of the enemy, seizing him in the flank, cutting off his retreat, and thus making possible his annihilation. In the face of enormously increased modern fire power, thoroughgoing success could no longer be expected from frontal attack with massed forces arrayed in depth, the tactic favored by Napoleon and still part of the traditional battle inventory of the Prussian generals in 1870-1871. Even the piercing of enemy lines had become very difficult, and the employment of massed artillery was not enough, for the mobile armor of today had not yet been invented.

Schlieffen was persuaded that frontal attack must be avoided whenever possible and that the issue should be forced by encirclement and flank attack. Frontal attack, he taught, resulted at best in pushing back the enemy—in other words, it merely led to an "ordinary" victory that could not really bring about a decision. Truly decisive victories could be won only by envelopment, and all the great successful battles and campaigns in history were in his view essentially due to the use of this one method—what he called the "Cannae" or "Leuthen" principle. Time and again, in every possible variation and demonstration, he hammered this thesis home to his staff officers. He had his historical section buttress it with numerous studies, which he supplemented with studies of his own on the Battle of Cannae.

The great "Schlieffen Plan" of 1905 is based wholly on this approach—it was, in fact, nothing more than an attempt to execute it on the grandest possible scale. One of the major ways in which it differs from Moltke's deployment plans is that it did not stop with fixing the initial order of the German forces, leaving further evolution to the genius, vision, and will of the captain, in keeping with the shifting situation and the enemy's response. Schlieffen instead sought to settle in advance and in full detail the course of the entire campaign. It was to be a single, centrally controlled and absolutely coherent grand action by massed armies, proceeding on the basis of a single operational principle.

Schlieffen's most faithful disciples and followers regarded this operational plan as an all but infallible formula for victory. In their view the failure that occurred in 1914 was due solely to the military incompetence of the younger Moltke, who "watered down" the great plan by strengthening his left wing instead of his right. This view was quite generally adopted by German war historians and strongly influenced the official versions put out by the army's historical section.

In my own book on the Schlieffen Plan, by contrast, I sought to show that objective scrutiny of all its details brings to light a whole series of uncertainty factors as well as certain dangerous weaknesses that characterize it as a venture with rather small chances of success instead of a formula for certain victory. My studies included Schlieffen's preliminary plans, his later conceptions, and the critical stand taken by the younger Moltke, and my findings can be summarized in a few sentences.

An advance by massive German armies through Belgium along the enemy front could not be intensified at will, because of the constricted space and the destruction of all the railways, bridges, and tunnels. There was danger at the outset, moreover, that the advance would disintegrate into separate actions by the various army groups, which, for technical reasons alone, could scarcely be centrally directed, as Schlieffen imagined would be the case. These partial actions also stood in danger of gradually losing their steam. Belgium would defend herself tenaciously, and a swift advance through that country could succeed only if particularly favorable circumstances combined. The crucial right wing was bound to lose more and more impetus as it penetrated deeper into France, particularly since bringing up supplies and reserves presented enormous difficulties.

Yet, as Schlieffen himself had recognized, the German right wing would be quite unable to outflank and encircle the giant fortress of Paris unless strong reserves could be brought up quickly. Above all, a point curiously unmentioned by the staff chief, the Germans themselves would stand in danger of being passed on their own extreme right flank—as indeed almost happened in 1914; for the enemy would be in control of a fully intact rail network, oriented on Paris, by means of which he could easily shift substantial troop masses from less exposed front sectors to his extreme left wing, an opportunity to which the French high command awoke only late. Thus it should have seemed rather improbable, to put it mildly, that Schlieffen's plan of pushing the entire French army away from Paris toward the southeast and destroying it in a matter of weeks could be executed. Yet if this ultimate goal was not reached quickly, the whole *Blitzkrieg* would fail; and week by week the danger to the eastern front of the Central Powers would loom larger and larger on the horizon.

There will, of course, always be disputes over the chances of military success. War, after all, is a most uncertain enterprise, with nothing dared, nothing won. Yet the questions raised in this book do not so much revolve around whether Schlieffen's great plan was or was not a formula for certain victory as around whether it constituted a war plan governed exclusively by technical military considerations, with politics playing no part at all. It was the product of a highly efficient military planning agency, and it was based on military theory rather than on the realities of history and politics. Indeed, one is tempted to compare it with the kind of abstract poker strategy represented by Tirpitz's naval battle plans.

The Schlieffen Plan is a classic example testifying to the truth of Clausewitz's paradoxical statement that "it is senseless to consult professional soldiers in drawing up plans for war, asking them to give 'purely military' opinions on what cabinets should do. Even more senseless is the demand by theoreticians that all available resources for war should be turned over to the generals, for them to use in drawing up military plans for a war or a campaign."[7] Yet this was precisely the German misfortune. The campaign plan of 1914 was conceived in "purely military" terms and the existing resources for war were turned over to the generals without striking a timely balance between the needs of war and the available means. All the structural defects we have already tried to show up in the army system of imperial Germany—the special position of the army as a state within the state, the continuing friction between military and political authority, the division of jurisdiction among various military agencies beholden only to a "supreme warlord" who lacked responsibility and expertise—combined to work their fateful effects.

During the period when Schlieffen was developing his operational plans for a grand campaign in the west—from 1897 to 1905—he already had to take into account the possibility of a two-front war. At the same time, it was not unreasonable for him to anticipate that some Franco-German controversy, like the one over Morocco, might set off the war. The German General Staff knew of the existence of a Franco-Russian military alliance, of course, but there was only limited information, if any, about its concrete provisions.

We know that Schlieffen was mistaken in his assumptions (see Chapter 4); and indeed, by 1912 he no longer believed that Russia would hold back in the event of hostilities with France.[8] As for the younger Moltke, a note in the files shows that he did believe in such a possibility. Yet he was convinced that the next war would break out between Austria-Hungary and Russia over some Balkan quarrel; but that did not persuade him to make any basic changes in his predecessor's operational plan. On the contrary, so convinced was he of the necessity for a grand offensive in the west, that in 1913 he dropped as superfluous another plan, the so-called "great eastern deployment."

Ever since the days of Schlieffen, such a plan had been developed year after year, side by side with the Schlieffen Plan. It provided for concentrating the main German force on the eastern rather than the western front, against the event that France might hold back in a Russo-German conflict. This had not merely become more and more improbable, but virtually impossible, in view of the military alliance of 1892. Any plan based on such a premise was indeed superfluous.

What was very essential, however, was attention to the inevitable consequences of Germany beginning a war in support of Austria-Hungary against

Russia with a major attack on France—an attack that would involve the invasion of neutral Luxembourg and Belgium, to be followed by a deep penetration into France with the purpose of totally annihilating the French armed forces. Bismarck had waged three wars in swift succession, and none of them could have been called wars of defense in the narrow sense, for on each occasion the issue was an open conflict of political power interests, the enhancement rather than the maintenance of Prussian-German power. Yet on each occasion Bismarck's diplomats skillfully saw to it that in the eyes of the world political and moral responsibility for the outbreak of war should not be attributed to him, but rather to the other side.

In the age of Bismarck, the Prussian-German monarchy enjoyed absolute military superiority over its enemies. This superiority had since dwindled, and no statesmen of the Wilhelminian empire could any longer dream of augmenting German power by military coups—nor did any of them dream of such a thing down to the outbreak of the First World War. All they were concerned with was maintaining undiminished the power of Germany and her ally. If Germany were to accept the immense burdens and dangers of a two-front war for the sake of Austria-Hungary, everything had to be done to avoid expanding it into a three-front war, and above all to make it plain to the world that the war was purely one of defense, an action in aid of Germany's ally. There would have been but one way to achieve that end—foregoing any breach of neutrality, remaining on the defensive in the west, with nothing more than tactical offensive sallies, and concentrating the strongest action on the eastern front. Germany, in other words, had to cling to the principle of Moltke's original war plan.

Such a policy would have given the war a totally different aspect. Of course, we can only surmise what the political consequences of such a change might have been—we cannot calculate them with anything like certainty. It can be taken for granted, however, that Belgium, with her three war-strength army corps, would not have joined Germany's enemies. It is highly unlikely, moreover, that Sir Edward Grey would have succeeded—even if such had been his intention—in involving his fellow countrymen in a continental war which, in effect, would have revolved around nothing more than helping the French reconquer Alsace-Lorraine rather than protecting them against German invasion and the total destruction of their military might.

We already know that in the last analysis Britain resorted to arms not on account of Belgium but on account of France (Chapter 3), and that Britain's fear of German preponderance on land was redoubled, since it thought it had every reason to feel immediately imperiled by German sea power (Chapter 8). Yet would the war have taken its fateful course if Germany had limited itself purely to the defensive in the west, avoiding any semblance of being intent on continental conquest and hegemony? After all, the British cabinet was prepared in 1912 to accept a treaty obligation not to support any "unprovoked" attack on Germany—and, for very good reasons, nothing threw the Poincaré government into such confusion as the news of this willingness.[9] Would the French people have taken the field with the patriotic fervor they displayed in 1914 if, instead of repelling a German invasion, it had been merely a matter of reconquering the provinces lost in 1871 or of helping the Russians destroy the Danubian empire? Not very likely.

True, in a military sense a modified German war plan would have probably meant foregoing complete victory—a victory of annihilation—not only in the west but in the east as well. After 1918, critics of the German supreme command claimed that Germany would have actually had much greater chances of swift and total victory in Russia than in France, but this can scarcely be proven. Possibly Schlieffen's reservations were exaggerated—he may have over-estimated the difficulties of carrying or outflanking the Russian fortifications on the Narev as well as the lack of communications and supply lines.

His main concern—that the Russians would avoid a decisive battle by simply withdrawing into the interior of their vast empire—involved a plain misjudgment of the Russians' political dilemma. They had committed themselves to the French for a major offensive against Germany directly upon mobilization. The czarist government, moreover, could scarcely have begun the war with a great retreat without courting the danger of new revolutionary uprisings. Yet now that we know the Russian deployment plans against the event of a major German offensive—the assembly area for their armies was to be pulled back all the way to Brest-Litovsk and the region north of the Pripet swamps—the younger Moltke's doubts whether the Russian main forces could indeed be encircled and overwhelmed within the first weeks of a war seem amply justified.[10]

Schlieffen's victory formula could not simply be transferred from the west to the east with any guarantee of total victory. Even the elder Moltke's deployment plans could not be used unchanged, for the offensive power of the French army had grown tremendously in the meantime and its leadership had become inspired with an aggressive spirit hitherto unknown. (It is true, however, that defensive strength had also increased to an extraordinary degree, mainly through the fire power of machine guns and the techniques of modern earthwork fortifications.) Considerable portions of the German army—perhaps even more than half—would have had to be left on the western front, to prevent a French breakthrough into Germany and destroy any French forces that might venture beyond the fortified line.

Nevertheless, considering the actual course of the German campaigns in the east in 1914 and 1915, as well as the sluggish and clumsy Russian leadership with its inadequate artillery, one is not easily persuaded that the elder Moltke was completely wrong with his plan for effectively defeating the Russian armies by a powerful offensive waged in common with the Austrians, i.e., with a probable numerical superiority. Perhaps complete annihilation was beyond reach, but there remained the possibility of paralyzing Russian offensive power so severely and pushing back the Russians so far as to eliminate any further immediate threat.

We must let the military experts debate the precise probabilities for the success of such undertakings. What matters is that here again purely military considerations are not sufficient. What is beyond dispute is that the motley and inadequately equipped army of Germany's Austrian ally could be stiffened and kept at peak effectiveness only by enabling it to win great initial successes in common action with German troops. If the task of warding off the Russian attack were left to the Austrian army alone for an indefinite period, there was great danger that it would collapse under the impact of such an attack—as indeed happened in September, 1914—and lose its best forces for good—to say nothing of Austrian resentment at being left in the lurch by the German ally. In the next chapter we shall deal with the relations between the German and Austrian General Staffs and their war plans. Let us here merely note that from the outset Schlieffen put little stock in cooperation with the Austrian army, of which he did not expect very much, and studiously practiced a chilly reserve toward the Vienna General Staff, which in return considered him arrogant.

Let us summarize: To be of any use, a war plan must be thoroughly considered, not only in a technical military sense but also from a political viewpoint. In France it was deemed essential to submit all operational plans to the government's supreme war council, which had to approve them after extended debate. In Germany, pressed and extended on every side, such a procedure would have been even more necessary. However admirable Schlieffen's great operational plan of 1905 may have been as a technical military achievement, the fact remains that its basic approach was promptly accepted by the top political leadership in Germany without any real discussion of the grave countervailing political arguments. Indeed, until 1913 at least,[11] there was not even an inquiry into the feasibility of alternative operational plans that might hold fewer political dangers, and the very details of the Schlieffen Plan itself were scarcely appreciated. This is one of the incomprehensible acts of omission in the Wilhelminian Reich—or perhaps it would be more accurate to say that it can be understood only in the light of the deficiencies within the German governmental and army systems which we have already discussed at length.

In May, 1900, on instructions from Schlieffen, Count Hutten-Czapski confidentially advised Privy Councilor Holstein at the German foreign ministry that the German General Staff proposed "not to allow its hands to be tied by existing international agreements in the event of a two-front war." Asked for his opinion, Holstein replied after a long, brooding silence (according to Count Hutten): "If the chief of staff, if a strategic authority of Schlieffen's stature, considers such a position to be necessary, it is the duty of German diplomacy to adjust to it and prepare for it to the degree that this is possible."

That was all; and that was the situation that continued down to 1914, through all the political vicissitudes.[12] In the Germany of William II, voicing political objections to a secret campaign plan worked out by the General Staff would have been regarded as unwarranted interference in matters with which politicians were not supposed to be concerned. To oppose the unanimous view of the military experts that this was the only path to German salvation, any leading statesman would have had to muster, in the total absence of support from his sovereign, an altogether uncommon measure of political authority and self-assurance.

Bethmann was always keenly aware of this dilemma. "No reasonably serious observer," he wrote in 1919, "could have failed to appreciate with the utmost clarity the enormous perils of a two-front war. For the civilian side to have tried to foil a thoroughly thought-out military plan described as absolutely essential would have entailed an intolerable responsibility. In the event of a subsequent failure, such a policy would have been considered its sole cause."[13]

Even so, Bethmann had to defend himself after 1918 against military charges that his intervention during the war had ruined the military plans. Hence he expressly assures us in his *Betrachtungen zum Weltkrieg:* "The German political leadership had no part in the preparation of the campaign plan, nor in the changes made in the Schlieffen Plan some time before the outbreak of the First World War, nor in the departures from this modified form that occurred when it was put into action. During my entire tenure no type of war council was ever held, at which politics might have intervened in the military cross-currents." Such, assuredly, was the case; but was this not a world turned topsy-turvy?

Part 2
Schlieffen and German Arms Policy

COOPERATION BETWEEN military and political authorities in war preparations was not the only element lacking in Germany. There was no unity even among the top military authorities. General Staff and war ministry had very different views on the needs of German arms policy. Perhaps the most curious aspect of the Schlieffen Plan is that it provided for operations at highly crucial points for which, by Schlieffen's own admission, the necessary forces were lacking.

Strategic encirclement is possible only when the front is enormously extended, exceeding the enemy front in length, while the power is retained to commit superior strength at the crucial point. In a war with huge mass armies this requires very large numbers of troops—indeed, true combat effectives rather than nondescript masses as such. The problem of how to procure such forces plays a major role in the correspondence between the General Staff under Schlieffen and the German war ministry. It also turns up as a very urgent matter in the operational plans of 1905.

"Before the Germans have reached the Somme and the Oise," we read there, "they will have become convinced that they lack the strength for the undertaking they have taken on. We shall find corroboration of what all the conquerors before us have found to be true—aggressive warfare requires and uses up enormous energies, and these tend to decline as the power of the defenders grows, especially in a land studded with fortifications."[14]

An enormous rear area, including Luxembourg, Belgium, and northern France, would have to be secured. Numerous strong points such as Antwerp would have to be besieged and kept under surveillance. The railways, roads, and countless towns, large and small, of a populous countryside would require special protection. To keep the active forces intact for battle, the Landsturm as well as the Landwehr would have to be mobilized and put in the field at the outset of war, and if this required changes in the law, these changes would have to be made. Even so, there would be no forces to ward off British intervention; and Schlieffen considered that the British might indeed land at Dunkirk, Calais, or Boulogne.

Schlieffen thought, however, that taking care of the British, if they turned up from that side, would be merely a side show on the German right wing, without seriously slowing the German advance into France. Today such an idea seems almost absurd, and it demonstrates clearly that the Schlieffen Plan of 1905 did not yet take British fighting power at all seriously. Its author had a much deeper concern. There was a shortage of troops for outflanking and encircling the greatly expanded Paris fortifications; and as Schlieffen came to appreciate in the course of his studies, unless Paris could be eliminated from the field of operations, the campaign could not be carried to a successful conclusion. Schlieffen thought that more than one third of the troop strength earmarked for the invasion would be necessary for this purpose—seven army corps swiftly to outflank Paris, defeat any British landing force that might approach from the west, and cut off retreat to the south for the French army on the Marne; and another six to encircle and besiege the city.

Such tremendous forces could not simply be detached from a general army reserve, for there was no such operational reserve. One of the most noteworthy characteristics of Schlieffen's strategy is that, on principle, he favored throwing every available army resource into the front line, staking everything on the swift success of his enveloping operation. He did not provide for "feeding the battle in depth" and left it to the several attacking armies to hold back their own reserves for any individual tactical operations they contemplated.

Thus Schlieffen had to resort to other expedients to carry out his operational plan despite plainly inadequate forces. He thought at first of shifting the whole advance of the attacking army far enough to the right to achieve a sufficiently strong overhang of troops for the envelopment and encirclement of Paris. Later on he must have grown doubtful whether this plan had a sufficient chance of success; the final version of his 1905 operational plan proposed the establishment, from the first day of mobilization, of at least eight new army corps, formed from cadres of the replacement battalions and from "super-numerary" reservists, i.e., those not directly mustered into the active units.[15]

But was this indeed a valid solution? Schlieffen himself was uncertain whether it would, in fact, be possible to move these new army crops in time through Belgium to the extreme German right wing, i.e., all the way to the area before Paris, where they would be most needed. His great operational plan did not settle the problem of how transport difficulties could be overcome in the presence of the complete destruction of the Belgian rail system. He merely suggested that those forces which could not be moved by rail would have to be used on the eastern wing, say at Metz or on the right bank of the Moselle. Even Ludendorff strongly sensed that these calculations, based on troops that were not available, represented a serious weakness in the great plan.[16] Schlieffen, he remarked, was too much a theoretician of pure strategy and not enough a practitioner of the military craft. He noted, during General Staff trips, that Schlieffen kept counting on the commitment of reserve divisions, reserve corps, Landwehr brigades, and "replacement corps" for combat purposes—units which then either did not exist at all or existed only in very imperfect form, with inadequate equipment. Perhaps Schlieffen figured that with the outbreak of war he would be given a free hand for improvisation on a grand scale, since from that moment on the war ministry would be reduced to the status of a mere instrument in the hands of the supreme command. But could improvisation be successfully carried out in wartime without appropriate preparations in peace-time—the organization of leading cadres, weapons, and equipment?

Here we touch on one of the greatest weaknesses in the preparations for warfare on land. General Staff and war ministry were not pulling in the same direction.

It was only natural that they should look at the arms problem through different eyes. It was easier for the General Staff to put forward large demands than it was for the war minister to push them through the treasury and the Reichstag and to justify them as politically necessary. Germany's everlasting financial predicament—a consequence of structural defects in the German federal state and its tax system, complicated by Bismarck's hapless financial policies—aggravated and delayed a systematic German army build-up in keeping with population growth and advancing military technology, as did Bismarck's self-inflicted shackle, the so-called "septennate" under which the army budget was always fixed for seven years in advance.

Yet the German army limitations that were later regarded as neglect were certainly not caused solely by financial stringencies or parliamentary opposi-tion, as the professional soldiers were fond of representing.[17] Nor would it be correct to say that the General Staff was always asking for more, while the war ministry was always trying to put on the brakes. Indeed, the only comprehen-sive and important augmentation and reorganization of the German army prior to 1912, which dates back to 1893, was suggested not by the General Staff but by War Minister von Verdy, and it was pushed through by Chancellor Caprivi against the vehement opposition of the Kaiser and his military courtiers.[18]

This had been Caprivi's hard-headed way of making up for his own cancellation of the reinsurance treaty with Russia—even though he was then ignorant of the contents of the Franco-Russian military agreement. Caprivi was simply and clearly anticipating the two-front war that now seemed to have become inevitable. Count Schlieffen himself had no part in preparing and pushing through this big army bill. It was merely sent to him as a matter of record. Even later on he took little part in such matters.

Schlieffen stuck conscientiously to the limits of his authority, even though time and again, when he was asked for his views, he put forward claims and demands that were sometimes quite extensive. On occasion he even protested against his complete exclusion from deliberations; yet he never claimed the right to speak the decisive word with respect to army bills. This brought serious consequences when army administration was dominated by a notably conservative, not to say reactionary, spirit under the war ministers von Gossler (1896-1903) and von Einem (1903-1909).

Any increase in peacetime army strength over and above the act of 1893 met with opposition from that side. Even though this act had not proved effective in preventing the Franco-Russian alliance from being able, at the turn of the century, to field a substantially higher number of troops than the Triple Alliance,[19] the Prussian war ministry remained convinced that the German army was equal to any war demands if only it elaborated and consolidated its traditional organization, without any increase in the peacetime cadres.[20] There was a basic reluctance to enter into an arms race with Germany's neighbors. As early as 1899, General von Einem, who even under von Gossler, as head of the army department, had a major voice in setting the ministry's attitude on arms questions, had written: "There must be an end to the arms race and the time must come when the chief of staff, always urging increases in the armed forces, must rest content with what the army administration makes available. Sound organization ceases when any troop increase effected by a presumptive enemy is instantly answered by a similar German increase."[21]

From the vantage point of subsequent experience, this sounds almost grotesque, and it has indeed been criticized as displaying a lack of insight into military necessities. On the other hand, it would be unfair to suggest that this opposition to a policy of unrestrained rearmament deserves to be condemned out of hand and to deny that it is possible to interpret it as an act of political wisdom in the Bismarckian tradition. The Prussian army spirit that found expression in such statements did not aim at continental dominance, let alone world power. It was concerned solely with defense and in this respect differed very deliberately from the policy of the Reich naval office. It was motivated, moreover, by a realization (which Tirpitz lacked) that an arms race with the other great powers was ultimately a vain dream for Germany, since every army increase on the German side could always be outdone by the others.

The remaining reproach is that von Gossler, and even more so von Einem, placed too much confidence in the qualitative superiority of the German army. There was a lingering pride in the superior skills displayed by the Prussian army in the Wars of Unification, which, decade by decade, grew less and less justified, especially in respect of the French army. What was overlooked was that in the end, even in 1870-1871, it had been the "stronger battalions" that had carried the day–33 infantry divisions against 26. Indeed, there was no real understanding on the ministry side why Schlieffen was so concerned with superiority in numbers.

In the document just cited, von Einem went on to say: "The notion that such masses can fight in long lines, man for man and man against man, must surely be relegated to the realm of fantasy. If numbers alone were decisive, the art of generalship would be superfluous. Yet it has always been essential and always will be, and it consists in concentrating superiority at the crucial point. To remind the chief of staff of this essential fact is not really the job of the war ministry. On the contrary, it should be the job of the chief to use it in dispelling any doubts the war ministry may entertain." Instead, continues the memorandum, the chief now declared German troop strength to be unequal to a large-scale offensive. Yet "never before were twenty-three active army corps made available to a general for war purposes. If he does not feel himself strong enough for the offensive with an army of such size, a few additional corps are unlikely to give him the necessary confidence."

The difference in military thinking that divided General Staff and war ministry can scarcely be expressed more plainly. It also becomes plain, however, that von Einem had no very clear picture of Schlieffen's campaign plans, which as early as 1897 provided for an advance through Belgium. These plans were indeed kept secret even from the ministry, probably until the well-known memorandum of December 21, 1912, conceived jointly by Moltke and Ludendorff, in which the veil was finally lifted.[22] This may have been unavoidable, yet there can be no question but that it seriously complicated understanding between the two agencies. Apparently no confidential talks between the leading men ever took place.

There were, of course, other reasons for the ministry's hesitancy. Repeatedly, and as late as 1906, after the first Morocco crisis, von Einem cited the absence of any immediate political threat, using this argument to oppose the kind of new military bill Chancellor Bülow was virtually throwing at him, a bill that was meant above all to modernize the army in a technical sense.[23] Thus von Einem left Tirpitz as the sole beneficiary of the changed mood in the Reichstag, as a result of the crisis recently surmounted. It is plain that until the end of his ministry—even after the Balkan crisis of 1908—von Einem never sensed the full gravity of Germany's political situation, nor was he aware of his own responsibility for timely arms measures.

Traditional Prussian thrift played a large part in this failure, as did the aversion of professional soldiers to the subtleties of parliamentary debate. And the rapidly rising financial needs of the Reich naval office created further complications. By 1908 they had reached a level of 400 million marks for the year, almost half of what was spent for the army. There was consternation within the war ministry, yet these demands were respected without protest, since they had the personal support of the Kaiser. It can be shown that—not least through the sovereign's direct intervention—the naval acts of 1898 and 1900 and the supplementary acts of 1906, 1908, and 1912 either prevented or limited an essential army build-up.[24] The navy's voracious appetite for officers also created difficulties for the army, since it severely restricted the manpower reservoir on which the army might have drawn.

The documents speak less plainly on a related matter. The war ministry's constant complaints about the lack of suitable officer candidates and a few other outright utterances [25] allow the conclusion that the army was worried lest unrestrained expansion impair the army's political character as an absolutely reliable bulwark of the throne. What would become of the aristocratic traditions of the officers' corps if it took in large numbers from the lower middle class? What would become of the once unshakable noncom loyalty if working-class youths from a socialist milieu rose to noncommissioned rank side by side with the peasant sons from Brandenburg and Pomerania, who formed the hard core of the army? [26] Whenever the war minister warned of the danger of qualitative deterioration if the army were swelled too fast, he was presumably also motivated by fears of a democratized people's army.

Initially these warnings dealt with other matters as well. The army was already being steadily and automatically increased, by virtue of the fact that universal service meant the discharge on "furlough status" of growing masses of trained soldiers year after year, a process which had been materially speeded up when the three-year term gave way to a two-year one in 1893. The question arose as to how these masses might be best employed in war. The younger men were to be called to their regiments immediately on mobilization, filling them up to full war strength. For the others there were special reserve divisions and Landwehr brigades, to be formed only in the event of war, though they were to take the field side by side with the troops of the line. What gave the minister concern was the large number and very uneven quality and equipment of these reserve units. Special peacetime cadres for them, of the kind Verdy had demanded, were lacking. The reservists themselves belonged predominantly to older age groups. Only very inadequate provision had been made for their weapons and equipment, especially artillery, supply, communications, intelligence, and medical. The appointment of officers and higher-echelon staffs caused many headaches.

For all these reasons the ministry feared that coordination of active and reserve units in the front lines would tend to paralyze the army's fighting power. Ministry plans were directed toward creating a smaller front-line army of full combat effectiveness and uniform organization, while the less efficient portions of the reserves would be assigned to the "occupation army" rather than the front. Further peacetime increases were to be halted until the existing active corps were strengthened by gradually filling the gaps and raising the number of scheduled cadres and men, while the reserve units would in the meantime be cured of their deficiencies. The fundamental idea was that reserve and Landwehr units would not immediately be committed at the front but be employed in subsidiary war functions. A large share of the reserves would be held back to replace combat losses.

These, then, were the concrete questions on which General Staff and war ministry were in dispute around 1900. Since Schlieffen changed his tactics repeatedly, the controversy often took on a confused aspect; but behind the many technical details his basic approach is discernible with considerable clarity.

His outlook was more modern than that of the ministry officers in that he did not shrink from operating with armies of millions. On occasion he spoke ironically of the time when Roon, in 1870-1871, had pleaded for a moratorium on the capture of French soldiers because he lacked the necessary troops to guard them.[27] He declined from the outset to rely on the alleged qualitative superiority of the German soldier and demanded that every man able to bear arms be mustered into the army.[28] He was simply drawing the logical conclusions from the fact that the German army system had been imitated by Germany's neighbors, as Caprivi had tried to do as early as 1893 in his comprehensive army bill.

Since any further increase in peacetime units was out of the question, Schlieffen in 1892 first pressed for improvement of the reserve corps. He demanded measures to make it possible "to bring our reserve formations into contact with the enemy directly after the conclusion of mobilization." They were to fight in close liaison with the line divisions. To preserve the capacity to bring every able-bodied man to the front, he rejected on principle the traditional sharp distinction between field and occupation army. As early as his first years in office, he desired the consolidation of army replacement battalions into higher mobile units under staffs of their own. In his operational plan of 1905 this took the form of eight war corps. Evidently his immediate concern was even more with numbers rather than the quality of the front-line troops.

Schlieffen, however, was not consistent in his attitude, and this seems to have greatly lessened the impact of his views on the war ministry. As early as October, 1893, he suddenly declared that the lessons of recent war history created grave doubts about mixing reserve units, closely akin in composition to the former Landwehr, with corps of the line, since such a policy tended to paralyze the striking power of the latter. Hence even then, on the heels of Caprivi's reforms, he pressed for a sharp increase in peacetime units, though he must have been aware that he could not expect such a thing until the next army bill, which was not due until 1899. Schlieffen also wanted so-called "war corps," to be assembled after mobilization from certain "supernumerary" units of the line.

The army act of 1899 did indeed provide for the organization of three new army corps in peacetime, though the actual number of peacetime effectives was but slightly increased—the second navy act, with its tremendous financial requirements, stood in the way of further army growth. This must have been a bitter disappointment to Schlieffen, who had hoped for seven new army corps—though there is some doubt as to whether he actually ever conveyed these desires to the ministry. Nevertheless, there is no record of any protests being lodged. Schlieffen knew what had happened to his predecessor, Count Waldersee, who fell out of favor with William II when he delivered an unfavorable critique of a war game. Schlieffen was always very careful in his treatment of the Kaiser, whose arbitrary intervention during imperial maneuvers he never opposed.

He kept up his efforts to strengthen the field army by creating additional war formations. To the war ministry his concrete proposals seemed somewhat vague and ambiguous. On the one hand, he reiterated in even sharper form his former criticisms of the reserve units. He stated again that it was inappropriate to mingle them with the fighting troops of the line and was firm in his demand for an operational army composed exclusively of "active units." On the other hand, he still wished to draw on reserve units in filling up new front-line corps and divisions, to be established in wartime from "supernumerary" line units.

Apparently this was a somewhat artificially contrived compromise, with the secret hope that some day, by way of the "war corps," additional peacetime army corps might be established.[29] In an era of feverish naval armaments this was, of course, out of the question. After 1900, von Gossler even had to forego his original intention to go beyond the act of 1899, which covered the effective strength of the army. Schlieffen's response was one of "serious concern," but he at once made a radical adjustment and came up with a proposal that now at last "the reserve divisions should be put into a state where they could be used shoulder to shoulder with the active field army" (March 27, 1900).

To this goal he now clung to the end of his tenure. In addition to qualitative improvement, he now asked for a substantial increase in the number of reserve divisions as well, with the ultimate aim of being able to mobilize and put in the field all of Germany's trained manpower at the very outset of war. This was almost certainly connected with his plans for a *Blitzkrieg* in France, which were then just maturing. We can scarcely be surprised, however, that there was headshaking over these demands of the chief of staff within the ministry, which knew little about his precise plans and was dominated by the traditional view that reserves should be committed only gradually and held in particular to make up for war losses.

Immediate mobilization of all reserves was possible only if they were trained and organized as combat units even in peacetime. In view of the numbers of "supernumerary" reservists and Landwehr men, this was a tremendous task. In Prussia alone 900,000 men had to be taken into account. Within the ministry the job was considered completely unrealistic. "How on earth," says a note in the files dating back to 1901, "are we to assemble in advance into regular units the entire strength currently on furlough status? Where is the money to come from for peacetime procurement and storage of the enormous quantities of clothing and equipment? How are the units to be kept up to strength? The thing would take forever."[30]

Schlieffen's idea of forming war corps from supernumerary active troop units and reserve units also seemed to the ministry an impractical proposal put forward by a pure theoretician. On this point von Einem, who had been war minister since 1903, was even more skeptical than his less conservative predecessor von Gossler, whom Schlieffen had persuaded to undertake the preliminary organizational work for establishing four such corps. Von Einem would have none of this. A note in his hand, dating back to the fall of 1903, indicates clearly that he regarded the whole war corps notion as a mere whim of the almost seventy-two-year-old staff chief, who was overdue for retirement.[31] The minister expressed the hope that Schlieffen's successor would not insist on such "inappropriate improvisations," which he felt would seriously interfere with the whole process of mobilization and deployment. Von Einem, moreover, did not see how the new units could be provided with adequate field artillery and ammunition trains without depriving the line formations and seriously weakening their combat power. In the face of such opposition, Schlieffen had considerable trouble persuading the Kaiser to allow him to retain at least two of his war corps.

At the end of his career Schlieffen had to stand by as the war minister delayed introduction of a supplementary army bill by a full year and even then limited its provisions to a minimal increase in army strength (1905). Schlieffen himself saw this draft bill only after it had been approved by the Kaiser. He limited his own response to a request that the continuing great arms gaps be filled up at a faster rate, to which no attention was paid. At the time, it had already been decided that he would be relieved, and his successor, Moltke, had already been appointed quartermaster general. In a letter in 1904, the war minister told Schlieffen (as he had told the Reichstag) that in his view army development in the direction of the establishment of new units and new troop formations had been essentially concluded, and that he regarded the numbers of effectives and cadres as sufficient for war needs.

All this was in the sharpest possible conflict with Schlieffen's own views, as embodied in the great operational plan he was just then formulating. "We invented universal military service and the idea of a nation in arms, and we have proved to other nations the necessity for introducing these institutions. Now that we have brought our sworn enemies to the point of increasing their armies beyond all limits, we have relaxed our own efforts. We keep on invoking our large population, the masses that are at our bidding—yet the able-bodied among these masses are neither trained nor armed to their full potential."

This appeal was meant to justify the demand for establishing eight war corps directly on mobilization. Yet Schlieffen did not say one word on just how these corps were to be improvised in time to come into play effectively in the outflanking and encirclement of Paris. Unable to obtain the number of troops needed for his *Blitzkrieg* by way of increased peacetime cadres, Schlieffen staked his hopes of success entirely on wartime improvisation. How realistic were his hopes?

His final petition to the war ministry (on November 4, 1905[32]) protested against von Einem's statement that army development was essentially complete, the establishment of further formations no longer necessary. Schlieffen admitted, however, that major changes were not to be expected in the immediate future—in other words, he was virtually accepting the new army bill, even the fact that "the establishment of special new field formations could not be anticipated in the existing circumstances."

He demanded, instead, that in order to use all trained manpower in the event of war the establishment of so-called "nonscheduled formations" be vigorously fostered, to be assembled from officers and men on furlough status who might be spared from replacement troop formations in wartime. Such units had already been contemplated in the mobilization plan of 1902, but had failed to materialize because of a lack of weapons and equipment, to say nothing of preparatory organizational measures. Equipment was now to be procured "so that these units can immediately follow and relieve the field troops." The relief was to be in the areas of garrison service, railways guards, and other occupation duties, and the initial peacetime equipment was to be provisional. As yet there was no mention of the formation of additional combat units, as provided for in the great Schlieffen Plan of 1905. Only in the further course of developments, we read, were such units to be rendered useful for appropriate missions in field warfare—that was all.

Despite these requests, an unresolved discrepancy remained between the theory of the great, bold campaign plan and the sober realities of German armaments.[33] The great Schlieffen Plan has, indeed, been described as more in the nature of a program than a realizable plan; but if that was what it was meant to be, it scarcely needed to remain locked up in the General Staff safes as a strictly kept secret. It could in fact have been realized, if at all, only by a radical change in the whole course of German arms policy. All trained reserves would have had to be armed for instant front-line use, and even such an enormous effort might well have been vain, since enemy countermeasures might have more than matched it.

Part 3
Strategy and Arms Policy after Schlieffen

THE YOUNGER MOLTKE, the new chief of the General Staff, initially did nothing more than take over the legacy of his predecessor unchanged, continuing it in terms of both organizational planning and arms policy. Yet there was a difference in basic attitude; and in the latter area Moltke, evidently under Ludendorff's influence, began to display a level of activity, in the final years before the First World War, that had been previously unknown in the General Staff.

His strategic ideas are laid down most plainly in a comprehensive memorandum of 1913, entitled "Germany's Attitude in a Triple-Alliance War."[34] Moltke here deals at length with the operational plans of his uncle and illustrious predecessor, whose ideas about a great German offensive in the east, to be waged together with Austria-Hungary, rested on the premise that Russian deployment would take a great deal of time and would proceed in Poland. Before its completion, the enemy was to be attacked from the north and south in a great pincers movement. The French army was much weaker at the time—before 1890—than when the younger Moltke wrote; hence it then appeared possible to stop it with relatively weak forces. Moltke's uncle had counted on a French offensive for the reconquest of Alsace-Lorraine, which he felt could be foiled because of the favorable configuration of the western border with Germany. Its relative shortness, only about thirty miles, made it possible for Germany to take a purely defensive stance, whereas the 120-mile eastern border could have been defended only by means of an offensive strategy.

In the meantime, everything had changed. The Russian rail network had been greatly extended, making possible an accelerated deployment much farther to the east along the Kovno-Grodno-Bialystok-Brest-Litovsk line. This would render ineffective an Austro-German offensive in the direction of Poland. A German attack on the new Russian staging areas would now have to overcome fortified positions in the impassable swamp regions of the Narev and Nemen. Austria-Hungary would have to advance against Ivangorod-Kovel, encountering the Rokotno swamps en route. A common offensive of the two armies, aimed at the Russian deployment, was thus scarcely feasible any longer. Even forcing the Narev would avail the Germans little, for the Russians could fall back on their vast hinterland. At best, a Russian campaign would be infinitely protracted.

The French had now brought their army to about the same strength as the German. A purely defensive strategy against such an army, using merely partial forces, would be possible for only a very short time. Yet the war on the eastern front would be a long drawn-out undertaking and the main effort could be shifted to the west only at a very late date. Unless the Germans wanted to adopt a purely defensive stand and forego victory, they had no choice but to conduct a powerful offensive in the west, leaving only weak forces in the east. Only in the west was a swift issue possible, since only here would both armies be deployed close to the national borders.

The strongest possible forces must be marshaled for the offensive blow in the west. The memorandum of 1912 found among Schlieffen's papers therefore provided for no troops at all to be left in the east, citing Field Marshal Moltke as authority, since in 1866 he too had concentrated all his forces for the main battle in Bohemia, stripping the Rhine front of troops.[35] In view of the totally changed alliance situation, however, this historical parallel was inapplicable. If no forces were left on the eastern front, the Russians would soon be in Berlin, and all the successes in the west, on which Schlieffen counted with such certainty, would be worth nothing. Without German support, moreover, Austria-Hungary would remain purely on the defensive and therefore offer no relief to Germany. The Austrians would swing into action only if German combat troops at least pinned down the Russian army of the Narev.

In the west the fortified line on the French eastern border must be turned, an undertaking which posed great difficulties. "It is not a pleasant thing to begin a campaign by violating the territory of a neighboring neutral state." The Germans should try to strike a political bargain with Belgium, perhaps along the lines of Germany promising the Belgians territorial expansion if they came over to the German side or at least did not resist the passage. At the very least they should be guaranteed the integrity of their present possesssions. Their country was to serve only for purposes of passage, and German war aims must on no account include the annexation of Belgian territory.

True, Moltke regarded such an agreement as virtually unattainable in practice. Germany must therefore count on enemy troop strength being swelled by the 150,000 men of the Belgian army. England too would—indeed must—be against Germany, for it was absolutely vital for the British to keep the Germans from gaining a foothold on the Channel coast. They would never believe any German disavowals of such an intent. German presence on the Channel would permanently tie down British naval forces there, which "would render Britain incapable of maintaining its world position."

In the face of these prospects, should Germany forego the advance through

Belgium, in the event that Britain pledged neutrality in return? Moltke regarded this as a dangerous course. It was uncertain whether Britain would, in fact, observe vague promises of neutrality; and if Britain did intervene, despite prior pledges not to do so, Germany would have thrown away its only chance for swift success, without gaining anything definite in return. The only condition under which Germany might find it tolerable to forego the great encirclement operation would be if Britain actively took the German side. But the British viewed Germany as stronger than France; they feared a French defeat with a consequent German hegemony in Europe. They wished to maintain the balance of Europe.

The British were not to be underestimated as enemies. They now had a fully and modernly equipped expeditionary army of 132,000 men. Britain and France had already entered into close ties and firmly counted on a German invasion of Belgium. The British expeditionary army was likely to land in the vicinity of Dunkirk-Calais rather than Antwerp, as Schlieffen had expected in 1906. The British seemed to have given up the idea of a landing there because of possible counteraction by the German fleet. Thus the Germans would have British troops to contend with in Belgium as well, and the attacking German right wing would have to be made very strong. To attack the French eastern front at the same time was not possible.

On no account must Germany follow Schlieffen's plan in crossing the Dutch province of Limburg, the southern tip of which covers the Meuse downward from Maastricht, and thus violating Dutch neutrality as well. Germany needed Holland as a "windpipe" for overseas imports.

The French on their part would want to halt the German attacking right wing, fighting shoulder to with the Belgians and British, and smash the German front with powerful forces from the direction of Verdun. This had to be taken into account in positioning the German forces. It was not feasible to engage in strategic speculations beyond the basic plan of the operation and the deployment preparations.[36] Germany's single aim must be to turn the enemy's left flank, if at all possible, while resting its own left wing securely against the powerful fortress of Metz.

In the main all this was in accord with Schlieffen's operational plans. Yet the basic orientation had changed perceptibly. The Schlieffen Plan was based on purely military considerations. Now political considerations came into play as well, on a sizable scale, as is true in other memoranda written by Moltke.[37] Above all, confidence in victory, the brimming sense of Germany's power, gave way to a very considerable extent to serious concern and an awareness of the inescapable dilemma lurking behind the great encirclement plan of advancing through Belgium.

Moltke clearly foresaw that this plan was bound to have fateful political repercussions, but he was rather at sea as to what the alternatives were. It was quite in character that in the General Staff war games he was prepared to forego the plan, if only the French would venture forth from their Meuse fortifications and accept battle on the soil of Lorraine. This was at odds with the ideas of Schlieffen, who was determined to stick unswervingly to his plan of invasion and encirclement, even if a French offensive carried deep into Germany.

We must conclude that, while Moltke kept to his predecessor's great plan, he evidently did so without enthusiasm. It was a plan of last resort, forced on him as the only way out of a serious dilemma, rather than a formula for victory that enlisted his fervent faith.[38] When Foreign Secretary von Jagow warned him early in 1913 that a Belgian invasion would inevitably bring out the British against Germany and suggested that the great plan be modified, Moltke grew "very thoughtful," promised a thoroughgoing reappraisal, and actually arranged for a General Staff discussion on the subject. As expected, this led to negative conclusions. The verdict was that the passage through Belgium could not be dispensed with.[39] Yet in retrospect it all seems like a policy of desperation—this business of seeking to "destroy" in a matter of weeks an enemy who had grown too strong to be fended off by the plan of the elder Moltke—a policy adopted despite the admitted fact that the German army was the enemy's clear superior neither in numbers nor in quality.

Then too, perhaps it was already too late to reshape the operational plans completely, which would have meant building well thought-out fortified positions between the Meuse, the Saar and the Rhine. In any event, no such change was made. The fearful political consequences were ignored, as were the serious difficulties that resulted with the Austrian General Staff—but that will be discussed later.

Moltke did make some purely technical changes in the Schlieffen Plan, for calculated strategic reasons rather than from any deep-seated aversion to the invasion of Belgium and the great flank-turning operation. The German left wing was to be substantially strengthened, above what Schlieffen had contemplated—without reducing the troop strength of the right wing in terms of absolute numbers, by the way. The German General Staff was aware that the French command was no longer content, as in Schlieffen's time, with remaining cautiously on the defensive, but instead, heartened by the growing power of its Russian ally and indeed constrained to display a greater initiative by current talks between the two staffs, was planning a strong offensive. The French could be expected to launch a breakthrough of the German deployment front from the direction of Verdun. In the face of this threat, Moltke, in agreement with his then deployment chief Colonel Ludendorff,[40] felt it necessary to alter the troop distribution under the Schlieffen Plan appropriately, a change that earned him the reproach, from Schlieffen's loyal disciples, of having "watered down" the great plan. The charge scarcely holds. Moltke was profoundly concerned with keeping the attacking German right wing as strong as possible, as shown not only in the 1913 memorandum already cited but also by the fact that, despite his worries about the eastern front, he left the initial covering force there at a level lower than what Schlieffen had provided for in 1905 against the eventuality of a two-front war.

In terms of over-all arms policy, Moltke also initially kept to his predecessor's frame of reference. Until 1911 he too acknowledged that it would be impossible in practice to push through a substantial expansion of the army's peacetime cadres; and he had the same experience, namely that War Minister von Einem paid precious little attention to General Staff wishes, advising him of draft bills only after the fact. Moltke's nature was basically conciliatory rather than militant, and he offered no protest when the minister declared anew in 1909 that "despite certain gaps, the basic framework of the army must be regarded as unalterable for some time to come"; nor did he object when the minister postponed until 1911 the new army bill actually due the year before and limited that bill entirely to the strengthening of auxiliary arms. The dreadnought construction program with its enormous costs, the supplementary navy bill of 1908, the need for sweeping financial reforms—all these impressed him to such an extent that in 1909 he conceded to the new Chancellor, Bethmann Hollweg, despite the Balkan crisis only just ended, that "a comprehensive new military bill could not be sufficiently motivated [before the Reichstag] from the military-political situation alone."[41]

Yet, from the beginning Moltke, like his predecessor, pressed for the establishment of larger combat units from the trained reserves, within the existing framework, to enable large sections of the "occupation army" to become combat ready through appropriate weapons and equipment. In time these demands grew more frequent and insistent, probably under the strong impact of the anti-German sentiments that suddenly flared up in Russia after the Bosnian crisis and the powerful regeneration and reinforcement of that country's army.

It was the chief of the deployment section, Lieutenant Colonel (later full colonel) Ludendorff, who soon had the deciding voice. An altogether new tone began to creep into the petitions to the ministry drafted by Ludendorff. They were no longer dry and technical accounts of desired improvements in armaments, but more and more insistent briefs. They argued that the development of modern mass armies by all the major powers compelled Germany to make maximum use of its manpower reserves. It was time that existing reserve formations were built into large, fully equipped combat units. The expedients and half-measures adopted heretofore were no longer sufficient. Germany needed reserve divisions and reserve corps provided with all ancillary services, heavy weapons, and technical equipment.

Precise and sweeping proposals were offered to that end. Schlieffen's old idea of establishing mobile combat units from the replacement troops was picked up again and immediately expanded almost beyond recognition. Unlike Schlieffen in his last request, the General Staff was no longer content to ask for the nonscheduled replacement formations already provided for in the mobilization plan of 1902, and to suggest only that they be equipped as garrison troops. It now demanded nothing less than the creation of a complete and fully combat-ready replacement army formed into "mixed brigades," which were in turn to be organized into higher units, each under a commander with the rank of general.

The style of Ludendorff's argumentation was highly characteristic of the man. Like all of his reports, it was full of patriotic pathos. "Every state fighting with every fiber for survival," we read in the memorandum of July 20, 1910, "must strain its every resource to live up to its highest obligations." And again: "Our enemies are so numerous that it may in certain circumstances become our inescapable duty to oppose them at the outset with our entire able-bodied manpower. Everything depends on our winning the initial battles. Once we have done that, it will not much matter if we use the replacement troops for combat purposes and permanently keep them from their proper tasks" (July 1, 1910).

Everything was thus staked on success in the great initial battle, as had been true with Schlieffen. Yet the use of these "replacement corps" was conceived along quite different lines. They were not meant to be used for the decisive battle in France, nor even to be "committed at once in common with the mobile field army," as the war ministry had at first feared—"that would be impossible, if only for reasons of rail limitations." Instead they were to appear in an independent role at secondary theaters of war, and only in special emergencies, such as the possible landing by the British in Schleswig-Holstein, which Moltke seriously feared, or on the Vistula, Netze, or Warta rivers in the east—in any event, they would always be "protected by fortresses, rivers, or other sectors." The very existence of such a replacement army, Ludendorff thought, might deter an enemy from launching an attack on Germany; and, if it were not needed in combat, it was still available to make up for combat losses.[42]

Schlieffen's rather unrealistic program for eight replacement corps had clearly been transformed into a practical proposition. It was no longer a question of wartime improvisation of makeshift units that could be thrown into exposed front-line sectors, but of a kind of second Landwehr, methodically trained for the immediate defense of the country. In this new form, the proposal made a much greater appeal even to the war ministry, now under von Heeringen. Only the scope of the new units still seemed unrealistic to him. After further debate, preparations were made in the summer of 1911 for "mobile replacement brigades," composed of replacement troops from various service branches, to be available against the event of war. They were, indeed, to be organized into higher units, so-called replacement corps and divisions, under "special-duty replacement commanders." At the outbreak of the First World War there were six such commanders, but the troops were still poorly equipped. The whole institution never attained any great importance.

It was, in a sense, already obsolete when it was created; for in the meantime an unexpected radical change had taken place in the course of German arms policy. All the dubious wartime improvisations which had so long been a bone of contention abruptly lost importance, because at a single stroke the carefully nursed peacetime army framework was burst open after all—or was at least greatly expanded. We come here upon one of the strangest and most memorable incidents in the history of the Prussian-German army. What makes it memorable is that it was quite evidently set in motion by a completely irrational element, a sudden change in German public opinion following the second Morocco crisis and Lloyd George's well-known threatening speech. Something almost inconceivable happened within the bureaucratic German state. A wave of national feeling pushed the government into a huge rearmament program with such urgency that the qualms of the fiscal and military experts were simply swept aside.

Bethmann Hollweg can scarcely have dreamed of the steamroller he would set in motion when he suggested to the war minister, von Heeringen, on October 9, 1911, that he sponsor a new army bill immediately rather than waiting until 1916. Even now he was apparently not convinced that a major increase in the army was essential. He wanted to sidetrack or at least delay the supplementary navy bill Tirpitz had announced, a bill that was most ill advised with respect to the state of Germany's foreign affairs.

The ministry was not in a strong position to oppose such a suggestion coming from above, especially since the Kaiser too had been urging a major army increase ever since 1910. Even in the Reichstag, when the army appropriations bill was passed early in the year, there was criticism of its inadequacy. At the time, the war minister scarcely bestirred himself to plan any basic change in arms policy. The war ministry and the General Staff moved only when Bethmann pointed out that the new militant spirit among the deputies might once again benefit the navy exclusively. What had never been said in official documents was now properly emphasized. Germany's destiny would ultimately be settled on land rather than at sea. A naval bill at this time might actually increase the threat of war.[43]

We have already seen in Part 3 of Chapter 8 that the naval bill did materialize, that for that very reason Bethmann Hollweg doubted the wisdom of announcing a new and redoubled army bill before the elections, that the juxtaposition of army and navy claims created serious fiscal difficulties which naturally reacted on the scope of the former, and, lastly, that hopes of reaching a naval understanding with Britain brought new delays. But to the government's surprise the new Reichstag, in which the social democrats were the strongest party, passed both defense bills and carried the tax increases without a murmur. Indeed, criticism was again voiced that the army bill still seemed inadequate. These events had far-reaching consequences.

In 1910 both war minister and General Staff had stated that "military-political considerations" were not sufficient to justify a large new army bill; but such reservations now fell by the wayside. In order to arouse universal patriotic concern and persuade the legislature to vote generous funds, all that was necesary now was to point to the tremendous numerical advantage which the allied armies of France and Russia had meanwhile gained over the armies of the Triple Alliance. General Keim's *Wehrverein,* founded early in 1912, took care to keep patriotic fears ablaze. It soon outstripped the German navy league in political influence, even though it did not enjoy the advantage of official support. Indeed, unlike the navy league, it was a thorn in the war ministry's flesh, and its exaggerated accounts of army deficiencies were considered dangerous, because they gained attention abroad.

Even so, ministry memoranda from 1912 on show growing apprehension of public indignation over lack of zeal and *schlappe Haltung* (slackness) in arms matters, particularly with respect to the Chancellor and the finance minister.[44] The agitation particularly benefited those elements in the General Staff and the war ministry which had long been urging that Germany accept the challenge of an arms race with its neighbors and desired to this end to "exploit the full military strength of the German people," i.e., to expand conscription to the point that everyone fit for service would be mustered into the army. This had never happened before. Instead, Article 60 of the Reich constitution had been followed under which no more than one percent of the population was to be under arms in peacetime (though this provision was formally in effect only until 1871).[45] The zealots now pressed for following the example of the French, who went much further. Ludendorff enunciated the ultimate goal in a phrase typical of him: "We must again become the nation in arms great men in great times once made us. Germany must ever advance, never retreat."[46]

But the military zealots were nowhere near content with the army act of 1912, which increased effective peacetime strength by about 29,000 men and brought many technical improvements.[47] Until the late fall of 1912, however, there was not the slightest indication that they were increasing their influence in the General Staff and war ministry, nor that they might push through still another new and larger army bill. As late as October 13, Moltke and Heeringen had a joint audience of the Kaiser at Hubertusstock. They declared that the state of preparedness that had now been attained was adequate and that the army was now equal to "any eventuality of a political nature." They even went so far as to say that the accelerated establishment of machine gun companies, desired by the Kaiser, was not particularly urgent.

Yet the very next day Moltke signed a letter to the war minister, drafted by Ludendorff, which stated that a considerable increase in the induction of recruits was necessary to make possible a "decisive rise in the peacetime strength of men and horses," and thus a more satisfactory make-up of reserve and Landwehr formations, which were described as totally inadequate. The letter was the opening gun in a series of General Staff requests calling for increases in scheduléd strength to be provided through a new army bill; and beginning in late November these demands grew more and more insistent. Under their impact von Heeringen, the war minister, changed his stand with surprising promptness, even though this put him in the embarrassing position of having to go back on his earlier declarations—even before the Reichstag—and of causing consternation in the Reich chancellery. There were no unexpected foreign threats to Germany he might have cited, any more than could Moltke, who had agreed with him as recently as early December that the military-political situation currently favored Germany. What circumstances could have been responsible for so sudden and radical a shift in the attitude of the leading men, Heeringen, and even more, Moltke?

No satisfactory answer is provided by the documents—nor in the careful account based on them by the Reich historical section. The files merely indicate unequivocally that Moltke was not swayed by any passing political events or dangers but rather by a general concern about the future. He felt that soon, perhaps in a matter of two or three years, unfavorable shifts could occur in European power relations and lead to war—especially the further growth of Russian power and events in the Balkans. Germany had to be prepared for such eventualities.[48] It is true that the General Staff was deeply concerned about the rapid progress of Russian armaments—but that was nothing new. Why, then, the sudden desire for such enormous new troop reinforcements?

The really new element that can be seen to play a major part in this turn was nothing more than a change in the cast of characters. The retirement of his superior, Quartermaster-General Stein, had given Colonel Ludendorff direct access to the chief of staff. It becomes clear that this hothead, a man of iron determination, fascinated and at once swept along his chief, the cultivated and aristocratic Moltke, inwardly insecure, often vacillating between resolve and reserve. Ludendorff carried Moltke far beyond his natural limits, as can be seen from subsequent reservations the latter was heard to express about documents drafted by Ludendorff which he nevertheless signed.

It is, of course, possible that there was more at work than the personal influence of his strong-minded staff officer in what agitated Moltke during these months and drove him to his unexpectedly sweeping arms demands. Late in 1912, Schlieffen sent Moltke a new great campaign plan, in which no troops at all were provided for the eastern front. It may well have been that in the discussions of all these deployment and operational plans Moltke for the first time grew alive to the almost incredible risks of the whole great flanking maneuver that was contemplated. "Once France has been beaten in the first great battles," he had written in a comprehensive memorandum in 1911, "that country, with no great reserves of manpower at its disposal, will scarcely be able to bear the brunt of a protracted war." The war minister had put a double question mark in the margin, with a reminder of the long "people's war" of the winter of 1870-1871.[49]

In the face of the increasing strength of French arms, might not doubts have arisen in Moltke's mind as well? We do not know. What we do know is that in the memorandum just cited, and in another, still more comprehensive one of December 21, 1912 (which he personally drafted for the Chancellor, but revised in collaboration with Ludendorff), Moltke discoursed at length about purely political issues—Germany's increasingly hopeless isolation among the great powers, the need for discounting Italy as a military ally (which would make the war with France a much more dubious affair than had been thought), the bitter necessity to fight the vital struggle essentially with Germany's own resources. In the course of all this, the breach of Belgian neutrality was described as essential for overwhelming France—probably for the first time in an official exchange with another agency.

These general considerations served as a basis for demanding a huge army increase. In the still more accentuated final version of the memorandum, in which Ludendorff had a hand, this came to an annual increase of 150,000 recruits, raising peacetime effective strength by about 300,000 men within two years. At least three new army corps were to be created from the ground up. Moltke's original draft shows that he originally envisaged this as a long-term program, to be realized over many years. It was Ludendorff who turned this into a high-priority program, a goal from which he would not desist, even though the war ministry kept insisting that so abrupt a leap forward was simply not feasible—and not merely for financial reasons.

Ludendorff's obstinacy at last led to a rupture. He was transferred to the field command of a regiment; and Moltke came to terms with the war minister and the Chancellor. This still resulted in the greatest army bill Germany had ever seen. It called for an increase of about 117,000 men and almost 19,000 officers and noncoms. Bethmann appealed directly to the people to raise the enormous sums—more than a billion for nonrecurrent expenditures alone—by a direct defense levy on capital rather than through loans. It was an audacious but statesmanlike and successful exploit. At a single stroke it swept aside the controversial question of how far the Reich's tax powers extended. The Reichstag was compelled to follow public opinion and vote the tremendous burden. Pushing through this great defense bill was the Bethmann Hollweg government's most successful action. At the time, everyone had the feeling that all had been done that could be done in a single action to make up for decades of neglect and equalize in some measure the numerical advantage in troops which Germany's neighbors had gained.

The Chancellor had actually tackled this important action only hesitantly and with many qualms—he had to be persuaded by the military. Bethmann Hollweg was afraid that such a sudden arms leap might serve only to increase political tension and sharpen the race, if anything. And he was to be proved right. Even before the bill had passed, countermeasures on a huge scale were initiated by Germany's neighboring states—France, for example, introduced the three-year service term. The race gathered breakneck speed, and by the time war broke out the great German army act of 1913 had not been able to effect any essential change in the relative strength of the two power blocs—not even in the ratio of Germany vis-à-vis France.[50]

Schlieffen's great operational design remained what it had been before, a risk with uncertain chances of success. One thing, however, the steady pressure of the General Staff did achieve. From the first day of war, the German army was able to take the field with much stronger and better-equipped reserve units than the French, who had centered all their efforts on the highest possible effective strength and needed a long time to mobilize all their reserve units. The immediate commitment of thirteen German reserve corps on the western front took the French General Staff completely by surprise. This had been considered impossible, and for that reason the French had not counted on quite so sweeping a flanking maneuver through Belgium.[51] Despite France's enormous military power and the intervention of strong Belgian and British units, Germany was thus enabled to develop initially a tremendous numerical superiority on the crucial right wing (1st, 2nd, and 3rd armies).[52] This may serve to explain why Moltke, despite his qualms, dared in the end to believe in the possibility of a great, swift success on the field of battle. Once that had been achieved, he remarked, as we have already noted, French resistance would have to fade rapidly, for France lacked the necessary manpower reserves.

It was with such expectations—or rather such slender hopes—that the German General Staff drifted into the crisis of July, 1914.

10

The General Staffs and the Outbreak of War

Part 1

The Austrian General Staff and the Notion of Preventive War

SO LITTLE WAS the German General Staff involved in the origins of the crisis of July, 1914, that its chief was not even asked for his opinion when Kaiser William gave the Austrians an unconditional pledge of help in the event of war with Russia—a pledge that was to have such fateful consequences. Moltke later insisted that, had he been asked, he would have, in view of the total military situation, advised against it.[1] Whether this be true or not—and we shall be dealing at length with Moltke's over-all attitude in July, 1914, later—it is certain that on the crucial days of July 5 and 6 no proper consultation took place either with the chief of staff or his deputy or with War Minister von Falkenhayn. As we know, Moltke himself was away at a spa until July 27. His deputy, General von Bertrab, simply received word of a *fait accompli*. A formal inquiry was addressed to Falkenhayn concerning the army's state of preparedness, but he was in no sense consulted.[2]

There is no point, therefore, in looking for bellicose sentiments among the German General Staff as an immediate cause of the First World War. It did, of course, bear a major share of the responsibility for the fact that the July crisis led straight to disaster—even though it is possible to show that neither the chief of staff nor the war minister at any time sought to bring on the war. The precise measure of that share of responsibility cannot, however, be determined unless we first thoroughly clarify the relationship between the German and Austrian General Staffs. There can be little doubt that in those crucial weeks the real center of intransigence—a militancy that in the end overwhelmed all diplomatic efforts at compromise—was located inside the General Staff of the Danubian monarchy.

Conrad von Hötzendorf, the Austrian chief of staff, certainly wanted war, but just as certainly he did not want a world war. The war he wanted was a war against Serbia—he had demanded it for years, paying no heed to the risk of a major conflagration. What ultimately prevailed in Vienna, owing to Conrad's influence, was a radical militarism that believed political problems could be solved only by force of arms; and what paralyzed political reason in Germany was the so-called *Zwangsläufigkeit* (inexorable sequence) of purely military considerations. If militarism, as defined at the outset of this work, means militancy to the exclusion of all else and to the point of numbing political reason with purely military arguments, then the crisis of July, 1914, must appear as the very epitome of the dangers of militarism.

It is a curious thing that the real impetus for the outbreak of this crisis did not issue from Prussia-Germany, which was decried as militarist, but from the Hapsburg dual monarchy, which had long boasted a style of diplomacy notable for caution and vacillation—actually a consequence of the military and internal political weakness that marked this archaic state. What persuaded Austria's statesmen to follow Conrad's advice was anything but an excess of self-assurance and a thirst for conquest, On the contrary, they were afraid that their multinational state might disintegrate completely, and they thought they could keep it from crumbling only by taking "vigorous action" before it was too late. For years the chief of staff had been urging such action.

Among the officers of the *k.u.k. (kaiserlich und königlich*, i.e., imperial and royal) army, Conrad von Hötzendorf had been considered a maverick early on. The over-all impression he made was not really soldierly. Of delicate stature and lively temperament, he was casual in appearance rather than cultivated. There was a nervous twitch in his impressive features, and a notably shrewd expression in his eyes. While still a young man, he drew much admiration from audiences and readers as an instructor in tactics at the war academy and the author of various manuals. What particularly distinguished him was imagination and inexhaustible energy.

Ever since 1889, the Austro-Hungarian army had drifted into a state of complete stagnation—it was "withering away," as the Austrian war minister Count Schönaich repeatedly put it before the Parliament in 1907-1908. In the circumstances, Conrad's unrelenting pressure for modernization and increased strength reflects much credit on him. Some of the deficiencies had been made up for in small measure by 1912, with Conrad playing an eager part in the process; his activities, however, were by no means limited to the military sphere.

Conrad's memoirs run to five heavy volumes. He left many papers, moreover, as well as mountains of correspondence in the Vienna war ministry. Plowing through this material, one is baffled by the man's obsession with writing. He set forth his proposals for military reforms in never-ending new memoranda addressed to the Emperor and the foreign minister, together with free-ranging disquisitions on foreign affairs and views on the proper relation of politics and war, all running to tremendous length. The foreign minister, Baron Aehrenthal, on occasion vainly sought to escape this rising floodtide by pleading that points at issue should be discussed in person.[3] In the end, he, like his successor Count Berchtold, had no choice but to leave some of the communications from the chief of staff unanswered.

Conrad utterly refused to confine himself to technical military matters. In 1909 Aehrenthal defended himself against a charge of having failed to exploit a favorable chance for war early in the year. Since, according to Clausewitz, war was merely the continuation of politics by other means, Aehrenthal felt that decisions of war or peace should be reserved to the foreign minister on principle. In a marginal note, Conrad protested vehemently. "In view of the intimate connection between the actual conduct of war and its preparation, and in view of the over-all political situation, part of this responsibility devolves on the chief of staff, as an adviser [to the crown]. History teaches us that in this respect he bears a much greater responsibility than the foreign minister. Clausewitz is quoted out of context here. Politics consists precisely of applying war as a method."[4]

War does indeed appear in Conrad's writings not merely as an indispensable political weapon, but as the most important, the one that alone really counts. Diplomatic cautions and reservations, we read in a memorandum of 1910, "must never serve as an excuse for evading military consequences, any more than should domestic difficulties and an unwillingness to spend. It must always be kept in mind that the destinies of nations and dynasties are settled on the battlefield rather than at the conference table.[5] . . . Do what you will, in the final reckoning it is military power that governs politics. Diplomacy instantly becomes mired when it leaves the solid ground of military power."[6]

This last sentence unquestionably states an important truth of politics and history. It is all the more curious to note that the outlook of this military man was narrowly limited to the relative military strength of Austria-Hungary vis-à-vis its closest neighbors, Italy and Serbia, when he came to hatch out his war plans. Conrad really saw but one means for curing the ills of his slowly crumbling multination country. Austria must show its military strength, must "settle accounts" with the enemies of the dual monarchy, overt and covert—and it must do so by a surprise attack in the form of a preventive war.

He called for such a war against Italy as early as the spring of 1907, on no better grounds than that Italy seemed to him to be Austria's enemy rather than its ally—it wished to deprive Austria of its position on the Adriatic, fostered the Irredentist movement in South Tyrol and Trieste, and was constantly strengthening its armed forces, almost certainly for an attack on the Hapsburg state. Austria must strike before it was too late. German assent was certain, Conrad boldly asserted. As for Russia, it was not ready for war.[7]

This Italian war was also to be a kind of preview of the next strike, the subjugation and annexation of Serbia. In Conrad's view, this was necessary to safeguard the annexation of Bosnia and Herzegovina and prevent the growth of a South Slavic empire at Austria's doorstep. Such an empire would exert a powerful attraction on the southern Slavs inside Austria. Austrian possession of Serbia, on the other hand, would provide a land bridge for trade with the East. General Conrad, with his eyes on this goal, thus welcomed the crisis over the annexation of Bosnia that broke out in the winter of 1908-1909. Not only did he make every preparation for a war on Serbia, but from January, 1909, on he kept urging that Austria attack this neighbor, regardless of whether Serbia became aggressive or not. Serbia and Montenegro had to be abolished as autonomous entities.[8]

Conrad thought he could bring off such a scheme at small risk, since Russia was still suffering from the aftereffects of the revolution of 1905-1906, neither Italy nor France was showing any strong taste for war, and Germany, clad in shining armor, had pledged support to her ally against Russia. He was bitterly disappointed when the Serbs, under pressure from the European powers, showed themselves conciliatory, whereupon the Vienna government too declared the controversy ended. In subsequent memoranda he kept reverting to these events, criticizing Aehrenthal's allegedly weak-kneed diplomacy. A great opportunity had been missed to strengthen the authority of the monarchy and the whole idea of the Austrian empire, at home and abroad. Conrad's pugnacity was enhanced when he succeeded, early in 1909, in extracting for the first time from the German General Staff definite pledges of assistance in the event of a Russian attack. We shall revert later to the political threat which this turn of events posed.

But Conrad did not relinquish his war plan—he merely postponed it. He intensified his political activities, which put him more and more at odds with Aehrenthal. The crisis over the annexation of Bosnia taught the foreign minister that any step to expand Austrian power in the Balkans carried the risk of unleashing a European war, and he therefore counseled extreme self-discipline. Everything must be done to foster a balance of power in the Balkans, especially by favoring Bulgaria. At the same time, nothing must be done to "oppose natural developments within the Balkan states." Serbia's fascination for Austria's South Slavic population was to be reduced by a sensible domestic policy, especially in Bosnia. Austro-Serbian tension was to be lessened, primarily by concluding a trade treaty favorable to Serbia. Aehrenthal utterly rejected a conflict with Italy over domination of the Adriatic, let alone a preventive war. The army must be strong, but only for the purpose of securing the realm and its vital interest, he wrote in one document, in which Conrad made this marginal annotation: "What country today could permanently maintain so formidable a power? Hence create it only for a time—and use it!"[9]

Just how did Conrad wish to use it? Some of Conrad's answers to this question strike one as extremely strange, not to say primitive. Early in 1910, for example, he reflected whether it might not be better to exploit Russia's weakness to launch a preventive strike against that possible enemy, rather than first settling accounts with Italy and for the time being seeking a "friendly and neighborly" relationship with Russia. In the end he recommended the latter course to the Emperor as "preferable from the military point of view." If necessary, Serbia and Montenegro could be finished off together with Italy.[10]

Similar thoughts recur in a curious directive of April 12 to the General Staff bureau chiefs. After a long review of the policies of virtually all the countries of the world, Conrad predicted that Russia was likely to be involved soon in a new war with Japan. Austria must take advantage of this situation, most suitably by an attack on Italy, Serbia, and Montenegro. The chiefs were instructed to work out deployment plans against this eventuality (and others as well, not least war with Russia) and to review all of Conrad's political studies and military memoranda back to 1905, so that they might become pervaded with the proper spirit of militancy that was so sadly lacking in the foreign ministry. That policy was one of inertia, of preserving the status quo, of wishful thinking on which no General Staff could base its plans. "If a state is not to invite being pushed aside, it must engage in positive policies in respect of the development of its sphere of power."[11]

This was almost outright incitement of the officers of the General Staff to oppose official government policy; and, understandably enough, Baron Aehrenthal regarded the chief of staff as a dangerous man. There were several serious clashes, over armament problems as well as the question of a pre-emptive strike against Italy, an issue which Conrad had pursued with redoubled vigor since the outbreak of the Tripoli war, and in 1911 the foreign minister succeeded in having his adversary dismissed from the General Staff.[12] Conrad's successor, General Schemua, however, was evidently no more than a caretaker, an absolute nonentity in the political sense.[13] Within the year, immediately on Aehrenthal's death, Conrad again relieved him.

Enjoying the favor of Archduke Ferdinand, heir to the throne, Conrad now went even further with his notions of preventive war. They were no longer directed against Italy, but now, in the period of Balkan warfare, against Serbia and Russia. On January 20, 1913, Conrad declared that Serbia's growth into a military power of any consequence must be prevented at all costs, most effectively by a war against Russia. Germany would have to come to a similar conclusion if it took the trouble to cast a glance into the future. Germany's own eastern policy was incompatible with any strengthening of Balkan power. It would be to Germany's advantage too if the showdown between the Triple Alliance and the Triple Entente were to come as soon as possible. But if Germany shrank back, Serbia must be promptly attacked and crushed, "this very spring," since the chance of success would decline with every delay. Conrad asked for a mobilization date of March 1, operations to commence on the fifteenth. Should Russia intervene, the main mass of the *k.u.k.* army could still be shifted to Galicia in time. This proposal was to recur in July, 1914. Conrad did not even trouble to suggest a plausible pretext for war.[14]

This memorandum was the opening gun in an almost endless exchange of correspondence with the new foreign minister, Count Berchtold, in which the theme was discussed in ever new versions. Berchtold was a typical grandseigneur in the old Austrian style, suave in the circles of high society and diplomacy, but miles away from any real feeling for the everyday life of the people, unfamiliar with the innermost problems of a multinational country and its economic plight, indeed, basically without any interest in politics as such. He did not trouble to conceal this from the Emperor and long resisted being summoned to his difficult office.[15] As it turned out, he particularly embodied the traditional isolation of the foreign ministry from the concrete problems of the two component parts of the dual monarchy and the separate Austrian and Hungarian parliaments. His exchanges with Conrad show that he was unsure of himself from the outset, pusillanimous at heart, but eager to appear as a courageous activist in the eyes of the stronger man and thus intent on hiding his anxieties behind real or supposed reservations emanating from third parties.[16]

Conrad did indeed feel himself to be the stronger of the two and sought to make Berchtold the instrument of his own plans. Once Berchtold had been appointed, he no longer acknowledged that there were any limits to the expansion of his activities beyond the military sphere. Among Conrad's papers there is an amazingly extensive correspondence on purely political matters with Austrian military attachés, especially those in London, St. Petersburg, and Bucharest. Some of it was even conducted on his part in the familiar "thou" form of address widely used among Austrian officers, in keeping with an old tradition in the aristocracy. The impression left by this correspondence is that the General Staff conducted its own separate diplomatic service, quite independent of the ambassadors.

The Austrian military attaché in St. Petersburg, for example, reported that Russia was likely to turn its attention entirely toward Turkey, leaving Austria a free hand against Serbia; and immediately on receiving this communication Conrad advocated a prompt strike against Serbia, ignoring any Russian threat.[17] His political thinking was dominated by the thought that sooner or later a crucial battle for the future of the Danubian monarchy impended, and that in the meantime the situation could only get worse. His invariable conclusion was that the time to strike was now, even though the power constellation was no longer as favorable as it had been in 1907 and 1909. This was the very view that tipped the balance in favor of war in Vienna in July, 1914.

There is some justification for the belief that Austria-Hungary, by its helpless passivity during the two Balkan wars, had lost international prestige. One can even understand the motivation for regaining prestige by a show of strength and for stifling anti-Austrian agitation in Serbia by force. But was the military power that stood behind such plans really impressive enough for such audacious ventures? None knew Austria's weaknesses better than Conrad. What inspired him was political ambition rather than a realistic assessment of his resources. His confidence was obsessive rather than soundly based.

Added to this was a grave lack of clarity with respect to political goals. How could the problem of South Slavic nationalism really be solved by the military subjugation of Serbia? Was that not bound to lead to protracted military rule and rebellion after rebellion? Hungary, moreover, bitterly opposed any annexation of Serbian territory. The Hungarians did not wish to see their privileged position within the whole body politic endangered by a further increase in Slavic elements.

Even if it had been possible to overcome this resistance, which would have been virtually impossible without civil war, the danger to the inner cohesion of the Danubian empire would only have increased. There were times when Conrad seems to have thought he might tempt the Serbs to join the empire on their own, by a combination of carrot and stick. If they refused, there would be war, which Conrad proposed to precipitate by means of an extemely brutal ultimatum, which already sounds like July, 1914.[18] Once forced into the Danubian empire, the Serbs, together with the Croats and the Slovenes, were to be given a special status, analogous to that of Bavaria within the German Reich. This should satisfy them. It was a curiously unrealistic perspective, all the more so since Conrad proposed at the same time to mutilate the territorial integrity of Serbia by giving away substantial portions of it to Rumania and Bulgaria.[19]

By 1913 it already seemed much less probable than it had in 1908-1909 that Russia, by virtue of its growing military strength, would remain neutral in an Austro-Serbian war. Conrad was also well aware that Germany would show little inclination to support a preventive war against Serbia, and this rubbed him very much the wrong way. "Greedily selfish," he wrote in July, 1913, "Germany seeks to displace us in Serbia in the commercial sphere—indeed throughout the Balkans." Germany preferred to maintain the independence of the Balkan countries, the better to exploit them; but the German ally's reluctance "must not keep the monarchy from the pursuit of its interests; for it may be taken for granted that if the tables were turned—if, for example, Russian policy in Asia required it—Germany would not scruple to compel the monarchy to side with it. In the sphere of politics chivalry can become a crime against one's own country and is quite out of place." In other words, Germany was to be blackmailed into supporting the Austrian expansionist policy in the Balkans. The only saving grace was that Conrad did not yet take the Russian threat quite seriously. Basing himself on the reports of his military attaché in St. Petersburg, he tried to hypnotize his foreign minister into the fanciful notion of concluding an agreement with Russia, under which Turkey would be left to Russia as a prize, while the Danubian monarchy would conquer the western Balkans.[20] At the same time, Conrad was in such a hurry to strike that he was unwilling to wait for such an agreement and recommended that war be opened immediately, even before the August war games began, indeed without even consulting the German ally, let alone the two prime ministers of the dual monarchy.

While the Balkan wars were on, Conrad was not yet able to prevail with his plans for war and conquest. A meeting of ministers in October, 1913, dealt with ways in which the Belgrade government might be compelled to yield to the wishes of the major powers and evacuate Albania. Conrad proposed that Serbia be subjugated by force, even if it yielded on the Albanian question, but he got no support. Most of the ministers agreed to Count Tisza's proposal for resting content with an act of diplomatic humiliation, to be imposed by mere threats put forward with iron consistency.

According to Conrad, a few did favor occupying certain territories, in order to "show Serbia who was boss"; but none would have anything to do with the kind of annexation or integration on the Bavarian model which Conrad demanded. There does, however, seem to have been talk of deposing the Karageorge dynasty, of reductions in territory, and of military sanctions directed against Serbia's sovereignty. Count Berchtold agreed with the chief of staff in general terms, but warned of possible Russian intervention and the unlikelihood of German and Italian support.

What worried Berchtold particularly—and rightly, as the events of 1914 were to show—was the three weeks' delay from the day of mobilization until hostilities could be begun. Conrad's entire counterargument was his militant will. "Military success must be pursued, regardless of what others do. . . . If it comes to war with Russia—as it must some day—today is as good as any other time."[21] According to Conrad, even Tisza agreed with this dangerous fatalism. Would this gifted Hungarian statesman be able and willing in the long run to resist the pressure from the militarists and the need for "face" which all the advisers to the crown felt so keenly? Such resistance could be expected of Berchtold only so long as Vienna society was not yet dominated by a general mood of war.[22]

Precisely such a mood, however, did erupt when the assassination of Archduke Francis Ferdinand and his wife on June 28, 1914, showed the world how deep was the hatred and danger that threatened the rickety Hapsburg state from the side of Serbian nationalism. There was an outcry for revenge, for cleaning out the den of conspiracy in Belgrade for good and all by force of arms. It was an elemental outburst of passions that could no longer be confined. Traditional Austrian pride and German nationalist sentiment surged forward. There were numerous spontaneous street demonstrations, not only in Austria but in Germany as well, especially in Munich and Berlin. Any government that would now have shrunk from vigorous action to put the Serbian nationalists in their place and cripple their activities for good would have earned nothing but universal contempt and might, indeed, have been swept aside by storms of parliamentary opposition.

Amid the general agitation no one even asked for the kind of documentary proof of Serbian government complicity that the Austrian government vainly tried to provide. Almost instinctively everyone was convinced that Serbia was guilty, and, of course, we know today that this instinct was only too well founded.[23] Vienna had long sensed resentfully that the Balkan countries no longer took the old Austrian empire seriously as a great power. Now resentment and injured pride simply boiled over, not only in terms of public opinion but in diplomacy as well. "If this leads to a world war, we don't care," said Count Hoyos, undersecretary of the foreign ministry, on July 15 to the historian Joseph Redlich, who was visiting him and whom he was confidentially apprising of his government's intention to force a war against Serbia.[24] When passion runs rampant, political wisdom usually goes out the window.

Precisely what share did General Conrad have in the warlike decisions of July, 1914? He himself reported—and this is confirmed from other sources— that in the summer of 1914 he regarded the constellation for a war to be waged by Austria-Hungary as much less favorable than in 1909—and even 1913. What troubled him particularly was the attitude of Rumania, which had sided with Serbia in the second Balkan war and in July, 1914, seemed on the point of reaching a close degree of intimacy with the czarist court. The clear-cut warning which the Russian foreign minister lodged at the time with the Rumanian court against the event of an Austrian attack on Serbia made a strong impression in Vienna.[25] In January, 1914, Conrad, in another comprehensive memorandum, had concluded that if, in addition to Serbia and Montenegro, Rumania were to fight on the side of the Entente, it would have "numerical and geographical preponderance" over the Triple Alliance. He made this statement even though at the time he still believed with undue optimism that Italy could be kept in line on the side of the Central Powers.[26]

Conrad insisted that since late 1913 he had held the view that Austria had clearly let the proper hour for a warlike initiative slip past for good. This, to be sure, did not keep him from telling the German ambassador Tschirschky and the military attaché Count Kageneck in gloomy tones that it might be better to settle the inevitable conflict with Russia as soon as possible, since the situation could only get worse. He seems also to have entertained doubts as to the length of time the motley armies of the dual monarchy could still be held together. Early in July he said to his friend Baron Chlumecky: "In 1908-1909 we would have been playing cards up, in 1912-1913 we still had a clear chance, now we have to go for all or nothing": and to the woman who was to become his second wife he wrote: "Still, [the war] must be waged. So ancient a monarchy and so glorious an army cannot be allowed to perish ignominiously. I see the future black and the eve of my life in shadow."[27]

Conrad was indeed convinced that Austria could not avoid "going for broke," that it must accept even a hopeless war, unless the monarchy were willing to retire from the field. The Gordian knot must be cut if its prestige was to be salvaged. The process of corrosion within the multinational state must be arrested by force. Just how a war against Serbia was to achieve that was something on which he was no clearer in 1914 than he had been before. When Count Berchtold in a frank talk on July 6 warned him that the Germans would ask what was to happen *after* the war, Conrad gave a reply typical of him as a soldier: "Tell them we don't know ourselves."[28]

Directly after the assassination, as early as June 29, Conrad advised mobilization against Serbia. In retrospect, we are probably justified in saying today that such swift action would have been politically much more effective and less dangerous to the peace of Europe than the endless delay that did take place, putting the nerves of the statesmen of Europe to the severest strain and ultimately ending in warlike action that came too late. But the foreign minister, Count Berchtold, showed himself uncertain and hesitant, both with respect to the Slavic population elements of the country and the German and Rumanian allies. For the time being he wanted to let it go at putting certain demands to Serbia for the limitation of nationalist propaganda and, more importantly, to await the results of the judicial inquiry into the background of the assassination. In terms of international law this stand was impeccable, though it showed, if anything, too much political caution. But the two prime ministers, Count Tisza and Count Stürgkh, agreed. An important element was fear of Russian intervention and uncertainty about the attitude of Germany.[29]

The same uncertainty assailed the aged Austrian emperor, with whom Conrad had an audience on July 5 for the purpose of persuading him to approve military action against Serbia. All the statesmen in Vienna were evidently well aware that an Austrian attack on Serbia could be held to be an act of provocation, bringing on a Russian attack on Austria, which would mean that under the terms of the Triple Alliance (though not the dual alliance of 1879) Germany would have a formal excuse not to come to Austria's aid. They had reason to remember the grave warnings that had emanated from Berlin during the Serbo-Albanian crisis of 1912-1913, when Bethmann Hollweg, together with Lord Grey, had put forth every effort to keep the Balkan quarrels from growing into a world conflagration.[30]

Even Conrad did not wish to risk war without firm assurances of German aid. Such an unconditional pledge, however, actually came from Berlin on July 6, removing all doubts and resulting in an abrupt change of front in Austrian policy. The scene of this change was the well-known joint cabinet meeting of July 7, when Count Tisza, despite his grave reservations about the war, ultimately agreed—or at least did not object—to an ultimatum to Serbia couched in such terms as to be politically unacceptable, in other words making war certain.

Berchtold, who had been so unsure and fainthearted, suddenly turned into the strong man, now that he was certain of German support—Berlin had actually recommended an immediate strike! He now held a settling of accounts with the hated neighbor to be indispensable, and any diplomatic negotiations or political agreements with Serbia to be pointless. Presumably he had looked for appeals to reason from Berlin, of the kind the German ambassador Tschirschky had instantly voiced, and along the lines heard from the German Chancellor in the winter of 1912-1913.

But Germany instead advised prompt action, and this probably made two things clear to Berchtold, the profound impression the assassination had made everywhere in Europe and the new and unexpected opportunities that were opening up for Austria. He was not slow to put two and two together and now yielded to Conrad's demands which he had so often ignored or rejected. Conrad, however, did not actually take part in the crucial deliberations of the ministers. He was summoned only in the afternoon, when the main decision had already been taken, and he was heard only as an expert on technical questions of mobilization.[31] Conrad, all the same, bears a large share of the responsibility for the decisions of July 7, for what the ministers wanted to hear from him was at bottom but one thing: whether the Austrian army were, indeed, capable of waging a swift war of annihilation against Serbia, even in the event of the Russian intervention everyone feared. Yet it was precisely to this question that Conrad failed to give a clear-cut answer. Indeed, he seems to have failed to face up to its gravity.

He knew very well that Austria-Hungary would not be able to wage all-out war on a Serbian and a Russian front at the same time. In the event of a threat of Russian attack on its northern borders, it would have to move from the offensive in Serbia to the defensive and shift all available troops to Galicia. Should Russia attack only after the outbreak of a Serbian war, as the General Staff feared,[32] there might not yet have been time for large-scale hostilities, or, conversely, the Austrians might already be so deeply enmeshed in battle that they could extricate themselves only with difficulty. The Austrians were, therefore, facing the unknown, including the grave danger of irrevocably committing troops in Serbia that would be absolutely vital on the Galician front at the crucial hour. (This eventuality did indeed occur in August, 1914.)

Conrad had worked out a mobilization plan that was to make possible a shift of the Austrian army to Galicia, against great technical transportation odds, even after the deployment against Serbia had swung into motion; but this had to be decided no later than the fifth day of mobilization, i.e., the Austrians had to know by then whether it would be necessary, whether or not Russia would indeed intervene. Otherwise, there would be dangerous strains and delays in the strategic evolution. Conrad said as much to the ministers, but what he apparently did not say,[33] and what none of the ministers who voted in favor of war seems to have noted, was the fact that such a shift would turn the Serbian war plan into the sheerest gamble.

Yet none in Vienna could seriously believe that Russia would stand by idly while Serbia was politically destroyed. (There was no more talk of annexation, which Tisza unconditionally rejected, but, as in 1913, only of a reduction in territory, the ousting of the Karageorge dynasty and a military satellite status for a diminished Serbia.) Inaction would have meant that Russia, in the eyes of the Balkan nations, had abdicated as a great power, as even Conrad acknowledged in conversation.[34] Thus neither Tisza nor Berchtold put their trust in Russian neutrality, and the latter dusted off Conrad's old argument: Since Russia had long been plotting the creation of a Balkan league directed against Austria, war was inevitable in any event, and the longer it was delayed the worse the chances. If Russian intervention were indeed certain, Austria could not even begin to crush the Serbo-Montenegrine military power until after the Russian forces were destroyed or at least stalemated. But how certain was that?

At the cabinet meeting a frivolous view all too typical of the mentality of many Austrian diplomats was voiced by Count Hoyos, who had only recently said the same thing in Berlin, as a special envoy of the Austrian foreign ministry.[35] "We must employ all of our resources in the Balkans and let Germany take on Russia alone," he said. Cutting him off, Conrad rejected this view with the remark that certain binding military agreements had been entered into with the German General Staff for a common struggle against Russia.

Presumably, this piece of news made a deep impression on the meeting. With Conrad's added insistence that the balance of power among the major countries was bound to shift to Austria's disadvantage in the years to come, it must have stiffened the war zeal of the participants.

Yet we are not really justified in saying that the Austrian chief of staff deceived his ministers by painting an overoptimistic picture of the military-political situation. He had beforehand submitted to the foreign minister a memorandum stating quite openly and with the utmost seriousness that in the event of Rumanian neutrality Austria-Hungary's over-all situation would greatly worsen; while if Rumania went over to the other side it could become disastrous. Rumanian neutrality would mean a deficit of twenty divisions or 400,000 men. Defection would double this loss and in addition pose a most serious threat of invasion by Rumanian forces of vital Austrian territories. It was not even glossed over that initially the main brunt of a war with Russia would fall on Austria-Hungary alone, while the allied German armies sought a decision in France, during which period they would be at a numerical disadvantage on the eastern front. "This harsh challenge to our main forces can be met with any prospect of success only so long as we may count on the cooperation of the Rumanian army." Once Rumania defected, the situation would be changed from the bottom up.

The minutes of the meeting of July 7, kept by Count Hoyos, do not reveal whether this memorandum was even discussed there. Count Tisza seems to have been the only minister present who was seriously disturbed about the Rumanian problem—as a Hungarian, he was worried about Transylvania. It does not appear that Conrad mentioned his concern about Rumanian neutrality in person.[35] He certainly cannot have done so with any strong emphasis, for Tisza was alone in his objections. All the same, the chief of staff seems to have left the meeting in a rather depressed mood. Directly afterward, to his colleague Colonel Metzger, he voiced his misgivings that Austria-Hungary would not be equal to a simultaneous war with Serbia, Russia, and Rumania. "I should like to persuade myself that this is not so, but it is." Was this the only worry weighing on his mind? Was he certain of victory over the attacking Russian armies, side by side with the Germans, if Rumania remained neutral? Would he have been justified in such confidence?

To find the answer we must interrupt our report on the July days of 1914 and first consider the existing agreements between the Austrian and German General Staffs.

Part 2

Understandings Between the Austrian and German General Staffs

AN IMPORTANT CHANGE had taken place in the character of the Austro-German alliance since the days of Bismarck and the elder Moltke. After the old chancellor's fall, Berlin grew more and more openhanded with political pledges of aid to Austria—almost to the point of irresponsibility. Yet after Moltke's departure the promised military support kept declining in certainty and value.[1]

Bismarck had always been reluctant to permit clear-cut arrangements between the two staffs against the event of war and had categorically forbidden any binding military agreement. He was afraid that, if Austrian reliance on the powerful German ally grew too strong, the politicians in Vienna would become too venturesome in their Balkan policies and slacken their defense program. The alliance was to remain limited to purely defensive measures; and, in sharp contrast to what happened in 1914, he expressly stated that Germany would in no circumstance declare war on Russia unless Austria had actually been attacked by that country. Nor would he have any part in a binding commitment with respect to the strength of the German eastern front.[2] The Austrians were, nevertheless, entitled to feel sure at the time that in the event of a Russian attack the Germans would not let them down but throw the greater part of their army into a common offensive against Russia; for such was Moltke's war plan.

William II apparently never grasped the idea of this policy of alliance. In 1889 he told the Austrian chief of staff, Beck, in the presence of Emperor Francis Joseph: "For whatever reason you may mobilize, whether on account of Bulgaria or from some other cause, the day you do so will be the day of mobilization for my army, let the chancellors say what they will." In 1895, and again in 1908, he went so far as to tell the Austrian ambassador: "Emperor Francis Joseph is a field marshal of Prussia. Thus he has but to command and the whole Prussian army will follow him."[3]

Waldersee and the war minister, Verdy, also made sweeping pledges to General Beck, and thus the zeal of the professional soldiers and the political naiveté of the Kaiser tended to distort the essential meaning of the alliance altogether. It was Caprivi whose vigorous intervention prevented this, and in so doing he acted in complete agreement with the new chief of staff, Schlieffen. The latter, however, was not motivated by political considerations, but by purely military reasons already known to us. Since he had shifted the center of gravity of the German deployment so sharply, to the west, one might have expected him to be all the more concerned with vigorous and effective Austrian action on the eastern front. But such was not the case, for Schlieffen had a low opinion of the effectiveness of the Austrian army. The fate of Austria-Hungary, he said, would ultimately be settled on the Seine rather than the San.

Schlieffen's deployment and operational plans for the east varied in many details over the years. Initially he planned to move the German front close to the Austrian one. He intended to push eastward from Poznan or Silesia, sweeping along his allies in an offensive for which, unaided, they might lack the spirit. Then again, he contemplated building up a German eastern front in East Prussia, proposing that the Austrians spread their armies over far too broad a front from Upper Silesia to Lvov and Cernautzi, which would have meant that they bore the brunt of the defense. This Colonel-General von Beck rejected, and henceforth Schlieffen would discuss common operations no further, but became very aloof and contented himself with a plan under which East Prussia would be covered by offensive thrusts against the Narev, thus giving the Austrians indirect relief. The Germans concealed from their Austrian allies the full degree to which their strategic plans had shifted westward. Indeed, after 1896, contact between the two General Staffs was almost completely lost. In the summer of 1908, General Conrad drew up an operational plan in outline against the event of war with Russia. His premise was that Germany would first deliver a main blow against the Russians, and only then throw itself against the French. It was on such a basis that Conrad developed plans for a joint battle of encirclement and annihilation. Clearly, he had not a glimmer of the real German plans.

Understandably enough, the General Staff in Vienna felt that the situation had become intolerable when the Bosnian crisis acutely brought on the specter of war, and a two-front war at that, against Serbia and Russia at the same time.

On the express authorization of Aehrenthal—who had previously been in touch with Prince Bülow, the German chancellor—Conrad, therefore, on January 1, 1909, officially inquired of Moltke how the German General Staff viewed a two-front war with Russia and France. Would the German forces be spread over both fronts, or would a main blow be first struck at one front and only then at the other? Which came first? Austria needed to know in order to decide whether it could first "settle accounts" with Serbia, and only then turn on Russia, or whether the first decisive blow must be struck against Russia.

At the time, Conrad was still counting on the armed aid of Rumania. He proposed to deploy a total of forty infantry divisions in Galicia against Russia; but if the first blow was struck against Serbia-Montenegro, he had decided to use eight or nine divisions on that front, initially reserving only thirty for the northern front. These could be reinforced from the Balkan front only after a lag of something like three months.

It was a calculation not without its merits, as Moltke's reply of January 21, 1909, admitted. According to his intelligence, the Russians had no more than twenty-five infantry divisions at their disposal against Austria-Hungary, and about twenty-nine against Germany. If France intervened, the German command, nevertheless, could initially leave only "the most necessary forces for the protection of our eastern provinces" stationed there, while the German main forces had first to be committed in France. The real decision, even with respect to the eastern front, had to be looked for there, Moltke explained, using Schlieffen's arguments but failing to mention the invasion of Belgium. Such a decision, he added optimistically, would "fall soon after the deployment was complete. . . . There is every reason to believe that if German arms are blessed with victory, we shall, after not too long a time, have powerful forces [available] for sustained and direct support." Their transfer was prepared for and could be completed in a matter of days. In view of the slow pace of Russian mobilization and operations, the issue in the west would probably have been decided by the time events on the Austro-Russian border reached the crucial stage. "The situation of the allied empires must be viewed as serious, in the event of French intervention, but it would not be critical."

The optimism was put on for a purpose. Moltke had to prevent the unwelcome news about leaving "only the most necessary forces on the eastern front" from keeping the Austrians from aggressive action against the Russians and limiting themselves, say, to a defense of the Carpathian passes. If that happened, the German situation in the east would become completely untenable. In political respects too the letter struck a highly optimistic note. Moltke said he did not believe the Russians would again be combat-ready so soon after their revolution—which had begun with troop mutinies. Nor did he believe the Italians would desert their Austrian ally, as did Conrad, who had long been obsessed by that notion.

Moltke's letter, in other words, formed a kind of military counterpart to the political fanfares of Bülow, who was then loudly proclaiming that Germany would keep "the ancient Teutonic faith" with Austria. It so happened that the German General Staff was extremely well informed on the internal weaknesses of both the Russian and the Italian armed forces. The letter did, indeed, do its job. Far from showing disappointment, Conrad assured Moltke that he understood perfectly the need for a great German offensive in the west, which had become clear to him in his own strategic studies. With characteristic zeal he at once developed large-scale attack plans, with many details and refinements, for a war against Russia, even if Serbia had to be dealt with at the same time. One almost gets the impression that it was a matter of pride with him to show that he could win major victories on the battlefield even before German help arrived, thereby reflecting glory on Austrian arms.

Criticial historians have viewed Moltke's letter, which succeeded so well, as military meddling with politics, as a dangerous expansion of Germany's treaty obligations beyond the bounds within which Bismarck always sought to stay. The "key to the war guilt question," they contend, is that with this letter (elaborated in the ensuing correspondence between the two staff chiefs) Germany obligated herself to give military cover even to the most ambitious Austrian expansionist policies in the Balkans.[4]

Like most of Moltke's memoranda, his missive to Conrad does give vent to certain reflections transcending the military sphere. Among other things, he remarked that Serbia "was drifting into a war of desperation with Austria." Predictably, "the moment must come when the patience of the Austrian empire, in the face of Serbian provocation, must come to an end. Austria will then have virtually no alternative to invading Serbia," and this might well trigger active Russian intervention. This would necessarily require Germany to abide by the terms of the alliance.[5]

But did this not expand "the terms of the alliance," distort the defensive pact of 1879 into an aggressive alliance? Looking back on the long series of Conrad's plans for preventive war, as we know them today, one is inclined to answer this question in the affirmative. Yet Moltke's formulation (surely bearing the imprimatur of the German foreign ministry) did not really constitute the kind of carte blanche for any and every Balkan venture such as was given the Austrians in Potsdam on July 6, 1914. The thought of supporting such ventures was far from the German staff chief's mind, as is clearly shown in a marginal note he made on Conrad's message of January 1: "It is important, in my view, that Austria should not provoke war with Serbia. So long as it limits itself to the defensive against Serbia, the Russians will have no reason to act." Presumably the phrase in question in his reply was meant to deal with Serbian provocations supported by the Russians in such a way that they had to be considered an indirect Russian attack, threatening the very life of Austria.

We cannot be sure just how Bismarck would have responded in such a situation, for in his time no such vital threat on the part of Serbia against Austria existed as yet. All we can say with considerable certainty is that Germany's first chancellor would probably not have agreed to Moltke's pledge that "Germany will mobilize its entire army the moment Russia mobilizes." This pledge, for its part, was derived from Schlieffen's plans, formulated only after Bismarck's death—they made it impossible for Germany to wait until the Russians actually attacked Austria.[6]

There is no denying that such clear-cut assurances of support under the alliance as were contained in Moltke's reply were precisely calculated to confirm Conrad, the politician of war, in his already exuberant political activities. Yet the correspondence between Moltke and Conrad never did lead to the conclusion of a formal "military convention" comparable to that between the French and the Russians, dating back to 1892. Indeed, it did not even result in the kind of firm commitments negotiated between England and France and at times Belgium. As will still be discussed, Moltke very deliberately evaded continuing Austrian efforts to get the Germans to agree to a fixed troop strength in the east, or to certain definite operations. So vague was this correspondence with respect to German aid in the event of undefined Austrian Balkan ventures that in July, 1914, no one in Vienna even thought of invoking it, when German aid under the alliance was actually requested. On the contrary, until the Potsdam assurance of July 6, Conrad, as we have already seen, was as uncertain as Count Berchtold as to whether the Germans would "go along."

Had Moltke's message of January 21, moreover, actually contained a political commitment to the policies of Vienna, Chancellor Bülow rather than the chief of staff would have to be held responsible, for the authority lay with Bülow. With the greater freedom of action vis-à-vis Austria which Germany had secured by dissolving the reinsurance treaty with Russia, however, German foreign policy had long since gone beyond the strictly limited alliances of the Bismarck era. True, when a Russo-Austrian conflict threatened to erupt in 1896 over the question of the Straits, Chancellor Hohenlohe had expressly declared that Germany would regard a Russian occupation of neither Constantinople nor the Dobrudja as a cause for war. If Austria declared war on Russia in such a case, it would be acting on its own responsibility. But he immediately added that Germany would not permit Austria's status as a great power to be seriously imperiled.

"We stick to the program," he sent word to Vienna, "that if our Austrian friends fall into mortal danger, even by virtue of undertakings of which we disapprove, we shall swiftly come to their aid." He had declared even before that "of course the ultimate judgment whether given events violate a vital interest of the Austro-Hungarian monarchy must lie with Emperor Francis Joseph and his government. If Austria's status as a great power were threatened without provocation from the Austrian side [an important qualification!], Emperor

Francis Joseph may depend on Emperor William."[7] Thus, a fundamental decision had long ago been taken, going far beyond the jurisdiction of the General Staff; and increasing tension between the great European power blocs had since only served to stiffen this position.[8]

Of course, Conrad did not rest content with this general pledge of vigorous assistance after the conclusion of a French campaign. He wanted to know precisely when the German reinforcements from the west would arrive and in what strength, so that he might be able to take the offensive in Galicia immediately, even in the event of a simultaneous campaign in the Balkans. Would the German forces left in the east be able to pin down the first and second Russian armies (totaling nineteen and a half divisions) at the East Prussian border from the outset? What would their mission be? Could he count on at least twenty German divisions arriving from France on the thirty-fifth day of mobilization to support the Austrian offensive? Whether such an offensive could be initiated and where depended on the answers to these questions.

Conrad clearly wished to settle on a very definite operational plan with the Germans, a plan that was to commit them firmly and guarantee the success of his own offensive. Moltke, however, was not willing to go that far. Although his replies are clear cut and concise, he always avoided being drawn more deeply into operational details. The first bit of concrete information he provided was that only thirteen German divisions were to be left in the east, against the eighteen formerly scheduled. This remaining strength, he insisted, would be entirely adequate to keep nineteen and a half Russian divisions away from Austria. On the matter of the date of arrival of the German forces from the western front, on the other hand, he spoke with a touch of helpless embarrassment. "I am unable to give a precise answer to this, the most important of all the questions under discussion, since the enemy will have a voice in it." Depending on whether the French took the offensive themselves or not, the issue might be decided in three to four weeks, and the troop transfer would take another nine or ten days. Moltke refused to discuss the number of troops to be shifted to the east and how they were to be used.

Essentially, this is the way matters remained until 1914. Moltke never did give precise details on any of these points, except that as French military strength grew his estimate for the timing of the eastward shift gradually lengthened from three or four weeks to "about six weeks after the commencement of operations," i.e., by the sixtieth day of mobilization. This timetable was indeed approximately maintained—actually bettered—in 1914, except that the total victory in France contemplated under the Schlieffen Plan was never achieved.

Conrad was far from satisfied. He was intent on keeping the initiative in the eastern theater in his own hands from the start of war. In no circumstances was he willing to wait until the German divisions came rolling up from the west, while the Russians had meanwhile fully deployed their forces. He wanted to open his great offensive (already planned by his predecessor Beck) between the Vistula and the Bug rivers on the twenty-fourth or twenty-fifth day of mobilization, even if the Austro-Hungarian armies were at that time already heavily engaged in the Balkans, in consequence of a delayed Russian war declaration. To that end, however, he had to be certain, as he explained to Moltke, that the German eastern army would launch an offensive on the very same day, "directing its main blow, with about ten divisions, against the Russian second army, i.e., against the Narev, making it impossible for the Russian first and second armies to throw further forces against the Austro-Hungarian army." What he was asking for, in other words, was a German relief offensive to pin down the Russian forces on the Narev, not a major offensive, in the style of the elder Moltke, across the Narev and deep into Poland, joining up with the Austrian armies directly. The campaign was thus to be opened with partial strikes, the actual issue being sought only on the arrival of the German main force from the west. Conrad was rather concerned—not without reason, as later events were to show—whether the Germans would be able to hold in check the Russian first army (the army of the Niemen), estimated at about eleven and a half divisions, with a mere three or four divisions left over if ten divisions advanced on the Narev.

Responding to this desire, Moltke, on March 19, 1909, offered an undertaking that was to become crucial to Conrad's planning and the whole relationship between the two allies on the outbreak of war. He pledged a German attack on the Narev line to support the Austrian offensive between the Bug and the Vistula and to prevent the Russian third army that would be engaged there from being reinforced from the Narev. Apparently he gave this pledge reluctantly, stressing that the thirteen German divisions to be left in the east were actually intended only to protect the provinces east of the Vistula, it being left to their commander whether he was willing and able to conduct an active defense. The Austrian General Staff, according to Moltke, was mistaken in its assumption that the Russians would also let their second army march on Galacia, for they were almost certainly committed to a major offensive against Germany, under the Franco-Russian treaty. An attack on the Narev with weak German forces, moreover, "would have to overcome great difficulties. Warsaw would threaten it on the right flank, counterattacks from the direction of Lomza on the left. Still, I shall not hesitate to launch such an attack in support of the simultaneous Austrian offensive. Your Excellency may indeed rely on this pledge, which has been carefully considered. A condition is that the movements of the allies commence at the same time and are carried out without fail. Should enemy action make it impossible for either of us to carry out our intention, it is absolutely essential that the other be advised as promptly as possible, since our security is entirely dependent on our cooperation."

Here, then, was a formal obligation, a highly significant sign of the importance which the German command now, in contrast to Schlieffen's day, set by encouraging its Austrian ally to conduct a major offensive at all costs, to relieve the otherwise gravely threatened German eastern front. Conrad took Moltke's pledge seriously enough to insist on having it annually confirmed as being still in force, each time painstakingly listing the entire correspondence. Without a doubt this is what he had in mind when he mysteriously mentioned firm agreements between the two general staffs against the event of war at the cabinet meeting on July 7, 1914.

Yet, looked at objectively, what was the real value of this trump card? For the early weeks of war Conrad had a German pledge of no more than a diversionary action that was to pin down part of the Russian forces. Its timely success was doubtful, for the question remained open as to whether a German Narev offensive could fend off a flank attack by the Russian army of the Niemen with grossly inferior forces. Moltke had not discussed this in his reply, though he had wisely mentioned the possibility that enemy action might make it impossible to carry out his intent—which is precisely what happened in August, 1914, when Rennenkampf's army advanced all the way to the Masurian lakes. It could very well be that the Germans would first have to gain a respite by a vigorous foray to the northeast, i.e., against the Russian first army, before they dared turn southward. At best a considerable element of uncertainty attached to the pledge. Even more uncertain was the prospect that powerful German forces, shifted from the west, could arrive on Polish soil in a matter of weeks, there to carry to a successful conclusion the great offensive battle presumably begun by the Austrians. It took a considerable measure of optimism to include this expectation as a fixed element in the strategic calculation. Initially, Conrad shared this optimism, which was entertained by all the German generals.

He never succeeded in securing further and better assurances from the German General Staff, though after he was recalled into the Austrian General Staff in 1913 he grew visibly more concerned and pressed for them.[9] His last discussion with Moltke before the outbreak of the First World War took place in Karlsbad in May, 1914. Moltke there spoke of only twelve divisions, "perhaps a bit more," to the east of the lower Vistula, and mentioned a plan to strengthen the German Vistula fortifications. "What will you do," Conrad anxiously asked, "if you have no luck in the west and the Russians attack you in the rear? " Moltke shrugged his shoulders. "I shall do what I can. We do not have superiority over the French."

That was not a very reassuring answer; and we already know with what pessimism, not to say hopelessness, Conrad viewed the future in the summer of 1914. The German pledges he held did not beyond all doubt constitute a winning hand. They did not alter the essential fact that the whole thing was still a great gamble. Was Conrad, then, irresponsible, acting out of character, when at the fateful cabinet meeting of July 7 he failed to give open support to Tisza's reservations about the war, instead encouraging the other ministers in their blind faith in the powerful help of Germany? We shall probably be nearer the truth if we speak of the courage of desperation. This may well have to do with the soldier's code, already known to us from a similar decision by Zukhomlinov (see Chapter 4), which holds that a true soldier does not shrink from even the greatest danger.

Surely, however, Conrad was not justified in keeping the full magnitude of the danger from the politicians. Later on, when his great Galician offensive failed before the Germans were able to advance on the Narev and before armed help arrived from the west, he blustered loudly about a German betrayal. Not only was this extremely unfair, it demonstrates plainly the degree to which Conrad's nimble mind lacked the ability for objectively assessing his own resources as well as those of his allies. It is true, of course, that the German campaign plan, banking on a great Austrian offensive, also overestimated German capabilities. As it turned out, each General Staff expected more than the other could deliver.

Part 3

Conrad's and Moltke's Share in Manning the Loom of Destiny

WHAT THE VIENNA council meeting of July 7 arrived at was in every way only half a decision. Instead of drafting and sending off an ultimatum to Serbia at once, it was delayed for many long weeks—first because of the inadequate conclusions of the criminal trial at Serajevo; then on account of the harvesting work on the farms, which was first to be ended; and lastly because of Poincaré's visit of state in St. Petersburg. There was so little question of immediate mobilization for the promptest possible strike, that the chief of staff was sent on holiday for the express purpose of avoiding any semblance of warlike intent.

These efforts at camouflage would have made sense only if Austria had been able, directly after the ultimatum, to confront the world with a *fait accompli* in the form of an occupation of Serbian territory. The war minister and the chief of staff did press for accelerated action and its instant implementation; but on Conrad's part this was done so lackadaisically that the suspicion obtrudes that he was, after all, as unsure as Count Berchtold, who again displayed a rather depressed air after the meeting.

In the general's view, Rumania's attitude had first to be clarified before a blow could be struck.[1] Thus, week after week of a fair and cloudless summer elapsed without anything being done.[2] It was the political authorities in Berlin rather than the professional soldiers in Vienna who pressed for a swift decision. When at last, on July 19, a second "Council of Ministers for Common Affairs of

Austria and Hungary" assembled to decide on an ultimatum to Serbia—to be delivered only on July 23—Berchtold gave as a reason for this measure the fact that "Berlin was beginning to get nervous."[3]

But in Berlin too it was not the generals who were "getting nervous"—they were purposely kept away at their summer holidays—but rather Bethmann Hollweg and his foreign minister von Jagow. They waited impatiently for "strong action" on the part of Austria-Hungary in the forcible solution of the South Slavic question. They knew the risks were great but hoped that in the end Russia would not go beyond "rumbling and grumbling"—in other words, that the war could after all be "localized"—provided the world were confronted with a *fait accompli,* as in 1908, as soon as possible, while there was still general indignation over the bloody deed at Serajevo.

"The more resolute Austria shows herself," Jagow remarked, "and the more vigorously we support her, the more likely Russia is to keep quiet." The czarist empire was simply not yet ready to strike, he said, though within a few years it would have an overwhelming arms superiority. In the long run war would be inevitable, in any event. "I do not desire a preventive war, but if war is offered, we must not pull in our tails." Germany must not now put a spoke in the wheel of its last and only dependable ally. "If we did that, Austria might rightly blame us—as we might ourselves—for barring her last chance of political rehabilitation. This would serve only to accelerate her malaise and disintegration."[4]

That kind of spirit can scarcely be called bloodthirsty, and still less did it betoken confidence in the outcome of the war. At best it was a dismal fatalism in the face of inexorable danger—but it also bespoke a resolute will to meet that danger by drawing on every last resource. Chief of Staff Moltke was not asked for his opinion on whether Russia was able, at this moment, to embark on a major struggle. We have no way of knowing how we would have answered such a question, but we do know he fully expected that Russian military might would continue to grow in the years to come, to a level extremely dangerous to the Central Powers. That, after all, was the reason he had been pressing so strongly for a greater German army since 1913. In May, 1914, he resumed this pressure with particular vigor.[5] Did the dreary prospects for the future persuade Moltke, as they did his Austrian colleague, that Germany must strike before the last chance was gone? Did he too counsel preventive war?

Our discussion has already shown that Moltke was anything but a hearty swashbuckler, an activist ready for instant war. Indeed, to his staff members he sometimes seemed downright defeatist (see end of Chapter 6). A study of his papers is calculated to deepen this impression—despite occasional indignant outbursts over the seemingly weak-kneed attitude of the foreign ministry, which were no more than reflections of the typical officer's attitude in those days.[6]

Moltke's correspondence with Conrad has been combed for evidence that he shared the latter's preventive war notions. Cited as the most important proof is a private letter in which he searched for an answer to his Austrian colleague's everlasting complaint, contained in a letter dated April 10, 1909, that a highly favorable occasion for "settling accounts" with Serbia had been let pass by the diplomats, leaving Austria with the certainty of now having to count on a two-front war against both Serbia and Russia. Moltke, after a five months' delay, was reassuring. So long as the two allies "stood shoulder to shoulder," they would be able to break out of any ring encircling them.

Moltke then went on to say that he "deeply regretted that an opportunity which was not likely soon to recur in such favorable circumstances had gone by unexploited. I am firmly convinced that efforts to localize a war between Austria-Hungary and Serbia would have succeeded. Strengthened both internally and externally after its victorious conclusion, the monarchy might have won a preponderance in the Balkans that would not have been easy to shake. Even if Russia had taken a hand and a European war had developed, the prospects for Austria and Germany would have been better than they presumably will be several years hence."[7]

Undoubtedly this was true, but it was stated entirely from a military point of view. The only chances that were weighed were the chances of military success; but even so, Moltke held Russian intervention at that time to be most unlikely, and he actually said no more than that the Russians would have had less of a chance than they "presumably" would have at a later date. To read into these primarily theoretical considerations a desire for a prompt "settling of accounts" with Russia would be stretching them beyond reason. Four years later it was shown how far away Moltke was from encouraging the Austrians in wild Balkan adventures. This was during the first Balkan war, in February, 1913. Moltke then sent Conrad a very outspoken and politically motivated warning (previously submitted to the foreign ministry) against unnecessarily forcing the Serbian (and indirectly the Russian) issue. The German people, he said unequivocally, would not show much sympathy if the Austrians were to provoke war now that Serbia had shown itself in a conciliatory mood. Germany's determination to abide by its treaty obligations must not be unduly strained.[8] For Germany, a two-front war would in any event constitute an enormous burden. It was true, Moltke said, that he was convinced a European war would necessarily come sooner or later, a war that would ultimately hinge on the issue between Germans and Slavs; but this risk could be accepted only if the world were "fully receptive to the historic character of the issue."

"To begin a world war," Moltke later added in a discussion with the Austrian military attaché, "is a matter to be most carefully considered." In a letter to Foreign Minister von Jagow he expressed his serious concern over the vagueness and aimlessness of Austrian Balkan policy, and also over Vienna's policy toward Russia, which was being subjected to quite unnecessary provocation. He had found, in personal encounters, that Archduke Francis Ferdinand, heir to the throne, was not at all in agreement with the attitude of his protégé, General Conrad. Austrian diplomats were split into two parties, a war party and a peace party. "It is without a doubt most irksome that our treaty obligations and the need for preserving the integrity of Austria have put us in a certain state of dependence on Vienna. I put it to Your Excellency that the main goal must be to prevent Austrian blunders, a task that is neither easy nor agreeable."[9]

There is no reason for assuming that any basic change took place within the year in Moltke's views on these political issues, even though, after Serajevo, he may have seen Austria's situation in quite another light. In March, 1914, he admonished Conrad that there was no reason to keep on grieving over the opportunities missed in 1908. One "had to take the situation as it is." It was a fact that Serbia had become a rising and vigorous country which exerted a powerful fascination. The Danubian monarchy must "stake everything on creating at least economic bonds with that country."

The talks Moltke held two months later in Karlsbad with his Austrian counterpart put him in a very serious mood, according to his colleague Waldersee. In a memorandum written at the time and intended for the Chancellor, he stated outright that the defection of Rumania would tie Austria's hands in the Balkans in such a way that Germany could no longer seriously count on an Austrian offensive into Russia.[10] It would be beyond belief that in the face of such deep concern he should have wanted Austria to provoke war with Russia as soon as possible. It is true, however, that in the course of the summer of 1914 he repeatedly voiced the view, already known to us, that when the big Russian rearmament program was completed in 1916 or 1917, the military situation of the Central Powers would become much worse. But we should again be doing violence to his utterances if we read into them a desire for a preventive war.[11]

When Moltke at last returned to Berlin on July 26, the major political decisions had already been made. The German foreign ministry had vainly tried to secure information in time on the precise wording and date of delivery of the proposed ultimatum to Serbia. The details were made available to Germany only twenty-four hours before the dispatch of the ultimatum, on the afternoon of July 23.[12] It was known in advance, however, that the Austrians were not looking for the Serbians to accept the ultimatum—they wished the break to be inevitable.

On the afternoon of July 25 a rumor spread in Vienna that the Serbians seemed ready to submit completely to the ultimatum; and there was as much consternation in the German embassy as among the Austrian war party lest the opportunity for the great purging action had once again been "frittered away."[13] But that evening came the news that the Austrian envoy, Baron Giel, had left Belgrade; hence the Serbian reply had been unsatisfactory. Conrad now pushed through the immediate mobilization against Serbia of eight army corps, a total of twenty-six and a half infantry divisions. He had actually asked for this authority the day before, on the basis of first reports of a Serbian mobilization.

It will be recalled that in January, 1909, in the first consultation with Moltke, Conrad had reserved only eight or nine divisions for this purpose, while thirty divisions were to be deployed at the same time in Galicia, to cover the northern border. Now there was initially no mobilization at all for this purpose, and a much more powerful force was summoned for the Serbian operation, "in order to achieve a swift and decisive success."[14] How are we to explain this highly significant change from the old plans? Did Conrad seriously expect to be able to carry out the subjugation of Serbia so rapidly that any Russian intervention would come too late, delayed or even prevented by the threat that the Germans would respond to Russian mobilization by mobilizing themselves?

We can scarcely explain his conduct in any other way. Yet how could Conrad hope to carry out his Serbian campaign free from any outside intervention, when he had had to admit on July 26 that there could be no thought of opening hostilities before August 12, since unfortunately—and against the original wish of the chief of staff—mobilization had not yet begun? He needed to know by August 4 or 5 at the latest, moreover, whether or not Russia would intervene; for only until that time would it have been possible to readjust to a deployment of the main mass of the army on the northern front in Galicia.[15] Apparently Conrad hoped that, by delaying an official declaration of war against Serbia and foregoing for the time being any warlike act in Galicia, he might postpone Russian intervention for a while. But was this not a policy of pure adventurism? In describing this dilemma, Conrad himself speaks of a "confused situation."[16] Actually, it was even more the policies of the Danubian monarchy that were heedless and confused. Berlin had apparently caught on to them only slowly.

It was taken for granted there that Serbia's rejection of the ultimatum would be instantly followed by an Austrian declaration of war, the violent step so often proclaimed as ineluctable. Indeed, Berlin advised, even before the nature of the Serbian reply was known there, that this step be taken as quickly as possible, to foreclose any meddling by the Entente powers. In a discussion with the German ambassador and Count Berchtold on July 12, Conrad at first resisted this counsel, apparently inspired by the vague hope just mentioned, namely, that Russia could still be kept in the dark for a while about Austrian intentions.

Berchtold at once argued that "the diplomatic situation will not keep that long." He clearly foresaw that in the wake of the rupture of diplomatic relations with Serbia any semblance of Austrian inactivity could arouse among the Entente powers only an impression of pusillanimity rather than the impressive strength it was intended to display, and that this would serve only to encourage Russian intervention. Indeed, having first horrified European public opinion by the harshness of its challenge to Serbia and then aroused even further indignation by brusquely rejecting the highly conciliatory Serbian reply, Austria could scarcely expect that the powers, Russia in the lead, would sit back and allow it time to prepare for an annihilating blow against Serbia. This analysis was so obvious that it really needed no "pressure" from Berlin to convince first Berchtold and the next day Conrad himself.[17] On July 28 the Austrian foreign minister therefore obtained the Emperor's assent to a declaration of war on Serbia, with the express intent thereby to anticipate all the attempts at mediation launched by the great powers of Europe in the meantime. Austria insisted on the right to put its political vigor and military power to the test. The Germans, on their part, were to do everything to deter the Russians from entering the war.

The German General Staff was suspicious from the outset that the Austrians might commit themselves in the Balkans to such a degree that they would be unable to put in an appearance on the Russian front at the crucial time.[18] Understandably enough, Moltke showed little inclination to relieve the Austrians prematurely of the Russian threat by threatening the czarist empire with a German mobilization in turn. On July 26 he found himself in complete agreement with the Chancellor, on the point that, if the war were to be localized, Germany must remain quiescent so long as Russia did not take any hostile action.[19] The chief of staff resolutely supported the German diplomats in their efforts at persuading the government in Vienna to make political concessions to Italy, to keep this ally within the Triple Alliance if at all possible. This was all the more pressing, since General Conrad felt that an Italian defection to the other side would be fatal and clung to the last moment to the illusory hope that he might yet strengthen his fighting front with Italian auxiliaries.[20] He too, therefore, now voted for concessions to Italy, achieving as little as the German diplomats had. Count Berchtold was by no means prepared to purchase uncertain Italian assistance with cessions of Austrian territory. In contrast to 1913, he held with stubborn tenacity to the role of the "strong man" he had assumed.

German policy, on the other hand, followed—though with a reluctance that grew from day to day—the tug of the diplomatic rope it had placed about its own neck early in July, when it had pledged unconditional assistance to its ally. Bethmann Hollweg could not bring himself to cut this rope even when the last hope of "localizing" the war had gone. What paralyzed him was partly the fatalistic belief that the final issue between the two great power blocs must be settled sooner or later, partly the fear that the two Central Powers, Austria-Hungary in the lead, would forfeit their political prestige and their status as great powers if they yielded to the pressure of the Russian war threat. It is difficult to gauge the measure in which influence was brought to bear on the statesmen by the perfervid patriotic mood of the day, which was manifested in countless street demonstrations. It certainly made a diplomatic retreat more difficult, if not impossible.

Did the top military leaders influence the Chancellor in the same direction? Throughout military circles it was taken absolutely for granted that Germany could not abandon Austria in its "struggle for survival." This spirit is documented with particular clarity in a General Staff memorandum of July 29 prepared for the Chancellor.[21] In it, Moltke viewed with horror the danger that "the leading nations of Europe would tear one another limb from limb . . . in a struggle that would destroy the culture of almost all of Europe for decades to come." Yet unless there was a miracle, this "terrible war" which Germany did not desire to bring about would inexorably overtake Germany. The German government knew "it would fatefully violate deep-seated sentiments of loyalty to an ally, one of the finest traits of the German character, and run counter to the whole mood of the country, if it failed to come to the assistance of any ally at a time when that ally must decide on its very survival." Europe should indeed be grateful to Austria-Hungary for being prepared at long last to halt the trouble-making activities of Serbia, whose continuing provocations it had hitherto tolerated with "a patience bordering on weakness." It was high time "to cauterize a canker that continually bade fair to poison the body politic of Europe." What had happened instead was that Russia had meddled in Austria's "purely private quarrel" with Serbia, thereby putting the whole peace of Europe at risk.

Thus the self-same Moltke who only a year before had urgently warned against Austrian adventurism in the Balkans! The sudden change in political temper and the profound impression left by the assassination at Serajevo could scarcely be more dramatically illustrated. Still, there is no sign of fire-eating, no pressure for prompt mobilization against Russia. All the memorandum sought to do was to call attention to the likelihood that the partial mobilization announced by Russia in the event that Austria invaded Serbia would lead relentlessly to a whole chain of further mobilization measures by the Central Powers, and ultimately by France as well, all of which would inevitably bring a general war.[22] The chief of staff by no means desired to accelerate this dreadful process by means of German military measures. He merely asked for a clear picture as soon as possible on the question of whether France and Russia would indeed risk a war with Germany; for Germany, in its parlous position, could on no account allow those countries to gain a headstart with their military preparations. Here we see, in outline, the general direction in which Moltke's further influence on the German government would move. The chief of staff was not agitating for a war that indeed made him shudder, because he knew its dangers and horrors better than others; but he felt it his duty to exert his influence to the end of preventing the enemy from gaining a dangerous headstart by pointless German procrastination.

What Moltke had feared happened. The Austrian declaration of war on Serbia on July 28 was followed the next day by the mobilization of no fewer than twelve Russian army corps, comprising a total of fifty-five infantry and reserve divisions. For the time being, this was a partial mobilization, directed solely against Austria-Hungary. The fact that St. Petersburg, against its earlier announced intention, did not wait for Austria troops actually to cross the Serbian border and that troops were mobilized in such strength clearly showed that the Russians had seen through Conrad's plan to strike a swift blow against Serbia with overwhelming superiority and wished to foil it. There was as much consternation in Vienna as there was in Berlin.

Even the day before, Berchtold had become belatedly anxious about the risks of marshaling almost half the Austrian army against Serbia alone, in the face of Russia's threatening attitude. General Conrad had replied that Germany must seek to prevent a Russian mobilization by threatening countermeasures; but he betrayed his own uncertainty by advancing to August 1 the deadline by which he wished to know whether or not there would be a two-front war.[23]

The Austrian foreign minister, at this juncture, seems to have been dependent entirely on the political counsel of his chief of staff. He sent an appropriate telegram to Berlin, repeating it on July 29 with this addition: "We shall, of course, not be swerved from our military actions against Serbia."[24] It sounded very optimistic, but Conrad actually realized by the evening of July 29 that Austria had no choice but to order total mobilization promptly and that the three Galician army corps not yet mobilized would not be strong enough to ward off a Russian attack, the more so since just then the last hope of drawing Rumania into the war as an ally was waning.

The news from St. Petersburg that the Russian army did not plan an attack for the time being, but would merely "stand at ease" at the border, would have been reassuring only if Vienna had been ready to negotiate a political compromise under pressure of the Russian military threat; but in the prevailing mood there was no question of such a thing. Vienna turned deaf ears to increasingly urgent entreaties from the German Chancellor against allowing the diplomatic dialogue with Russia to lapse, turning down British mediation offers out of hand, and insisting on the military subjugation and occupation of the whole of Serbia. Not without the complicity of Bethmann Hollweg and his foreign minister von Jagow, Vienna at first chose to interpret these pleas as meaning that the Germans wished not so much to avoid a great war as to shift the odium of aggression to the Russians.[25] The diplomats at Vienna, kept informed only sketchily by their representatives abroad, failed to grasp and acknowledge the immense gravity of the diplomatic and military situation.[26] Always concerned with prestige, they were fond of invoking "the sentiments of the army and the people," which allegedly forbade any deal with the enemy once war had been declared.

Actually this "policy of strength" was little more than a façade. On July 30, Count Berchtold and the Austrian prime minister Stürgkh voiced their serious concern to Conrad as to whether Austria would be able financially to conduct a two-front war. The chief of staff tried to reassure them that war with Russia was not inevitable, since the Russians might, indeed, stay behind their line, but this was no more than wishful thinking—though a sign of how obsessed Conrad was with his Serbian war plan. Conrad did, indeed, successfully insist that no negotiations take place that might hold up operations against Serbia.

A new and extremely firm exhortation by Bethmann, supported by a telegram from the Kaiser addressed to Francis Joseph, did, however, on the evening of July 30 lead to a consultation in the presence of the Emperor on demands that might be put to Serbia, if that country were prepared to submit abjectly. The discussion only showed that no one was prepared to offer terms that would be acceptable to Russia. The British had proposed that for the nonce only part of Serbia be occupied—say, the region of Belgrade. With that prize in Austria's hands, a European mediation effort could then get underway that would meet all of Austria's just demands. This was declared to be unacceptable and was rejected with polite circumlocution. Instead, the curious decision was taken to continue the war against Serbia and at the same time to put a general mobilization into effect as of August 4. After further consultations in the presence of Tisza on July 31, it was decided to proclaim the general mobilization order on August 1. Such portions of the army as were not reserved for Serbia were to be assembled in Galicia, but headquarters for the time being was to be shifted to Serbia. Even then war with Russia was not yet considered inevitable, for it was stated that if such a war did occur, the headquarters staff could still reach Galicia in time.[27]

This Austrian attitude, combining political obstinacy with poor military judgment, understandably created deep concern in Berlin. The situation was aggravated by the intolerable tardiness of communications between the two governments, for which the German ambassador Baron Tschirschky must probably take part of the blame.[28] A particular reason for Bethmann's agitation was that the stubborn silence and perpetual evasion of the Vienna politicians on the subject of political concessions was destroying his last hopes for keeping at least Britain out of the great struggle. This would be conceivable only if Russia clearly appeared to be the aggressor. It was to this end that Bethmann on July 28—in agreement with Moltke, by the way—declined to accede to the Austrian demand that he deter the Russians from mobilizing by threatening St. Petersburg with German measures, as we have already seen.

Both the German chief of staff and the German war minister displayed much sympathy with Bethmann's political worries during these days. In a consultation with the Kaiser on the afternoon of July 29, Falkenhayn, disturbed by military intelligence from France and England (though not yet from Russia), asked that a state of emergency be proclaimed but failed to prevail over the objections of Bethmann and Moltke, who thought that less drastic measures were sufficient. By noon of that day Bethmann had felt motivated after all to warn the Russians rather sharply against mobilizing.

When he learned that night that the Russians were set on ordering mobilization against Austria-Hungary, he summoned the two generals once again and decided, against Moltke's "token opposition," that the Russian measure should not yet be viewed as an act of war that would require Germany to act under the alliance with Austria. Falkenhayn actually regarded the peaceful protestations of Sazonov in St. Petersburg as deliberately misleading, nor did he any longer believe in the possibility of British neutrality; but he offered no protest, feeling obliged to stick to his military sphere and not to meddle in political decisions. Besides, like Moltke, he did not take too grave a view of a certain delay in German mobilization against Russia.

Thus the evening of July 29 saw a rather conciliatory sounding warning dispatched to St. Petersburg. It announced that the Austrians would now in all likelihood take countermeasures, but pleaded with the czarist government to await the results of the mediation effort Germany had launched in Vienna before precipitating armed conflict. How deeply the chancellor had already come to feel that the steamroller could no longer be halted is seen from his hapless attempt that same night, transmitted to London through the British ambassador. To keep Britain out of the conflict, he offered a neutrality treaty, an offer that in London was considered almost an insult to the international dignity of the British Empire.[29]

The following morning Bethmann's policy of caution toward Russia still had the support of the chief of staff, who about ten o'clock received the Austrian General Staff liaison officer, Captain von Fleischmann, and advised him that Germany did not regard Russia's partial mobilization as yet as denoting the existence of a state of war and hence did not propose to mobilize. He took it for granted, he said, that Austria-Hungary would now proceed to total mobilization but urgently recommended that the declaration of war be left to the Russians, in consideration of European public opinion, especially that in England, which might be persuaded to stay neutral only in this way, if at all.

This was entirely in keeping with Bethmann Hollweg's stand, and a coded message was at once dispatched to Vienna.[30] Moltke himself had formulated it, unfortunately somewhat ambiguously. Conrad at first thought the German General Staff was advising him against total mobilization, which did not sway him at all.[31] Fleischmann had gained the impression that Moltke still viewed the over-all situation with a certain measure of confidence and still hoped that war could be avoided.

About noon on that day this confidence was abruptly reversed. The reason emerges quite clearly from the document files. It was a message from St. Petersburg, received at the foreign ministry at 11:50 a.m. and at once transmitted to the General Staff, showing the unexpected scope of the Russian "partial mobilization"—only the military districts of Warsaw, Vilnius, and St. Petersburg were exempted from the call-up.[32] This news in a flash revealed the magnitude of the danger threatening the two Central Powers from the east if they delayed their mobilization any further. In the eyes of the generals, Sazonov's diplomatic assurances that mobilization still fell far short of war now lost all credibility.

Moltke had, of course, not the slightest inkling of the drama that was unfolding in the Russian capital at that very hour. With the failure of all his efforts to reach an understanding with the Austrian diplomats over the fate of Serbia, Sazonov, further incensed by reports of a bombardment of Belgrade, had allowed the Russian generals to persuade him that partial mobilization of the Russian army was not technically feasible, besides the fact that it was politically dangerous. In turn, he resolved on persuading the Czar to renew the order for the mobilization of all military districts, which had already been issued the day before only to be withdrawn. We have already heard, in Chapter 4, of the technical difficulties that caused this pressure; but there were also groundless rumors being circulated by fearful and agitated persons to the effect that German mobilization measures were actually much further advanced.

It was in the early afternoon that the notorious and dramatic confrontation between the Czar and Sazonov took place, in which the latter finally prevailed, wresting the ukase for total mobilization from his reluctant sovereign. On the Czar's side, the decision was the outgrowth of fear rather than of any desire for war; but in the perspective of history it was the signal for the dam burst that could no longer be halted. The fateful order was dispatched to the military districts at five o'clock in the afternoon. From that moment on, the continuing exchanges between Berlin and Vienna were mere byplay, soon to be overtaken by events. Yet they clearly illustrate the contrast between the two general staffs.

Directly on receipt of the first dispatches from Russia, Moltke became preoccupied with the question of whether the Austrians would now promptly decide to relinquish their Serbian adventure and swiftly take up positions on the Galician front. Through Fleischmann he inquired in Vienna for news of the decisions being taken there.[33] Soon afterward, about two o'clock, he had a talk with the Austrian military attaché Freiherr von Bienerth, who came over from the foreign ministry and found him "more agitated than I have ever seen him before."[34] The much-cited telegram Bienerth dispatched to Vienna about this talk has often been described in so-called "war guilt research" as providing striking proof of Moltke's heedless bent for war.[35]

The burden of this message was Moltke's urgent exhortation to the Austrians to mobilize against Russia at once, publicly justifying this action with Russia's own mobilization—in other words, representing Russia as the aggressor. "Every hour's delay worsens the situation, since the Russians will gain a head start." But Moltke, in his talk with Bienerth, evidently did not stop at purely military recommendations. He urgently counseled "that an honest settlement be sought with Italy, which should be assured of considerations in return for actively staying in the Triple Alliance. At all costs, leave not a man on the Italian border! " This was an old goal envisaged by both the German General Staff and the German foreign ministry, often put forward vainly in Vienna and on this day once again earnestly commended to the Austrian military attaché.[36]

But Moltke was also clearly concerned with encouraging the Austrians to resist Russia and abandon their Serbian campaign plan. In any event, he mentioned that the imminent Russian attack "put the alliance into effect for Germany. . . . To stand up to a European war is the ultimate resort for pre-serving the integrity of Austria. Germany will unconditionally participate." If that indeed meant a political pledge, the chief of staff was certainly exceeding his authority—even though his pledge did not actually go beyond the promise already given at Potsdam on July 6.

It will be recalled, however, that ever since Bethmann had begun to urge moderation, Vienna had grown more and more skeptical of German assurances of aid and that the Austrians were assailed by many doubts about a two-front war. Thus, it is all too likely that Moltke's encouraging words were in direct answer to searching questions put to him by Bienerth.

Far more serious questions are raised by another passage in the telegram: "Refuse [or refused] renewed English efforts to maintain peace." As it stands (and it has been repeatedly so interpreted by Moltke's critics), this sentence sounds like a stab in the back of the Chancellor, who during these days was making desperate efforts to persuade Vienna to reach an understanding with Russia on the basis of the British mediation proposals. But such an act of sabotage would be so greatly at variance with the attitude Moltke displayed as recently as the morning of July 30 that it commands little credence. A possible explanation is that the military attaché, under the necessity of summarizing a long discussion, expressed himself badly or simply misunderstood Moltke, who may have meant to say that in his view the situation had become far too critical for him to believe any longer that British mediation efforts could be successful—at any rate, no more time should be lost over them. Later that night, Moltke himself sent another telegram to Conrad, briefly going over the content of Bienerth's dispatch. There is no mention of the British mediation proposals in this message.

Neither of these telegrams had any practical effect in Vienna, for they were submitted to the ministers only on the morning of July 31, while the conference with Emperor Francis Joseph had decided on total mobilization the night before, as we have seen. But Bienerth's telegram was very useful to Count Berchtold, when a council meeting (including Tisza) ratified the order for total mobilization and rejected the recommendation from the Kaiser and Bethmann to advance no farther than Belgrade and then negotiate. Berchtold could point to an apparent disagreement in Berlin between the Chancellor and "the most authoritative military spokesman."

Moltke's activities, of course, were not limited to his exchanges with Vienna. Reports say that all day long there were endless discussions with Falkenhayn and the Chancellor, of whom the two soldiers insistently demanded that Germany must now take the first step toward mobilization by declaring a state of emergency. Bethmann Hollweg, still unwilling to give up hope for the success of his representations in Vienna and St. Petersburg, strenuously resisted taking any military steps that might block his mediation proposals; but in the end he had to promise to reach a final decision by no later than noon of July 31. During a meeting of the Prussian Cabinet in the afternoon, however, he clearly showed that his hopes for saving the peace were dwindling. Meanwhile, news was flowing in to the General Staff from the eastern border, suggesting and even corroborating a further extension of Russian mobilization.

Under the impact of this intelligence, Moltke late that night apparently protested against the Chancellor dispatching a final and urgently admonitory telegram to Vienna, which complained bitterly that virtually every mediation effort was being rejected there. In the eyes of Europe this would be interpreted as meaning that Austria was set on war—a war into which Germany would inevitably be drawn, placing the German government "in an altogether untenable situation" vis-à-vis the German people. Very probably Moltke gave it as his opinion that it was already too late for such protests, since war with Russia was indeed imminent.[37]

He was not able to prove this contention at the time; but the events that immediately followed were to bear him out. By midnight, dispatches received at the General Staff spoke of border closings, the destruction of customs posts, etc., and Moltke knew virtually for certain that the dreaded turn had taken place in Russia.[38] Early on the morning of July 31 he received further confirmation by telephone from headquarters at Allenstein in East Prussia. At 11:40 a.m., Ambassador Count Pourtalès' official communication confirming that general mobilization had been ordered arrived from St. Petersburg.

All further discussion as to whether or not Germany should take military measures was now at an end. To avoid the risk of losing any more time, a state of emergency was declared at one o'clock. Moltke's concern immediately shifted to the continuing uncertainty about the military measures and intentions of Germany's ally. It proved very hard to get details, despite the dispatch of liaison officers and the creation of a direct telephone line between the two general staffs; for its users, in order to maintain security, were unwilling to employ it for anything except the transmission of coded telegrams.

Even with their "partial mobilization" of July 29, the Russians were putting fifty-five divisions in the field, more than the total strength of the Austrian army, indeed more than twice what was left of that army after deducting the forces set in motion against Serbia.[39] Yet, incomprehensibly, Vienna was still unwilling to forego the Serbian adventure, even though it entailed a difficult passage without rail transport across mountainous country that had few roads and was bound to take many weeks. The meager news reaching Berlin on July 30 revealed only that Vienna was still waiting to see whether German threats in Paris and St. Petersburg might not persuade the Russians to revoke their mobilization measures and that the Austrians were on no account prepared to give up the war against Serbia.[40] Indeed, a dispatch from the German ambassador received on the morning of July 31 suggested that on the preceding afternoon doubts had once again arisen as to "whether in the existing situation mobilization was still indicated," while any curb on military operations against Serbia along the lines of the British mediation proposals was uncompromisingly rejected.[41]

We have already seen that general mobilization was actually decided on, at least in principle, during the late afternoon at a consultation with the Emperor, though only after much pulling and hauling, with Conrad seeking to persuade the ministers that the Serbian action need not be terminated even after mobilization, since the Russians might merely take up stations at the Galician border without attacking. In an emergency, twenty-seven and a half infantry divisions would still be available to ward off the first Russian assault. The firmness of Conrad's hope that a major clash with Russia might still be postponed is seen from the fact that he set August 1 as the date for proclaiming general mobilization, which was to come into force only on August 4—by which time the divisions earmarked for Serbia would have long departed for the south.[42]

It is scarcely an accident that Conrad, who drafted a brief report on these decisions on the evening of July 30, telegraphed this dispatch to Berlin only at eight o'clock the following morning.[43] He knew that Berlin was bound to object to the monstrous attempt to continue the Serbian action at undiminished strength, rallying in Galicia only what was left of the army. Moltke received this dispatch at the very moment when news that the Russians had moved on to general mobilization became known in Berlin, to be confirmed in several more dispatches.[44] His head probably spun at the thought of the danger to Germany's eastern border, for the protection of which he could spare so few divisions, having counted firmly on a great Austrian offensive in Galicia and Poland. So the warning he had conveyed through Bienerth, the military attaché, had not had the slightest effect! His apprehensions were greatly intensified when General Conrad sent him a telephone message at 4:15 p.m.: "Austro-Hungarian mobilization provoked solely by Russian mobilization. Sole purpose to guard against any Russian attack, no intention whatever to declare or begin war."[45] Moltke could not know that this amazing message was an incredibly delayed answer to his warning against unnecessarily provoking a Russian war by aggressive action, which he had transmitted to Vienna through Captain Fleischmann on the morning of July 30. Accordingly, he telegraphed back: "Germany will proclaim mobilization of all its armed forces presumably on August 2 and take up the fight against Russia and France. Does that sound as though it were abandoning Austria? *"(Will es Österreich im Stich lassen?)*

Conrad von Hötzendorf was much taken aback by this query, spoke of a misunderstanding, and referred to Moltke's dispatch of the preceding day. Yet there can be no doubt that as late as the afternoon of July 31 he proposed to proceed exactly as was telephoned to Berlin, i.e., to remain purely on the defensive in Galicia, so that he might carry out his punitive campaign in Serbia without let or hindrance. How firmly this program was still fixed in the minds of the Austrians is shown by a report *(Vortrag)* which Berchtold submitted to Emperor Francis Joseph on the afternoon of this day. Although Ambassador Tschirschky had meanwhile told him about preparations for mobilization in Germany and the German intention to address an ultimatum to Russia, he nevertheless asserted that the German General Staff counted on the Austrian army continuing its campaign against Serbia, proceeding against Russia only "as soon as was feasible." The same distortion of the true state of affairs recurs in one of Szögény's dispatches as late as the evening of July 31.[46]

By the time the Austrian ambassador sent this misleading report from Berlin, Moltke had long since moved heaven and earth to make the gravity of the military situation clear to the Austrians. William II himself was prevailed upon to send an emphatic message to Emperor Francis Joseph, imploring him not to fritter away his country's military might on subsidiary missions. "In the gigantic struggle on which we now embark shoulder to shoulder Serbia plays an entirely subordinate role." Germany urgently needed the main Austrian force used against Russia in the difficult two-front war that faced it. Italy, too, must be kept within the Triple Alliance, no matter what the concessions.[47] The chief of staff sent for Captain Fleischmann and demanded that he not only make renewed representations to Conrad by wire but betake himself to Vienna at once for the same purpose.

Conrad von Hötzendorf's innermost thoughts are revealed in the draft of a telegram dictated on the night of July 31 but not sent in the original version: "It still is not clear here today, whether Russia is doing anything more than merely threatening, hence we must not be swerved from proceeding against Serbia." The final version read instead: "At time my last message dispatched, news of Germany's intention to mobilize not yet received here.[48] Hence able to count on continuing with war against Serbia, before necessary to proceed against Russia." Similarly, in a letter to Moltke of August 2, the hope was rationalized that establishment of a defensive line in Galicia, combined with vigorous diplomatic pressure by other powers, especially Germany, would be sufficient to make it possible to finish off Serbia. Austria must not flinch in the face of a mere threat. "The diplomatic exchanges during that phase seemed to us to show that while Germany, in the event we were attacked by Russia, would fulfill its obligations under the alliance, it would much prefer to avoid a great war."

Germany's sudden decision to mobilize had created "a totally new situation" for Austria.[49]

Plainly, until the last minute, the Austrian chief of staff toyed with the notion that the Russian tactics might be nothing more than a bluff, or that the Germans would after all succeed in deterring the Russians from the attack. This was now shown to be a complete misapprehension. The Serbian plans had to be dropped for good and all, and all the Austrian forces had to be shifted to the northern front as fast as was still possible. What the Austrian chief of staff now did was try to place the full blame on the Germans, for hesitating so long to mobilize and instead making mere diplomatic threats and pressing Austria to offer political compromises. Conrad's open distrust of his ally was shown during the night of August 1, when Berlin was asked by wire to confirm that Germany was really "prepared to wage large-scale war against Russia immediately and unreservedly"; for Austria "should not be placed in the position of desisting from a war in Serbia for the sake of a war against Russia that might never take place."

It is hard to decide whether this was genuine political distrust or merely the frustration of a man who hated to let go of a prize he had thought was already his. It seems inconceivable to me that the general could have entertained any serious fears that the government of William II and Bethmann Hollweg might at the last minute renege on its pledges of assistance because the Austrians had not heeded its mediation proposals; but if he did believe this, what sense was there still to his Serbian war plans? Any pretense that Germany was able to choose between a "great war against Russia" and a mere covering operation in support of the Austrian defensive front in Galicia was against his better knowledge.

"It is appreciated here that taking up the war with our main forces in Galicia serves primarily to cover Germany's rear." This was the wording Conrad would have liked to include in the reply telegram to the German Kaiser, drafted in the Austrian foreign ministry on August 1; but the foreign minister cut the passage.[50] Conrad's assertion was extremely one-sided, to say the least. Yet it did express a very real difference in interests between the two allies.

For Germany, under the Schlieffen Plan, the eastern front was a subsidiary consideration at the outset; while to the Austrian general the alliance with Germany, despite its outward glitter, was something of a disappointment, for it instantly transformed the struggle for supremacy in the Balkans into a struggle with the western powers. This conflict emerged sharply in the first weeks of the war, when Conrad began his great offensive in Galicia only to find that he had grossly overestimated the scope of German armed aid in the east.

This led to bitter accusations of a German betrayal, even to threats by Berchtold that Austria might conclude a separate peace. From the beginning, the plan of "fighting shoulder to shoulder" proved to be a severe ordeal.[51] One of the reasons the great Galician offensive failed early in September, 1914, was that Conrad had allowed his military transports to roll southward for five vital days, instead of northward, and encountered unexpected trouble when it came to redirecting them. Another was that general mobilization had been ordered far too late, only on August 4, further delaying the northern deployment. Lastly, too large a part of the Austrian army had already become committed to fight with Serbia.[52] All this stemmed from the whole concept of the Serbian campaign, at first delayed, then prematurely initiated, and in the end not broken off in time. General Conrad, of course, tried to shift all the blame to his German partner for having hesitated too long to support Austria by exerting military pressure on Russia.

Historians today are likely to blame the German government for a rather different failure—not for spending too much time on pressing its ally to practice political moderation, but for starting these efforts too late and not carrying them out consistently enough. The destiny and power relations of Europe might have taken an incalculably different form had Germany succeeded in 1914—as happened in the years 1912-1913—in showing itself, in common with Great Britain, to be a guarantor of the peace, in finding an acceptable solution to unrest in the Balkans, a solution that would have kept Serbian nationalism within firm limits.

It is hard to envisage, however, how a durable solution could have been achieved without reshaping the Hapsburg dual monarchy from top to bottom. And when the joint Austro-Hungarian cabinet declared in Vienna on July 31 that no such solution, in either the political or the military sense, was possible on the basis of the British and German proposals, it was for good reason. One can scarcely read the minutes of that session without emotion. The question of whether it was even feasible, in the military sense, to continue the war against Serbia (as was there decided) was not even discussed. Instead, General Conrad expressed optimism with respect to the prospect of persuading the Italian General Staff to dispatch troops not only against France but to the Galician front as well—in return for a vague promise to discuss, under certain circumstances at the end of the war, the cession of the Albanian port of Vlonë (Avlona).[53] It is doubtful whether a major European power ever before stumbled into a war for survival struck with such blindness. For this the Austrian military leaders bear a significant share of the blame.

Part 4

The Inexorable Sequence of War Declarations

FROM ABOUT NOON of July 31 on Bethmann Hollweg no longer seriously believed that peace could be preserved. He had the feeling of having lost the reins of government to the military; and the professional soldiers did sense keenly the pressure of responsibility that weighed on them. Moltke, sensitive in mind and ailing in body, almost succumbed to it even before the war began. His successor, Colonel General Beck, an eyewitness, told me in 1943 that Moltke lost his composure on August 1 when he had to pass on the mobilization order to the officers of the General Staff—as did Count Pourtalès about the very same time, in his farewell audience with the Russian foreign minister.

The responsibility that now lay on the soldiers was indeed crushing. All possibilities for seeking a peaceful settlement seemed to have been wiped out by purely military considerations. Were any such possibilities now left?

When the first news of general Russian mobilization arrived in Berlin early on the morning of July 31, Bethmann Hollweg had already made up his mind to respond with a short-term ultimatum, which was indeed dispatched at 3:30 p.m., at a time when no final decision on Britain's latest mediation proposal had been received from Vienna. The minutes of the meeting of Austrian ministers, at which the proposal was rejected that morning, do not show whether the participants in that meeting had any inkling that such an ultimatum impended; but, in any event, they soon learned of it.[1] Thus there seem to have been no written exchanges between Vienna and Berlin over whether the compromise proposal was to be accepted or rejected. The only thing that now counted for the Germans was to get the Austrians to commit their main forces against Russia as quickly as possible.

In the Kaiser's telegram to Emperor Francis Joseph, which has already been mentioned, the "state of emergency" was described as the initial step toward mobilization, to be promptly followed by the definitive step itself, with August 2 as the first day of mobilization. The Kaiser minced no words in saying that he was ready to begin war against Russia and France at once, in fulfillment of his obligations under the alliance. The burden of Moltke's telegrams to General Conrad that night was that Germany had dispatched an ultimatum to Russia and France, setting a very short time for a reply. It demanded that St. Petersburg revoke all military measures taken against Germany and Austria within twelve hours. "Should Russia refuse, an immediate declaration of war will follow on the part of Germany. . . . I regard Russian acceptance of the German demands as out of the question."[2]

The German government, in other words, was unwilling to negotiate any longer over mediation proposals, while the pressure of general Russian mobilization was on. In Berlin, any concession granted under such pressure was viewed as a loss in prestige, an acknowledgment of the adversary's superior power. Actually, the German ultimatum to Russia did not threaten war, only mobilization, leaving the question of declaring war still open—although this was already taken for granted in Moltke's night telegram. For if Russia had yielded in the face of the German threat, its defeat in the Serbian controversy would have been sealed before all the world; and if it did not yield, the power struggle would be on immediately, without further bargaining.

Bethmann Hollweg had until then always spoken of the need for Austria to be reasonable and not insist absolutely on the military subjugation and political humiliation of Serbia, so that Russia rather than Austria-Hungary would appear to be the disturber of the peace. Now he was apparently convinced that Russia had so unequivocally demonstrated its aggressive intent by ordering general mobilization that no further evidence was required. The military experts had been convinced of this aggressive intent a good deal longer than the Chancellor. They had long been pressing for initial steps leading to mobilization, for they regarded the continuing diplomatic representations as a mere smoke screen hiding the true Russian intent.

Now Russia repeated the assurances given before, when partial mobilization had been declared. Mobilization, St. Petersburg declared, was a step short of war, a security measure. Russia was ready, indeed desired, to continue negotiations on the Serbian problem. The Czar even solemnly promised the Kaiser: "So long as negotiations over Serbia continue with Austria, my troops will not engage in any provocative actions."[3] There is no reason to doubt the sincerity of these assurances, for it was very much in the Russian interest to prove to the world that Russian mobilization was no more than a reply to Austrian mobilization against Serbia. Should negotiations with the government in Vienna drag on, this would be most useful in view of the slow pace of Russian mobilization. Should they fail, Russia would be none the worse off.

To have seriously considered this offer would have been of great value to Germany in a political sense. This would have entailed exerting even stronger pressure on Austria for a peaceful settlement, which would have been all the more appropriate in the light of Sir Edward Grey's redoubled efforts at mediation. On July 31 he went so far as to hint to the German ambassador that if Berlin really succeeded in extracting tangible concessions from Austria and in making reasonable proposals for a settlement the rejection of which would put Russia in the wrong, he, Lord Grey, was prepared to support the German cause in Paris and St. Petersburg and to explain that Britain would decline to have any part in the possible consequences of the Russian attitude.[4]

By the time this new British statement reached foreign minister von Jagow late on July 31, he was no longer in a position to act on it, not only because the ultimatum had meanwhile been dispatched to Russia, but even more for general military considerations. Germany knew it would be threatened on two fronts and had to guard against giving away any chance of military victory, by allowing the Russians to drag out negotiations further and delay a German offensive in the west for even a few days. So, at least, it appeared to the German General Staff; and here we see in bold relief its baneful obsession with the Schlieffen Plan.

As matters stood, there was no great hurry about the war in the east. The marching orders for the German eighth army, stationed there, clearly show that no attack across the border was planned for the first few days, but that the

Germans instead expected to rest content with merely guarding their border, depending on what the enemy would do.[5] On the western front, however, the General Staff was all the more eager to reach the action stage at once, though even there not to the same degree all along the front. Naturally, the territories directly under the Reich had to be protected from a French offensive by the timely deployment of troops, while the powerful forces meant for the advance through Belgium had to be assembled as soon as possible in the Aachen-Wesel area. Even so, this meant a lapse of at least eight to ten days until hostilities proper could really commence. A formal declaration of war on France and Belgium could well be postponed that long without doing any military harm. What could not be postponed, however, was the attack Moltke planned on Liège.

Schlieffen had wanted to proceed through Dutch territory beyond the Meuse north of this fortress, which he held to have little importance, merely keeping it and Namur "under surveillance." As we have already noted, Moltke wished to respect Dutch neutrality at all costs; and also unlike Schlieffen, he was convinced that the two strong points on the Meuse could put up a stiff resistance, even with small garrisons—above all, that they could block the Meuse river course, which the Germans could not forego.[6] To seize this route, together with the fortress of Liège, with the smallest amount of trouble, Moltke had devised a coup that could be successful only if it were launched on the morning of the third day of mobilization, when the border troops had not yet been mobilized, i.e., before the Belgians had time to build obstacles to plug the gaps between their widely spaced strong points.

This plan, verging on the fantastic, had been weighed ever since 1908, but was settled on in detail only on April 1, 1913, in connection with the mobilization preparations for 1913-1914. It was the work of Colonel Ludendorff, as he then was, who, indeed, later on carried out the coup himself with the greatest audacity, actually leading the front-line assault. It was a carefully guarded secret, limited to a small circle of General Staff officers and kept from the government and even the Kaiser.[7]

If it is true that Bethmann Hollweg first heard about it on July 31, after the proclamation of a state of siege, it must have come as a most unpleasant surprise to him. He had known long since, of course, that the German generals planned to begin war against France by marching through Belgium; and he was also probably aware that this invasion had to have surprise character to succeed.[8] But the effect of this Liège plan was to speed up the pace of war preparations from a matter of days to one of hours. Germany was under the necessity of jumping the enemy—in this case actually a neutral—at the very outbreak of war, so to speak, before he had had time to take a defensive stance.

In retrospect, it seems tragic that this single project, which was only half-successful at that and aimed at goals that might well have been achieved in some other way, should have so gravely paralyzed German freedom of political action in those crucial days of July, 1914. The fact that the responsible head of the German government felt that he had to accept such a plan without protest as a "military necessity" shows how abjectly dependent on war plans politics could become. One consequence was that the diplomatic form in which war was declared was most unfortunate for Germany. The welter of consultations from which the various declarations of war emerged has been discussed often enough. We shall here merely give a brief review of the share the top military agencies had in the course of events.

Germany did not mobilize against Russia immediately. It first sent out an ultimatum with a short time limit, demanding that the czarist empire rescind its mobilization order, not only against Germany but against Austria as well. Since no one could expect the Russian government to accept these demands—certainly not within the impossible time span from midnight to noon that was allowed—a declaration of war was being drafted even before the ultimatum had reached St. Petersburg. This was begun during a long session with the Reich Chancellor on the evening of July 31. The chief of staff was present, but not Falkenhayn, who only hours before had pressed for accelerated mobilization.[9] Moltke insisted that on expiration of the ultimatum a declaration of war on Russia must follow immediately, as well as full mobilization. His main argument was that Germany had to take the initiative in the west at once—he was probably thinking of the Liège coup and the need for seizing the Luxembourgeois railways.

Moltke wanted to start and if possible complete his campaign in the west while the Russians were still busy mobilizing and assembling their forces. The Chancellor did not dare oppose these military arguments, and a directive was written for Ambassador Pourtalès, instructing him to deliver the declaration of war by five o'clock in the afternoon, whether the Russians had given a negative reply or none at all. (Two parallel versions were provided, against either of these cases.) The chief of staff was anxious to be able to wire the mobilization order to all army posts by Saturday afternoon, August 1.[10]

A declaration of war against France was also in preparation, and we shall still have to talk of it. For the time being, this was not yet dispatched, and the instructions to Pourtalès, to which the Kaiser had assented on the morning of August 1, were telegraphed at noon to St. Petersburg with such promptness that there was not even time to secure the assent of the federal council to the war declaration, as required under the constitution. This was later given without a dissenting vote.

The entire procedure plainly smacked of haste, and this was due exclusively to the urging of the chief of staff, who feared for the timetable of his war plan. Apparently time was not even taken to consider the political consequences that would inevitably arise from Germany rather than Russia being put in the light of being the aggressor. Yet such consequences were foreseeable in their effect not only on the Russian people but on all Europe, especially Germany's allies, Rumania and Italy, whom the German declaration of war (which clearly made Germany look the aggressor)[11] provided with a ready-made pretext for not fulfilling their treaty obligations. Since the Austrians delayed their declaration of war until August 6, still hoping thereby to delay a Russian advance, a grotesque situation arose in which Germany was at war with Russia six days earlier than its ally, on whose account it entered the war in the first place.

It was Falkenhayn, the war minister, who first realized that such haste was foolish. Early on the morning of August 1 he went to Moltke to win him over to this view. The two then went on to the Chancellor, whom they also persuaded. The Chancellor, however, soon learned at the foreign ministry that it was too late. The message to Pourtalès had already been sent.[12] One probable result was a decision to proceed with greater caution with an ultimatum to France. Immediately, Falkenhayn redoubled his pressure for mobilizing the German army. Against the initial resistance of the Chancellor, he succeeded in having the Kaiser sign the order at five o'clock in the afternoon on the dot, as planned, even though a delay or wire failure had kept a reply from Pourtalès from being available at the time—in other words, the Germans did not really know for certain whether their country was at war with Russia or not.

When Bethmann heard about this incident after the fact, he raised a great uproar and did not calm down until he learned from the General Staff in the course of the night that small Russian detachments had meanwhile crossed the German border—in other words, that a state of war did, in fact, exist. The two generals were in a great hurry to get mobilization underway that very night, and nothing would do but that they carry the order personally to their staffs. But, while the consultation on the declaration of war was still going on in the palace, a telegram from the German ambassador in London suddenly arrived, and the whole war situation bade fair to change in a flash.

This was the well-known, not to say desperate, effort by Sir Edward Grey to save the peace of Europe at the last hour with the fantastic proposal to secure French neutrality through a German offer to refrain from any attack on the western front. At the very least, the two armies were merely to face each other at the border, arms at the ready, thus enabling Britain to remain neutral.

The Kaiser and the Chancellor greeted this proposal with immense relief, indeed with something close to enthusiasm, and the two generals were summoned again to consider it—Tirpitz too was present. The three military men reacted in their various typical ways. The grand admiral, though he did not really believe that the proposal was in earnest, counseled a conciliatory response and helped draft a message from the Kaiser to the king of England. He was immediately mindful of the political effect of an outright rejection, but he was probably also concerned about the fate of his navy in a hopeless struggle.

Falkenhayn was inclined to view the whole thing as a diplomatic soap bubble, but nevertheless kept his nerve and looked for a practical way out. Perhaps the British proposal need not be rejected out of hand, but could be accepted with so many reservations and qualifications that no serious danger to the German deployment would arise. He dictated a message along these lines to von Jagow, which was actually dispatched.

Moltke showed himself least equal to the unexpected situation. He completely lost his composure when Bethmann and the Kaiser suddenly suggested that he might abandon his entire campaign plan and shift his main forces to the east. In the technical sense, this was indeed an impossible challenge. Mobilization and deployment plans for an army of millions, the product of months of detailed work, cannot be overturned from one day to the next without precipitating chaos;[13] and Schlieffen's contingency plan for an eastern deployment on the grand scale had been abandoned in 1913.

"Your uncle would have given me a different answer!" was the grossly unfair taunt the Kaiser flung in the face of his chief of staff; and nothing could have shown more clearly the inadequacy of his military knowledge than this inability to grasp the technical problems involved. What actually raised this entire debate to so high a pitch was the profound discrepancy between the "purely military" Schlieffen Plan and Germany's real needs, on which that plan cast such a stark light—the rigidity with which German policy was tied to a great western offensive, with all its political consequences. Moltke showed himself to be far less resourceful in this emergency than Falkenhayn, who did not dismiss the possibility of a certain lag in the western offensive if that were to give Britain a chance to formulate her proposal more concretely.

Against Moltke's vociferous opposition, it was finally resolved to delay the opening gun in the war against France, in order to assure Britain that the German army would not cross the French border until the evening of August 3. For the nonce, no change in the deployment plans was ordered, except that the Kaiser, over the head and against the will of his chief of staff, halted any invasion of Luxembourg by German troops. Such an invasion had been scheduled to take place at once, in preparation for the invasion of Belgium. Understandably enough, Moltke lapsed into a state of profound depression. He could not but have the feeling that he was no longer taken quite seriously as the responsible head of army operations. Yet the fact that he now suffered a complete collapse—to use his own words—does tend to show how narrowly he clung to his military set pieces.

The controversy over deployment in the west came to a swift end, for in a matter of hours telegrams arrived from London that tended to show up Grey's proposal as a mere "misunderstanding," an episode without practical importance; but the question of a declaration of war on France continued to be a subject of bitter debate. At the noon session of the federal council *(Bundesrat)*

Tirpitz had already opposed a formal declaration of war on Russia;[14] and at the meeting in the palace he had declared that he was against the immediate initiation of hostilities on the eastern front—let the Russians attack first. In this he had enjoyed the Kaiser's assent.

Very early Sunday morning—between 2:30 and 3:30 a.m.—the debate was continued in another form in the Reich chancellery. The three top military men, Moltke, Falkenhayn, and Tirpitz, there met with the Chancellor and representatives of the foreign ministry. Nerves were raw by this time, and military and political viewpoints once again clashed head on. The "civilians" insisted that in order to proceed on the western front a formal declaration of war must first be handed to France; nor, until then, could a *sommation* (summary notice) be directed to Belgium demanding that that country permit the German troops passage.

The military men held that a formal declaration of war was superfluous. That should be left to the French. Moltke insisted, moreover, that certain border incidents showed that "a state of war already existed." The soldiers, especially War Minister Falkenhayn, had clearly begun to realize the invidious political situation that would overtake Germany by virtue of the fact that it appeared to be striking out almost blindly and with such suddenness, refusing to be restrained by the several efforts at mediation and compromise that were still pending with London, Moscow, and Paris. They thought they could avoid the onus by letting the other side declare war in the formal sense, and they resented the insistence of foreign ministry "civilians and lawyers" on the niceties of international law that to them seemed a mere formality.[15]

Falkenhayn took this stand "rather brusquely"—Tirpitz's words—toward the Chancellor; but Moltke, too, got into a vehement argument with Bethmann Hollweg and rudely rejected an attempt by Privy Councilor Kriege, of the foreign ministry law division, to advance legal arguments. These differences gave rise to deep resentments between the Chancellor and the military, which continued throughout the war. Military literature, and especially the widely read writings of the grand admiral, are full of the kind of charges that were first raised in public when Bethmann Hollweg fell in 1917. The reason Germany appeared as a brutal aggressor in the eyes of the world, it was contended, lay in Bethmann's lack of diplomatic skill, in his insistence on proceeding by pettifogging legalism. Bethmann was even charged with being motivated by considerations of domestic politics. He forced the war against czarist Russia, it was implied, because of his liberal democratic sentiments.

As against this view, it was von Jagow who rightly emphasized that none other than the chief of staff himself had demanded and forced the hasty declaration of war against Russia, for purely military considerations; and, further, that Germany's situation would have been much worsened rather than bettered if the Germans had begun the war in the west with an invasion of a neighboring country "like a bolt from the blue" and without benefit of a formal declaration of war.[16]

The soldiers thought that France would sooner or later be forced to declare war on Germany, because of its aggressive designs and the mood of the French people. Yet everything we know about French policy during those days points to the fact that Paris was well aware of the advantage of being able to wait for a German attack, especially since that attack was to come via neutral territory. To have anticipated this attack by a French advance along the Belgian Meuse would have been highly advantageous in a military sense—indeed, it might be described as having been a "military necessity"; but for political reasons already discussed in Chapter 3, the French did not dare such a thing, though General Joffre was forever urging haste.

The German generals, in other words, miscalculated. It was politically naive to believe that a mere foregoing of a formal declaration of war would give the appearance of a purely defensive war, before the eyes of Europe, to a war that actually began with an invasion of neutral Belgium, conducted in open violation of international law. The reason Germany declared war on Russia in such a hurry was in order to be able to attack Russia's ally, France, without delay, which was, in fact, scarcely possible so long as a state of war did not even exist. In the military view, the western offensive had to begin with an invasion of Belgium; and this invasion, in Moltke's view, was feasible only if passage was first demanded of Belgium. Such a demand, in turn, depended on a state of war existing between Germany and France. It was an inescapable vicious circle, and the heart of the whole problem was the invasion of Belgium.

Its fateful importance became quite clear even to the generals in the course of that nocturnal debate, the more so since the British diplomats kept insisting more and more emphatically that their attitude to the war would depend greatly on whether Germany would respect Belgian neutrality or not. Tirpitz, who later insisted that this was the first he had heard of the Belgian invasion plans,[17] objected strenuously, if only for the sake of his fleet. He predicted war with England. Bethmann Hollweg too seems to have voiced reservations at this last moment, of course in vain. Tirpitz did, however, extract an assurance (later not kept) that the *sommation* to Belgium would be issued as late as possible, giving time for naval mobilization. It was also agreed to delay the declaration of war on France, despite the disappointing news from London—in the hope that the French might attack in the meantime.[18]

This lively debate was continued on the morning of Sunday, August 2, at the palace, where Moltke and Tirpitz, against Bethmann's stubborn resistance, tried to persuade the Kaiser to forego the declaration against France altogether. The chancellor was unable to prevail and was instructed to reassure the British government about the impending invasion of Belgium with promises that Germany was acting purely in self-defense and did not come as a conqueror.

After Bethmann departed, both military men vociferously complained of the total incompetence of the foreign ministry and its head von Jagow, whom Tirpitz wanted replaced by Rear Admiral Hintze. Moltke reproached von Jagow with still being under the illusion that he might halt the inexorable wheel of fate by means of diplomatic notes.

Similar discussions about a complete "rout" of the foreign service had already been held among the military men at the end of their night meeting. Moltke was heard to remark that "he must now take the political reins in his own hands."[19] That same day he did, indeed, transmit to the foreign ministry a most curious document, evidently composed in a great hurry and outwardly appearing to be a kind of directive for political action "from the military point of view." It contained recommendations for what now had to be done in order to effect a successful strategy and the best possible power configuration. It was essentially a rather naive list of goals—a military alliance with the Scandinavian countries, Japan, and Persia; the fomenting of rebellions in India, Egypt, and South Africa—together with more concrete proposals for the treatment of Italy, the Balkans, and other countries. The whole thing was a demonstration of a total lack of political realism rather than a show of trained diplomatic skill.[20] Once again, of course, there was the demand to forego a declaration of war against France for the time being and to keep the Belgian invasion an entirely separate matter.

This was all the more curious since the note intended for the Belgian government, drafted by Moltke himself and sent to the Belgian embassy on July 29 in a sealed envelope, justified the German invasion of Belgium by the necessity for countering a deployment of powerful French forces along the Givet-Namur section of the Meuse, allegedly reported "by reliable sources." But what if war with France had not yet broken out by the time this note was delivered? By August 2, the German General Staff was frantically collecting intelligence of diverse character and value on the subject of French border violations, in an effort to prove that a state of war already existed. We shall yet have to discuss the consequences of this whole course of action.

In the early morning hours of August 2, German troops moved into Luxembourg.[21] The great western offensive was thus underway, and the time had arrived to have the scheduled *sommation* handed to the Belgian government. It offered the Belgians the alternative of maintaining a benevolent neutrality toward the German passage, in return for certain political assurances, or of considering themselves enemies of the Germans. This note was transmitted at eight o'clock in the evening of August 2, at a time when no formal state of war with France yet existed. In accordance with Moltke's wishes, a time limit of twelve hours was set, so that the advance on Liège could be prepared on August 3 and the border crossed the next day.

The draft of this note clearly reflects the proposals Moltke had made in his comprehensive memorandum of 1913 (see Chapter 9, Part 3). It endeavored to reassure the Belgians on the future of their country, promising them, if they assented, complete territorial integrity, together with indemnitites for any and all losses they might suffer and, furthermore, "territorial compensation at the expense of France." Had the offer actually been made to Belgium in that form, Brussels would have taken deep offense, and indignation would have been certain in France and England. Fortunately von Jagow ordered the offending passages stricken out at the last moment.[22]

The fact that so important a document was not even written in the foreign ministry but taken from a desk drawer of the chief of staff glaringly illustrates the wretched quality of German diplomatic war preparations, the utter dependence on improvisation. On the military side, Bethmann Hollweg has often been reproached with having taken no diplomatic precautions whatever to lighten the odium that would attach to Germany for violating the neutrality of a neighbor; but Moltke's draft provides telling proof that there was simply no way of glossing over such an act of force. The assertion that the German army was under the necessity of countering the imminent threat of a French invasion was far too threadbare to be taken seriously anywhere outside Germany; and the claim that Belgium had violated its obligations as a neutral was even less convincing, despite all the propaganda and research later marshaled to bolster it.[23] In the end, there was but one possibility left in an attempt at justification—to invoke the exigencies of Germany's military and strategic situation, the very thing Bethmann Hollweg tried in his familiar and controversial Reichstag speech of August 4, 1914. Many Germans indignantly rejected what they felt to be the self-abasement implicit in so open an admission of a breach of international law. On the other hand, it was the only way in which nationwide resentment in Belgium could have been assuaged—if that was, indeed, possible at all.[24]

With the directives dispatched to Brussels, a solution was found to the question of a declaration of war against France as well, though only in the form of a most unfortunate compromise. On July 31 the German ambassador von Schön had received an inquiry to be addressed to the French government. Under pressure from the German military, extremely dubious aspects had been given to this message. In addition to the outright question whether France was prepared to preserve neutrality during a war between Germany and Russia, it contained an added "secret" clause. In the improbable event that the answer might be in the affirmative, the ambassador was to demand that the French fortresses of Toul and Verdun be occupied by the Germans for the duration of the war, as "tokens" of French neutrality.

It is almost incomprehensible that Bethmann Hollweg should have agreed to include so humiliating a provocation in the dispatch to von Schön. Sharp military criticism has also been voiced of the political innocence of the chief of staff responsible for the secret clause.[25] It would have made sense only if the object had been to prevent French neutrality at all costs. Even so, no clumsier justification for a German declaration of war could be imagined. The only possible interpretation is the reason given by Bethmann himself. Such security for French neutrality seemed indispensable "in the view of the military."[26]

The French government avoided giving any assurances of neutrality with a statement that "it would act as its interests dictated." Thus the "secret" instruction was, in fact, never carried out; but, during the course of the war, the French succeeded in decoding the dispatch sent to Schön, and this hapless contingency demand did after all supply welcome fuel for anti-German propaganda.

The German foreign ministry had better luck with the draft of a declaration of war against France, worked out on the evening of the same day. It gave a straightforward picture of the dilemma in which Germany felt herself to be enmeshed. With the outbreak of war with Russia, Germany now faced the prospect of having to declare war on Russia's ally, since France refused to declare itself neutral. In a two-front war, the German army could not possibly wait to see whether or not France would stab it in the back.

This was as forthright as it was plausible, and such words could have scarcely failed to impress world opinion, had they been made public; but neither the chief of staff nor the war minister would retreat from their stand that Germany must not proclaim itself the aggressor by a declaration of war, and they had secured the Kaiser's support. The Chancellor and the foreign minister, for their part, stuck to their objections, which were further stiffened by a new report from London: a crossing of the French border by German troops without a prior declaration of war would make a very poor impression in Britain, probably exerting a crucial influence on Grey's attitude.

German troops were scheduled to invade Belgium on the morning of August 4, and Moltke still insisted that this be done without a declaration of war, since he still hoped that the Belgian government might yield. But if that happened, would the French be likely to anticipate the Germans with a declaration of war, since they would now feel in peril and under attack: Von Jagow and Moltke discussed these possibilities on the morning of August 3, and a compromise was ultimately agreed on. The declaration was dispatched to Paris, but the wording of the first draft was dropped and instead an attempt was made to brand the French before the world as the aggressors. This was done by enumerating a series of insignificant border incidents reported by the General Staff, the more important of which were later shown to be products of imaginative border patrols or other persons out to find "news." No more misguided way of justifying a life-and-death struggle between two great nations in the eyes of the world can be imagined.

The great and fearsome drama had now been launched, marking a historic juncture and ushering in a new age of steel. The German people went into the First World War with a clear conscience, convinced that a multitude of enemies all about were swarming over them without warning. As for Germany's political and military leaders, they too had reason for saying that they never consciously courted disaster. They were simply overwhelmed by it, and we have no right to doubt that their peaceful intentions were genuine in principle. No one in a leading position wished to bring about a world war; and to that extent there is no longer today any question of "war guilt."

A certain spirit of fatalism, however, was abroad, a belief that a great war was inevitable; and coupled with a strong sense of national prestige and self-assertion, this was calculated to engender political blindness. It was, to be sure, by no means limited to Vienna and Berlin, but the perilous situation of the Central European powers gave it a particularly fateful tinge there; and in the eyes of history, even political blindness can turn into guilt.

We are no longer content to comprehend the outbreak of the First World War simply in terms of inexorable fate, the necessary and natural result of tensions, power politics, and conflicts of national interest in an age of imperialism. Despite the powerful forces of destiny that hold mankind under their spell and in their thrall, there always remains—such is our firm belief—a sphere for freedom of decision on the part of responsible statesmen acting with political reason. Were that not so, we should have to despair of mankind's future.

It is by no means certain that the outbreak of the First World War could have been avoided if the relation between sword and scepter in imperial Germany had been better ordered; for many other forces—forces outside Germany, above all—had a share in that outbreak. It is quite certain, however, that had that relation been better ordered, the war would have begun less inauspiciously. It is also very probable that it would not have led the German people into so terrible a catastrophe. Just how terrible it was will be shown in the next volume of this work.

Notes

Notes to the Preface to the Second Edition

1. As I correctly noted in the first edition, notice of the Austrian ultimatum of July 23 went simultaneously to all countries on July 20 (see *Österreichische Dokumente,* Vol. 8, No. 10,400), but, as I overlooked, was to be presented outside Germany only on July 24. It is correct that part of its content was known in Berlin beforehand; but the full wording was not known, and it was precisely this that created the greatest consternation in the German foreign ministry, a fact not mentioned by Geiss, *loc. cit.,* pp. 25f. See also L. Albertini, Vol. 2, pp. 265f.

Notes to Chapter 1

1. See especially General Lamarque, *De l'Esprit Militaire en France* (1826), pp. 9f. Similar views were given as early as the eighteenth century by Turpin de Crissé; also by others, such as Blondel (1836) and General de Prival (1824), according to I. Monteilhet, *Les Institutions Militaires de la France. 1814-1932* (1932), p. 40. This interesting book, crammed with information, advocates the militia ideas of J. Jaurès and is devoted to the struggle against the *esprit militaire* and the *armée de caserne.* My description of the army system of the Restoration period and the attitude of French liberalism toward it is based, among other sources, on an unpublished dissertation by my Freiburg student Werner Schulz, *Die Französische Armee im Zeitalter der Restauration* (1951). Schulz was able to consult abundant source material in Paris. Developments to 1873 have been described by M. Jähns in *Das Französische Heer von der Grossen Revolution bis zur Gegenwart* (1873), with his usual brilliance, but also with a noticeable anti-French bias. The older accounts are all largely based on the comprehensive and knowledgeable but partisan Orléanist book by the Duc d'Aumale, *Les Institutions Militaires de France* (1867). M. von Szczepanski, in *Napoleon III. und Sein Heer (Heidelberger Abhandlungen,* Vol. 42 [1913]), deals with a somewhat fragmentary portion of the mutual relationship between army and constitution in France. H. Pfister's *Das Französische Heerwesen* (1867) and Exner's *Die Französische Armee in Krieg und Frieden* (1889) merely review external army organization for military instructional purposes. This is also done at great length in Hepke, *Frankreich. Das Heer am Ende des 19. Jahrhunderts (Die Heere und Flotten der Gegenwart;* edited by von Zepelin,

1900). More useful in my context was the anonymous General Staff memorandum, *Die Französische Armee* (2nd ed.; Mittler & Son, 1913). W. Frank, in *Nationalismus und Demokratie im Frankreich der Dritten Republik* (1933), which seeks to describe the Dreyfus case and its historical background, completely neglects the historical problems proper, like the position of the army within the nation as a whole and the repercussions from the Dreyfus case on it, in favor of a discursive and tendentious account of parliamentary scandals, given in a journalistic style. Arpad F. Kovacs, in "French Military Institutions before the Franco-Prussian War" (*American Historical Review*, Vol. 51 [January, 1946] p. 2) merely offers a brief survey of no independent value. Raoul Girardet, in *La Soeiété Militaire dans la France Contemporaine, 1815-1939* (Paris, 1953), based on impressive source material, traces the position of the army in French society and the spirit which animated it.

2. Letter to his fiancée from Coppet, October 3, 1807.

3. It has been calculated, however, that even during the fifteen years of Napoleonic rule no more than 52,000 volunteers joined the colors, making an annual average of only 3,500. In the 1820's the number of volunteers rose to about 5,000 to 7,000 a year. In the year of the Spanish campaign, 1824, it was substantially higher.

4. Even under Louis XIV it was possible to buy one's way out of militia duty in France.

5. For further details, see p. 21.

6. Between 1821 and 1831 there were 4,499 promotions of officers. Of these, 1,952 went to war academy graduates, 2,537 to former noncoms (Schulz, *loc. cit.*). In the 1860's, according to Jähns (*loc. cit.*, p. 413), half of the subaltern officers were former noncoms. Under the law of 1883, at least one-third of all officers were to be *sortis du rang*. The actual proportion in 1913 was three-fifths, since attendance at the St. Cyr academy rapidly declined after the Dreyfus case. Many candidates from the educated classes, however, sought to attain officer status by the less costly noncom route, even though it led only in exceptional cases beyond the rank of captain or at best major. In 1912 ten percent of the higher staff officers and two percent of the generals were former noncoms. For details see also Girardet, *loc. cit.*, pp. 185ff. and 274ff.

7. See the studies by two of my students: Paul Sauer, *Das Württembergische Heer zur Zeit des Deutschen und des Norddeutschen Bundes;* and Reinhard Mielitz, *Das Badische Militärwesen und die Volksbewaffnung bis 1848*, cited at greater length in Note 5 to Chapter 5.

8. Prosper Mérimée's correspondence: "A force de prêcher que l'argent est le sourverain bien, on a profondément altéré les sentiments belliqueux de la France, je ne dis pas dans le peuple, mais dans les classes élevées. L'idée de risquer sa vie est devenue très répugnante, et ceux qui s'appellent les honnêtes gens disent que cela est bas et grossier." Cited after Monteilhet, *loc. cit.*, p. 47.

9. See his *Cours Complet d'Economie Politique Pratique*, Vol. 2 (2nd ed., 1839-40). From similar considerations Auguste Comte toyed with the utopian idea of replacing the army with 80,000 gendarmes.

10. Jähns (*loc. cit.*, p. 401), puts the number of professional soldiers among the total of 330,000 to 350,000 at 250,000.

11. Girardet writes memorably on this subject, *loc. cit.*, pp. 162ff.

12. Thiers was motivated in part by the fear that the introduction of universal military service would even further arouse Bismarck's distrust of French rearmament plans. An exchange of dispatches with Ambassador Gontart-Biron is found in *Documents Diplomatiques Français*, Series 1, Vol. 1 (1929), and Thiers, *Notes et Souvenirs* (1904). Gontart-Biron, *Mon Embassade en Allemagne 1872-73* (1906); *Occupation et Libération du Territoire 1871-73; Correspondances* (1903), No. 121.

13. Details in Girardet, *loc. cit.*, pp. 213ff and 228ff. For the following see also pp. 240ff.

14. According to Monteilhet, *loc. cit.*, p. 254, only 65 percent of the reservists called up appeared for field exercises in 1907. In May, 1913, there were disturbances among the soldiers when the service term was to be extended to three years. According to

Girardet (*loc. cit.,* p. 245), the proportion of draft resisters was anticipated as 13 percent prior to 1914. The actual rate in 1914, in the face of the threat of German invasion, was only 1.5 percent.

15. As early as 1900, recruitment in France exceeded all other countries in harshness and ruthlessness. At the time, Russia excused on the average every other man liable for service, for family reasons, Italy 37 percent. In France no one was excused. The peacetime rate of service among able-bodied males from 21 to 60 stood at 30.2 per 1,000 in Italy, 34 in Austria-Hungary, 43.6 in Russia, 48 in Germany, and 58.4 in France (A. von Drygalski, *Die Organisation der Russischen Armee in ihrer Eigenart und im Vergleich mit den Streitkräften Frankreichs, Österreich-Ungarns, Italiens und Deutschlands* [1902]).

16. It is perhaps overestimated in O. von Moser, *Die Obersten Gewalten im Weltkrieg* (1931), p. 22. See also A. Vagts, *Defense and Diplomacy* (1956), pp. 500ff.

17. See the authorities (Schwarte, Marcel Sembat, Mordacq, Cadorna) cited by J. M. Bourget, *Gouvernement et Commandement. Les Leçons de la Guerre Mondiale* (1930), pp. 61f.

18. P. Schmidt, *Statist auf Diplomatischer Bühne* (1949), p. 66.

19. Bourget *(loc. cit.),* apparently overestimates the importance of this tradition, as indeed he does the organizational element as a whole. P. Renouvin, in *Les Formes du Gouvernement de Guerre* (in *Histoire Economique et Sociale de la Guerre Mondiale,* [French Series; Carnegie Foundation, 1926]), gives only a cursory review of the relations between *gouvernement* and *commandement.* He devotes more attention to the administration of the war than to its conduct, dealing especially with the share of the parliament. A graphic but rather popular account of the relations between parliamentary ministers and General Staff is given by Lieutenant Colonel Charles Bugnel, in *Rue St. Dominique et G.C.G. ou les Trois Dictatures de la Guerre* (1937). Georges Bonnefou, in his comprehensive account, *Histoire Politique de la 3ᵉ Republique. II: La Grande Guerre 1914-1918* (1957), limits himself almost exclusively to the deliberations in parliament during the war, but these are very enlightening, especially the excerpts from the records of the secret session in 1916-1917. Jere Clemens King, in *Generals and Politicians: Conflict between France's High Command, Parliament and Government 1914-1918* (Berkeley: University of California Press, 1951), gives a lively and informative picture. This work became known to me only after this chapter was written, but did not require me to make any changes.

20. Maréchal Joffre, "La Guerre et la Politique," *Revue des Deux Mondes,* Vol. 102, XI (1932), pp. 46ff. Of special interest is his complaint to the war minister on June 26, 1915.

21. Maréchal Foch, *Mémoires pour Servir à l'Histoire de la Guerre de 1914-1918* (1931), Vol. 1, p. 14. Foch himself was very slow in achieving promotion. Having attended a Jesuit school, he was regarded as a "clerical," and the old Jacobin Clémenceau never found him congenial. Joffre was a Freemason. A clerical legend is already growing up around Foch's life; see G. Beyerhaus, "Die Europapolitik des Marschall Foch," in *Das Reich und Europa* (1942), and the French source material used there.

22. Georges Clémenceau, *Grösse und Tragik eines Sieges* (German translation, 1930), pp. 3, 6, 34, 39, 57, and *passim.* Among the personages described by Clémenceau, Pétain cuts by far the best figure.

23. Much proof is given by King, *loc. cit.*

24. After Joffre's fall, he appointed a ministerial Comité de Guerre within his cabinet, as the body formally in charge of conducting the war; but, unlike the British War Council, on which it was modeled, the French body never achieved practical importance.

Notes to Chapter 2

1. Among works used in writing this chapter are J. H. Fortescue, *A History of the British*

Army (1930), Vols. 11-13; I. S. Omond, *Parliament and the Army 1642-1904* (Lectures, 1933); in the *Oxford History of England:* E. L. Woodward, *The Age of Reform 1815-1870* (1938), and R. C. K. Ensor, *England 1870-1914* (1936). Important for the period from 1900 to 1914 are: P. Kluke, "Heeresaufbau und Heerespolitik Englands. Vom Burenkrieg bis zum Weltkrieg," Supplement No. 27 to *Historische Zeitschrift,* 1932; I. E. Tyler, *The British Army and the Continent 1904-1914* (1938); D. H. Cole and E. C. Priestley, *An Outline of British Military History 1660-1939* (London, 1935). J. K. Dunlop's *The Development of the British Army 1898-1914* (1938) was not to be found in West German libraries. A brief review of the British army system is given by Julius Hatschek in *Englisches Staatsrecht, Handbuch des Öffentlichen Rechts,* edited by Piloty, VI, 2, Vol. 2: "Die Verwaltung" (1906), Paragraphs 185-194. Evidence is produced there for the connection between eighteenth-century English militia institutions and the conscription system of Frederic William I of Prussia, which was used as a model. Among memoirs, those of Field Marshal Robertson (*Soldiers and Statesmen 1914-1918,* Vol. 1, [1936]; *From Private to Field Marshal* [1921]) offer a particularly dramatic view of British soldiering before the First World War.

2. Fortescue, *loc. cit.,* Vol. 13, final page.
3. Fortescue, *loc. cit.,* Vol. 11, pp. 16f.; Sir C. E. Callwell: *Field Marshal Sir Henry Wilson* (1927), Vol. 1, p. 49. See also Kluke, *loc. cit.,* p. 24.
4. According to Cole and Priestley (*loc. cit.,* p. 216), a lieutenant-colonelcy cost about £7,000 around 1856.
5. This is acknowledged by Field Marshal Robertson (Vol. 1, p. 18), who nevertheless criticizes the incorporation of the General Staff into the war office, which overburdened the General Staff with purely administrative duties, from which it was freed only by Haldane. Robertson also complained that the General Staff was out of direct touch with the troops, for whose training it issued directives without being advised by the inspectors general how they worked in practice.
6. Its importance is clearly much overestimated by Kluke, *loc. cit.,* p. 69.
7. My account of this structure is essentially based on Kluke, *loc. cit.,* a work built on a careful study of the sources.
8. Robertson's memorandum of October, 1902, given in his memoirs, *loc. cit.,* p. 22.
9. *Before the War* (1920); *An autobiography* (1929).
10. See especially Robertson, *Soldiers and Statesmen,* pp. 40ff.
11. It is true, however, that a British force of 70,000 men remained stationed in India in the First World War, its use being made very difficult by the interposition of the India Office, the Government of India, and in certain instances the foreign office. See Robertson, *loc. cit.,* Vol. 1, p. 158.
12. Robertson, Vol. 2, p. 296: "His desire always was that we should aim at having the strongest army in Europe when the war came to an end, and so be able to ensure that suitable terms of peace were exacted." Similarly, Vol. 1, p. 156: "Scouting the feasibility of a limited participation in the war . . . he at once commenced to make the British Empire into a military power of the first rank."
13. See especially the comprehensive memorandum of December 5, 1915, in Vol. 1, pp. 168ff., and the concluding remarks, Vol. 2, pp. 300ff. The entire memoirs revolve around the theme of soldiers and politicians.
14. See the similar-sounding formulation by Churchill in his *World Crisis* (1915), Vol. 2, pp. 21f.: "As a summit true politics and strategy are one. The manoeuvre which brings an ally into the field is as serviceable as that which wins a great battle. . . . " Churchill added, however, that there was need for a "clearing house of ideas, where these different relative values could be established and changed."
15. See the interesting remarks by Liddell Hart, "The Historical Strategy of Britain," in *The British Way of Warfare* (London, 1932).

Notes to Chapter 3

1. D. S. MacDiarmid, *The Life of Lieutenant General Sir James M. Grierson* (1923), p.

133; S. Aston, "The Entente Cordiale and the 'Military Conversations,'" *Quarterly Review*, No. 512 (April, 1932), p. 367.
2. Robertson, *Soldiers and Statesmen*, Vol. 1, pp. 20ff.
3. W. H. H. Waters, *Private and Personal* (1928), pp. 240f., cited from the excellent monograph by J. E. Tyler, *The British Army and the Continent 1904-1914* (1938), pp. 16f., and after Kluke, *loc. cit.*, p. 138.
4. Since there was then not yet any contact with the French General Staff, it seems unlikely that anything was known in Camberley about the espionage intelligence the French had had since 1904. These intelligence reports, by the way, were the work of a swindler who fooled the espionage section of the French General Staff, but not its top leadership. See W. Foerster, in *Berliner Monatshefte*, Vol. 10 (1932), pp. 1053ff.; and the careful documentation in a dissertation I suggested to J. Hanebuth, *Beiträge zur Entwicklung der Rolle der Belgischen Neutralität in der Französischen Aussenpolitik 1900-1914* (Göttingen, 1947; typescript), pp. 29ff.
5. Robertson (Vol. 1, p. 19) mentions discussions that took place as early as 1902 on Britain's attitude in the event of a German advance through Belgium. Salisbury then refused to fix the British position in advance. The war games Robertson conducted in 1905 went far beyond what the French General Staff, in its deployment plans down to 1911, thought a German offensive would be like. Apparently even Joffre was encouraged to somewhat greater boldness in his counteroffensive plans only under British influence (Wilson, September, 1911) – see Hanebuth, *loc. cit.*, pp. 64f. Compare also the semiofficial soundings in the British press in 1887, on whether the Germans might not invade Belgium in the event of a Franco-German war, and Salisbury's rather ambiguous attitude on the question of British obligations toward
. Belgium in such a case – see my book, *Der Schlieffenplan – Kritik eines Mythos* (1956), pp. 83f.
6. See the report of 1900 by the Belgian General Staff officer Ducarne in B. Schwertfeger, *Der Geistige Kampf um die Verletzung der Belgischen Neutralität* (2nd ed., 1919), pp. 62ff. (Vol. 5 in the series of Belgian documents on the origins of the First World War, 1925, pp. 44ff.). On French General Staff plans, see the above-cited dissertation by Hanebuth.
7. For details of this theory, see Kluke, *loc. cit.*, pp. 139ff., and confirming diplomatic dispatches in *Grosse Politik*, Vol. 20, 2, Nos. 6863, 6867, 6873, and *passim;* as well as the very concrete assurances of the Belgian envoy, Baron Greindl, in Schwertfeger, *Dokumente zur Europäischen Politik 1897-1914* (1919), reports of April 5, 1906, April 18, 1907, November 19, 1907, and *passim*. In addition *British Documents*, Vol. 3, No. 95; *Documents Diplomatiques Français*, 3rd series, Vol. 4, No. 301. On Fisher's plans: R. H. Bacon, *Life of Lord Fisher*, Vol. 2, pp. 72f., 81, 146, 182; and Tyler, *loc. cit.*, pp. 21ff. Of great interest are the discussions within the British admiralty from June 24 to 27, 1905, on the role of the British navy in the event of a Franco-German war, recently brought to light by Arthur J. Marder in *The Anatomy of British Sea Power: A History of British Naval Policy in the Pre-Dreadnought Era, 1880-1905* (New York, 1940), pp. 502ff. Questioned by Admiral Ottley, director of the naval intelligence department and chief of the admiralty staff, Admiral Wilson, chief of the Channel fleet, held that mere fleet action – such as damaging German sea trade and blocking the Elbe estuary, etc. – was insufficient. He demanded a landing of British troops on the German coast, preferably in Schleswig-Holstein. Ottley reverted to this idea in a long memorandum in July, 1905, for the Committee of Imperial Defence, asking for a special subcommittee that would even in peacetime prepare for such landing operations in cooperation with the admiralty and the General Staff. As early as June 26, he had expressed a desire for talks between the British and French naval commands for the coordination of their war plans.
8. See his private letter to Delcassé of May 29, 1905, *Documents Diplomatiques Français*, 2, VI, p. 465.
9. German diplomatic reports in the summer of 1905 and Bülow's corresponding directives always envisaged only British naval intervention, deprecating the dimen-

sions of British aid to France. See *Grosse Politik*, XX, 2, No. 6864 (July 19, 1905),
No. 6866 (July 22, 1905), No. 6849 (May 1, 1905), and *passim.*. At the height of
the crisis, in January, 1906, Count Schulenburg, the military attaché in London,
accurately reported on the aims of the military reforms planned by the Defense
Committee, on British plans for landing in Belgium in the event of a Franco-German
war, and on the size of the expeditionary force and the timing of its intervention:
but he remarks that "we may be certain of victory over it." *Grosse Politik*, XXI, 1,
No. 6946, Appendix. On Holstein's Morocco policy in 1905-1906, see my book,
Der Schlieffenplan, Chapter 2.

10. See the report by General Sir George Aston in *Quarterly Review*, No. 512 (April, 1932),
    p. 378; also Robertson, *loc. cit.*, Vol. 1, p. 24, and Tyler, *loc. cit.*, p. 20.
11. Grey, *Twenty-five Years*, Vol. 1, p. 76 (to Bertie, January 15, 1906); *British Docu-
    ments on the Origins of the War*, Vol. 3, No. 210, p. 171.
12. Tyler now holds the same view,*loc. cit.*, pp. 176ff.
13. These details are given most completely, with important documents, by Carl Hesse, *Die
    Englisch-Belgischen Aufmarschpläne gegen Deutschland vor dem Weltkrieg* (1930).
    More recently, see Kluke, *loc. cit.*, and Tyler, *loc. cit.*. Documents also appear in
    British Documents, Vol. 3, pp. 179, 187-201. Schwertfeger, *loc. cit.*, also provides
    important information on the character and political-military views of Ducarne. It
    is Kluke's theory that the Anglo-Belgian discussions led to an integrated campaign
    plan. This is not completely proven, but seems very likely.
14. Hosse, pp. 44, 47.
15. See the highly instructive and comprehensive report by Baron Greindl of December 23,
    1911, in Schwertfeger, *loc. cit.*, Chapter 3; and the reports of the British military
    attaché from the fall of 1912 onward: *British Documents*, Vol. 8, Nos. 326ff.; also
    Joffre, *Mémoires* (1932), Vol. 1, p. 126.
16. *British Documents*, Vol. 3, Nos. 217b, 221 c5, c7.
17. Kluke, *loc. cit.*, p. 157f. The assertion that the Schlieffen Plan of 1905-1906, contrary
    to British expectations, provided that the German army would not be the first to
    invade Belgium is simply false, as shown by the text I have published – see my book
    Der Schlieffenplan. Kluke cites J. V. Bredt, *Die Belgische Neutralität und der
    Schlieffensche Feldzugsplan* (1929), p. 52, who in turn bases himself on a "personal
    communication from a person once close to Count Schlieffen." He is the victim of
    an act of mystification.
18. Robertson, *From Private to Field Marshal*, pp. 177ff.
19. C. E. Callwell, *Sir Henry Wilson. Life and Diaries* (1927), Vol. 1, pp. 125, 152f.
20. See *British Documents*, Vol. 7, p. 639 (memorandum by Chief of Staff W. Nicholson of
    November 6, 1911).
21. It is possible and perhaps even probable that this occurred under the influence of
    Wilson, who as a Briton was bound to keep urging that Belgium be included in the
    operations and who had apparently already had an influence on Michel's ideas
    (French General Staff work, 2nd ed., Vol. 1, pp. 37ff.). On this whole subject see
    Hanebuth, *loc. cit.*, p. 64. Hanebuth offers the most complete picture of Franco-
    British deployment plans and their various changes, carefully using all the source
    material that had been published by 1947.
22. See Joffre's very frank account of the session of the supreme defense council of
    February 21, 1912, *Mémoires* (1932), Vol. 1, pp. 118ff.
23. *Documents Diplomatiques Français*, 3, II, No. 240 (March 21), No. 269 (March 28),
    No. 276 (March 30), and No. 300 (April 4). *British Documents*, Vol. 6, No. 556
    (March 28), No. 559 (March 29), and *passim.*
24. *Documents Diplomatiques Français*, 3, II, No. 300 (de Fleuriac, April 4).
25. On March 16, see *British Documents*, Vol. 6, No. 544; *Grosse Politik*, Vol. 31, No.
    11,403. The account by Kluke, *loc. cit.*, p. 174, therefore exaggerates the impor-
    tance of French intervention.
26. *British Documents*, Vol. 8, No. 321 (March 10, 1912). What was at issue here was
    primarily whether it was permissible (say, for technical naval considerations) to
    extend the naval blockade of the North Sea to Belgium and Holland at the outset of

the war. This memorandum is an impressive example of the cool-headed objectivity with which such questions were discussed within the British foreign office. Crowe unhesitatingly envisaged the possibility that at some time during the war a pretext might have to be found to blockade the ports of a neutral Holland. He correctly anticipated, however, how much would depend on Britain not opening a world war—a life-and-death struggle—with actions that would put Britain in the light of being a violator of the rights of neutral nations rather than a protector of small states. In his view, military considerations would here have to give way to political. Political and diplomatic preparations for war were obviously conducted with much greater care in London than in Berlin.

27. Callwell, *Wilson*, Vol. 1, p. 118; *British Documents*, Vol. 8, No. 326, note (October 10, 1912); No. 327, note (November 2, 1912); and No. 330 (April 7, 1913); Joffre, *Mémoires*, Vol. 1, p. 125, and in this connection Callwell, *Wilson*, Vol. 1, pp. 119f., and *Documents Diplomatiques Français*, III, 5, No. 53. Kluke, p. 176, wrote without having seen Joffre's memoirs and hence gives a rather distorted account.

28. See the chapter, *"The Wider Aspects—Strategic,"* in Tyler, loc. cit., pp. 172ff. Joffre himself, however, seems to have realized that the planned French counteroffensive could at best reach the Rhine and that thereafter an endless struggle would commence—*Mémoires*, Vol. 1, p. 123, note from notes by Paléologue on February 21, 1912.

Notes to Chapter 4

1. Besides many other diplomatic reports, see, for example, those of the military plenipotentiary Hintze of August 31, 1909 and August 20, 1910, in Count Lambsdorff, *Die Militärbevollmächtigten Kaiser Wilhelms II am Zarenhofe 1904-1914* (1937), pp. 353f., 405.

2. After G. Frantz, *Russlands Eintritt in den Weltkrieg* (1934), p. 9.

3. It was soon cut to five and then to four years, and after the Revolution of 1905-1906 to three to four years.

4. See the report by Radowitz of February 12, 1892, in *Grosse Politik*, Vol. 8, p. 378. On the military reorganization of 1874, see, among others, Major General Krahmer, *Geschichte der Entwicklung des Russischen Heeres von der Thronbesteigung Kaiser Nikolaus' I. Pawlowitsch bis auf die Neueste Zeit*, Vol. 1 (1896).

5. Voiced particularly by W. A. Zukhomlinov in *Erinnerungen* (German ed., 1924).

6. According to figures given by A. von Drygalski in *Die Organisation der Russischen Armee . . . im Vergleich mit den Streitkräften Frankreichs, Österreich-Ungarns, Italiens und Deutschlands* (1902), trained soldiers (including reserves and militia) ran to but 21 percent of the male working population in Russia in 1900. The corresponding figure for France was 41 percent, for Germany 36 percent. On the other hand, in Austria-Hungary and Italy, countries with weak governments, the percentages were only 21 and 24. Russian conscription was intensified only with the defense act of 1912.

7. See Zukhomlinov: *Erinnerungen*, pp. 325ff. and *passim*. I. N. Danilov, quartermaster general in 1914-1915, in *Dem Zusammenbruch Entgegen* (German ed., 1928), gives a very gloomy account of the deficiencies in the Russian army system, the political apathy of the people, the acute social tensions, the paralyzing effect of poor communications, etc.

8. Ambassador Schweinitz's comprehensive report of February 12, 1892 (*Grosse Politik*, Vol. 7, No. 1623, reproduced in his *Denkwürdigkeiten*, Vol. 2, pp. 435ff.) deals illuminatingly with these matters. See also Zukhomlinov's *Erinnerungen*, p. 26, on the grandseigneur Shuvalov.

9. Zukhomlinov's memoirs are pervaded by such grudges, especially against Nicolai Nicolaevich, his grand-ducal rival and adversary, whom he describes as the arch-source of all Russia's misfortunes.

10. Details in *Die Heere und Flotten der Gegenwart*, edited by O. von Zepelin, Vol. 3, *Russland. Das Heer*, by R. von Drygalski (1898), pp. 78ff.

11. Zukhomlinov, *Erinnerungen,* p. 207.
12. A. Vagts, *Defense and Diplomacy: The Soldier and the Conduct of Foreign Relations* (New York, 1956), pp. 503ff. and *passim:* "Russian imperialism was officer imperialism."
13. On this subject and the nationalist Katkov's change of heart after the assassination of Alexander II, see the illuminating reports by Austrian diplomats in R. Wittram, "Die Russisch-Nationalen Tendenzen der Achtziger Jahre im Spiegel Österreich-isch-Ungarischer Diplomatischer Berichte aus St. Petersburg," in *Schicksalswege Deutscher Vergangenheit,* Festschrift for S. Kaehler, ed. by W. Hubatsch (1950), pp. 321ff. No very clear picture emerges from H. Kohn, *Die Slawen und der Westen. Die Geschichte des Panslavismus* (1956). A good review is given in Seton-Watson, *The Decline of Imperial Russia 1855-1914* (12th ed., 1956), pp. 92ff, 318ff.
14. *Grosse Politik,* Vol. 7, p. 376 (February 12, 1892), cited by Vagts as one of his chief exhibits. Vagts cites examples tending to show that individual Russian generals stationed at the remote borders of Inner Asia (Persia, Afghanistan) occasionally pursued colonial politics on their own and staged "incidents" without the prior knowledge of headquarters at St. Petersburg. But to me this seems too common a phenomenon in colonial affairs to prove that the Russian army was animated by a special "imperialist" spirit. See Schweinitz's highly intelligent remarks, *loc. cit.,* pp. 378ff.
15. See H. Herzfeld: "Bismarck und die Skobelew-Episode," *Historische Zeitschrift,* Vol. 142, pp. 279ff.
16. See Schweinitz: *Denkwürdigkeiten,* Vol. 2, pp. 247ff., for example.
17. Zukhomlinov, *Erinnerungen,* p. 24, states that as early as 1874, at the General Staff academy at Obruchev, he was assigned the planning of such a cavalry raid in a test.
18. Baron Boris Nolde, *L'Alliance Franco-Russe* (Paris, 1936); W. Langer, *The Franco-Russian Alliance 1890-1894* (Cambridge, 1929); W. Langer, *The Diplomacy of Imperialism 1880-1902,* Vol. 1, Chapters 1 and 2; O. Becker, *Das Französisch-Russische Bündnis* (1925); A. Vagts, *Defense and Diplomacy,* pp. 104-18. Vagts (especially on p. 111) seeks to hold the Pan-Slavism of the Russian General Staff essentially responsible for the military convention, but this view is refuted elsewhere in his own story.
19. It is true, however, that in 1890, when Kaiser William II, to the Czar's displeasure, announced that he intended to participate in the Russian imperial maneuvers as a guest, Obruchev suggested that French officers be invited as well, which led to a first meeting between himself and Boisdeffre. See B. Nolde, *L'Alliance Franco-Russe,* p. 599. For the following, see the same source, pp. 656ff.
20. See Major Günther Frantz, *Russland's Eintritt in den Weltkrieg* (1924), pp. 53ff., 16, and 89; Major Günther Frantz, *Russland auf dem Wege zur Katastrophe* (1926), pp. 12ff; and the minutes of the General Staff talks 1911-1913, in Zukhomlinov, *Erinnerungen,* pp. 254-267. Zukhomlinov expressed himself in highly critical terms on the "selfish" attitude of the French ally and the allegedly minimal value of the military alliance for Russia (*ibid.,* p. 240). Vagts, *Defense and Diplomacy,* p. 118, suggests that the military convention did not provide for the necessary arms and munitions deliveries to Russia in time. But he seems to overlook the fact that prior to 1914 none of the powers had a proper idea of the volume of matériel required in modern warfare, and that every country was experiencing the greatest difficulties in supplying its own needs.
21. See, for example, *Grosse Politik,* Vol. 9, No. 2317 (Radolin, July 14, 1897).
22. On this subject see, among others, Wittram, *loc. cit.,* pp. 323ff.
23. Zukhomlinov, *Erinnerungen,* pp. 186ff. A more detailed presentation is given by Sergei Dobrorolsky, chief of the mobilization section of the Russian General Staff in 1914: "La Mobilisation de l'Armée Russe en 1914" (French translation), in *Revue d'Histoire de la Guerre Mondiale,* Vol. 1 (1923), pp. 61ff, 64ff. A German translation appeared in 1922 (*Beiträge zur Schuldfrage,* No. 1).
24. G. Frantz, *Russland auf dem Wege zur Katastrophe* (1926), Chapter 1.
25. See the accounts in the two books by G. Frantz, cited above.

26. Zukhomlinov, *Erinnerungen*, pp. 342f.
27. The best account of these famous "Straits conferences" is given in S. B. Fay, *The Origins of the World War*, Vol. 1, pp. 524ff. Fay demonstrates, in my view convincingly, that at the time neither Zasonov nor Zukhomlinov planned to provoke war, though both of them (unlike Kakovzov) were frivolously playing with fire.
28. Zukhomlinov, *Erinnerungen*, pp. 358ff.
29. Particularly noteworthy with respect to the German embassy are the reports by Count Pourtalès late in 1913 and early in 1914: *Grosse Politik*, Vol. 38, pp. 253ff., 269f., 293.; Vol. 39, pp. 540-589 and *passim.*
30. Careful proof is given in Horst Jablonski, *Die Stellungnahme der Russischen Parteien zur Aussenpolitik von der Russisch-Englischen Verständigung bis zum Ersten Weltkrieg, Forschungen zur Osteuropäischen Geschichte*, Vol. 3 (1957).
31. It is true, of course, that the talks between generals and civilian ministers referred to above (Note 27), on the subject of possible war plans against Turkey, show that there were exceptions.
32. Nevertheless, as far as I can see, there is no direct proof that he intervened actively in July, 1914, in the sense of representing a "war party." He had been set back sharply on his heels in 1908.
33. On the technical impossibility of partial mobilization, see G. Frantz, *Russlands Eintritt in den Weltkrieg*, pp. 35ff., as well as the detailed discussion in Luigi Albertini, *The Origins of the War of 1914* (English translation, 1953), Vol. 2, pp. 292ff. and 539ff., the latter reference dealing with the events that led to total Russian mobilization. See also the report of the German military attaché of July 27 in *Die Deutschen Dokumente zum Kriegsausbruch* (1919), Vol. 1, No. 242; and S. K. Dobrorolsky, chief of the mobilization section, *Die Mobilmachung der Russischen Armee 1914* (1922), pp. 17f.
34. See his much-criticized newspaper article in *Birzheviya Vyedomosti* of July 14, 1914, reproduced by H. Cleinow in the foreword to Zukhomlinov's memoirs, p. xxiii (also *ibid.*, pp. 252 and 373, and Danilov, *loc. cit.*, p. 27). No. 2 in Vol. 1, *Deutsche Dokumente zum Kriegsausbruch*, published by the German foreign office in 1919, is so palpably addressed to French public opinion that in my view this document is useless in demonstrating any lack of realism in Russian preparedness.

Notes to Chapter 5

1. See the figures given in G. Schmeller, *Preussische Verfassungs, Verwaltungs- und Finanzgeschichte* (1921), p. 112. About one-sixth of the male population capable of bearing arms was in the army.
2. See C. Hinrichs: "Friedrich Wilhelm I," in *Welt als Geschichte*, Vol. 4 (1938), pp. 1ff., where he gives a graphic account of the shock effect on all classes. See also C. Hinrichs, "Der Regierungsantritt Friedrich Wilhelms I," in *Jahrbuch für die Geschichte Mittel- und Ostdeutschlands*, Vol. 5 (1956), pp. 183ff.
3. Details in Otto Büsch, *Militärsystem und Sozialleben im Alten Preussen 1713-1807. Die Anfänge der Sozialen Militarisierung der Preussisch-Deutschen Gesellschaft* (Berlin, 1962; Vol. 7, publications of the Historical Commission).
4. There is no more telling document on the wretched social situation of the common soldier in the Prussia of Frederic the Great—especially the foreigner impressed into service—than the oft-reprinted moving account by the Swiss, Ulrich Bräcker, *Der Arme Mann im Toggenburg*, from which G. Freytag, in his *Bilder aus der Deutschen Vergangenheit* (Vol. 4 [9th edition; 1876], pp. 203ff.) reprints a section. It should be noted, however, that for domestic recruits *(Kantonisten)* membership in a regiment meant a legal position with respect to the civil authorities that was in some measure better and calculated to enhance self-esteem. After long service, *Kantonisten* could even expect to be emancipated from serfdom—see O. Büsch, *loc. cit.*, pp. 58ff.

5. With respect to the army system in Württemberg, see the graphic and substantial account by my student P. Sauer, *Das Württembergische Heer in der Zeit des Deutschen und des Norddeutschen Bundes,* published in 1958 by the Commission for Local Baden-Württemberg History, Vol. 5, Series B. With respect to Baden, see the still unpublished dissertation of my student Reinhard Mielitz, *Das Badische Militärwesen und die Frage der Volksbewaffnung von den Jahren des Rheinbundes bis zur Achtundvierziger Revolution* (Freiburg 1956), to be published as part of the same series as the preceding work. With respect to Bavaria, see, among others, K. Demeter, *Das Deutsche Offizierkorps in Seinen Historisch-Soziologischen Grundlagen* (1930), pp. 41ff.

6. See R. Stadelmann, *Soziale und Politische Geschichte der Revolution von 1848* (1948), pp. 53ff.; and Jacques Droz, *Les Révolutions Allemandes de 1848* (1957), pp. 195ff.

7. It is noteworthy in this connection that the term "militarism," apparently first coined by Proudhon, was imported into Germany from France in the 1860's, in the sense of "dominion by the sword," i.e., as a term of reproach directed originally against Napoleon III and subsequently against Bismarck. It passed from the liberals into the hands of the clericals and ultimately the anti-Bismarck socialists. For details, see Erhard Assmus, *Die Publizistische Diskussion um den Militarismus . . . zwischen 1850 und 1950* (unpublished dissertation; Erlangen, 1951). Among other documents, Assmus cites a pamphlet by Wilhelm Schulz-Bodmer, an officer of Hesse-Darmstadt and a deputy in the Frankfurt Parliament of 1948 – *Die Rettung der Gesellschaft aus den Gefahren der Militärherrschaft* (Leipzig, 1859) – in which the author resumes Rotteck's fight against standing armies. It provoked a counterblast that same year, *Der Militärstaat,* by Konstantin Frantz, who sought to demonstrate that Prussia must remain a military state for the sake of its perilous position and future mission.

8. See P. Sauer, *loc. cit.,* pp. 220ff.

9. M. Bloch, in *L'Etrange Défaite,* posthumously published in 1957, paints a vivid picture of the left's everlasting fault-finding with the army, which could find warm support only on the right in France, before 1918 and after (pp. 213f.). Of interest is his conclusion that in France, too, the average officer was more or less nonpolitical, interested purely in technical military matters.

10. See, for example, Clause 5 of the program of the German *Freisinnige Partei* of March 5, 1884, at the height of the struggle against Bismarck's conservative course. This recurs in Clause 5b of the program of the *Freisinnige Volkspartei* of September 24, 1894, though this time in combination with concrete demands for reform (W. Treue, *Deutsche Parteiprogramme 1861-1954,* pp. 72, 81).

11. On its origins in Protestant ecclesiastical circles (P. von Bodelschwingh), see Th. Schieder, *Das Deutsche Kaiserreich von 1871 als Nationalstaat* (1961), pp. 125 ff.

12. See, among others, S. A. Kaehler, "Der 1. April 1895 und Sein Zeitgeschichtlicher Hintergrund," in *Nachrichten der Göttinger Akademie der Wissenschaften, Philosophisch-Historische Klasse* (1948), pp. 35ff.

13. *Countess Mathilde von Keller, 40 Jahre im Dienst der Kaiserin* (1935), pp. 110f. On pp. 144f., the countess describes a Potsdam parade of the imperial children with the eleven-year-old queen of the Netherlands, attired in military cap and sword for the purpose, a spectacle by no means limited to the court.

14. *Deutscher Liberalismus im Zeitalter Bismarcks,* Vol. 1, edited by V. Heyderhoff (1925), p. 494.

15. For conditions in the 1860's, see Vol. 1, p. 281, Note 35. According to Demeter, *loc. cit.,* p. 25, 49 percent of the officer candidates in 1867 were of aristocratic origin, while 51 percent were commoners. Among the latter, 79 percent were sons of officers, landed gentry, and higher officials, i.e., they came from "high society," in which, at the time, heavy industry and commerce were not yet included. The ensuing influx of the bourgeoisie into the officers' corps (which began as early as the war of 1870-1871) gave rise to continuing complaints, especially about the sons

of businessmen. At the same time, many young men from military families went into business careers, while many aristocratic officer families died out. According to Demeter (p. 34), the officers' corps in 1860 was composed of 65 percent aristocrats and 35 percent commoners, whereas in 1913 the proportions were 30 and 70 (in the lower grades actually 75). In 1906 the General Staff was still 60 percent aristocratic, in 1913 only 50 percent. In 1908 the guards numbered only four so-called "token Smiths," in 1913 there were 59, undoubtedly in consequence of vehement attacks on the military cabinet in the Reichstag. On the subject of the differences between so-called "good" and "bad" posts, and "high-toned" and less desirable regiments–and the preponderance of the aristrocracy in the former–see F. C. Endres: "Soziologische Struktur und Ihre Entsprechende Ideologie des Deutschen Offizierkorps vor dem Weltkrieg," in *Archiv für Sozialwissenschaft und Sozialpolitik,* Vol. 58 (1927), pp. 295ff. The seniority list of 1913 shows 87 percent aristocratic staff officers in the cavalry, 48 percent in the infantry, 41 percent in the field artillery, 31 percent in the supply services, and 6 percent in the foot artillery, engineers, and signal corps. Only 13 percent of all naval officers were of aristocratic birth (Eckart Kehr, "Zur Genesis des Königlich Preussischen Reserveoffiziers." in *Die Gesellschaft,* Vol. 2 [1928] , p. 497).

16. Details in General G. von Gleich, *Die Alte Armee und Ihre Verirrungen* (2nd ed.; 1919), pp. 17ff. The immense importance of "connections," commoner status, and political orientation of parents even for naval officer candidates is graphically described by L. Persius, *Menschen und Schiffe in der Kaiserlichen Flotte* (1925), pp. 11ff.

17. A particularly dramatic picture of the close ties between the officers' corps, especially in the guards, and court life on the one hand and the aristocratic student fraternities on the other emerges from the memoirs of the court marshal Hugo Freiherr von Reichasch, *Unter drei Kaisern* (1925). This suave cavalryman and boudoir hero began his career as "dance leader" at court balls and wound up as chief imperial master of the horse. On the intrusion of the plutocracy into the officer corps, see Demeter, *loc. cit.,* pp. 196ff., and G. von Gleich, *loc. cit.,* pp. 49ff.

18. For details, see Vol. 1, p. 281, Note 11 to p. 126. The archeologist L. Curtius, who had much occasion during the First World War to become acquainted with German and Austro-Hungarian troop staffs, remarks in his interesting memoirs, *Deutsche und Antike Welt* (1958, p. 287), that he found it a great advantage of the German officers' corps, compared to the allied officers, that the former was much more representative of the wealthy, educated bourgeoisie, which served to enhance it and round it out. He also regarded the many ties of kinship among aristocratic Prusso-German officers as a strong cohesive force. These officers knew about one another.

19. After 1885, virtually no Jew was ever promoted to regular officer status, though the war minister declared in 1908 and 1909 that the exclusion of a Jew solely on account of his faith was not permissible. In 1911, the League of German Jews knew of only 26 baptized Jews who had become reserve officers–see Demeter, *loc. cit.,* pp. 186f.

20. See Endres, *loc. cit.,* especially pp. 293, 297, 302.

21. E. von Liebert, *Aus Einem Bewegten Leben* (1925), p. 149.

22. L. Maenner, *Prinz Heinrich von Schönaich-Carolath* (1931), pp. 35, 87; Waldersee: *Denkwürdigkeiten,* Vol. 1, pp. 257f.

23. See, among others, Kehr, *loc. cit.,* pp. 492ff. As might be expected from the title, this article offers political and sociological criticism rather than a historical genesis.

Notes to Chapter 6

1. Details in Demeter, *loc. cit.,* pp. 158ff. See also von Gleich, *Die Alte Armee und Ihre Verirrungen,* pp. 88ff., especially on General Staff censorship of works on war history and the serious consequences of this measure. According to Demeter (p.

162), the younger Moltke declared, after the appearance of the first volume of Hohenlohe's memoirs, that precensorship even of memoirs of this type was desirable. An impressive example of how military writers were limited by official prejudices is the case of Colmar von der Goltz. As a result of his first military writings, while he was a captain in the General Staff, he was transferred to a small-town garrison, on account of "unsuitable views" (*Denkwürdigkeiten* [1929], pp. 86ff., 97ff.).

2. A particularly glaring example is found in the letters of Theodor Fontane to Georg Friedländer (edited by Schreiner [1954], pp. 61f., 70ff.). Friedländer, a magistrate, was summoned before a military court of honor in 1887 on account of an entirely harmless anecdote he had included in a book of war memoirs, which had offended a certain general. Fontane adds some bitter remarks on the rise of the militarist spirit in Prussia-Germany, unknown in his youth. The much lower social position of Prussian officers before the revolution of 1948 is made clear in Fontane's memoirs, *Von Zwanzig bis Dreissig,* in the chapter entitled "Bei Kaiser Franz."

3. *Denkwürdigkeiten,* edited by H. O. Meisner (1922), Vol. 1, p. 338 (April 26, 1887). See also Vol. 1, above, pp. 295ff.

4. Evidence is included in my book *Der Schlieffenplan,* p. 106. The quotation given there in Note 6, however, belongs in another context, an oversight rightly called to my attention by E. Kessel in *Graf A. Schlieffens Briefe,* pp. 106ff, p. 53n.

5. Details in my Schlieffen book, pp. 106ff. and 184. Of interest is Holstein's criticism of Schlieffen's article in *Geheime Papiere,* Vol. 1 (1956), pp. 158ff. H. Rogge, in *Holstein und Harden* (1959), p. 430, in my view misinterprets the phrase he cites from Schlieffen's article when he describes it as "pessimistic."

6. Conrad von Hötzendorf, *Aus Meiner Dienstzeit,* Vol. 4 (1923), pp. 128ff. The fable of "Jewish imperialism" is not absent from this book—the Jews were the only nation in history to have survived so long, and "were now seeking to bend the powers of the world to their will and to subjugate the masses by way of socialism." A study by H. G. Zmarzlik will shortly appear on the subject of the transformation of Darwinian concepts into political ideas—or rather slogans.

7. *Das Deutsche Problem* (1962), Chapter 4, pp. 110-146. On the subject of British "navalism" (see below), consult especially the very interesting book, based on a broad study of publicist sources, by the American Arthur J. Marder, *The Anatomy of British Sea Power,* especially pp. 10-65.

8. See the interesting lecture by Henri Brunschwig, "Vom Kolonialimperialismus zur Kolonialpolitik der Gegenwart," published by the Institute for European History, Mainz, No. 21 (1957). Brunschwig pays special attention to the French congresses of geographers in the 1880's.

9. See the substantial study by my student Dirk Oncken, *Das Problem des "Lebensraumes" in der Deutschen Politik vor 1914* (Unpublished dissertation; Freiburg, 1948). It is remarkable that even so widely read a radical nationalist as Count E. Reventlow protested against the excesses of imperial naval policy and the fuzzy talk about "German world power," strongly emphasizing the continental character of the German Reich, *Kaiser Wilhelm II und die Byzantiner* (12th ed., 1906), pp. 94ff.

10. See his memoirs: E. von Liebert, *Aus Einem Bewegten Leben* (1925).

11. Keim, *Erlebtes und Erstrebtes. Lebenserinnerungen* (1925).

12. *Ibid.,* p. 180.

13. Liebert, *Aus Einem Bewegten Leben,* p. 135.

14. He did so as early as 1896, two years before Tirpitz's first great naval bill: *Deutsche Revue* (June, 1922), pp. 450f. According to William II—*Ereignisse und Gestalten 1878 bis 1918* (1922), pp. 43ff.—Caprivi asked the Kaiser to relieve him of his post as chief of the admiralty because he wanted no part of the Kaiser's naval policy. See also Tirpitz, *Erinnerungen* (1919), p. 25; and A. Vagts: "Land- and Sea-Power in the Second German Reich," in *Journal of the American Military Institute,* Vol. 3 (Winter, 1939), p. 218.

15. Reprinted in H. Mohs, *Generalfeldmarschall Alfred Graf von Waldersee in Seinem Militärischen Wirken* (1929), Vol. 2, pp. 317ff.; see especially p. 320.

16. Mohs., *loc. cit.*, p. 288; correspondence, edited by H. O. Meisner (1928), Vol. 1, p. 224; *Denkwürdigkeiten*, Vol. II, 4 (1888), p. 366 (January 31, 1896), p. 393. Since Waldersee in 1897 hoped to be appointed chancellor himself, the Kaiser's ambitious naval plans put him in a serious dilemma.

17. Eberhard Kessel, in the introduction to *Generalfeldmarschall Graf Alfred Schlieffen, Briefe* (1958), p. 18.

18. Freiherr von Freytag-Loringhoven, *Menschen und Dinge, wie Ich Sie in Meinem Leben Sah* (1923), pp. 156f.

19. Tirpitz, *Politische Dokumente I: Der Aufbau der Deutschen Weltmacht* (1924), pp. 166, 267. See also A. H. von Zwehl: *E. von Falkenhayn* (1926), p. 87. Characteristic of the resentment that prevailed even in the War Ministry against William II's naval policies are the statements by War Minister von Einem, *Erinnerungen eines Soldaten 1853-1933* (1933), pp. 60ff. Von Einem was at the same time an enthusiastic admirer of Tirpitz!

20. *Denkwürdigkeiten* (1929), pp. 220f. (to Mudra, September 24, 1899), 214. See also Tirpitz, *Erinnerungen* (1919), p. 97.

21. Waldersee, correspondence, Vol. 1, p. 56; von der Goltz, *Denkwürdigkeiten*, pp. 326, 332; von Eisenhart-Rothe, *Im Bann der Persönlichkeit* (1931), p. 40, who reports a conversation with Conrad von Hötzendorf during maneuvers in 1913, in which both expressed bitter disappointment over the peaceful settlement of the Morocco crisis, to which they would have preferred a preventive war. Eisenhart-Rothe, however, seems to confuse the crises of 1905 and 1911.

22. "Seemacht und Landkrieg," in *Deutsche Rundschau*, Vol. 102 (January-March, 1900), pp. 335ff.

23. *Denkwürdigkeiten*, p. 331. Von der Goltz is known to have endeavored, after 1901, as founder and leader of the *Jungdeutschlandbund*, to give the rising German youth movement, with its romantic tendencies toward the simple life, a direction toward military self-discipline.

24. Von Kuhl, Schlieffen's most loyal disciple, deals very seriously with Bernhardi, the "brilliant general," in his defense of Schlieffen, *Der Deutsche Generalstab in Vorbereitung und Durchführung des Weltkrieges* (1920), pp. 140ff. See also my Schlieffen book, pp. 51f.

25. Certain of Moltke's more brusque formulations were relinquished in the process. Bernhardi's later radical move toward militarism offers a curious spectacle. Apparently he came under the influence of Ludendorff and the supreme army command after 1916; see *Vom Kriege der Zukunft. Nach den Efahrungen des Weltkriegs* (1920), Chapter 6.

26. Von Bernhardi, *Denkwürdigkeiten*, p. 118. Unfortunately, I was unable to secure a copy of the pamphlet itself.

27. See *Denkwürdigkeiten*, pp. 350ff. Bernhardi prided himself on having fought Bethmann's "shameful peace policy" of 1911 at the time in books and newspaper articles. He regretted that the German people failed to organize public demonstrations in favor of war during the second Morocco crisis. One of his friends, giving way to deep indignation, expressed the hope that the German Reich might soon collapse, so that a process of complete reconstruction might commence (p. 352).

28. To this end Bernhardi published a second shorter treatise similar in content, *Unsere Zukunft. Ein Mahnwort an das Deutsche Volk* (1912).

29. *Denkwürdigkeiten* (1927), p. 369.

30. Personal communication to me from Wolfgang Foerster, January 30, 1949. Foerster personally read the order-in-council in the files of the military cabinet. Curiously enough, Bernhardi does not mention it in his memoirs. He merely says he had heard that the foreign office had tried to suppress the book.

31. *Menschen und Dinge, wie Ich Sie in Meinem Leben Sah* (1927), p. 136. Freytag himself evidently was no blind daredevil. In 1918, at any rate, he thought that the efforts of

German diplomats before 1914 to preserve the peace as long as possible "were justifiable from the higher human point of view" (*Keieg und Politik* [1918], p. 211; a book of the same title, published in 1911, was unfortunately not available to me). His writings reveal an uncommonly deep understanding of scholarly German history, literary culture, and clear political judgment; but all this takes second place to historical reflections that display a certain tendency toward a harmonizing approach that blurs the distinctions between political and military thinking. Moltke's statement about Bernhardi was made in 1912 in a discussion with Freytag–H. Kaupisch, *Berliner Monatschefte*, Vol. 5 (1927), p. 181.

32. War history of the Reich archives, Vol. 1, p. 641.

Notes to Chapter 7

1. The first volume of this work has shown how hard was Bismarck's struggle, especially with Edwin von Manteuffel, to maintain this preponderance. Let me here add a remark from a characteristic letter by Manteuffel to Bismarck, dated February 28, 1858. In Prussia, he said, preponderance must "lie on the civilian side only in exceptional circumstances. . . . Since in Prussia the military sign is on the right side, the question of where the nominative should really lie is settled, as far as I am concerned" (*Bismarck-Jahrbuch*, Vol. 4, p. 98).
2. Collected works, 6c, No. 264 (February 24, 1883), p. 275. On von Kameke's fall, see E. Kessel, "Die Entlassung Kamekes und Stoschs, 1883," in *Festschrift für Friedrich Hartung* (1958); H. O. Meisner, *Der Kriegsminister 1814-1914* (1940), pp. 31ff.; Schmidt-Bückeburg, *Das Militärkabinett der Preussischen Könige und Deutschen Kaiser 1787-1918* (1933), pp. 142f.
3. On the written opinion given by the War Ministry after von Kameke's departure on the subject of direct access by the chief of staff to the sovereign, see my essay, "Die Deutschen Militärattachés and das Auswärtige Amt," *Proceedings of the Heidelberg Academy*, No. 1 (1959), pp. 30f. Proof is also offered there that formal supervision of the General Staff by the War Ministry was by no means revoked in 1883, and that correspondence with other Reich agencies continued to be channeled through the War Ministry.
4. Details in Schmidt-Bückeburg, pp. 152ff. See also Meisner, *loc. cit.*, pp. 68ff. On page 73 Meisner tells of a very curious case in which Bismarck, as late as July 1888, i.e., after William II's ascent to the throne, desired to have an "order in command matters," which also touched upon the budget (army organization), published without the countersignature of the minister in order to underline the Kaiser's "absolute command power."
5. Meisner, *loc. cit.*, p. 67.
6. See the legal opinion of 1896, initiated by W. von Bronsart, on the constitutional position of the war minister, in Rüdt von Collenberg, "Die Staatsrechtliche Stellung des Preussischen Kriegsministers von 1867-1914", in *Wissen und Wehr*, Vol. 8 (1927), p. 307. It is in sharp conflict with Roon's views of 1861; see Vol. 1, p. 178.
7. Schmidt-Bückeburg (p. 153) believes Bismarck wanted to restrict the war minister's prerogatives in order "to gain influence over the army himself." H. O. Meisner (p. 71), on the other hand, emphasizes that maintenance of the unlimited monarchial command power was a kind of article of faith with Bismarck. In my view this was true only in the sense defined above, as a means to limit parliamentary prerogatives.
8. Details in Rüdt von Collenberg, *loc. cit.*, pp. 299ff.; Schmidt-Bückeburg, *loc. cit.*, p. 160 and *passim;* Meisner, *loc. cit.*, pp. 74ff. and *passim.*
9. Meisner, *loc. cit.*, p. 53, and the sources there cited. Until the outbreak of the war, the War Ministry asserted its right to appear to other Reich agencies as the authority properly in charge in order not to let any differences with the General Staff emerge. See my essay: "Die Deutschen Militärattachés und das Auswärtige Amt," p. 31, note 2.
10. H. Goldschmidt, *Das Reich und Preussen im Kamf um die Führung* (1931), p. 166. I overlooked this rather obscure piece of evidence in Vol. 1, p. 301, Note 28.

11. Memorial of March 10, 1889, in Schmidt-Bückeburg, pp. 180ff.
12. Reichstag speech of March 21, 1889. See Schmidt-Bückeburg, pp. 180ff.
13. Count Zedlitz-Trützschler: *Zwölf Jahre am Kaiserhof* (1924), p. 201.
14. Haller, *Aus dem Leben des Fürsten Philipp zu Eulenburg-Hertefeld* (1924), p. 160. See also the account of a cabinet reception, entirely along military lines, in Zedlitz-Trützschler, p. 133.
15. Schmidt-Bückeburg, p. 214, from the files of the military cabinet; see also *ibid.*, p. 209, Note 64.
16. *Ibid.*, p. 178.
17. *Ibid.*, pp. 197f.
18. Haller, *Eulenburg*, p. 245 (note by Eulenburg); Zedlitz-Trützschler, pp. 160f. A similar judgment is rendered by Friedrich Hartung in "Verantwortliche Regierung. Kabinette und Nebenregierungen in Preussen 1848-1916," in *Forschungen zur Brandenburgisch-Preussischen Geschichte*, Vol. 44 (1931), p. 318.
19. Waldersee, *Denkwürdigkeiten*, Vol. 2, p. 96; The Raffauf reports, *Grosse Politik*, Vol. 6, pp. 362ff. The limitless political arrogance of the Waldersee military clique as early as the final years of Bismarck's chancellorship is best shown in the letters from Freiherr von Loë, commanding general in the Rhineland, to Waldersee in 1889. He there called Bismarck's Triple Alliance a "scarecrow of political humbuggery" and declared that all military working chiefs must now close ranks against Bismarck, who did not dare risk the crucial struggle against France and Russia at the right time. "The time is not far off when even the blindest must see that we can expect salvation only from our own resources, that the way in which the politicians are managing the crucial struggle is a model of incompetence, and that the diplomats who have been ruling the world for the past 18 years are bound to make a mess of things. May God grant our army the power to undo the diplomatic mischief, or it will be all the worse for us." Waldersee, correspondence, Vol. 1, p. 245; see also *ibid.*, p. 230.
20. I published them in my already cited essay: "Die Deutschen Militärattachés und das Auswärtige Amt." The account given above is based on the findings from this study, in which I was able to supplement and correct the existing literature from my excerpts from the General Staff files, which were lost by fire in 1945; H. O. Meisner: *Militärattachés und Militärbevollmächtigte in Preussen und im Deutschen Reich* (1957); G. A. Craig: "Military Diplomats in the Prussian Army and German Service: The Attachés 1816-1914," in *Political Science Quarterly*, Vol. 64 (1949).
21. When the War Ministry, after Caprivi's fall, proposed that the instructions be changed, Schlieffen merely suggested that the reporting system be simplified and speeded up, but he did not insist on it.
22. For example, von Huene (see *Grosse Politik*, Vol. 7, pp. 295ff. and also my above-cited study, p. 26, Note 52) and Engelbrecht (see Haller, *Eulenburg*, p. 248).
23. See Waldersee, *Denkwürdigkeiten*, Vol. 2, p. 360.
24. *Ibid.*, pp. 366, 377, 386ff., 394, 396f., 401f.; Hammann: *Der Missverstandene Bismarck*, pp. 31f; Haller, *Eulenburg*, pp. 193, 201, 203f; Hohenlohe, *Denkwürdigkeiten* Vol. 3, pp. 248, 250, and *passim;* Hartung, *loc. cit.*, p. 335; E. Zechlin, *Staatsstreichpläne Bismarcks und Wilhelms II 1890-1894* (1929), pp. 91ff. Interesting insight into Waldersee's thinking is afforded by an unpublished letter to Edwin von Manteuffel of February 8, 1877, found among Manteuffel's papers. In it Waldersee advocates the abolition of all regulations submitting so-called *Ehrenwechsel*—i.e., I.O.U.'s made out by officers—to the judgment of military courts of honor. Public criticism of such a change must not be winked at. "One of my favorite notions is that our caste spirit must be more strongly developed, that we, the officer class, must set ourselves off from the others as a class on our own. I see in this the sole means for preventing the officer class from being swamped by the plutocracy and the officer son from vanishing." In the long run, prohibitions of luxurious living and salary increases would not avail. Even though there might be certain deficiencies, the goal could be attained only "by segregation from other classes and the formation of a cohesive officer class." Waldersee was convinced "that we must soon

abandon the system of universal military service," for "inevitably there will be a struggle of the propertyless against the propertied, and then only a professional army will be able to forestall the total collapse of all existing social institutions. In brief, what we need is a small and well-paid army that will shoot down the rabble without a quavering, whenever that is required. We should then have the warrior caste I should like to see us prepare for in the officer corps even now." Since all the countries of the continent were threatened by socialism, Waldersee expected, "by the general law of cycles," that there would be a return to the system of professional armies–though he described this notion as "somewhat extravagant."

25. Haller, *Eulenburg*, p. 193 (from a letter by Holstein).
26. Haller, *Eulenburg*, p. 155; see also *ibid.*, pp. 91ff., 154; F. von Bernhardi, *Denkwürdigkeiten*, pp. 164ff. My student Horst Uhlmann's unpublished disseration, *Studien zur Innenpolitik des Reichskanzlers Leo von Caprivi* (Freiburg, 1953), presents documentary material on Caprivi's army reforms and trade treaties that makes possible a fairer estimate of this eminent man and his achievements than has heretofore prevailed in the wake of the unedifying polemics over Bismarck. It becomes particularly plain that there was no question whatever of an attitude of "military obedience" to William II. Indeed, among Bismarck's successors, Caprivi was the only one unwilling to sacrifice or adapt his objective convictions to the Kaiser's whims.
27. Hohenlohe, *Denkwürdigkeiten*, Vol. 3 (period of chancellorship, 1931), p. 116; Haller, *Eulenburg*, p. 202.
28. Hohenlohe, *loc. cit.*, 291.
29. On the Köller crisis and the Marschall trial, see O. Hammann, *Der Neue Kurs* (1918), pp. 72ff.; Schmidt-Bückeburg, pp. 208ff.; Hohenlohe, pp. 186ff., 249ff., 269, 305, and *passim*; and Haller, *Eulenburg*, pp. 158ff, 199ff.
30. See the study by my student H. G. Zmarzlik, "Bethmann Hollweg als Reichskanzler 1909-1914," *Beiträge zur Geschichte des Parlamentarismus und der Politischen Parteien*, Vol. 11 (1957), p. 40, from unpublished sources.
31. *Ibid.* p. 135.
32. *Ibid.*, p. 132. Chapter 3 of this valuable study, on the question of Alsace-Lorraine, based throughout on new documentary material, renders obsolete the neat and careful factual report by E. Schenk, "Der Fall Zabern," *Beiträge zur Geschichte der Nachbismarckischen Zeit und des Weltkriegs*, No. 3 (1927), especially with respect to its searching discussion and clarification of the political problems involved.

Notes to Chapter 8

1. E. Kehr, "Soziale und Finanzielle Grundlagen der Tirpitzschen Flottenpropaganda," in *Die Gesellschaft*, Vol. 2 (1928), pp. 221ff.; E. Kehr, *Schlachtflottenbau und Parteipolitik 1894-1901* (Unpublished dissertation; Freiburg, 1945); W. Marienfeld, "Wissenschaft und Schlachtflottenbau in Deutschland 1897-1906," Supplement No. 2 to *Marinerundschau* (Dissertation; Göttingen, 1957).
2. According to Bülow himself, in his announcement of the bill on December 11, 1899, and the customary story. According to W. Hubatsch, *Die Ära Tirpitz* (1955), p. 70, the increase was only from 25 to 36 battleships (from three to four squadrons). His reasoning, as given in a personal communication, is that in 1898, besides the 19 line ships asked for, a third battle squadron was already in existence, in the form of eight armored coastal cruisers, which were subsequently rebuilt as deep sea ships.
3. General histories of Germany in the age of William II written after 1919 (E. Brandenburg, J. Ziekursch, F. Hartung, H. Oncken, J. Haller, W. Schüssler, and lately E. Eyck) uniformly treat Tirpitz's naval policies in a highly critical vein, though with many nuances in detail. H. Hallmann (*Der Weg zum Deutschen Schlachtflottenbau* [1933] and *Krügerdepesche und Flottenfrage* [1927]) and his

disciples H. G. Fernis (*Die Flottennovellen im Reichstag 1906-1912* [1934]) and P. Sethe (*Die Ausgebliebene Seeschlacht* [1933]) breathe undiminished admiration. U. von Hassel's biography (1920) is also couched in thoroughly adulatory terms. Very serious criticism was leveled in 1948 by R. Stadelmann, "Die Epoche Deutsch-Englischer Flottenrivalität," in *Deutschland und Westeuropa.* This is dealt with by W. Hubatsch: *Die Ära Tirpitz. Studien zur Deutschen Marinepolitik 1890-1918* (No. 21, *Göttinger Bausteine zur Geschichtswissenschaft* 1955), and by W. Schüssler, G. Howe, F. Boie, W. Hubatsch, and O. Hauser in *Weltmachtstreben und Flottenbau,* edited by W. Schüssler (1956).
4. Tirpitz, *Politische Dokumente,* Vols. 1 (1924), 5, and 8.
5. L. Dehio: *Deutschland und die Weltpolitik im 20. Jahrhundert* (1955), especially the first three essays, which had been previously published in the *Historische Zeitschrift,* Vols. 170, 173, and 174. They blend—in my view somewhat too closely—prewar and war propaganda, and the work of historians with that of politicians like Naumann and Rohrbach. A. Thimme, *Hans Delbrück als Kritiker der Wilhelminischen Epoche* (1955), pp. 101-116. Especially noteworthy is the fight of the Berlin professors Delbrück, Schmoller, Sering, and Wagner in 1896 against the socialists and for enlargement of the battle fleet (*ibid.,* p. 107). Especially informative on the effect of Max Weber's well-known Freiburg maiden speech on Naumann's imperialism is W. Conze in the Kaehler *Festschrift,* Schicksalswege Deutscher Vergangenheit" (1950), pp. 358f. See also W. Marienfeld, *Wissenschaft und Schlachtflottenbau* (1957).
6. See Waldersee's criticism in his *Denkwürdigkeiten,* Vol. 2, p. 449, and my book, *Europa und die Deutsche Frage* (1948), pp. 122ff.
7. See W. Hubatsch: "Auslandsflotte und Reichspolitik," in *Die Ära Tirpitz,* pp. 25ff.
8. See the unpublished Freiburg dissertation of my student Dirk Oncken, *Das Problem des Lebensraums in der Deutschen Politik vor 1914* (1948).
9. This was Bismarck's view too, in his well-known conversation with Tirpitz in 1897—the Germans must "push overseas service . . . with many small ships." Tirpitz, *Erinnerungen,* p. 90.
10. Petition to the Kaiser of April 24, 1898, in Hohenlohe, *Denkwürdigkeiten aus der Reichskanzlerzeit,* pp. 441f. See also Tirpitz, *Erinnerungen,* p. 67. On the meaning of this petition, see W. Hubatsch, *Der Admiralstab und die Obersten Marinebehörden in Deutschland 1848 bis 1945* (1958), p. 88. Stadelmann's view (p. 116) that Tirpitz formally applied for the establishment of a chain of bases does not seem to me justified by the text. On Bülow's far-reaching pre-1899 plans for the acquisition of coal and naval bases from Spain and Portugal, see *Grosse Politik,* 14, I, pp. 260f.; 14, II, p. 52; 17, p. 467.
11. This is stated with particular clarity in a naval high command note of June, 1897, cited from unpublished files by Stadelmann, p. 101.
12. Hubatsch, *Die Ära Tirpitz,* pp. 14ff., 53ff., 60ff.
13. This was stated plainly in the crucial audience with the Kaiser on June 15, 1897, and is cited in Hallmann, *Der Weg zum Deutschen Schlachtflottenbau* (1933), p. 248, where it is put in terms of the basis of the naval plan being "the strengthening of German political power and importance vis-à-vis England." Naturally, technical considerations also played a role—greater concentration of fighting power in the big ships, systematic simplification of construction plans by limiting vessels to a main mission, the military necessity for always being a match for the strongest potential enemy, etc.
14. Tirpitz's own memoirs show this as clearly as the strongly adulatory article by U. von Hassell, "Tirpitz's Aussenpolitische Gedankenwelt," in *Berliner Monatshefte,* Vol. 17 (1939), especially pp. 326ff. Details in Stadelmann, pp. 112ff.
15. On the background and unrepresentative character of the articles from the *Saturday Review* of 1896-1897, which Tirpitz was so fond of citing, see E. Woodward, *Great Britain and the German Navy* (1935), p. 92; Stadelmann, p. 125, Note 79; H. Grimm (there cited), *Marinerundschau,* Vol. 46 (1941), pp. 447ff.; and the

judgment of Ambassador Metternich, *Grosse Politik,* Vol. 28, pp. 13, 45. Even the naval attaché, Widenmann, Tirpitz's most willing tool, occasionally warned against overestimating the fiery speeches of British admirals—see Tirpitz's *Politische Dokumente, Vol.* 1, p. 153. See also Kühlmann's criticism of the "Copenhagen myth," *ibid.,* p. 367n.

16. The excellent and thorough study by the American Ross I. S. Hoffmann, *Great Britain and the German Trade Rivalry, 1875-1914* (Philadelphia, 1933), shows that peaks in "trade envy" always precisely coincided in time with peaks in political resentments, and also demonstrates why competition grew notably less keen after about 1900 (see pp. 96ff.). Here are a few statistics: In 1913 Britain was Germany's best customer, taking 14.2 percent of all German exports. Germany, taking 6.4 percent of British exports, was Britain's second-best customer, behind India. Three-fourths of all German exports went to Europe, only one-fourth overseas. Britain's share in the China trade was 43.5 percent, Germany's 9.75. North and South America, by far Germany's best overseas customers, together took only one-sixth of all German exports. The Kaiser's exaggerated concern in 1897 over cancellation of the obsolete Anglo-German trade treaties of 1862-1865 was to be used in naval propaganda (*Grosse Politik,* Vol. 13, p. 39. See also Woodward, p. 25).

17. It accounted for only one-half of 1 percent of German foreign trade. Only one-fifth of the foreign trade of the German colonies went to Germany. See also my article, "Geschichtliche Erfahrungen Deutscher Kolonialpolitik," in *Lebendige Vergangenheit* (1948).

18. W. Hubatsch, *Die Ära Tirpitz,* p. 18.

19. I. Metz, "Die Deutsche Flotte in der Englischen Presse, der Navy Scare vom Winter 1904-1905," No. 290, *Eberings Historische Studien* (1936); W. Frauendienst, "Deutsche Weltpolitik," in *Welt als Geschichte,* Vol. 19 (1959), pp. 32f.; O. Hauser: "Deutschland und der English-Russische Gegensatz 1900-1914," *Göttinger Bausteine,* No. 30 (1958), pp. 18ff. The latter two seek to show that, contrary to the view once commonly held in Germany, the sharp British reaction to German naval construction began long before the onset of dreadnought construction in 1906. See also Stadelmann, pp. 121f. (unpublished documentary material). A thorough study of British naval propaganda from 1898 to 1905 is found in Marder, *The Anatomy of British Sea-Power,* pp. 44f. Also impressive is the account of rising Germanophobia in Britain in Woodward, *loc. cit.* The naval acts merely reinforced the effect of the unrestrained anti-British propaganda in the German press during the Boer War; there were unedifying incidents with the militarist Waldersee during the China campaign of 1900, etc.

20. *British Documents,* Vol. 3 (1928), pp. 417ff. I do not think W. Frauendienst is justified in his criticism of H. Oncken's interpretation of this memorandum; nor do I quite see the point of O. Hauser's interpretation (pp. 31f.).

21. See W. Rathenau's memorandum of 1909, cited by Prince Bülow in his *Denkwürdigkeiten,* Vol. 2, p. 428.

22. Tirpitz, *Erinnerungen,* p. 106 and *passim.*

23. The enthusiasm with which the British admiralty in 1905 responded to this turn of events is shown in the interesting documents published by Marden in *The Anatomy of British Sea-Power,* pp. 502ff.

24. See Churchill, *Weltkrisis 1911-1914* (German ed., 1924), pp. 92ff.

25. *Grosse Politik,* Vol. 28, p. 176, minutes of June 3, 1909. These minutes, kept by Admiral von Müller (Tirpitz, *Politische Dokumente,* p. 161), actually contain the formulation: "within five to six years the danger will be altogether past."

26. Churchill, *loc. cit.,* pp. 92ff.

27. See, among others, the interesting proof Habatsch has dredged up from Weyer's pocketbook of the war fleets for 1902—*Die Ära Tirpitz,* p. 74, Note. 69.

28. See letter to Tirpitz from the Reich minister of finance, Wermuth, of November 28, 1911, which also sharply contests the myth of the exhaustion of British financial resources—*Grosse Politik,* Vol. 31, No. 11, 324, pp. 35ff.

29. Reprinted in *Nauticus*, Vol. 18 (1926), pp. 188ff.
30. He did so in a report requested by the Kaiser early in 1912. See Weniger, "Die Entwicklung des Operationsplans für die Deutsche Schlachtflotte," *Marine-Rundschau*, Vol. 35 (1930), p. 5.
31. They were voiced by the British naval attaché Captain Dumas in a comprehensive report of January 29, 1907; see *British Documents*, VI, 2 (German edition), p. 1279. Even then Dumas was proposing barriers across the entire North Sea, from Dover to Calais at one end, from Scotland to the Skagerrak at the other.
32. Churchill, *Weltkrisis*, pp. 58, 114f.; P. Sethe: *Die Ausgebliebene Seeschlacht* (Dissertation; Bonn, 1933 [No. 17, *Beiträge zur Geschichte der Nachbismarckischen Zeit*]).
33. Details in Stadelmann, pp. 137ff. In a memorandum in 1912, Tirpitz himself had warned against a fleet deployment at Skagen, since this would necessarily precipitate an immediate battle issue. Under certain circumstances it might be better to postpone such a decision (Weniger, *loc. cit.*, p. 5).
34. *Grosse Politik*, 23, II, No. 8,006, appendix (esp. p. 365) and No. 8,008 (esp. pp. 374ff.). In its fight to preserve the law of prize, the *Reichsmarineamt* unconscionably (and not without misrepresenting the British attitude) mixed military, political, and legal arguments. In practice the controversy had no significant consequences, for Britain never ratified the limitation of the law of prize negotiated in 1909 (London declaration on maritime law of February 26, 1909), which essentially met Germany's requirements. See the volume on armaments and war economy in the Reich archives series, Vol. 1 (1930), pp. 315ff.
35. Reich Archives series, Vol. I (1930), pp. 305ff. and appendix 70.
36. Hubatsch, *Admiralstab*, p. 118.
37. See my book, *Der Schlieffenplan*, p. 180.
38. Reich Archives series, Vol. 1, p. 341 and *passim*.
39. *British Documents*, VI, 2 (German edition), p. 1280 (report by Captain Dumas of January 29, 1907). The question had already become acute once before in 1899, during the Boer War, when the German postal packet *Bundesrath* was seized by the British for allegedly carrying contraband goods destined for the Transvaal by way of a neutral port. The German foreign ministry clearly foresaw that this was a precedent for the treatment of neutral imports into Germany by way of Dutch or Belgian ports, in the event of a war between Germany and Britain. See *Grosse Politik*, Vol. 15, p. 451 (Bülow's directive of January 6, 1900).
40. Weniger, *loc. cit.*, p. 6. W. Hubatsch, *Admiralstab*, p. 145.
41. See Admiral von Ingenohl's memorandum of January, 1918, in *Der Krieg zur See, Nordsee*, Vol. 1 (1920), pp. 62f. The Germans never quite believed that the British would succeed in having the blocking of the North Sea internationally recognized as an "effective blockade," nor that they would, for reasons of prestige, permit the German fleet to continue its activities in the North Sea, especially the mine-layers.
42. File note of May 17, 1914, in Hubatsch, *Die Ära Tirpitz*, p. 108.
43. Reproduced after Hubatsch, *Admiralstab*, pp. 122f.
44. The British marveled that the Germans seemed to make a kind of article of faith of their naval act. See Woodward, p. 30.
45. A discussion within the admiralty staff in the fall of 1912 concluded that British troop transports could be damaged only by means of mines and submarines. For the bulk of the German fleet, the long approach and withdrawal were much too risky. Weniger, *loc. cit.*, pp. 7f.
46. To Vice Admiral Weniger (retired), in *Die Seestrategie des Weltkriegs* (1929), a large-scale offensive from Norway seemed to be the only possibility for successful naval warfare in the World War.
47. W. Hubatsch, *Admiralstab*, pp. 117ff. Tirpitz, *Dokumente*. Vol. 1, pp. 13f.
48. Weniger, *Marine-Rundschau* (1930), pp. 9f.
49. The remarks in my book, *Der Schlieffenplan*, p. 75, paragraph 1, require correction.
50. W. Hubatsch, *Admiralstab*, p. 113.

51. *Ibid.*, p. 91. The secret journal of the chief of staff in the former Reich archives notes: January 10, 1899, a memorandum of the naval high command dealing with operations against Britain; March 20, 1900, conference between General Staff and admiralty officers; March 21, 1900, memorandum from the admiralty chief, "German Naval Warfare Against England"; February 15 and March 20, dispatch of two General Staff officers for consultation on naval operations, on the suggestion of the admiralty chief. For von der Goltz's differing position, see p. 112, above.

52. W. Hubatsch, *Admiralstab*, pp. 44f. and *passim;* also W. Foerster, *Aus der Gedankenwerkstatt des Deutschen Generalstabs* (1931), pp. 60ff.

53. Details in my Schlieffen book, pp. 72f.

54. Ludendorff, *Mein Militärischer Werdegang* (1933), p. 126; Reich Archives series, volume on armaments and war economy, I (1930), Appendix No. 28, April 7, 1906. Moltke's notion of preventing a landing of British troops in Schleswig-Holstein with mobilized replacement troops recurs as late as July 1, 1910, in a letter to the war minister (*ibid.*, pp. 109f.).

55. Weniger, *Marine-Rundschau*, Vol. 35 (1930), p. 8: Report by a naval officer from the admiralty on liaison with the General Staff. According to this, Moltke probably learned of the changes in naval operations orders after 1912, in which the offensive element was blunted (*Krieg zur See, Nordsee*, Vol. I, p. 82).

56. Tirpitz, *Politische Dokumente*, Vol. 1, p. 160, minutes kept by cabinet chief Admiral von Müller.

57. *Grosse Politik*, Vol. 28, p. 175, minutes of the foreign ministry.

58. Admiral von Müller, in *Front Wider Bülow*, edited by Thimme (1931), p. 186.

59. See Bülow, *Denkwürdigkeiten*, Vol. 1, pp. 108-117.

60. Tirpitz, *Politische Dokumente*, Vol. 1, pp. 13ff., esp. 21 and 25 (memorial by Senden of February 6, 1906).

61. With the giant strides in technology, the transition to the dreadnought could not be hurried – indeed, it could not be forced at all, if only for technical reasons.

62. It was addressed to Holstein, on September 3, 1907; Holstein, *Lebensbekenntnis in Briefen* (1932), p. 292. See also H. G. Fernis: *Die Flottennovellen im Reichstag 1906-1912* (1934), pp. 59f.

63. One of these was naval captain Coerper, in his final report of March 14, 1907 (he was relieved that same year). See O. Hauser, *Deutschland und der Englisch-Russische Gegensatz 1900-1914* (1958), p. 33.

64. See his letter to press chief Otto Hammann of September 19, 1908, in the latter's *Bilder aus der Letzten Kaiserzeit*, pp. 59f., and Tirpitz, *Politische Dokumente*, Vol. 1, p. 51.

65. *Grosse Politik*, Vol. 28, No. 10,242, December 25, 1908; No. 10,247, January 4, 1909; No. 10,251, January 11, 1909. Most of the documents in this volume are also found in Tirpitz, *Politische Dokumente*, Vol. 1, pp. 97ff., and in W. Widenmann, *Marineattaché an der Kaiserlichen Botschaft in London 1907-1912* (1952). For the following, see also *British Documents*, VI, 1-2; the rather onesidedly pro-British account by Hauser, *loc. cit.*, pp. 195ff.; and W. Hubatsch: *Die Ära Tirpitz*, pp. 85ff.

66. *Grosse Politik*, Vol. 28, p. 67; Vol. 24, p. 162n.; *Süddeutsche Monatshefte*, Vol. 23 (1925-1926), p. 101.

67. *Süddeutsche Monatshefte*, Vol. 23, p. 102 (to von Müller, April 25, 1909), p. 103 (to von Müller, May 6, 1909); *Grosse Politik*, Vol. 28, p. 67 (January 20, 1909); *ibid.*, p. 170 (June 3, 1909).

68. *Grosse Politik*, Vol. 28, No. 10,254.

69. See the construction schedule in Hallmann, *Weg zur Schlachtflotte*, p. 335. Tirpitz's petition of November 4, 1909 (*Politische Dokumente*, Vol. 1, p. 168; *Grosse Politik*, Vol. 28, No. 10,357) shrewdly fails to mention such "make-up units," contrary to Hubatsch's statement. They could be built without any change in the naval act, while the above-mentioned four additional units required a supplementary bill, long planned for 1912 but abandoned in 1908 to appease the British. During the audience of April 3 (see below), the Kaiser understood Tirpitz to mean

that he once again planned a supplementary bill for 1912. In the session of June 3 (see below), Tirpitz declared that this was a "misunderstanding," and in a letter to the naval cabinet chief of May 6, 1909 (*Politische Dokumente*, Vol. 1, p. 152), he said that "any suggestion that we are going back on our renunciation of a supplementary bill would greatly complicate the situation." I suspect that he mentioned his intention of introducing a supplementary bill later on after all to the Kaiser only by way of a "mental reservation." After the meeting of June 3 he was intent on seeing to it that the British were given no assurances on the question of a later supplementary bill (*Grosse Politik*, Vol. 28, No. 10,311 [June 27]). His letters to von Müller (*Süddeutsche Monatshefte*, Vol. 23, pp. 101ff.) afford insight into his sometimes vacillating plans in April and May, 1909. They clearly show that his main aim was to get the British down from eight new units to possibly no more than four.

70. Aside from numerous other utterances, see the concluding remark in a report by Metternich on Lloyd George's first suggestions for a naval understanding, August 1, 1908, *Grosse Politik*, Vol. 24, p. 116—Metternich was to "give those gentlemen a suitable reply like 'kiss my – – –,' etc., to insure that they come to their senses!" Metternich should not even have allowed himself to become involved in talks on the naval question with the chancellor of the exchequer. "Metternich should get a hearty kick in the – – –. He is much too *schlapp!*" See E. Brandenburg, *Von Bismarck zum Weltkrieg* (Rev. ed., 1939), pp. 329ff.

71. *Grosse Politik*, Vol. 28, Nos. 10,275, 10,277-86 (March 19-22, 1909), and 10,292 (March 28). W. Hubatsch, in *Die Ära Tirpitz* (pp. 66f.), overlooks that the items he cites from Tirpitz's papers have already been published in *Grosse Politik (loc. cit.,)*, and in my view errs in interpreting them, since he did not see them in the proper context. When Tirpitz remarked, in No. 10,285, that "understanding is bound to take some time," he was, in my view, merely seeking to give a reason why he hoped to win over the Kaiser—the four capital ships for 1909 would still be built after all. Hubatsch completely misunderstands the quotation from No. 10,286 (p. 87).

72. *Loc. cit.*, No. 10,290 (Bülow, *Denkwürdigkeiten*, pp. 429f.). Tirpitz's report on his report to the Kaiser on April 3 (*Politische Dokumente*, Vol. 1, pp. 146f.) is evidently incomplete.

73. *Grosse Politik*, Vol. 28, No. 10,306. The second record, made by Admiral von Müller (Tirpitz, *Politische Dokumente*, Vol. 1, pp. 157ff.) is clearer and more precise in essential points. An important supplement is offered in Metternich's notes (*Grosse Politik*, Vol. 28, No. 10,308). Bülow, in his *Denkwürdigkeiten*, Vol. 2, pp. 431-437, simply reprints the official version of the minutes. His report on what he told the Kaiser on June 11 (*ibid.*, pp. 438ff.) seems incomplete. Presumably it was calculated to create the impression that the Kaiser categorically rejected any naval understanding, which was almost certainly not the case.

74. For Tirpitz's proposals, see *Grosse Politik*, Vol. 28, No. 10,325, Appendix; 10,339 (September 1); 10,357 (November 4); and Bethmann's countercalculations, No. 10,340 (September 16). On the question of the motives for Tirpitz's apparent change of heart in August, 1909, we can only conjecture that he (or perhaps the Kaiser) had again grown more strongly aware of the "danger zone," by virtue of final authorization in the House of Commons of eight rather than four dreadnoughts for 1909, as well as authorization of additional naval units for the dominions. The change must have occurred before Bethmann's intervention, since the first contact in Britain, by way of Albert Ballin and Sir Ernest Cassel—a channel often used before—took place as early as July, on the Kaiser's authorization and with the help of Tirpitz and von Müller. See *Grosse Politik*, Vol. 28, No. 10,323ff., and W. Hubatsch, *Die Ära Tirpitz*, pp. 87f.; also the correspondence with von Müller, *Süddeutsche Monatshefte*, Vol. 23, pp. 104ff., and the notes on the Wilhelmshöhe audience of August 12, *ibid.*, p. 107.

75. The importance he attributed to dissuading the British from their eight dreadnoughts for 1909 is shown by the changed proposal he made to Bethmann on September 1 (*Grosse Politik*, Vol. 28, p. 228). He was never willing to accept a 1 to 2 ratio, not

even against "adequate political guarantees," as W. Hubatsch (*Die Ara Tirpitz*, p. 89) thinks.

76. S. E. Jäckh, *Kiderlen-Wächter* (1924), Vol. 2, pp. 54 and 58. For the following, see *Grosse Politik*, Vol. 28, Nos. 10,347ff., and *British Documents*, Vol. 6, p. 1. The account by Hauser (*loc. cit.*, pp. 206-214) of Bethmann's negotiations is based on so imperfect and superficial a knowledge of the sources that criticism is scarcely worthwhile.

77. In a note on his report to the Kaiser on October 24, 1910 (*Politische Dokumente*, Vol. 1, p. 184), Tirpitz wrote: "If the British fleet can be made permanently so strong that it would incur no risk in attacking Germany, then German naval development will have been a mistake from the historical point of view."

78. F. Thimme, in a footnote to p. 369, *Grosse Politik*, Vol. 28, suggests that in the summer of 1909 Tirpitz would have been ready to forego full implementation of the naval act, but this misinterprets documents 10,325 and 10,339.

79. *Grosse Politik*, Vol. 28, No. 10,361.

80. For example, Metternich, *Grosse Politik*, Vol. 28, p. 244.

81. The rumors were based on false or exaggerated accounts of German naval construction (based in part on espionage–*Grosse Politik*, Vol. 28, p. 425) given in the House of Commons by the first sea lord, McKenna. This affair plays a major role in Widenmann's reports, Tirpitz's documents, and the negotiations between German and English diplomats.

82. *Grosse Politik*, Vol. 28, No. 10,401; *British Documents*, VI, 2, No. 387. How much store the Kaiser set by a limitation on British naval units and how greatly he feared a naval arms race is shown by his discussion with Ambassador Goschen on October 17, 1910; Tirpitz, *Politische Dokumente*, Vol. 1, p. 183. He threatened that, if the British raised their construction rate to a very high level, the Germans would respond with a "firm supplementary naval bill."

83. *Grosse Politik*, Vol. 28, No. 10,408 (September 23, 1910).

84. Tirpitz, *Politische Dokumente*, Vol. 1, pp. 184f.

85. *Grosse Politik*, Vol. 28, Nos. 10,416-17.

86. See, for example, Nicolson's private letter to Buchanan (*British Documents*, VI, 2, No. 450 [March 14, 1911]) or Grey's to Count Benckendorff of March, 1911, in Siebert, *Diplomatische Aktenstücke zur Geschichte der Ententepolitik der Vorkriegsjahre*, pp. 733f., quoted after Thimme, *Grosse Politik*, Vol. 28, p. 403n.

87. *Grosse Politik*, Vol. 28, No. 10,439, March 8, 1911 (transmitted on March 24). For the following, see *ibid.*, No. 10,443, May 9, 1911.

88. On May 22, Grey replied (*Grosse Politik*, Vol. 28, No. 10,447) that it might be possible after all to reach agreement on, say, the torpedo boat fleet or the size of replacement units; but this was no more than an insignificant epilogue.

89. *Grosse Politik*, Vol. 38, No. 10,434. For the following, see *ibid.*, Nos. 10,435 and 10,442; Tirpitz, *Politische Dokumente*, Vol. 1, pp. 188-196.

90. *British Documents*, VI, 2, No. 442, Appendix, and No. 446 (March 3 and 12, 1911).

91. *Grosse Politik*, Vol. 28, p. 409n. The same arguments are given with even greater sophistry in *Politische Dokumente*, Vol. 1, pp. 195f.–incidentally, in curious contrast to the reproaches against Bethmann Hollweg raised *ibid.*, pp. 189f. See also *Süddeutsche Monatshefte*, Vol. 23, 1925-1926, pp. 119ff. In his memoirs (p. 178 and *passim*) Tirpitz assures us that he had "at once accepted" Churchill's proposal for a naval ratio of 10 to 16. There was never any proposal to fix such a ratio by treaty, nor would Tirpitz have accepted it; see *Politische Dokumente*, Vol. 1, p. 381.

92. The present author then belonged to the inner circle of students of the historian Hermann Oncken and was an attentive reader of Hans Delbrück's *Preussische Jahrbücher*. He clearly recalls with what apprehension many educated persons then contemplated the possibility that Tirpitz might exploit the general agitation for introducing and pushing through a third supplementary naval bill, thus further increasing tension with Britain, to no practical purpose. See H. Oncken's speech before the Navy League: "Deutschland und England. Heeres– oder Flottenver-

stärkung?" (Published in 1912.) I was a witness to its powerful effect on the audience.
93. Tirpitz, *Politische Dokumente,* Vol. 1. pp. 200ff; Widenmann, pp. 184ff.
94. His letter to Tirpitz of September 11, *Politische Dokumente,* Vol. 1, p. 210, urged that an effort at least be made (though only in 1913) to prevent a "permanent two-a-year rate." What was probably meant was a three-a-year rate even then, not only in 1918. Since there is mention only of the adherence to rather than the upgrading of the naval act, while at the same time warnings were voiced against a precipitate rate of construction, if only for lack of personnel, this letter seems to me compatible with the memorandum cited in the following.
95. Published by W. Hubatsch in *Die Ära Tirpitz,* p. 92. The interpretation there given by Hubatsch seems to me mistaken. I owe a great deal to Hubatsch's conscientious, well-informed, and well-researched studies of German naval policy, but I cannot always follow his conclusions. Widenmann, p. 186, confirms that Capelle entertained reservations with respect to a supplementary bill from the beginning.
96. For details on the British reaction to this speech see *Grosse Politik,* Vol. 31, pp. 3f.
97. The attitude of admiralty chief von Heeringen, apparently misrepresented by the Kaiser (Tirpitz, *Politische Dokumente,* Vol. 1, p. 215), is clearly established by the statements reproduced *ibid.,* pp. 220f., and in Hubatsch, p. 94. He was for the supplementary bill. Cabinet Chief von Müller, on the other hand, seems to have endeavored to play a mediating role between chancellor and grand admiral. On Holtzendorff's opposition to the bill, which he found "provocative," see also Hubatsch (p. 94), and Widenmann (p. 188). Holtzendorff stuck to his opposition; see *Grosse Politik,* Vol. 31, p. 123.
98. It is ironic to note that Widenmann failed to recognize this turn in time and in his reports merrily continued to inveigh against the allegedly malicious intentions of the British to hold the Germans to a two-a-year rate by means of a 2 to 3 ratio. *Politische Dokumente,* Vol. 1, p. 232, Report of October 28, 1911.
99. See the preamble of the draft bill of November 4, in Widenmann, pp. 220f. The speeches of British statesmen had mentioned a 2 to 3 standard in the spring of 1911, but this related only to dreadnoughts available for service by 1914, not to the total fleets. Tirpitz now calculated that the British would be unable, in the long run, to match three new German units a year with six of their own—in other words, that the German fleet would increase at a faster rate. Only when a 2 to 3 standard had been reached with respect to the total fleets was construction to continue at an annual ratio of 2 to 3.
100. Among other things, he intervened vigorously when Widenmann, in February, 1912, had the audacity to negotiate with Admiral Jellicoe on a treaty along such lines (Widenmann, pp. 260ff). The Kaiser rejected Bethmann's complaint as unjustified, as he did a request to reprimand the attaché and authorize an instruction that Widenmann confine himself to purely military matters. "No! " the Kaiser declared. "He is an officer and can be reproved only by his supreme warlord, not by civilian superiors" (*ibid.,* p. 262).
101. Tirpitz's report on his audience of October 14 (*Politische Dokumente,* Vol. 1, p. 226) seems, according to Hubatsch (p. 99, Note 111), to be based on faulty recollection.
102. See his correspondence with Tirpitz and Bethmann Hollweg (*Grosse Politik,* Vol. 31, No. 11,324) and A. Wermuth, *Ein Beamtenleben* (1922), pp. 280, 305ff.; also Tirpitz, *Politische Dokumente,* Vol. 1, pp. 258ff. Tirpitz took his revenge by giving a completely distorted version of Wermuth's attitude toward the chancellor, of his work, and of his resignation. In the military literature too, Wermuth is described, among other things, as a petty bureaucrat who was forever obstructing military progress—even though he backed army rather than navy enlargement as early as 1910.
103. See letter to Kiderlen of January 2, 1912, in Jäckh, *Kiderlen-Wächter,* Vol. 2, p. 174. Bethmann Hollweg realized that opposition to the bill would lead to his dismissal; telegram to Metternich, November 22, *Grosse Politik,* Vol. 31, p. 31.

104. He sought to make possible a substantial increase in personnel by simply increasing the naval budget, thus also making possible the activation of a third squadron—or at least to request the desired additional units only in individual annual quotas. According to Hubatsch (*Die Ära Tirpitz*, p. 97). Tirpitz's counterarguments to the first proposal (*Politische Dokumente*, Vol. 1, p. 268) are not necessarily convincing. See Hubatsch, pp. 96f., for reports on a discussion of these questions on November 13, 1911 between the Kaiser, von Müller, and von Valentini, in which von Müller was entirely on Tirpitz's side (notes by von Müller).
105. See Hauser, *loc. cit.,* Chapter 4. Reports by Metternich, Kühlmann, and Widenmann in *Grosse Politik*, Vol. 31. Widenmann's reports are also in his memoirs and in Tirpitz, *Politische Dokumente,* Vol. 1, pp. 228ff. Herbert Butterfield, in *History and Human Relations* (1951), pp. 211ff., strongly underlines the great fear felt in prewar Britain of Russia's steadily growing colonial power; but Butterfield, with critical overtones, also suggests that the only result was that Britain paid exaggerated attention to the czarist empire's power ambitions.
106. *Denkwürdigkeiten,* Vol. 2, p. 513.
107. *Grosse Politik,* Vol. 31, No. 11,309, September 27, 1911; and No. 11,318, November 10, 1911; Tirpitz, *Politische Dokumente,* Vol. 1, p. 228.
108. Widenmann, pp. 261f.; see also *ibid.,* pp. 250f.; Tirpitz, *Politische Dokumente,* Vol. 1, p. 294; and *Grosse Politik,* Vol. 31, Nos. 11,325, 11,328, 11,329, 11,331, and 11,337. Metternich vainly recommended that Widenmann be recalled immediately, an action the chancellor dared not even propose.
109. Tirpitz, *loc. cit.,* p. 250. The item indicates that Tirpitz had communicated to the attaché Metternich's critical remarks on his report of October 28; see *Grosse Politik,* Vol. 31, No. 11,316. Also noteworthy is Widenmann's report on December 4, 1911 (Tirpitz, pp. 262f.) that there was talk in Britain of Bethmann's dismissal, with general fears that Tirpitz might become his successor.
110. *Grosse Politik,* Vol. 31, p. 35, November 27, 1911.
111. Apparently he understood the file note Cassel brought along (he later called it a "verbal note") to mean an assurance of a neutrality agreement. See his marginal notes in *Grosse Politik,* Vol. 31, p. 224, line 5. The chancellor remained skeptical (*ibid.,* p. 106). For the British side, see chiefly W. Churchill, *The World Crisis 1911-1914,* Chapter 5.
112. Without being able to provide documentary evidence, O. Hauser has strongly underlined the connection between Haldane's mission and British disappointment with the Anglo-Russian entente (*Deutschland und der Englisch-Russische Gegensatz* [1958], summarized in "Flottenbau und Weltpolitik," in *Weltmachtstreben und Flottenbau,* ed. W. Schüssler [1956], pp. 223ff.). F. Thimme, *Grosse Politik,* Vol. 31, pp. 101 and 131 had already pointed out this connection, giving important sources. On the other hand, Woodward (*loc. cit.,* p. 339, Note 1) states that British files yield no evidence for Thimme's conjecture that the conclusion of the Persian crisis had decreased Grey's interest in the German negotiations. This would not exclude the possibility that such consideratons did play a role, though in my view the failure of the Haldane mission can be explained without such suppositions.
113. P. Kluke, "Entscheidungsreiche Tage Deutsch-Englischer Beziehungen. Aus Lord Haldane's Briefwechsel," in *Berliner Monatshefte* (1938), pp. 16ff.
114. Detailed statement by Haldane, *British Documents,* VI, 2, No. 506.
115. Hopman, *Das Logbuch eines Deutschen Seeoffiziers* (1924), p. 382. Reproduced verbatim in Scheer, *Vom Segelschiff zum U-Boat* (1925), p. 272, with the remark that, after the cuts were made, the supplementary naval bill was left with little practical importance. Personnel could have been procured by annual budget authorizations, and the prompt formation of an active third squadron would have been possible even without the new units.
116. "Undated green slip of paper" in Capelle's hand, in Hubatsch (p. 103), who thinks it was dictated by Tirpitz and represents the fragmentary draft of a letter intended for Cabinet Chief von Müller. I find the coincidence with the passage cited from

Hopman so striking that I cannot accept the idea of Tirpitz having dictated the memorandum. Only the address, "Your Excellency," is inserted in his hand. (Could there have been a plan subsequently to use Capelle's notes as the draft for a letter?). W. Hubatsch was kind enough to write me that the text he reproduced actually continued: "If on the other hand the three ships are cut in the text of the supplementary bill or even in the cost calculation, none can be in any doubt but that we shall have struck our sails before England." In my view this clearly shows that Capelle favored dropping the bill rather than further mutilating it, evidently unlike Tirpitz in the item of late February, contained in Hubatsch (p. 104).

117. *Politische Dokumente,* Vol. 1, p. 286. The important Clause 4 in the preamble is missing in the version submitted to the Kaiser in 1917. *Grosse Politik,* Vol. 31, No. 11,426, Appendix.

118. See William II's report to Admiral von Müller, in W. Hubatsch, p. 102, and to Ballin, in Huldermann, *Albert Ballin,* pp. 256f., and *Grosse Politik,* Vol. 31, p. 113. Tirpitz was correct in his subsequent complaint that Bethmann Hollweg had communicated the essential content of the naval bill in its watered-down form to the British before the negotiations, thus making it impossible for him to exploit these concessions (see *Grosse Politik,* Vol. 31, p. 99n., as against Thimme, *ibid.,* p. 111); but this merely shows how completely Tirpitz misread the situation. Communicating the original draft to Haldane would have had an even more devastating effect than making known the watered-down version. The latter version, moreover, was insisted upon before Haldane's appearance precisely by Tirpitz, who, in the session of February 9, constantly cited the speech from the throne of February 7, which in his view made any surrender of new construction impossible–though the speech contained nothing about this.

119. On the differences in the reports of Haldane and Tirpitz on this point see, in addition to Thimme, *Grosse Politik,* Vol. 31, p. 113, also Haldane's detailed report in *British Documents,* VI, 2, No. 506.

120. *British Documents,* VI. 2, 504 (Goschen to Nicolson, February 10, 1912).

121. This is how I understand Hopman's statement (*loc. cit.,* p. 382) that Tirpitz had hoped, by handing over a printed copy of the bill, "to strike a bridge for further negotiations." As Tirpitz's *Politische Dokumente* show, however, subsequent compromise proposals for further weakening the bill emanated from Bethmann and in part from Admiral von Müller, while Tirpitz balked at discussing them (see especially last paragraph on p. 395). The items Hubatsch has published from Tirpitz's papers (p. 104) can be properly understood only when they are compared with *Politische Dokumente,* Vol. 1, pp. 299f., 323, and the last paragraph on p. 330. Apparently Tirpitz, in replying to Bethmann's suggestion to leave all three construction dates open, said on both February 26 and 27 that only the third date could remain open. When the Kaiser, after the chancellor had submitted his resignation, wished to leave all three dates open after all, Tirpitz, on March 9, objected, threatening to resign himself. Ultimately, however, after the agreement had failed to carry in England on March 18, Tirpitz recommended to the Kaiser that the bill should mention no construction dates–not to facilitate negotiations with the British, but, on the contrary, "to have a free hand . . . in the event of further British insolence"–in other words, in order to retain the option, in certain circumstances, of revoking the slowing down of construction dates that had been promised Haldane. From this point of view, there can be no question of the "Reich naval office once again making concessions to the political leadership," as suggested in the item published by Hubatsch. On the contrary, Tirpitz allowed it to be known through von Müller that the chancellor would have to go if the Kaiser stuck to the bill against the chancellor's objections, an eventuality Tirpitz firmly believed would occur.

122. *Documents Diplomatiques Français,* 3, II, No. 19, February 10, 1912.

123. As Tirpitz suggests, *Politische Dokumente,* Vol. 1, pp. 310f. See also Lord Morley's statement to Metternich, February 29, *Grosse Politik,* Vol. 31, p. 144.

124. *Grosse Politik,* Vol. 31, No. 11,403.
125. See William II's furious note to Metternich's report of March 17 (*Grosse Politik,* Vol. 31, No. 11,403): "Grey seems to have not the slightest idea of who is boss here, and that it is I who rule. He is already dictating to me who is to be my minister if I conclude an agreement with England." Metternich had provoked Grey's remark about Bethmann; *British Documents,* VI, 2, No. 539.
126 Against Metternich's view that nothing could be achieved unless the bill were completely dropped, he asserted that Haldane had by no means made such a request even beforehand. His own views probably came closest to those of Admiral von Holtzendorff: No new battleships, but increases in personnel, and keeping ships longer in service. See *Grosse Politik,* Vol. 31, No. 11,367, February 12, 1912.
127. It is noteworthy that his handwritten letter of February 26 to the chancellor in part takes over Tirpitz's argument verbatim. *Politische Dokumente,* p. 301, compare with *ibid.,* p. 299.
128. Reproduced in Tirpitz, *Politische Dokumente,* Vol. 1, pp. 318ff.; and Jäckh, *Kiderlen-Wächter,* Vol. 2, pp. 159ff.
129. This is how I explain the triumphant mood of the Kaiser on the evening of March 11, as reported in *Politische Dokumente,* Vol. 1, p. 324. That this mood was not altogether justified is shown in *Grosse Politik,* Vol. 31, Nos. 11,394ff.
130. Woodward, *loc. cit.,* p. 352, reporting on the directive to Metternich of March 18 (*Grosse Politik,* Vol. 31, No. 11,406), with its sharp demand for a neutrality declaration, takes this as evidence that Bethmann on that day had "lost his composure."
131. *Grosse Politik,* Vol. 31, to No. 11,422.
132. Widenmann, pp. 277ff.
133. He himself relates in his memoirs (pp. 309f.; Tirpitz, *Politische Dokumente,* Vol. 1, pp. 354ff.) how tactlessly and contentiously he put forward these views at his last reception on board the *Hohenzollern* in the chancellor's presence. Only Capelle's opposition seems to have prevented him from intriguing directly against Bethmann Hollweg with the Kaiser, as Tirpitz wished.
134. Tirpitz, *Politische Dokumente,* Vol. 1, pp. 355f., 403.
135. *Ibid.,* pp. 395f.

Notes to Chapter 9

1. Details in my book, *Der Schlieffenplan, Kritik eines Mythos,* 1956, pp. 102ff., which forms an indispensable supplement to the above text and enables me to limit my remarks about Schlieffen. Schlieffen's private correspondence, published in the meantime (1958) under the editorship of Eberhard Kessel, has only served to confirm me in my over-all view (despite Kessel's critical introduction). I do, however, wish to set two details right: (1) To characterize Schlieffen as a "courtier" may be going too far, since his letters contain rather critical statements about William II, and since Schlieffen had every reason to be circumspect, in view of the abrupt fall of his predecessor Waldersee. (2) As to p. 106, Note 6, of my Schlieffen book, see Chapter 6, Note 4, above. Schlieffen's letters make possible an even higher estimate of the moral force with which he endeavored to fill his high office.
2. One of the accepted dogmas of the General Staff under Schlieffen was the notion that a German defensive position on the western border would soon be outflanked by the French, operating through Belgium. See, for example, Ludendorff, *Mein Militärischer Werdegang,* p. 96.
3. My Schlieffen book, p. 84, after Schwertfeger, *Der Geistige Kampf um die Verletzung der Belgischen Neutralität* (1919), p. 112. See also Bismarck's conversation with Waldersee on July 10, 1888, when Bismarck inquired whether it would be feasible for the Germans to march through Belgium, in violation of that country's neutrality. Waldersee answered in the negative. Waldersee, *Denkwürdigkeiten,* Vol. 1, p. 412.

4. See my Schlieffen book, pp. 82, 147, 179f. J. Verseput, in a review of my book in *Tijdschrift voor Geschiedenis,* Vol. 70 (1957), p. 405, suspects that Schlieffen conceived his erroneous view because of the pronounced anti-British stand of the Kuyper government in Holland, while Moltke reached his opposing view in 1911 because of clear-cut statements in favor of strict neutrality by the Dutch government after the second Morocco crisis. This is possible, but the text of Moltke's notes in 1911 makes it improbable. There was a tradition within the German General Staff to the effect that Schlieffen had relied on certain statements by the then Dutch chief of staff.

5. Evidence of this, and for the following as well, is found in the volume on armaments and war economy of the Reich Archives series, I, pp. 326ff.

6. It is noteworthy that even Bismarck held that the prospects for Germany in a two-front war would be most unfavorable, and especially that total destruction of Russian power would be an impossibility—nor, for that matter, would it even be politically desirable. It was for these reasons that he himself at times inclined more toward a western than an eastern offensive—and, in any event, did not expect much more than a defensive success. Evidence for the period 1886-1890 is contained in P. Rassow, "Die Stellung Deutschlands im Kreise der Grossen Mächte 1887-1890," *Proceedings of the Mainz Academy* (1959), No. 4, Note 1, which became available to me only after this book was already in print.

7. *On War,* Book 8, 6b; see also Vol. 1, p. 67.

8. My Schlieffen book, p. 185, and even more plainly, Moltke's memorandum of December 2, 1911, meant for the chancellor, pp. 128f. in the Reich Archives volume on Armaments and War Economy, I. Moltke there expressly stated that he did not know the details of the military pact of 1892, hence could not be certain in his judgment.

9. See Chapter 8, Part 3, above, and Chapter 3, Notes 23ff.; and *Documents Diplomatiques Français,* 3rd series, Vol. 2, Nos. 269 and 276 (directives by Poincaré).

10. Details in my Schlieffen book, pp. 32ff.; see also *ibid.,* pp. 21ff., and Part 3, below. An extensive polemical literature has grown up since 1919 around the military and political arguments that militated against the Schlieffen Plan, as well as around its virtues, and I cannot here deal with it in detail. Its chief defect is that the full text of Schlieffen's various memoranda and drafts was not available until 1956. The defense, chiefly led by Groener and Kuhl, has generally prevailed in military literature, especially the official treatment by the Reich Archives. Political criticism, initiated in the main by Hans Delbrück, pleads that an eastern campaign would have been better than a western, but for the most part overestimates the chances of success that beckoned in the east. A military-political critique that comes close to my own views is found in Lieutenant Colonel von Auwers (retired), "Einige Betrachtungen zu General Groeners Testament des Grafen Schlieffen," in *Wissen und Wehr,* Vol. 8 (1927), pp. 146-172. This author views the Schlieffen Plan as a battle rather than an operational plan and strongly doubts that total victory could have been achieved, even had the plan succeeded.

11. As reported, early in 1913, Foreign Minister von Jagow directed such an inquiry to Moltke. See Part 3.

12. Bülow, in his *Denkwürdigkeiten,* Vol. 2, pp. 72ff., speaks of objections he claims to have put forward in discussion with Schlieffen in 1904 or 1905, but this is scarcely credible. See my Schlieffen book, pp. 98f.

13. *Betrachtungen zum Weltkrieg,* Vol. 1, p. 167; the following quotation from Vol. 2, p. 7.

14. See my Schlieffen book, pp. 62, 153, 172.

15. The data in the Reich Archives volume on Armaments and War Economy (1930), I, p. 87, are inaccurate and incorrect. Schlieffen did not at all desire "to employ in mobile form parts of the occupation army numerically corresponding to about eight army corps, in case of emergency." He wanted to form eight new army corps at home from replacement troops and supernumerary reservists, possibly even *Landwehr* men, directly upon mobilization. There is no proof whatever that "he

was of course under no illusions as to the slight combat value [of these troops],"
and this assertion is at odds with the missions Schlieffen wished to assign to these
army corps.

16. Ludendorff, *Mein Militärischer Werdegang* (1933), pp. 88, 101ff., and various articles.
In connection with the latter, see W. Foerster, *Aus der Gedankenwerkstatt des
Deutschen Generalstabs* (1913), pp. 32ff. Even Schlieffen's admirer W. Groener,
who was then chief of the field railway service, admits that it would actually have
been impossible in 1914 to transport large troop masses to the German right wing in
time. See *Wissen und Wehr*, Vol. 8 (1927), p. 532. According to him, only the
supply services for the right wing of the German army could be provided for.
According to von Tappen, *Bis zur Marne 1914* (1920), pp. 7, 14, and *passim*, even
that was possible only because the army high command made almost its entire truck
park available.

17. For example, War Minister General von Einem in his *Erinnerungen eines Soldaten
1853-1933* (1933), who seeks to fix all the blame for the blunders and neglects of
his own office on the left parties in the Reichstag.

18. See the unpublished dissertation by my student Horst Oehlmann, *Studien zur Innenpolitik des Reichskanzlers L. von Caprivi* (Freiburg, 1953).

19. According to the Reich Archives volume on Armaments and War Economy, p. 57, the
ratio of wartime strength was 7.5 to 6.4 million.

20. Gossler to Hohenlohe, August 3, 1898, Armaments and War Economy, pp. 52f.

21. Note of November 19, 1899, Armaments and War Economy, pp. 65f. The law of 1899,
governing peacetime strength, had just provided for the organization of three new
army corps, though essentially only from already existing units. Since the files of
the army archives in Potsdam were completely destroyed by British incendiary
bombs in 1945, the only source on armaments questions still available is the
above-cited volume from the Reich Archives, with its documentary appendix. An
older monograph by H. Herzfeld, *Die Deutsche Rüstungspolitik vor dem Weltkriege*
(1923) deals only with the arms bills of 1912-1913. It includes a wealth of
documentary material, but is in objective and political respects obsolete, except for
certain details.

22. Armaments and War Economy, Appendix Volume, p. 164, No. 54.

23. Armaments and War Economy, pp. 29 and 31; see also von Einem, *Erinnerungen,* pp.
99ff., for a rather implausible effort at self-justification.

24. Armaments and War Economy, pp. 53, 61, 63, 67, 69 (1898-1900); 72ff. (1904-1905);
90 (1908); and 137 (1912). Tirpitz disputes these facts in vain.

25. See, for example, von Einem's letter to Schlieffen, April 19, 1904, Armaments and War
Economy, Appendix No. 26, p. 91: "Undoubtedly this lack [of officers] could
soon be remedied, if we scaled down our standards in respect of the background,
etc., of officer candidates. This, however, cannot be recommended, since in that
case we should not be able to prevent an increased influx of democratic and other
elements that are unsuitable to the profession." See also Chapter 7, Note 24, above,
Waldersee to Manteuffel.

26. I refer to the concern expressed by Waldersee in his letter to Manteuffel (Chapter 7,
Note 24), in which he speaks of the political repercussions of universal military
service.

27. Armaments and War Economy, Appendix Volume, p. 92, No. 27.

28. Letter to his sister Marie, November 13, 1892, Armaments and War Economy, p. 43;
and Schlieffen's correspondence, edited by E. Kessel (1958), pp. 295ff.

29. It is in this way that the Reich Archives volume (*loc. cit.,* pp. 64f.) seeks to explain
Schlieffen's curious proposals. Rüdt von Collenberg, "Graf Schlieffen und die
Kriegsformation der Deutschen Armee," in *Wissen und Wehr*, Vol. 8 (1927), pp.
605ff., gives an account of the negotiations with the War Ministry in 1899 and after,
but seeks only to prove Schlieffen's genius.

30. Armaments and War Economy, p. 71.

31. Armaments and War Economy, Appendix Volume, No. 23.

32. Armaments and War Economy, Appendix Volume, No. 27. According to Ludendorff, *Mein Militärischer Werdegang*, p. 103, this document goes back to a suggestion by Ludendorff.
33. W. Foerster, in *Aus der Gedankenwerkstatt des Deutschen Generalstabs* (1931), p. 41, seeks to show, by means of quotations from this memorandum, that Schlieffen tried as early as 1905 to apply for the supplementary combat forces required under his plan; but he fails to mention that the plan called for units that would be immediately usable in combat. See Charts 3 and 6, reproduced in my Schlieffen book, both of which show six replacement corps before Paris. The document of November 4, 1905, mentions only garrison troops.
34. I reproduced the content in part in my Schlieffen book, p. 71, Note 50, from my library notes of 1943. The date and addressee I there suggested now seem to me highly questionable, upon re-examination of my excerpts from the secret journal of the chief of staff. On the other hand, it seems plausible to link up this document with a re-examination of the Schlieffen Plan in February, 1913, suggested by Foreign Minister von Jagow and mentioned further on. A few sentences from the memorandum are reproduced in the Reich Archives volume, I, p. 18. General Ludwig Beck cites them in his study, "Besass Deutschland 1914 einen Kriegsplan?" in *Studien,* ed. H. Speidel (1955), pp. 91ff. It is reprinted in toto in W. Elze, *Tannenberg*, pp. 157-162.
35. Reproduced in my Schlieffen book, pp. 181ff. *Ibid.*, p. 185, Moltke's critical marginal notes.
36. As was done in Schlieffen's great operational plan.
37. See his memorandum for the chancellor of December 2, 1911 (Reich Archives volume I, pp. 11ff., Armaments and War Economy, pp. 126ff.) and of December 21, 1912 (Armaments and War Economy, Appendix No. 54; also in Ludendorff, *Mein Militärischer Werdegang,* Appendix 8).
38. According to a statement by General von Kuhl before a committee of the Reichstag in 1923 (Committee Reports, 4th series, Vol. 1, p. 155), the general, in 1909, when he was head of Section III of the General Staff, was assigned the mission "to reconnoiter the entire front from Toul to Belfort for offensive opportunities," in order to avoid an attack through Belgium if possible. The result was a report by von Kuhl to the effect that an attack on this line would be impossible without long-drawn-out siege operations. (This passage was kindly called to my attention by Dr. Schmidt-Richter of the Research Institute for Military History, Freiburg; see also his article in *Beiträge zur Militärgeschichte,* Vol. 3, p. 29.)
39. Report by von Jagow in *Deutscher Offiziersbund* (1927), No. 23, p. 966, dated back to February, 1913. Ambassador Botho von Wedel claims to have heard the same conclusion from Moltke himself; see *Front wider Bülow,* ed. Thimme (1925), pp. 276ff.
40. Ludendorff, *loc. cit.,* pp. 128ff.
41. Armaments and War Economy, p. 101.
42. Memoranda by Ludendorff and Moltke. Armaments and War Economy, Nos. 34, 36, 37, and 39 (March 11 to August 20, 1910), with text volume, pp. 107ff., 112f. For the following, *ibid.,* pp. 119, 215; also Ludendorff, *loc. cit.,* pp. 132-137. According to Ludendorff's account, the initiative in arms questions virtually rested with him alone—all his superiors merely served to hold things up. General Staff petitions to the War Ministry embodied his ideas alone—Moltke only watered them down.
43. Memorandum by von Heeringen of November 19, by Moltke of December 2, 1911, Armaments and War Economy, pp. 123ff., 126ff.
44. On the intense pressure the *Wehrverein* exerted on the War Ministry, see H. Müller-Brandenburg, *Von Schlieffen bis Ludendorff* (1925), pp. 27ff. Müller-Brandenburg was the *Wehrverein's* press chief.
45. According to the volume on Armaments and War Economy, pp. 99 and 123, the army proportion in 1910 was 0.795 percent, and in 1911 it was 0.99, though for army and navy together it was 1.06 of the population. France drafted 83 percent of men

liable for service, Germany only 57.3 percent (75 percent of the fit).

46. Moltke (drafted by Ludendorff) to the War Ministry, November 25, 1912, Armaments and War Economy, Appendices, p. 147.

47. Including the transformation into peacetime formations of two of the "war corps" Schlieffen had fought for.

48. Moltke to Heeringen, December 2, 1912, Armaments and War Economy, Appendix No. 50.

49. Armaments and War Economy, p. 130.

50. According to Reich Archives Volume, *Der Weltkrieg,* I, p. 22, field army troop strength in 1914 was: Germany, 2,147,000; France, 2,150,000; Russia, 2,712,000. Rüdt von Collenberg, in *Die Deutsche Armee 1871-1914* (1922), gives slightly different figures: Germany, 2,019,470 (without immobile replacement formations, *Landwehr* and *Landsturm*); France, 2,032,820 (excluding territorial army); Russia, 3,461,750 (excluding imperial defense force).

51. According to the French General Staff work, *Les Armées Françaises dans la Grande Guerre,* Tome 1, Vol. 1, pp. 63f., the French General Staff seems to have realized only in May, 1914, that the Germans would commit their reserve corps beside their active corps at the front. Only General Michel (under the influence of General Wilson of the British General Staff) correctly perceived the operational plans of the German General Staff in 1911 and planned an appropriate reorganization of the French army (utilization of reserves directly with combat units), but was unable to prevail. See my Schlieffen book, p. 89; also Chapter 3, Note 21, above, and Churchill, *The World Crisis 1916-1918,* Vol. 1 (1927), pp. 19ff.

52. According to the Reich Archives work, Vol. 1 (1925), p. 646, 358 German battalions opposed 257 French, and 2,164 German guns opposed 1,120 French. The French General Staff work, I, 1 (1936), p. 589, gives 358 German infantry battalions against 269 French, 215 German cavalry squadrons against 169 French, 2,164 German guns against 828 French. German estimates of enemy strength were in part inaccurate. The figures given by Churchill, *loc. cit.,* p. 23, greatly exaggerate the superiority of the German field army as a whole—2,000,000 against 1,300,000! Apparently he did not count the British and Belgians on the French left wing.

Notes to Chapter 10, Part 1

1. Discussion with Major von Haeften, November, 1914, mentioned by Theodor von Schäfer, "Generaloberst von Moltke in den Tagen vor der Mobilmachung und Seine Einwirkung auf Österreich-Ungarn," in *Berliner Monatshefte,* "Die Kriegschuldfrage," Vol. 4 (1926), p. 515.

2. E. Zwehl, *Falkenhayn* (1926), p. 55. For Falkenhayn's report to Moltke of July 5, see M. Montgelas, *Leitfaden zur Kriegschuldfrage* (1923), p. 196; First Subcommittee of the Reichstag Committee of Inquiry, Supplement 1, "Zur Vorgeschichte des Weltkrieges: Schriftliche Auskünfte Deutscher Staatsmänner," No. 17 (no date); von Bertrab, *Deutsche Dokumente zum Kriegsausbruch* (1919), Vol. 1, pp. xivf.; C. I. Snijders and R. Dufour, *De Mobilisatien bij de Groote Europeesche Mogendheiden in 1914 en de Invloed van de Generale Staven op het Uitbreken van den Wereld-Oorlog* (Leyden, 1927). The last-named book, by two Dutch generals, missing in West German libraries, deals in the main with technical military questions and is based in part on sources that are today outdated.

3. War Archives, Vienna, "Behinderungen des Ausbaues der Wehrmacht durch das Ministerium des Äusseren," in file of the Department Chief of the General Staff, Op. 90. This volume contains correspondence of 1911.

4. Memorandum by Aehrenthal of August 15, 1909, with many marginal notes by Conrad, War Archives, Vienna, Chief of Staff, Op. 89a (1909). The marginal notes are not given with the memorandum in Conrad, *Aus meiner Dienstzeit,* Vol. 1 (1921), pp. 245-254.

5. Personal report to the Emperor, October 31, 1910, War Archives, Vienna, Chief of Staff, Op. 95 (memoranda), apparently never printed.

6. To Count Berchtold, September 6, 1913, Conrad, *loc. cit.,* Vol. 3, p. 420.
7. In connection with these proposals, an unprinted direct petition to the Emperor (transmitted on February 1, 1910, but prepared in November, 1909) says: "We were not only certain of Germany, but authoritative circles in Germany, at least on the military side, would have favored such a war!" War Archives, Vienna, General Staff, Op. 89a (1910), No. 4. Conrad at once worked out a campaign plan against Italy.
8. Unprinted draft of a memorandum of January, 1909, War Archives, Vienna, General Staff, Op. 89a (1909), No. 1.
9. See Note 4 to the above-cited memorandum by Aehrenthal of August 15, 1909, War Archives, Vienna.
10. Direct petition to the Emperor of February 1, 1910, already cited, Note No. 7, War Archives, Vienna.
11. War Archives, Vienna, General Staff, Op. 89a (1910), No. 10.
12. Details in A. F. Pribram, "Der Konflikt Conrad-Aehrenthal," in *Österreichische Rundschau,* Vol. 64 (1920), pp. 93-118.
13. On February 12, 1912, he wrote a comprehensive memorial for the Emperor; War Archives, Vienna, General Staff, Op. 95 (memoranda). It is an almost incredible collection of political nonsense. Schemua would avoid the "Anglo-German rivalry" by means of an alliance of the three empires, Germany, Austria-Hungary, and Russia. He speaks incoherently of the "yellow peril," America's economic threat, international stock exchanges, etc., etc.
14. Memorandum for Count Berchtold, in Conrad, Vol. 3, pp. 12ff.
15. See Freiherr von Musulin, *Das Haus am Ballplatz* (1934), pp. 173ff.
16. Friedrich Kern sees this correctly in "Conrad und Berchtold," *Europäische Gespräche,* Vol. 2 (1924), pp. 97ff. For the almost condescending manner with which Conrad sought to win over the minister to his views, see the discussion of January 9, 1913 (Memoirs, Vol. 3, pp. 77f.): "Your Excellency must make up his mind. The monarchy has lost face in the Balkans, and in the end there will have to be a test of strength. It would certainly be best if Russia were subjugated—then we should have a hundred years of peace."
17. Report by Captain Prince Hohenlohe from St. Petersburg, January 18, 1913. Conrad's reply on January 21 remarks that it would be hard to see what could persuade Russia, which pursued such important aims in Asia, to meddle in petty Balkan squabbles! War Archives, Vienna, Conrad file, B 3-4; Conrad, Vol. 3, pp. 52, 82. Austria had no general directive like Germany's (see Chapter 7, above), which prescribed that reports from military attachés were subject to ambassadorial control. On January 21, 1913, attaché Horváth in London reported that the ambassador had requested him not to send any reports to Conrad without first showing them to him. In consequence, arrangements were made for private communications. War Archives, Vienna, Conrad file, B 3, B 4, 1913 (papers of wing adjutant Kundmann).
18. Memoranda of July 28 and September 4, 1913; Conrad, Vol. 3, pp. 407, 420ff. See also a manuscript memorandum of July 2; War Archives, General Staff, Op. 90.
19. See F. Kern, "Die Südslawische Frage und die Wiener Kriegspartei 1913-1914," in *Schmollers Jahrbuch,* Vol. 48 (1924), pp. 244ff.
20. On July 28 and 30, 1913; Conrad, Vol. 3, pp. 407ff., 409ff.
21. The official minutes in the file "Austro-Hungarian Foreign Policy" (*Österreichische Dokumente,* Vol. 7, p. 397, No. 8,779) are very restrained, apparently softening many statements. I have used a note in the War Archives, General Staff, Op. 90, apparently made by an officer at Conrad's behest. Conrad has reworked it in his Vol. 3, pp. 464f. See also the discussion with Berchtold on September 29, *ibid.,* Vol. 3, pp. 443f. Typical of his activist mood is that as early as October 15 he tried to arouse the Emperor against the "petty viewpoint of the civilian ministers" and to prevail with his own views.
22. F. Kern, *Europäische Gespräche,* Vol. 2, pp. 97ff., tries, not quite convincingly, to prove that he was in essence won over to the "war party" as early as 1913. All I can

see is that he used vague and noncommittal statements of assent in order to avoid a clash with the powerful general and favorite of the successor to the throne.

23. The latest and very careful study of Serbian guilt and responsibility, Luigi Albertini, *The Origins of the War of 1914* (English ed., 1953) Vol. 2, Chapters 2-3, oddly enough overlooks the hand-written confession of Colonel Dimitrijević (Apix), which the German military authorities found in Belgrade during the Second World War and which Übersberger has published in facsimile. H. Übersberger, "Das Entscheidende Aktenstück zur Kreigsschuldfrage 1914," in *Auswärtige Politik,* Vol. 10 (July, 1943), pp. 429-438. The most recent and highly detailed account of the Serajevo plot is found in H. Übersberger, *Österreich zwischen Russland und Serbien* (1958).

24. *Schicksalsjahre Österreichs 1908-1919. Das Politische Tagebuch Josef Redlichs,* Vol. 1, 1908-1914, ed. F. Fellner (1953). Among the younger diplomats in the foreign office there seems to have been a kind of "war party" that feared nothing more than that foreign mediation efforts might once again prevent a settlement by force of arms. See the report by General Höfer to Conrad of July 14, 1914, in Conrad, Vol. 4, p. 79. Count Hoyos' indiscreet statement in Berlin that the Vienna government planned to carve up Serbia completely probably stemmed from the sentiments of this war party–Berchtold was compelled to deny Hoyos' statement. Hoyos himself persuaded the journalist V. Naumann to provide him with reports of alleged preventive-war notions in German military circles. *Österreichische Dokumente,* Vol. 8, No. 9,966. An example of the irresponsibility that prevailed among Austrian diplomats is the remark made on July 8 to Conrad by the Belgrade ambassador, Baron Giesl, who said that the time was "highly propitious" for war. Conrad rejected this. See Conrad, Vol. 4, p. 57.

25. Czernin, *Im Weltkrieg* (1919), p. 117. S. D. Sazonov, *Sechs Schwere Jahre* (German ed., 1927, pp. 133f).

26. Conrad, Vol. 3, pp. 754ff.

27. Conrad, Vol. 3, pp. 504, 596f.; Vol. 4, p. 72. Countess Gina Conrad von Hötzendorf, *Mein Leben mit Conrad von Hötzendorf. Sein Geistiges Vermächtnis* (1935), p. 114, letter of June 28, 1914. Count Georg Waldersee, in *Berliner Monatshefte,* Vol. 8 (1930), pp. 133ff., reports on pessimistic views within the Vienna General Staff as early as the spring of 1914, basing himself in part on reports by the military attaché Count Kageneck.

28. Conrad, Vol. 4, p. 40.

29. Conrad, Vol. 4, pp. 33ff. For the following, see *ibid.,* pp. 39f.

30. Details in Albertini, *The Origins of the War of 1914,* Vol. 1, pp. 435ff.

31. Minutes in *Österreichische Dokumente,* Vol. 8, No. 10,118, pp. 343ff.; Conrad, Vol. 4, pp. 43ff. In place of Conrad, War Minister Krobatin put forward the desire of the General Staff for swift and decisive action (immediate mobilization, an ultimatum only when mobilization had been completed, and preferably a strike without a formal declaration of war). He did not, however, prevail against the serious reservation of Count Tisza against war. The result was a wretched compromise, endlessly postponing action without dropping it altogether.

32. Letter by the military attaché Count Kageneck to General von Waldersee, July 17, 1914, *Berliner Monatshefte,* Vol. 8, p. 136.

33. At Conrad's request, the minutes contain no details about his military testimony. In his memoirs, Vol. 4, p. 54, he supplements them only very guardedly.

34. Diary note by the German military attaché Count Kageneck of July 25, kindly communicated to me by him: "My own firm impression, which I have always expressed in discussion with Chief Conrad and other acquaintances in the War Ministry, is that Russia cannot hold still if Austria-Hungary settles accounts with Serbia. Otherwise Russia would cease to be a great power, and in any event would have lost all influence in the Balkans." See Kageneck's letter to General von Waldersee of July 22, 1914, *Berliner Monatshefte,* Vol. 8 (1930), p. 137. According to it, Conrad shared this view. Berchtold, too, did not doubt that Russia would intervene, as shown by the original version of the minutes of July 7 (in Albertini,

The Origins of the War of 1914, Vol. 2, p. 385, in English translation): "He was clear in his own mind that a war with Russia would be the most probable consequence of our entering Serbia." On July 24, Count Hoyos told Redlich: "It is virtually certain that Russia will make common cause with Serbia. . . . If Russia were to leave Serbia to its fate without lifting a finger, the nationalists would topple the Czar." The note to Serbia would create a furor in Europe. "We are therefore still able to form a resolve. We do form a resolve and we must not malinger—far better to perish swiftly." J. Redlich, Diary, *loc. cit.*, pp. 238f.

35. Memorandum by Conrad of July 2, *Österreichische Dokumente,* Vol. 8, No. 9,995, pp. 268f. The appendix to Tisza's direct petition of July 8 may perhaps also be used to supplement the minutes of July 7. *Ibid.,* No. 10,146, p. 374. It shows how Conrad responded to Tisza's concern, though it is not clear whether this was during the meeting.

Notes to Chapter 10, Part 2

1. In the following I base myself on my study, "Die Zusammenarbeit der Generalstäbe Deutschlands und Österreich-Ungarns vor dem Ersten Weltkrieg," in *Festgabe für Hans Herzfeld* ("Zur Geschichte und Problematik der Demokratie," 1958, pp. 523-549). That study, in turn, is based in part on unpublished source material from the war archives and from the court and state archives in Vienna.

2. See my Vol. 1, pp. 231ff. I find it necessary to correct a point in my article in the Herzfeld *Festgabe.* According to Waldersee's *Denkwürdigkeiten,* Vol. 1, pp. 313 and 319, in February, 1887, Waldersee orally arranged with Moltke for a substantial shift of forces from the east to the western front. It is to this that the complaint of Archduke Albrecht in March, 1887, mentioned in Paragraph 2, probably refers.

3. *Österreichische Dokumente,* Vol. 1, p. 278.

4. This is the view of the Austrian journalist H. Kanner in a pamphlet entitled *Der Schlüssel zur Kriegsschuldfrage* (1926). The pamphlet also includes a refutation of contrary articles by General Count Montgelas, which are there reprinted. Noteworthy is the critique by S. B. Fay in *American Historical Review,* Vol. 32 (1926-1927), pp. 717-719, 944-946; and Th. von Schäfer, "Wollte Generaloberst von Moltke den Präventivkrieg? " in *Berliner Monatshefte,* Vol. 5, p. 545. Albertini, *The Origins of the War of 1914,* Vol. 1, p. 271, reverts to Kanner's accusations.

5. Conrad, Vol. 1, p. 380.

6. Details in Part 3. Albertini, *The Origins of the War of 1914,* Vol. 2, p. 486, interprets this sentence of Moltke's as meaning that he shared Conrad notions of preventive war.

7. *Grosse Politik,* Vol. 10, p. 203; Vol. 11, p. 114 (direct report to the Kaiser by Hohenlohe, February 2, 1896). *Ibid.,* p. 123 (directive to Eulenburg, March 5, 1896).

8. It is not possible, within the frame of reference of this work, to discuss the very important political question of whether the Germans were right in tying their destiny to the slowly decaying Danubian monarchy. Nor is it possible to discuss the question raised by Count Tosza at the joint ministerial council of July 7, whether the alternative of war or peace might not have been avoided by a different Balkan policy. Most interesting with respect to the former question is the discussion between Ambassador Prince Lichnowsky and Foreign Minister von Jagow, July 18 to 23, 1914, *Deutsche Dokumente,* Vol. 1, No. 72-161. There is probably no living historian who is completely convinced by von Jagow's arguments.

9. Detailed evidence is found in my above-cited study in the Herzfeld *Festgabe,* which I here repeat in part verbatim.

Notes to Chapter 10, Part 3

1. Conrad, Vol. 4, p. 80 (directive to Höfer).
2. The present author well remembers this curious military and political calm that lasted

into the final days of July, 1914, for he was on a journey in Austria during that month.
3. *Österreichische Dokumente,* Vol. 8, p. 511, No. 10,393. Pressure from the Berlin foreign ministry began as early as July 8. See Nos. 10,127ff. The aged Emperor Francis Joseph understood it this way on July 10: "On Germany's account alone, we can no longer give way! "
4. *Deutsche Dokumente,* Vol. 1, No. 72, letter from Jagow to Lichnowsky, July 18, 1914.
5. Draft of a memorandum of May, 1914, in Th. von Schäfer, *Berliner Monatschefte,* Vol. 5 (1927), pp. 549f.; and a pamphlet, *Hat der Deutsche Generalstab zum Krieg Getrieben?* (1919), pp. 11ff. The memoranda by Quartermaster General Count Waldersee, there reprinted, sound even more pessimistic, especially with respect to Austria-Hungary's capacity. According to his own testimony (Schäfer, *loc. cit.,* p. 548; and *Berliner Monatshefte,* Vol. 8 [1930]), he recommended a change in Germany's policy of alliances in the summer of 1914.
6. H. von Moltke, *Erinnerungen, Briefe, Dokumente 1877-1916* (1922), esp. p. 331 (revulsion against the "terror of a European massacre," 1905), p. 373 (revulsion against the Balkan wars, 1913). The outburst (p. 362) over "the wretched Morocco affair" in 1911 is misinterpreted by Albertini, *The Origins of the War of 1914,* Vol. 2, p. 486, as proof of Moltke's enduring thirst for war. Moltke's grave disillusion in 1911 is explained from the fact that at first he stood wholly behind Kiderlen-Wächter, the "man with strong nerves," and regarded the Morocco crisis as a favorable time for "settling accounts with Britain." See travel report of Austrian General Staff captain Milan Ulmansky of August 7, 1911, on an interview with Moltke, War Archives, Vienna.
7. Conrad, Vol. 1, p. 165, September 14, 1909.
8. *Grosse Politik,* Vol. 38, I, No. 12,824, February 10, 1913; Conrad, Vol. 3, pp. 144ff. See *ibid.,* pp. 147ff., for Conrad's reply and Moltke's retort to the Austrian military attaché Baron Bienerth. Albertini, *The Origins of the War of 1914,* Vol. 1, p. 437, and Vol. 2, pp. 486f., seeks to deflate the importance of this statement by Moltke by explaining it as an adaptation to William II's then peaceful attitude. This is an arbitrary assumption.
9. *Grosse Politik,* Vol. 34, I, No. 12,793, February 6, 1913. Also to be noted is a marginal note by Moltke to Conrad's letter of January 11, 1911, quoted by Th. von Schäfer from the Reich Archives files, in *Berliner Monatshefte,* Vol. 4 (1926): "We have no interest in precipitating a European war, merely for the sake of fighting on behalf of Austria. It would be a different matter if we were challenged. Then, in God's name, to it."
10. Conrad, Vol. 3, p. 612 (letter to Conrad). Waldersee's testimony, *Berliner Monatshefte,* Vol. 8 (1930), p. 133. Memorandum of May, 1914, *Berliner Monatshefte,* Vol. 5 (1927), p. 550, printed by W. Elze, *Tannenberg,* pp. 163f. Similar expressions of concern are contained in *Berliner Monatshefte,* Vol. 5, p. 551.
11. The May memorandum, just cited, emphasizes with extreme gravity the dangerously swift rise in Russian military power. Apparently, he expressed himself in a similar vein to Conrad, who immediately interpreted the statement in his own way: "Any delay would lessen our chances" (Conrad, Vol. 3, p. 670). What the Bavarian envoy Lerchenfeld passed on to Hertling was unevaluated "talk in military circles," in other words, adjutants' antechamber gossip (*Deutsche Dokumente,* Vol. 4, No. 27, p. 151). The "impressions" of the Bavarian military attaché Wenninger of July 29 to the effect that Moltke was spoiling for war (*Deutsche Dokumente,* new edition of 1927, Supplement 4a, 2, p. 153), are palpably and demonstrably biased and even more useless. Wenninger was out to show the military as stanch optimists, at odds with the hesitant civilian weakling Bethmann. These sources are unquestioningly accepted in Bernadotte Schmitt, *The Coming of the War, 1914,* Vol. 2 (1930), p. 136; and Albertini, *The Origins of the War of 1914,* Vol. 2, pp. 490f.
12. *Deutsche Dokumente,* Vol. 1, Nos. 77, 83, 88, 113. See also Albertini, *The Origins of the War of 1914,* Vol. 2, p. 265.

13. *Deutsche Dokumente,* Vol. 1, No. 87 (Legation Councilor Stolberg to the foreign ministry, July 18). See also Count Kageneck's unpublished diary note of July 25: "In the afternoon I went to the War Ministry and met Conrad, whom I accompanied home, both of us down in the mouth, for there had been an extra in Frankfurt claiming Serbia had accepted all of Austria's demands. We thought the whole thing was over and discussed the domestic political measures that would have to be taken." For the Austrian war party, see J. Redlich's diary, *loc. cit.,* p. 239 (July 26).
14. Conrad, Vol. 4, p. 122.
15. Conrad, Vol. 4, p. 132; *Deutsche Dokumente,* Vol. 1, No. 213. A swift deployment with immobile troops would have been possible with partial forces only from Hungary, and the enveloping attack in the west, from Bosnia, would have been delayed because of the inadequacy of the Bosnian narrow-gauge railway. Conrad had explained all this in 1913, when faced with Berchtold's desire for a swift strike.
16. *Loc. cit.,* p. 124.
17. Albertini, *The Origins of the War of 1914,* Vol. 2, pp. 454ff., seeks to prove that Austria declared war on Serbia only under German "pressure"; but Szögény's telegram of July 25 (*Österreichische Dokumente,* No. 10,656), which Albertini cites, cannot possibly be so interpreted. It contained an urgent recommendation without any trace of a threat. Even if the recollections by Margutti and Giesl, some written long after the event, should be accurate, what Albertini (Vol. 2, p. 375) cites as Austrian "retreats" after Giesl's departure from Belgrade shows no more than that Francis Joseph and Berchtold at first found it difficult to cope with the shock of the certainty of war, consoling themselves with the easy excuse that a rupture of diplomatic relations did not necessarily mean war. Berchtold cannot possibly have believed in earnest that Serbia would in the end humble itself, even without war; and if he did not desire war, why did he so stubbornly sabotage every effort at mediation? The arguments he presented in London through Mensdorff (*Österreichische Dokumente,* Vol. 8, No. 10,599) and to the Russians through Macchio (*ibid.,* No. 10,704), were no more than efforts at reassurance. On July 14 he told the Emperor that even after mobilization an understanding with Serbia was not impossible, if Serbia yielded completely and paid the costs of mobilization (!) (*Österreichische Dokumente,* Vol. 8, No. 10,272, July 14)—a statement repeated on July 23 (Conrad, Vol. 4, p. 108)—and this, evidently based on a discussion with Conrad (*ibid.,* p. 61), was meant to conceal the gravity of the decision from the Emperor. Berchtold sought to excuse the belated commencement of operations with the argument that there was to be no mobilization until it was definitely known that there would be war (*Österreichische Dokumente,* Vol. 8, Nos. 10,783 and 10,910), i.e., not until July 25, but Albertini, *The Origins of the War of 1914,* Vol. 2, p. 457, completely misinterprets this. There was no question of keeping any chance for peace open.
18. *Deutsche Dokumente,* Vol. 1, No. 74, Quartermaster General Count Waldersee to von Jagow, July 17. According to General Höfer, by way of Kageneck, Waldersee then counted on only six army corps against Serbia.
19. *Deutsche Dokumente,* Vol. 1, No. 197, July 26. Not yet aware of the gravity of the European situation, Kaiser William II criticized this attitude in scornful marginal notes.
20. *Deutsche Dokumente,* Vol. 1, Nos. 202 and 212; Vol. 2, No. 326; *Österreichische Dokumente,* Vol. 8, No. 11,030; Conrad, Vol. 4, pp. 108, 154. According to a paper by M. Toscano at the historians' congress in Rome in 1955 (*ATTI del X. Congresso Internazionale* [die Scienze Storiche] [Rome 1957], p. 716), Italian efforts to mediate in Belgrade and secure further Serbian concessions (*Deutsche Dokumente,* Vol. 1, No. 249, July 27) met with greater success than has been hitherto assumed. See, however, the detailed treatment of this episode by Albertini, *The Origins of the War of 1914,* Vol. 2, pp. 417-424; Vol. 3, pp. 266ff.
21. *Deutsche Dokumente,* Vol. 2, No. 349.
22. There is no substance to the charge, originally leveled by H. Lutz and repeated by

Albertini (Vol. 2, p. 490), that Moltke expanded the scope of Germany's obligations under the alliance, since he was willing to have German mobilization follow on
only Russian partial mobilization, a course the German government had previously
rejected (*Deutsche Dokumente,* No. 299). The memorandum assumes that total
Austrian mobilization would lead to a clash with Russia that would force Germany
to intervene. Moltke opposed German mobilization as late as July 30; Conrad,
Vol. 4, p. 152.

23. Conrad, Vol. 4, pp. 137f.
24. *Österreichische Dokumente,* Vol. 8, No. 10,937; *Deutsche Dokumente,* Vol. 2, No.
    427. The content of the draft note Conrad presented to him on July 30 (Conrad,
    Vol. 4, p. 147) recurs almost verbatim in *Österreichische Dokumente,* Vol. 8, No.
    11,093.
25. Conrad, Vol. 4, p. 148 (discussion with Berchtold, July 30). The excessive caution in
    the German exhortations and mediation proposals to Vienna is evident. Even the
    well-known "forceful" notes of July 30 (*Deutsche Dokumente,* Nos. 395, 396, and
    441) carefully avoid the slightest threat that Germany might refuse to abide by the
    terms of the Austrian alliance. Despite later denials by Jagow and Bethmann,
    Szögény's controversial report of July 27 (*Österreichische Dokumente,* Vol. 8, No.
    10,793), to the effect that von Jagow had all but told the Austrians not to take the
    political mediation proposals seriously that were reaching Vienna via Berlin, may in
    part have been the result of misunderstandings–though it was scarcely cut from the
    whole cloth. Possibly von Jagow meant to say no more than that the German
    government did not necessarily identify itself with all the mediation proposals
    emanating from London, but that it must be intent on not letting the line to
    London be cut. It should be borne in mind that at the time von Jagow evidently still
    had full faith in Britain's neutrality. See Goschen's report, *British Documents,* Vol.
    11, p. 361. Unprejudiced readers of the original sources are unlikely to accept
    Albertini's grotesque exaggeration (Vol. 2, p. 495) that the Vienna politicians were
    mere puppets on Bethmann's string.
26. Almost any reader of *Österreichische Dokumente,* Vol. 8, is likely to be struck by the
    inadequacy of Austrian reporting from foreign capitals. Szögény is known to have
    been long superannuated. Most of the other foreign representatives seem to have
    been intent on telling the Vienna ministry what it wanted to hear rather than on
    voicing disagreeable truths. In this respect, they form a sharp contrast to personal-
    ities like Prince Lichnowsky and Count Pourtalès. Many of the reports also sound
    amazingly shallow.
27. Conrad, Vol. 4, pp. 147ff.; *Österreichische Dokumente,* Nos. 11,025-26, 11,119.
28. Albertini, *The Origins of the War of 1914,* Vol. 2, pp. 658ff., deals with this subject at
    great length. He also puts forward many untenable suspicions. On pp. 659ff., for
    example, he stands things completely on their head. He suggests that Conrad's
    decision to order general mobilization was inspired by Tschirschky, while at the
    same time, incomprehensibly, imputing to Tschirschky the intention of keeping
    this decision by the German government secret as long as possible, to prevent
    objections from Berlin–as though Berlin had not been impatiently waiting for total
    Austrian mobilization! Albertini's study, substantial and meritorious in so many
    respects, suffers from the author's predisposition to suspect all German generals
    and politicians of militarism a priori. This leads him into many surprising misinter-
    pretations and errors of judgment.
29. *Deutsche Dokumente,* Vol. 2, No. 299, July 28; *ibid.,* Nos. 342, 373, and 380, July 29;
    Zwehl, *Falkenhayn,* pp. 56f. Albertini, *The Origins of the War of 1914,* Vol. 2, p.
    503, of course, views the attitude of the two generals as no more than adaptation to
    the Kaiser's current mood rather than as representing their own conscientious
    convictions.
30. Th. von Schäfer, "Generaloberst von Moltke in den Tagen vor der Mobilmachung und
    Seine Einwirkung auf Österreich-Ungarn," in *Berliner Monatschefte,* Vol. 4, p. 523.
31. Conrad, Vol. 4, p. 152. Szögény's alleged telegram of July 30, mentioned there, does

not exist, according to *Österreichische Dokuments*, Vol. 8. Evidently this is a case of confusion with *ibid.*, No. 10,945, of July 29.

32. *Deutsche Dokumente*, Vol. 2, No. 410. Fleischmann's letter of the evening of July 30 (*Berliner Monatschefte*, Vol. 4, p. 523) speaks of fourteen mobilized Russian army corps, "according to intelligence now confirmed"–intelligence apparently not yet available to Moltke in the morning. Albertini, *The Origins of the War of 1914*, Vol. II, pp. 8ff., has collected material to explain Moltke's sudden change, partly from dated propaganda. Much of this is unprovable, and unnecessary as well. Albertini's distrust of the militarists in the General Staff persuades him to attribute to them even the well-known false report in the Berlin *Lokalanzeiger*, on noon of July 30.

33. Schäfer, *Berliner Monatshefte*, p. 524. This inquiry seems to have been motivated by a communication from the Russian ambassador in Berlin rather than by the above-mentioned dispatch from St. Petersburg.

34. Schäfer, *loc. cit.*, p. 529, and particularly Albertini, *The Origins of the War of 1914*, Vol. 3, pp. 8ff., suggest that an essential element in this agitation was the telegram from the Czar early on July 30 (*Deutsche Dokumente*, Vol. 2, No. 395), which the Kaiser misunderstood and excitedly annotated, but this seems to me quite doubtful. One can scarcely believe that he failed to recognize, when reading the dispatch, that the Czar was speaking of decisions taken on the twenty-fifth, but being implemented only now, July 30.

35. Schäfer, *loc. cit.*, p. 525; Conrad, Vol. 4, p. 152; *ibid* (the so-called Moltke telegram of the evening of July 30). See also *Österreichische Dokumente*, Vol. 8, No. 11,033.

36. *Österreichische Dokumente*, Vol. 8, No. 11,030 (report from Szögény).

37. *Deutsche Dokumente*, Vol. 2, Nos. 441, 451 (Bethmann's first denial), 464 (second denial). See also Schäfer, *loc. cit.*, p. 533.

38. Albertini, *The Origins of the War of 1914*, Vol. 3, p. 25, questions the accuracy of von Haeften's note of August 2, 1914, on his nocturnal talk with Moltke (published in Schulthess, *Europäischer Geschichts-Kalender* [1917], Vol. 2, pp. 995ff., from a newspaper excerpt); but Albertini's arguments are vitiated by his own statement, *ibid.*, p. 27.

39. Reich Archives History, Military Land Operations, Vol. 2, p. 27.

40. Note from Szögény to the foreign ministry, afternoon of July 30 (*Deutsche Dokumente*, Vol. 2, Nos. 427, 429). A note made by Tschirschky on the morning of July 30 shows that German assent to total mobilization was awaited.

41. *Deutsche Dokumente*, Vol. 2, p. 465.

42. Conrad, Vol. 4, p. 151. Conrad's calculations seem to have provided that in an emergency he might detach "Echelon B" (eleven and a half divisions) from the twenty-six and a half division combat force meant for the Balkans, dispatching the former to Galicia as reinforcements.

43. Schäfer, *Berliner Monatshefte*, Vol. 4, p. 530; *Österreichische Dokumente*, Vol. 8, No. 11,119.

44. Schäfer, *loc. cit.*, p. 539 (from the Reich Archives); and *Deutsche Dokumente*, p. 482. Francis Joseph, too, wired in Conrad's sense–*Deutsche Dokumente*, Vol. 2, p. 482.

45. Schäfer, *loc. cit.*, p. 539.

46. *Österreichische Dokumente*, Vol. 8, Nos. 11,201 and 11,132. According to the Reich Archives History, Vol. 2, p. 29, Vienna still did not know about total Russian mobilization until the morning of August 1, "on account of an unfortunate concatenation of circumstances." Did communication services in Vienna really fail so completely? Actually, Szögény's official report, filed about 7 p.m. on July 31, did not arrive until 8 a.m. on August 1 (*Österreichische Dokumente*, Vol. 8, No. 11,133). But the German government's intention to mobilize and put an ultimatum to Russia was known on the morning of July 31 (Conrad, Vol. 4, p. 152; and *Österreichische Dokumente*, Vol. 8, No. 11,201). Stumm telephoned the Vienna embassy about 12:30 p.m., also communicating the news of the Russian general mobilization. A. von Wegerer, "Die Russische Allgemeine Mobilmachung und das Deutsche Ultimatum an Russland," *Berliner Monatshefte* (1928), pp. 1061-63.

Bethmann included it in his telegram to Tschirschky, which arrived at 4:20 p.m. *Deutsche Dokumente,* Vol. 2, No. 479. The embassy could not possibly have suppressed this. See also Szögény's telegrams (*Österreichische Dokumente,* No. 11,130, on German mobilization, time of receipt 6 p.m.) and those of Fleischmann, received before midnight (Schäfer, p. 540).

47. *Österreichische Dokumente,* Vol. 8, No. 11,125; *Deutsche Dokumente,* Vol. 3, No. 503; Conrad, Vol. 4, p. 156. For Bethmann's telegram as early as 1:44 p.m., see *Deutsche Dokumente,* Vol. 2, p. 479.

48. This assertion commands little credence, since the "message" mentioned went out at 4:15 p.m., while Count Berchtold had heard about the German ultimatum to Russia from Tschirschky in the morning (*Österreichische Dokumente,* Vol. 8, No. 11,201).

49. Schäfer, p. 541; Conrad, Vol. 4, p. 543.

50. Conrad, Vol. 4, p. 160. See also the characteristic wire inquiry of August 1: "Is Germany mobilizing only against Russia or also against France? " *ibid.,* p. 161.

51. Details in my above-cited article in the *Festgabe* for Herzfeld (1958).

52. Conrad's account in his memoirs is not free of attempts at self-justification, as becomes apparent from the Reich Archives History, Vol. 2, and the official work, *Österreich-Ungarns Letzter Krieg,* Vol. 1 (1930). See also Th. von Schäfer, *Berliner Monatshefte,* Vol. 5 (1927), pp. 1,122ff.

53. Oddly enough, the minutes (*Österreichische Dokumente,* Vol. 8, No. 11,203) do not list the chief of staff as participating. See Conrad, Vol. 4, p. 153. Yet the fact that he did participate is clear, not only from his own report, but from Berchtold's to Emperor Francis Joseph (*Österreichische Dokumente,* Vol. 8, No. 11,201).

Notes to Chapter 10, Part 4

1. *Österreichische Dokumente,* Vol. 8, Nos. 11,203 and 11,201. From these it would appear that Bethmann was considering the "ultimatum" even before official news of Russian general mobilization was received from St. Petersburg. His talk with Goschen about 10 a.m. shows how disquieted he was by earlier reports from the border. *British Documents,* Vol. 11, p. 677.

2. Schäfer, *Berliner Monatshefte,* Vol. 4, p. 542.

3. *Deutsche Dokumente,* Vol. 3, pp. 487, 536.

4. *British Documents,* Vol. 11, No. 340: *Deutsche Dokumente,* Vol. 3, No. 489. Report by Goschen on the execution of his mission, *British Documents,* Vol. 11, No. 385. According to Bethmann Hollweg, *Betrachtungen zum Weltkrieg,* Vol. 2, pp. 83f., it would seem that during the discussions on the night of July 31 about a declaration of war on Russia Moltke counted on the Russians neither opening hostilities nor declaring war before the conclusion of their mobilization.

5. Details and evidence in E. Hemmer, *Die Deutschen Kriegserklärungen von 1914* (1935), pp. 33f. Of special importance are the statements by Count Waldersee, chief of staff of the eighth army in 1914.

6. My Schlieffen book, p. 148. The Schlieffen Plan never mentions any intention to take Liège "in an abbreviated coup" during the general advance, as is asserted by E. Hemmer (*loc. cit.,* p. 128), following Kabisch, Groener, *et al.* Schlieffen did want to have Huy taken by storm, to serve as a crossing point above Liège. In his memoirs, p. 18, Moltke stresses that he was primarily interested in occupying the Aachen-Liège railway line, which was, indeed, successfully done.

7. Hemmer, basing himself on statements by Count Waldersee, suspects this (pp. 118f.).

8. This expression was used by Moltke in a memorandum for Minister Delbrück of May 14, 1914 (Armaments and War Economy, Vol. 1, Appendix, Volume, p. 289).

9. In the following I am basing myself, without detailed references to sources, among others on A. von Wegerer, *Der Ausbruch des Weltkriegs 1914,* Vol. 2 (1939). In total concept, this book is now outdated, but it does offer very complete details of the events and evidence.

10. Von Wegerer, Vol. 2, pp. 141ff. See also Bethmann Hollweg, *Betrachtungen zum Weltkrieg*, Vol. 1 (1919), p. 156, and the already mentioned wire from Moltke to Conrad, dispatched at 2:20 a.m., which summarized the results of the discussion.

11. Details in Hemmer, *loc. cit.*, pp. 78ff., on the equivalence of war declaration and attack.

12. Von Wegerer, Vol. 2, p. 182, who here retracts his own former "corrections" of Falkenhayn's diary, which Albertini, *The Origins of the War of 1914*, Vol. 3, p. 192, still invokes.

13. We have already seen this in connection with the Russian mobilization plan and Conrad's difficulties in altering his deployment.

14. He probably misunderstood Bethmann's reply, to the effect that the military wished to send troops across the border swiftly. The chancellor probably meant Belgium and Luxembourg (Tirpitz's memoirs, p. 240).

15. On the question of the obligation to declare war formally, fixed at the Hague peace conference in 1907, see Hemmer, *loc. cit.*, pp. 69ff.

16. *Front wider Bülow*, pp. 217ff.; *Deutscher Offiziersbund*, August 15, 1927, No. 23, pp. 966f.

17. Tirpitz, *Erinnerungen* (1919), p. 228. He was, of course, mistaken in his assumption (*Politische Dokumente*, Vol. 2; *Deutsche Ohnmachtspolitik im Weltkrieg* [1926], p. 21) that Bethmann too "apparently" had no prior knowledge. Like all his accounts of his talks in those days, this was merely meant to distort the chancellor's image.

18. *Deutsche Dokumente*, Vol. 3, No. 629; Tirpitz, *Politische Dokumente*, Vol. 2, p. 21. In 1920, in an exchange with General von Kuhl, Bethmann Hollweg defended himself against the charge by the military that he had declared war on Russia and France quite unnecessarily (printed in *Berliner Monatshefte*, Vol. 17 [1939], pp. 663-673). In essence, he used the arguments that had been advanced by the foreign ministry as early as the night from August 1 to 2, 1914. He emphasized how awkward it would have been to leave "the onset of a state of war to the discretion of local military authorities," i.e., to incidents on the Russian border—though that is precisely what happened in France! He disputed, probably rightly, that Italy and Rumania would have fulfilled their treaty obligations but for the above-mentioned war declarations. He seems to have forgotten the details of the events in question. For example, he fails to mention Moltke's attitude on the night of July 31 and believes, oddly enough, that military criticism of the war declarations arose only after the disaster of 1918.

19. Tirpitz, *Politische Dokumente*, Vol. 2, p. 21.

20. *Deutsche Dokumente*, Vol. 3, No. 662.

21. Permission had been granted by the Kaiser around midnight, as a result of the disappointing news from London. Moltke had drafted a note for the Luxembourg government as well, but it was never sent in that form. See *Deutsche Dokumente*, Vol. 3, No. 639.

22. *Deutsche Dokumente*, Vol. 2, No. 376; Vol. 3, p. 648.

23. See von Jagow, *loc. cit.*

24. The author was able to confirm this in many discussions with educated Belgians during the occupation period in 1915-1916.

25. Von Moser, *Ernsthafte Plaudereien über den Weltkrieg* (1925), p. 38.

26. *Betrachtungen*, Vol. I, p. 165.

SUPPLEMENT TO THE NOTES TO CHAPTER 10
Bethmann Hollweg during the Crisis of July, 1914

In his lecture, "Zur Beurteilung Bethmann Hollwegs" (*Beschichte in Wissenschaft und Unterricht*, Vol. 15 [1964] pp. 525ff.), K. D. Erdmann has made public important new source material that throws light on Bethmann's attitude during the July crisis. This material is from the diaries of Legation Councilor Riezler, who was among the Chancellor's most intimate associates. Egmont Zechlin thereupon undertook a further account, using additional source material and becoming embroiled in a controversy with Fritz Fischer. This was in "Deutschland zwischen Kabinettskrieg und Wirtschaftskrieg," *Historische Zeitschrift,* Vol. 199 (1964); and "Probleme des Kriegskalküls und der Kriegsbeendigung im Ersten Weltkrieg," *Geschichte in Wissenschaft und Unterricht,* Vol. 16 (1965), pp. 69f. Both authors demonstrate, to my mind convincingly, that Bethmann Hollweg's hope of "localizing" the Serbo-Austrian war, strongly emphasized in earlier accounts, was poorly founded from the outset. As early as July 6, the day of the famous "blank check" for Vienna, Bethmann realized that the danger of Russian intervention in an Austrian war in the Balkans was greater this time than in 1912, since Austria was now merely fighting back against Serbo-Russian plots, as Bethmann told Riezler, according to Erdmann (*loc. cit.,* p. 536). Another reason that had long troubled him even more was that Russia had in the meantime greatly improved its rearmament. An added element, strongly emphasized by Zechlin, was that the German foreign ministry was in possession of secret and absolutely reliable intelligence that Britain was about to negotiate a naval convention with the czarist government, in the form of an agreement between the two admiralty staffs rather than the two governments—in other words, rather in the informal way that the Entente Cordiale with France had been negotiated by the two general staffs. As the German Chancellor told the German ambassador in London as early as June 16 (*Deutsche Dokumente,* Vol. 1, No. 3), that was bound to result in a dangerous increase in Russian and French chauvinism. If the Russians intervened, the French would inevitably follow suit. In other words, Bethmann Hollweg made out the German "blank check" in full awareness that he was thereby running the risk of not only a local but a continental war. He seems actually to have used the term "world war" to Riezler on July 6.

Of itself, none of this is new. We already know (see above, p. 237) that Vienna was reasonably certain Russia would intervene. Bethmann would have had to be stricken with blindness if he had trusted with absolute certainty that this time things would once again proceed as they had in 1908 and 1912. What is new, however, is the impression of gloomy fatalism that speaks from Bethmann's utterances to Riezler. Germany seemed to him to be in extreme peril, even without war. As its enemies well knew, it was completely checkmated by the Entente ring, while Austria-Hungary was growing steadily weaker and less mobile. Russia's military might was growing apace, haunting the Germans like a nightmare. Within a few years, Russia's growing claims and immense explosive force could no longer be contained, especially if the present configuration in Europe should continue (July 6, 7, and 20, 1914, in Erdmann, *loc. cit.,*). The conclusion was that a "leap into the dark" must be risked, in other words, the possibility of a great war. That was Germany's "gravest duty"; for on no account could Germany accept the disintegration and loss of its last ally, together with clear-cut Russian predominance on the continent. It was true, however, that such a war, no matter what its issue, would "bring a complete upheaval of the existing order."

We see that in all this there is no suggestion of the pursuit of world power, only of Germany's ineluctable "duty" to arrest decades of decline in its status as a great power, imperiled especially from the east. It wished to maintain that position, together with that of its Austrian ally, even at the risk of a European war. Even after the disaster of 1918, Bethmann insisted that he had had no alternative, in an age governed by notions of great power politics and prestige (see his *Betrachtungen zum Weltkrieg,* Vol. I, p. 129), and in view of the fact that his efforts prior to 1914 to achieve a peaceful harmonization among the powers with Britain's help had in the end failed (*ibid.,* p. 131). Yet, at the end of his chancellorship and even more so after his fall, he was deeply moved by the "horrible grandeur" of the world catastrophe that had become so inexorable. He foresaw that the nations would accuse their governments of having led them to disaster. This is seen most clearly in a letter to Prince Max of Baden of January 17, 1918, published by Zechlin, *loc. cit.,* pp. 451ff. I am unable, however, to perceive in this letter the element of "self-criticism" Zechlin finds in it. I do note an inclination to join forces with the socialists—to whom the Chancellor had come closer and closer during his tenure in office—in charging the nationalist warmongers and superpatriots for their failure to represent the popular will.

In sum, the Chancellor's decision to side with Austria-Hungary even at the risk of a European war can be called an act of desperate resolve rather than of arrogant faith in victory. Beyond doubt it contained a strong element of fatalistic surrender to what was seemingly inevitable. The nightmare confronting the Chancellor was the disaster that threatened from the side of Russia, magnified by the tremendous preponderance soon impending from the Russo-French military alliance, according to the military authorities. Yet there seems a danger to me of overestimating the practical importance of mere emotional outbursts, to which this statesman, always brooding and worried, was given in intimate discussion with his loyal follower, Riezler. Not only are there many utterances during the July crisis that clearly show Bethmann's hope that it might in the end be possible to localize the war—there are actions as well. Bethmann's hope was based in the main on the fact that Russia had not yet by far completed its arms program. The Russian czar and his generals might well shrink from prematurely involving themselves in a military adventure, the consequences of which were incalculable. (See, for example, von Jagow's well-known letter to Lichnowsky of July 17, *Deutsche Dokumente,* Vol. 1, No. 72.) Whether in the end such considerations of military reason rather than political ambition and the striving for great power status would carry the day in St. Petersburg depended not least on Britain's attitude.

It has hitherto always been assumed (even by Albertini and Fischer) that Bethmann Hollweg to the last moment clung to the hope that a way could somehow be found to persuade Britain at least to stay neutral in the event of a continental war, if not to exert a moderating influence on St. Petersburg. Otherwise—i.e., had the Chancellor counted from the outset on British entry into the war—his policy would have to be characterized as that of a gambler, indeed an adventurer, which would not be at all in character. I was shaken, for that reason, to read Zechlin's sentece: "The break with Britain in the event of a crisis was now deemed probable, even though not yet certain, since formal conclusion [of the planned Anglo-Russian naval conventions] was still lacking" (*Historische Zeitschrift,* Vol. 199, p. 353, Note 2, Line 6). Expressly opposing W. Naef, Albertini, and Fischer, Zechlin (p. 354) bases his contention not on the obvious fear, taken very seriously by von Jagow as early as 1913, that a German march into Belgium would bring out the British against the Germans (see p. 219, above), but exclusively on the well-known and much-discussed fact that the German foreign ministry had been extremely well informed ever since June about the impending naval negotiations between London and St. Petersburg. Were these actually viewed in such a grave light in Berlin, as "a decisive change in the political and strategic situation" (Zechlin, p. 354)? The sources Zechlin cites from the correspondence between Lichnowsky and the German foreign ministry (pp. 348 and 352n.) by no means compel such a conclusion. They merely show that the Chancellor and his associates were at pains to warn Sir Edward Grey against the strengthening of Russian as well as German chauvinism that might flow from such naval negotiations, particularly if they reached the press. The letters strive to continue the policy of *détante* hitherto pursued in common—that is all. One might cite from Riezler's diary notes Bethmann's remark that secret intelligence on the Anglo-Russian naval negotiations seriously opened up the possibility of British landing operations in Pomerania, in the event of war (Erdmann, *loc. cit.*); but, even if such a sigh of despair were to be taken literally, it would scarcely suffice to support the notion that Bethmann Hollweg had already buried his hopes for British neutrality.

Certain passages make it seem probable that even Zechlin does not assert such total resignation outright. He seems to regard the "decisive change in the political and strategic situation" brought about by the Anglo-Russian naval negotiations not as having already taken place, but only as directly impending. Yet he does take it seriously enough to suggest something like a preventive war notion on Bethmann Hollweg's part. In two or three years, he assumes (if I understand him rightly), Britain would have been as closely tied to Russia as it already was to France, a prospect that virtually provoked the political offensive in July. But was there then any real German "political offensive" that came just in time to trigger war? Is there any evidence that Bethmann harbored such thoughts at all? I do not think so. It seems to me that the point is drawn too fine, that it constitutes an effort to read more into the sources than is there. I am afraid this will only lead to new confusions in the war guilt debate. Things are not made easier by the fact that Zechlin, in order to make Bethmann's alleged policy of excessive risk plausible, seeks to prove that Bethmann thought of the war with Britain in terms of a kind of "cabinet war," i.e., a war of limited aims that would not be fought to the bitter end, but would be of relatively short duration. Bethmann, according to Zechlin, was greatly disappointed when the British moved instant- · ly into a total mass war, seizing the private property of aliens, inciting the nations against one another by means of ruthless propaganda, and preventing any of their allies from suing for separate peace, by invoking the various treaties. It was from this frustration that the "September program" discovered by Fischer supposedly emerged—the notion of a continental economic league under German leadership. It was a counterblow, a pure combat measure with the goal of forcing Albion to its knees by means of a kind of continental blockade.

It is a brilliant construction, but rather oversophisticated and certainly not provable from the sources. I regard its suppositions as quite improbable; but since a full discussion would lead us into the first weeks of the war, it does not really belong in this volume.

Index

adjutant general, British, 41, 43

Admiralty, British: administration of, 41, 43; and military plans, 64-5, 67, 72; war plans of, 150

Aehrenthal, Baron A. von, Austrian foreign minister, 228, 229, 230, 231, 241

Africa, German colonies in, 110, 141, 177

airships, 173

Aksakov, S. T., Russian nationalist writer, 81

Albania, Serbia and, 234, 236

Albedyll, Emil, chief of German military cabinet, 121

Albert, Prince Consort, 37

Algeciras Conference (1906), 65, 69, 173

Alldeutscher Verband, 109, 110; *see also* Pan-Germanism

Alsace, German army in, 101, 134-6

Anglo-French colonial pact (1904), 62, 63, 65, 66, 145, 160

Anglo-French military entente: beginnings of, 58-9; staff talks and, 48, 61-76; to maintain balance of power, 146-7; German naval policy and, 148; and possible rapprochement of Britain and Germany, 166, 169, 185

Anglo-French naval accord (1912), 148

Anglo-Russian agreement and entente (1907), 160, 166, 169, 185; conflicts of interest in, 177

antimilitarism: in France, 17, 19, 21; as basic ingredient of liberalism, 36; of left in Germany, 103, 126

anti-Semitism, 22, 102

Antwerp: as possible British base, 68, 70, 218; in later military plans, 73

armaments industry: in Russia, 79; in Germany, 137, 160

army: garrison, (in France) 8, 12, 13, 14, 19, 20, 27, (in Britain) 36, (in Prussia), 96; mass, (in France) 8, 19, 22, 28, (in Prussia) 8, 11, (in modern warfare), 197; mercenary, (in 18th century) 12, 17, 35, (in Britain) 71; rank and file of, (in France) 16-17, (in Britain) 35, 45, (in Prussia) 95-6; standing, British suspicion of, 48-9, 50; "steamroller," of Russia. 78; regarded as necessary evil in Western Europe, and nation's pride in Prussia/Germany, 93; term of service in, *see under* military service

army officers: French, 10, 15-16, 21-2, 27-8, 71; British, 36-7, 45, 49, 71; Prussian, 95, 97; German, 100-1, 103, 105, 211; of Landwehr, 14, 15, 101; German, alienated from civilian and political life, 28, 125, 126; Russian, 77, 79, 80, 85

army reserves: French, 13, 14, 18, 22, 226; British, 42, 45, 47, 48; German, 101-2, 211-12; in German war plans, 207, 213, 220-1, 226

Arndt, E. M., 115

Asquith, H. H., British prime minister, 50, 52, 55, 179

Austria-Hungary: German alliance with, 81, 167; Russia and, 81, 82, 84, 87; threats of war between Russia and, 202, 243; internal disintegration in, 107-8, 228,

236; supported by Germany in Balkan crisis (1908-9), 161, 177; Bismarck and, 198; general staff of, and notion of preventive war, 81, 227-39; general staffs of Germany and, 107-8, 205, 217, 219, 239-47; army of, 205, 228; William II pledges unconditional support to, 227, 236, 242, 252; issues ultimatum to Serbia, 237, 250; Germany and (July 1914), 247-63; mobilizes, against Serbia, 250-1, against Russia, 255, 257, 258, 263; declares war on Serbia, 252, on Russia, 268

Austro-Prussian War (1866), 19, 81, 217: *see also* Wars of Unification

Baghdad railway, 170, 177

Balfour, A. J., British prime minister, 42, 47

Balkans: turmoil in (1877), 197; crisis in (1908-9), 85, 112, 161, 177; Russia and, 82, 87, 161, 220; Austrian passivity during wars in (1911-12), 232; German trade with, 4, 233; recognition of danger of war arising in, 177, 190, 202

Ballin, Albert, chiarman of Hamburg-America line, 179, 180

Baltic, German navy and, 150, 155, 156, 157

Barnardiston, N. W., British military attaché in Brussels, 68

Barthou, J. L., French prime minister, 23

Bebel, August, 103

Beck, General von, successor of younger Moltke as chief of staff, 264

Beck-Rzikowsky, General von, Austrian chief of staff, 240

Belgium: neutrality of, 63, 115, 196; German invasion of, considered likely, 47, 62, 64, 66, 68, 195; French general staff and, 62, 63, 73, 271; army of, 68, 69, 74, 195, 196, 203, 216; British military discussions with, 68-9; resists Anglo-French approaches, 60, 73, 74; African colonies of, 115, 177; in German war plans, 152, 194, 195-6, 201, 205, 217, 219, 225; German naval views on, 152; German decision on, 155, 210; German *sommation* to, 270, 271, 272; and British entry into war, 62, 66, 203, 271

Belgrade, Austrian bombardment of, 257

Berchtold, Count Leopold, Austrian foreign minister: and Conrad von Hötzendorf, 229, 232, 234, 236, 238; and German pledge of support, 237; after Serajevo, 247, 248; at outbreak of war, 251-2, 254-5, 258, 262

Bernhardi, General Friedrich von, of German general staff; writings of, 112-16

Bernhardi, Theodor von, 112

Bernstorff, Count von, deputy German ambassador in London, 145

Bertie, Sir Francis, British ambassador in Paris, 74, 185

Bertrab, General von, German deputy chief of staff, 227

Bethman Hollweg, Theobald von, minister of the interior, Reich chancellor, 4, 75, 102, 190; and Zabern incident, 135, 136; and colonies, 141; in exchanges with Britain over naval expansion, 164-76 *passim*, 180, 182, 188; meets Haldane (1912), 181-4; Grey and, 186; offers resignation, 187; and military plans, 194, 206, 220, 222; puts through army bill and capital levy (1913), 225-6; in July 1914, 248, 254, 259; offers neutrality treaty to Britain (29 July), 256; at outbreak of war, 263, 265, 266, 268, 271; fall of (1917), 270

Bienerth, Freiherr von, Austrian military attaché in Berlin, 257, 258

Bismarck, Prince Otto von, 20, 34, 89, 93, 102, 203; and Russia, 82, 83; *realpolitik* of, 94, 98; domestic policies of, 100, 103; legend of, 100, 104, 106; and preventive war, 106, 113; civilian preponderance under, 119; and war ministers, 120-2; and military attachés, 128, 129; and Belgian neutrality, 196; and Austria, 198, 239; fall of (1890), 21, 128; in retirement, 131

Björkö convention (1905), between William II and Czar, 66-7

blitzkrieg, in Schlieffen plan, 201, 214, 215

blockade of Germany by Britain, 64, 114, 149, 150, 151, 152, 153

Blücher, General, Treitschke on, 99

Boer War: and British army, 34, 42, 45, 46, 70; Germany and, 144, 145

Boisdeffre, General, signs Franco-Russian pact, 82, 83

Boisgelin, on French army system, 15

Bosnia, crisis over Austrian annexation of (1908-9), 87, 230, 240

Bosporus, 150, 177

Boulanger, General, in politics, 28

Boyen, General von, Prussian war minister, 14

Briand, Aristide, French prime minister, 22, 29

Britain: army, society, and government in, 33-59; staff talks between France and,

48, 61-76, between Belgium and, 68; prospects of blockade of Germany by, *see* blockade; and German colonies, 141, 142; anti-German feeling in, 75, 144, 160; policy of, in Balkan crisis (1908-9), 161; and German naval expansion, 143-58 *passim*, 160; exchanges between Germany and, over naval expansion, (1909) 151-67, (1910, 1912), 167-91; trial mobilization of navy of (1911), 172; Moltke expects entry into war of, 217-18; intervenes in Austro-Serbian situation (July 1914), 254, 255, 258, 260, 264; proposes French neutrality, 268; Belgian neutrality and entry into war of, 62, 66, 203, 271; *see also entries beginning* Anglo-

Bronsart von Schellendorf, Paul, German war minister, 121, 133

Büchsel, Admiral, chief of German naval staff, 152, 154-5

Bulgaria: crisis over (1887), 20; Austria and, 230

Bülow, Prince Berhard von, German foreign minister (from 1897) and Reich chancellor (1900-9), 102, 130, 134, 177, 210; and Morocco, 64, 147; and colonies, 141; and naval developments, 155, 159, 160, 161, 163; and Schlieffen plan, 194; and Austria, 241, 242, 243

Burke, Edmund, financial reforms of (1782), 37, 38

cabinet, British, in 1914-18 war, 52, 53

Cambon, P. P., French ambassador in London, 63, 64, 65, 75

Cambridge, Duke of, British commander-in-chief, 37, 41

Campbell-Bannerman, Sir Henry, British prime minister, 44, 47, 48

Cannae, battle of, 200

Capelle, Vice-Admiral, deputy to Tirpitz, 172, 174, 183

capital levy, for German military expansion, 225

Caprivi, Count Georg von, Reich chancellor and foreign minister (1890-4): army reforms of (1892-3), 98, 132, 209, 212; and Austria, 240; and African colonies, 110 and military attachés, 129, 130; fall of, 133

Cardwell, Edward, British war minister, reforms of, 40, 45, 46

Carnot, L. M. N., 8

Cassel, Sir Ernest, banker, 179, 180

Cavaignac, French historian, 8

China: Germany in, 111, 141; Russia and, 177

Churchill, Winston, first lord of the Admiralty; and naval accord with France, 148; and British naval plans, 150; and exchanges with Germany over naval expansion, 178, 179, 180, 181, 183, 185; proposes "battleship holiday," 190; in 1914-18 war, 52, 53, 55, 56

Clarke, Sir George, permanent secretary to Committee of Imperial Defense, 65

Clausewitz, Karl von, 9; war theory of, 113, 202, 229

Clémenceau, Georges: and generals, 27, 28, 30; prime minister and war minister, 30, 57; after the war, 31

colonies: German, 109, 110, 111, 114, 141; in Anglo-German talks, 178, 182, 183, 184, 191; Belgian and Portuguese, 115, 177

commander-in-chief: in Britain, 36, 37, 38, 39, 40; post abolished, 43

commercial companies, to provide substitutes for French army, 16

commissions in the army: sale of, in Britain, 36-7

Committee of Imperial Defense, Britain, 44, 50, 52, 64, 70, 72

Congo, Belgian, 115, 177

Congress of Berlin (1878), 81

Congress of Vienna, 35

conscription: in France, 8, 9, 10, 11-12, 45; in Britain, (proposed) 46, 49, (introduced, 1916) 51; in Prussia, 48, 98; in Russia, 77-8, 79; in Germany, 223; as "foundation of political liberty" (Treitschke), 99

Conseil Supérieur de la Défense Nationale, 24, 25

constitution of German Reich, 126, 132, 134

courts martial, in Germany, 133

Crimean War (1854-6): 18, 34, 39, 48; and Russian army, 78

Crowe, Eyre, assistant under-secretary, Foreign Office, 64, 74, 146

Dähnhardt, Rear-Admiral, 183

Daily Telegraph affair (1908), 134, 161

Dardanelles expedition, 28, 53, 55, 56

Darwinism, in politics, 107, 108, 116

Deimling, General von, 135

Deines, von, German military attaché in Vienna, 128

Delbrück, Hans, historian and publicist, 109

Delcassé, Théophile, French foreign minister, (1898-1905), 63, 64, 66
Denmark, in German naval plans, 154, 155
diplomacy: Conrad von Hötzendorf on, 229; of Austrian general staff, 232
dominions, British: and Committee of Imperial Defense, 44; military support from, 45; training of forces of, 50
Dragomirov, General M. I., of Russian general staff, 80, 81
dreadnoughts: British, 149, 159, 160, 162, 168; German, 159, 162, 220
Dreyfus case, 16, 22, 28
Droysen, J. G., propagandist for union of Germany under Prussia, 99
Ducarne, General G. F. V., Belgian chief of staff, 68, 69
duels: in French army, 15; in German army, 101, 102

economists, and German naval policy, 140
education: and army service, (Prussia and France) 15, (Russia) 78; Bernhardi on, 115
Edward VII, 63; meets Kaiser, 162
Egypt, British campaign in, 46
Einem, Karl von, German war minister (1903-9), 123, 126, 209, 210, 211, 214, 215, 220
encirclement: German fears of, 106, 147; Schlieffen's strategy of, 200, 206, 218-19; Conrad von Hötzendorf's strategy of, 240
Esher, Lord, 65
Esher Commission (1903-4), 42-3
Eulenberg, Count Philip, 124, 133
expeditionary force, British: plans for (1906 onwards), 48, 49, 62, 63, 72; French ask for command of, 68, 70; German war plans and, 156, 157, 207, 218

Fadeyev, General, Pan-Slav and anti-German writer, 80
Falkenhayn, General E. von, German war minister, 227; and navy, 111; at outbreak of war, 255, 256, 259, 267, 269, 270
Ferdinand, Austrian Archduke, 231
finance: for British navy, 149, 160, 166, 176, 178, 180, 185; for German naval propaganda, from heavy industry, 137; for German military and naval expansion, 149, 159, 173, 176, 108, 211, 220, 222
Fischel, Admiral von, chief of German naval staff, 153

Fisher, Admiral Sir John, 64-5, 68, 159
Fleischmann, Captain von, Austrian general staff liaison officer in Germany, 256, 257, 261
Flottenverein (German Navy League), 110, 138; and Britain, 111, 112, 142, 146; and German world power, 140, 144; Tirpitz and, 139, 160
Foch, General, 28, 71, 72; French chief of staff, 29-31, 72
foreign policy, German: aggressive, required by Bernhardi, 114; affected by concentration on battle fleet, 142, 159, 160; Bethmann Hollweg and, 164
France: army in state and society of, 7-31; defense acts in, (1867) 19, (1872) 20; staff talks between Britain and, 48, 61-76; German military writers and, 106, 114; navy of, in early Schlieffen plan, 156; fortified eastern frontier of, 196; attack on, as first stage in German war plans, 197, 199-200, 204, 217; Britain proposes neutrality of (July 1914), 268; German declaration of war on, 267, 269, 270, 271, 272, 274; *see also entries beginning* Anglo-French, Franco-
Francis Ferdinand, Austrian Archduke, 250; assassination of 234, 235
Francis Joseph of Austria-Hungary: as field marshal of Prussia, 240; William II's telegram to (July 1914), 255, 264
Franco-Prussian War (1970-1), 13, 19-20, 197, 200, 212; *see also* Wars of Unification
Franco-Russian military pact (1892), 21, 82, 194, 202, 209, 243; Russia committed to immediate offensive in, 83, 88, 204
Frederic the Great of Prussia, 94-5
Frederic William I of Prussia, 95
Frederic William IV of Prussia, 127
French, General, 51
Freycinet, C. L. de: first French civilian war minister, 22; prime minister, 82, 83
Freytag-Loringhoven, Freiherr von, German quartermaster-general, 111, 116
Frisian Islands, 150

Galicia: conquest of, as Russian goal, 82; Austrian plans for offensive from, 84; in Austrian mobilization plans, 232, 237, 241, 255; at outbreak of war, 261, 262
Gallieni, General J. S., French war minister, 29
Galster, Vice-Admiral, on German naval policy, 153, 161

Gambetta, Léon, 19
garde mobile, France, 19
general staffs: Campbell-Bannerman on, 44; French, 23, 25; none in Britain, 38, 41; created in Britain (1904), 43, 49; discussions between French and British, 48, 61-76; British in 1914-18 war, 28, 53-5; Russian, 78, 79-80, 82; discussions between French and Russian, 84; German, 48, 83, 117; German and war ministry, 120, 123, 206, 208; German and navy, 156, 157; Austrians, 205; Austrian, and notion of preventive war, 81, 227-39; relations of German and Austrian, 107-8, 205, 216, 217, 219, 238, 239-47
generals: Napoleon's, 9, 10; French, and politics, 23-4, 26, 27-30; German, and monarch, 26; British, 52, 54; French and British, exchange visits, 71
George V, 188
German army bills: (1892-3), 98, 132; 209, 212, 213; (1899), 98, 213; (1905), 98, 214, 215; (1911), 98, 220, 222; (1912), 222, 223; (1913), 23, 225, 226
German Defense Union, *see Wehrverein*
German navy bills: (1898), 138, 145; (1900), 112, 138, 145, 154, 150, 162; (1906), 138, 146, 159, 160; (1908), 138, 168, 220; (1912). 138, 164, 168, 173, 175, 176, 180-90 *passim,* 222
Germany: Reinsurance Treaty between Russia and, 82, 209, 243; militarization of middle class in, 15, 93-104; war and politics in military literature of, 105-17; military and civilian authority in, 119-36; naval growth in, 47, 65, 67; naval policy of, to 1914, 137-58; fear of preponderance of, 50, 66, 147, 185, 218; arms race and first naval talks of Britain and, 158-67; further naval talks of Britain and, 167-91; war plans in, (Schlieffen's) 193-216, (after Schlieffen) 216-26; general staff in, *see under* general staffs; Austria and (July 1914), 247-73; pledges unconditional support to Austria, 227, 236; 242, 252; mobilizes, 260-1, 262, 268; issues ultimatum to Russia, 264; declarations of war by, on France, 267, 269, 270, 272, 274, on Russia, 268
Giel, Baron, Austrian envoy in Belgrade, 250
Giers, Baron N. K., Russian foreign minister, 83, 84, 89
Goethe, J. W., 116
Goltz, Freiherr Colmar von der, 111-12

Goschen, Sir Edward, British ambassador in Berlin, 165, 170, 184
Gossler, H. von, German war minister (1896-1906), 209, 210, 212, 214
Gourion-St. Cyr, Marshal, army law of (1818), 11
Grey, Sir Edward, British foreign minister (1905-16), 52, 191; and German naval growth, 47, 50; and military talks with France, 65, 66, 67; and Belgian neutrality, 62-3, 74, 75, 203; and naval exchanges with Germany, 163, 166, 168, 169, 173, 179, 180, 181, 185, 186; in Serbo-Albanian crisis (1912-13), 236; at outbreak of war, 71, 265, 268
Grierson, General J. M., 61, 68
Guchkov, Alexander, Octobrist leader, 87
Guizot, F. P., on Prussian army system, 14

Hague Conference (1907), 151
Hahnke, General von, head of German military cabinet, 130, 133
Haig, General D., 51, 75
Haldane, R. B., British war minister, 47, 48, 49, 50, 52, 66, 67; Fisher and, 64; army reforms of, 70; in Berlin (1912), 73, 74, 179, 181-5, 188
Hamburg, Strike in shipyards at, 131
Hamilton, General Ian, 49
Hanseatic League, 138
Hardinge, Sir Charles, permanent under-secretary, Foreign Office, 162
Hartington Commission (1870), 41, 43, 44
Heeringen, J. von, chief of German naval staff, 176; war minister, 123, 221, 222, 223, 224
Heligoland, fortification of, 162, 173
Herzegovina, Austrian annexation of, 230
Hintze, Rear-Admiral von, 85, 130, 272
historians, and German naval policy, 140
Hitler, Adolf, militarism of, 120
Hohenlohe, Prince C. K. L. von; commandant of imperial headquarters, 133; Reich chancellor, 126, 243; and Schlieffen plan, 194
Holland: British general staff and neutrality of, 69-70, 152; German naval policy and, 152, 218; in Schlieffen plan, 195, 196, 266
Holstein, Baron Friedrich von, of German foreign ministry, 83, 128, 133, 147; and Schlieffen plan, 194, 205
Holtzendorff, Admiral von, commanding german high-seas fleet, 174, 176, 190
Hopman, Albert, of *Reichsmarineamt,* 183
Hötzendorf, F. Conrad von, Austrian chief of staff, 107-8, 128; militarism of,

227-36 *passim;* operational plan of (1908), 240; exchanges between Moltke and, on war plans (1909-14), 241-6; in July 1914, 237, 247, 250-1; at outbreak of war, 261, 262

Hoyos, Count Alexander von, undersecretary, Austrian foreign ministry, 235, 238, 239

Huene, von, German military attaché in Paris, 128

Huguet, Major, French military attaché in London, 65

Hungary, and prospect of Austrian attack on Serbia, 233

Hutten-Czapski, Count, 205

illiteracy, in Russia, 78

imperialism: France and, 21; Britain and, 40, 42; Russia and, 84; and attitude to armies, 93; Conrad von Hötzendorf on, 107; political ideologies of, 108, 109; Germany and, 111

Indian Mutiny, 46

Ingenohl, Admiral, commanding German high-seas fleet, 153

Isvolsky, Alexander, Russian foreign minister, 87

Italy: and Germany, 106, 225; Austria and preventive war against, 229, 230, 231; at war with Turkey, 231; in Triple Alliance, 235, 241, 252, 257, 263; and German declaration of war, 268

Jagow, G. von, German foreign minister: and Belgian neutrality, 219; in July 1914, 248, 254, 265, 269; at outbreak of war, 265, 269, 270, 272, 273

Japan: and Kiao-chow, 141; and Russia, 231; *see also* Russo-Japanese War

Jaurès, Jean, 17

Joffre, General, 26-7, 29; French chief of staff, 73, 75, 271

Jutland, idea of British landing in, 156-7

Kageneck, Count, German military attaché in Vienna, 235

Kaltenborn, General H. K. von, German war minister, 130

Kameke, General G. von, German war minister, 120-1

Katkov, M. N., Russian nationalist writer, 81, 82

Keim, General, 109-10, 172, 223

Keller, Countess, 100

Kiao-chow, as German naval base, 111, 141

Kiderlen-Wächter, Alfred von: German ambassador in Bucharest, 165, 166, 167; foreign minister, 170, 173, 186

Kiel Canal, 64; widening of, 162, 173

Kitchener, Lord, 50, 51, 53, 54, 75

Kokovzov, Count V. N., Russian prime minister, 89

Kölnische Zeitung, Kaiser and, 133

Königgratz, battle of (1866), 19, 81

Köpenick, escapade of "Captain" of, 101

Kriege, Dr. J., of German foreign ministry law division, 270

Kruger telegram, 61

Kühlmann, Richard von, German legation councilor in London, 178, 186, 188

Kuropatkin, General A. N., Russian war minister, 85, 87

Landsturm, in Schlieffen plan, 207

Landwehr, 12, 14; amalgamated with army, 15, 101-2; in Schlieffen plan, 207, 211, 212, 214

Lansdowne, Lord, British foreign minister, 63, 64, 65, 66

law: Bernhardi and international, 115; maritime, London declaration on (1909), 152, 153

League of Nations, 67

League against Social Democracy (Germany), 109

Lebensraum: theories of, 108; Bernhardi and, 114

Lee, A. H., first lord of the Admiralty, 65, 154

liberal bourgeoisie, and army: in France, 12-13, 15, 17, 19, 20; in Germany, 97, 98, 99

Lichnowsky, Prince K. M., German ambassador in London, 189

Liebert, General, of German general staff, 103, 109, 110

Liège: fortification of, 195; Moltke's plan for attack on, 266, 272

Lloyd George, D.: chancellor of the Exchequer (1908-15), 53, 161; and Morocco crisis, 114, 172, 222; at ministry of munitions (1915-16), 53; prime minister (1916-22), 52, 56-7, 58; after the war, 31

Lorraine, as defensive buffer for Germany (Moltke), 198

Ludendorff, General Erich: militarism of, 54, 115; and Schlieffen plan, 208, 210, 216; and manpower for army, 220, 223; and Moltke, 224, 225; plans attack on Liège, 266

Luxembourg: neutrality of, 195, 203, 269; Germans invade, 272
Lyautey, General, French war minister, 29

MacDonald, J. R., on democratic government, 25
McKenna, Reginald, first lord of the Admiralty, 170, 178
machine-gun companies, German army, 223
Mahan, Captain Alfred, 108
Manila incidents (1898), 141
Manteuffel, Edwin von, 122
Marne, battle of the (1914), 26
Marschall, Freiherr F. W. von; German foreign minister, 133; ambassador in London, 189
Marseillaise, 8
Marxism, doctrine of class struggle in, 108
master-general of the ordnance, Britain, 41, 43
Mediterranean, British navy and, 142, 148, 181, 187
Metternich, Count Paul, German ambassador in London, 145, 151; Tirpitz urges replacement of, 165; and naval exchanges with Britain, 163, 164, 165-6, 167, 169, 188; and Widenmann, 174, 179, 182, 186; reports from, 178; reprimanded by William II, 187; proposes dropping of German navy bill, 185-6, recalled, 189
Metz, fortress of, 198, 218
Metzger, Colonel, 239
Michaelis, Georg, 102
Michel, General, 73
militarism, 23, 59, 93, 94, 95, 108, 158-9; and a negotiated peace, 58; in Russia, 77-89; of Napoleon, 7, 10, 11; of Ludendorff, 54, 115; of British admirals, 65, 68; of Tirpitz, 75, 109, 139, 161, 173; of Bernhardi, 115, 116; of Hitler, 120; of Widenmann, 174; of Kaiser, 188-9; of Conrad von Hötzendorf, 227-36 *passim*
militarization of German society, 15, 93-104
military attachés: German, reports from, 128, 129, 130, 156; Austrian, correspond with Conrad von Hötzendorf, 232
military cabinet, Prussian/German, 121-2, 123, 125
military rank, awarded in Germany as mark of distinction, 102
military service, term of: in France, 12, 13,

20, 22, 23, 226; in Britain, 45; in Russia, 78, 86; in Germany, 132, 211; *see also* conscription
militia: proposed French, 20; British, 45, 46, 48
Milyutin, General D., Russian army reformer, 78
mine-layers, in German naval policy, 155
mobilization procedures: French, 19, 23, 72; German, 48, 82; British, 65, 72; Russian, 78, 83, 84, 86, 241; Austrian, 231, 234, 237
Mohl, Moritz, Württemberg publicist, 97
Mohrenheim, Baron, Russian ambassador in Paris, 83
Moltke, Count Helmuth C. B. von, German chief of staff, 26, 53, 54, 193; Treitschke on, 99; and preventive war, 106, 127; operational plan of (1887), 199, 203; eastern front in plan of, 82, 198, 203, 204, 216; western front in plan of, 196-7, 203, 216; total victory foregone in plan of, 197, 198
Moltke (the younger), Count Helmuth J. L. von, German chief of staff (from 1905), 214, 216; and preventive war, 106; and navy, 111, 157; on three-front war, 116; and plan of elder Moltke, 216; and Schlieffen plan, 157, 200, 201, 210, 217-18, 226; rearranges Schlieffen plan to respect Dutch neutrality, 152; drops plan for "great eastern deployment," 202, 204; and army expansion, 223, 224, 225; exchanges between Conrad von Hötzendorf and, on war plans (1909-14), 241-6; in July 1914, 227, 247-63 *passim;* at outbreak of war, 264, 266, 267, 269, 270, 272
monarch and army: in Germany, 7, 25, 26, 119, 120, 134; in Britain, 37, 41, 43
Montenegro, Conrad von Hötzendorf and, 230, 231
Moreau, General, 9
Morocco, crisis over (1904-6): British support to France in, 21, 47, 147; and British army reform, 48, 66; and British navy, 159; von der Goltz on, 112; temptation to Germany during, 194
Morocco, second crisis over (1911): Germany in, 98, 106; Lloyd George in, 114, 172, 222; and German public opinion, 222
Müller, Admiral von, chief of German naval cabinet, 159, 182, 186
Müller, Lieutenant von, German naval attaché in London, 189-90

Namur, fortification of, 195
Napoleon Bonaparte, 8-9, 10, 35, 200
Napoleon III, 11, 18-19, 62
National Guard, French, 17
National Service League, Britian, 49
naval attachés, German: reports from, 131, 149: *see also* Widenmann, von Müller
naval cabinet, German, 124, 125
navalism, British version of militarism, 3, 108, 143 "great eastern deployment," 202, 204; and army expansion, 223, 224, 225; exchanges (Britain), 108; for German Navy League *see Flottenverein*
newspapers: British, and German naval growth, 145, 146; warmongering, 109
Nicholas II of Russia, 77, 78, 85, 88, 89: signs convention with Kaiser, 66-7; and mobilization, 257
Nicholas Nicolayevich, Russian Grand Duke, 85, 88
Nicolson, Sir Arthur, permanent under-secretary, Foreign Office, 66, 74, 185
Niel, Marshal A., 19
Nietzsche, F. W., 108, 116
Nivelle, General, 29

Obruchev, General S., Russian chief of staff, 82, 83
Octobrists, 87
officers, *see* army officers
Olmütz, conference at, 97

pacifism: in France, 17, 21; of free trade, 34; in British cabinet (1914), 71
Painlevé, Paul, French war minister, 30
Pan-Germanism, 109, 116, 139, 142, 146, 147
Pan-Slavism, 80, 85
Paris, fortress of, in German war plans, 201, 207, 215
Paris Commune, 20
Parliament: and army, 34-5, 38; army re-forms without reference to, 43; and dreadnoughts, 160, 162, 163; and rela-tions with Germany, 177, 180; in 1914-18 war, 51, 58
pékins, 27, 29
Persia: Germany and, 170; Russia and, 177, 180
Pétain, General, 29
Peter the Great, Czar, 78
Pichegru, General, 9
Pitt, William, 38, 39
Plessen, General von, commandant of im-perial headquarters, 132-3
Pohl, Admiral, 153
Poincaré, Raymond: French prime minister

(1912-14), 73, 74, 185; President (1914-24); and generals, 28, 29; visits St. Petersburg, 247; in 1914-18 war, 31
Poland: Russian troop movements in (1880s), 81, 82; Russian fear of enemy advance into, 84; in Moltke's plan, 82, 198, 203, 216
politics: French generals and, 23-4, 26, 27-30; British army and, 36; German army officers and, 103, 125, 126; and war, in German military literature, 105-17
population: of France, 23; of German Reich, 140
Portugal, African colonies of, 177
Pourtalès, Count F. von, German ambassa-dor in St. Petersburg, 259, 264, 267
prizes at sea, law of, 151, 152
propaganda: for British territorial army, 48-9; modern popular leaders supported by, 57; by *Reichmarineamt*, 137-8, 193; British, during 1914-18 war, 51
Puttkamer, Robert von, Prussian secretary of the interior, 104

quartermaster general, British, 41, 43

railways: Russian strategic, 81, 82, 84, 216; to Baghdad, 170, 177
realpolitik, 94, 98, 195
Redlich, Joseph, historian, 235
regiments, in British army, 37
Reichmarineamt (German imperial admi-ralty), 124, 161; political activity of, 137-8, 190, 193; and *Flottenverein*, 139; and prospect of blockade, 151, 152, 153; and foreign policy, 159; Wil-liam II and, 190
Reichstag: Bismarck on, 124; William II and, 126, 131, 134; Waldersee and, 131, 132; and naval burdens, 163; presses for swifter arming, 98-9; *see also* German army bills, German navy bills
Reinsurance Treaty, between Germany and Russia (1887), 82; cancelled (1890), 209, 243
Repington, Colonel, 65
reserves, *see* army reserves
Rhine, as defensive barrier (Moltke), 198
Ribot, Alexandre: French foreign minister (1892), 82; prime minister (1917), 29
Richter, Eugen, German liberal deputy, 103
Roberts. Lord, 49
Robertson, General W., 51, 53, 61, 62; Brit-ish chief of staff, 54-5, 56
Roediger, General A. F., Russian war minis-ter, 85, 87

Rohrbach, Paul, 109
Roon, Count A. von, Prussian war minister, 18, 122; in Franco-Prussian War, 26, 212
Rotteck, Karl von, 96
Rouvier, Maurice, French prime minister, 64, 65
Rumania: in Austrian war prospects, 235, 238, 239, 241, 247, 250; and German declaration of war, 268
Russia: threatened war between Austria and (1896), 243; German and Austrian ideas of preventive war against 106, 127, 231; defeat and revolution in (1905-6), 47, 63, 85, 199, 230, 241; in Bosnian crisis (1908-9), 161, 220; military recovery in, 69, 72, 185, 220, 224, 233, 250; militarism in, 77-89; and Turkey, 85, 86, 232; and Serbia, 87, 89, 238; and Persia, 177, 180; anti-German feeling in, 220; and Rumania, 235; Austria and prospect of war with, 232-8 *passim*, 241, 243, 250; partial mobilization in, 86-7, 88, 253-4, 257; general mobilization in, 88, 257, 259, 265; German ultimatum to, 264; German and Austrian declarations of war on, 268; *see also entries beginning* Anglo-Russian, Franco-Russian
Russo-Japanese·War (1905-6), 47, 61, 63, 79, 85, 111, 147; navies in, 154
Russo-Turkish War (1877-8), 78, 81

Sabron, Count de, 12
Salisbury, Lord, 52
Salonica expedition, 29, 30
Samoa, Germany in, 110
Sanders, General Liman von, in Istanbul, 86
Sarrail, General M., in French politics, 29
Say, J.-B., economist, 17
Sazonov, Serghei D., Russian foreign minister, 88, 89, 256, 257
Schemua, General, temporary Austrian chief of staff, 231
Schiller, J. C. F. von, 115
Schleswig-Holstein, possibility of British landing in, 63-4, 221
Schlieffen, Count Alfred, German chief of staff (1891-1907), 110, 130, 193; and navy, 111, 152, 155, 156; and Bernhardi, 113; operational plan of (1905), 156-7, 194, 197, 199-216, 220, 240; revised plan of (1912), 106-7, 224; total victory in plan of, 200, 204; German general staff and plan of, 265
Scholz, A. von, German finance minister, 102

Schön, Freiherr Wilhelm von, German ambassador in Paris, 273
Schönaich, Count, Austrian war minister, 228
Schönaich-Carolath, Prince Henry of, 103
Schweinitz, General von, German ambassador in St. Petersburg, 80, 81
Senden-Bibran, Admiral von, head of German naval cabinet, 124
Serbia: Russia and, 87, 89, 238; Conrad von Hötzendorf and war with, 228, 229-30, 231, 232, 236, 242; Aehrenthal and, 230; assassination of Austrian Archduke in, 234, 235; Austrian ultimatum to, 237, 250; Austrian invasion of, 263
Shilinsky, Russian chief of staff, 86
Skobelev, General M. D., 80-1, 82, 88
Social Democratic Party, Germany: and army, 98; Prince Schönaich and, 103; and navy, 140, 174, 176; in Reichstag (1911), 222
Solferino, battle of (1859), 18
Somme, battle of (1916), 51-2, 56
South Germany: and Prussian army system, 14, 97; army in, 96, 97, 100
Spanish-American War, 154
Stein, Baron Heinrich von, 115
Stein, General, 224
Stosch, Admiral, German naval minister, 121, 149
Strasbourg, fortress of, 198
Stumm-Halberg, Freiherr von, Saarbrücken "coal king", 131
Stürgkh, Count, Austrian prime minister, 236, 254-5
submarines, in German naval policy, 153, 155, 161, 173
substitutes: in French army (*remplaçants*), 15, 16, 18, 20; in Russian army, 78; in Prussian army, 96
Swabia, protests against Prussian military drill from, 14
Sybel, Heinrich von, propagandist for union of Germany under Prussia, 99, 100
syndicalism, French, 21
Szögény, Count L., Austrian ambassador in Berlin, 261

Tausch, Inspector, of German political police, 133
Territorial Army, British, 48-9, 50
Thiers, L. A., 13, 20
Tirpitz, Admiral, 138-40; and William II, 47, 124, 159, 162; militarism of, 75, 109, 139; and German naval policy, 111, 131, 137-58 *passim*, 159, 160; and German naval attachés, 131, 149, 178;

and naval exchanges with Britain, 162-90 *passim;* offers resignation (1912), 187; at outbreak of war, 268, 270, 271

Tisza, Count Istvan, Hungarian prime minister, 234, 236, 238, 247

Toul, fortress of, 270

trade: between Britain and Germany, 144; German overseas, 141, 142, 143

Treitschke, Heinrich von, propagandist for union of Germany under Prussia, 99; von der Goltz and, 112; Bernhardi and, 116

Trochu, General, 20

Tschirschky, H. von, German ambassador in Vienna, 235, 237, 255, 261

Turkey: Russia and, 85, 86, 232; von der Goltz in, 111; German economic activity in, 4, 141; Italy at war with, 231

United States of America: Clémenceau and army of, 30; German faith in maritime policy of, 152

Vagt, Alfred, 80

Vannovsky, General, Russian war minister, 84

Venezuela conflict (1901-3), 141

Verdun, fortress of, 273

Verdy du Vermois, General von, German war minister, 123-4, 132, 209; and Austria, 240

Victoria, Queen, 37, 39, 41

victory: anniversaries of, as German popular festivals, 99; total, foregone in Moltke's plan, 198, 199, 204; total, in Schlieffen's plan, 200, 204

"vitalism", 21

Viviani, René, French prime minister, 28

Waldeck-Rousseau, Pierre, French prime minister, 22

Waldersee, Count Alfred: deputy chief of staff, 121; chief of staff, 103, 110, 119, 240; and preventive war, 106, 127; as possible chancellor, 114, 128; and military attachés, 128-30; falls from favor, 130, 131, 193, 213; and social democrats, 131-2

war: totalitarian, 15; economic, 34; preventive, (British admirals and) 65, 68, 108-9, 143, 154, (German general staff and) 81, 106-7, 113-14, 127-8, 194, (Austrian general staff and), 81, 227-89, (Bernhardi and) 112, 113, 114

war minister: French, 24-5; British, 38, 39, 40, 43, 54; Russian, and general staff,

80; Prussian, 120, 121, 122; German, 124, 125, 193; German, and general staff, 194, 208, 210

War Office, British, 40, 41, 42; reform of, 43, 44, 45

Wars of Liberation, Prussia (1813-15), 96, 97, 134

Wars of Unification, Germany (1867-71), 13, 45, 93, 97, 105, 210; responsibility for outbreak of, 203

Waters, W. H. -H., British military attaché in Berlin, 61-2

Wedel, Count, governor-general in Alsace, 135

Wehrverein (German Defense Union), 110, 172, 223

Welcken, Freiburg liberal, 14

Wellington, Duke of, 33, 34, 35, 39

Wermuth, Adolf, German finance minister, 173, 176

Widenmann, Commander, German naval attaché in London, 170, 171, 173, 174, 178, 186, 189, 190

William II of Germany, 61, 88, 99; and Austria, 240; and Tirpitz, 47, 124, 159, 162; signs convention with Czar, 66-7; and navy, 110, 124-5, 131, 134, 137, 139, 147, 161, 211; as head of army, 105, 123, 125-6, 135; military entourage of, 126-7, 187; "imperial headquarters" of, 127, 132; and Waldersee, 130; and Schlieffen, 213, 214; and naval exchanges with Britain, 162-90 *passim;* and army increase, 222, 223; gives unconditional pledge to Austria (1914), 227, 236, 242, 252; telegraphs to Francis Joseph, 255, 264; at outbreak of war, 268, 269, 271

Wilson, General, 35, 71; and staff talks with France, 72, 73, 74, 75; chief of staff, 56

Wilson, President Woodrow, 31

world power, Germany's prospects of attaining, 100, 139, 140-1, 146, 183, 191; *Alldeutscher Verband* and, 109; Bernhardi and, 114, 115

Württemberg, attitude towards army in, 96, 97

Yanushkevich, General N. N., Russian chief of staff, 88

yeomanry, British, 46

York, Duke of, 36

Zabern affair, 134, 135, 136

Zukhomlinov, General V. A.: Russian chief of staff, 79; war minister, 85-6, 87, 88-9, 247

DATE DUE

11/v			
JAN 2 6 1973			
FEB 5 1973			
GAYLORD			PRINTED IN U.S.A